OIL
AND
TURMOIL

OIL AND TURMOIL

AMERICA FACES OPEC AND THE MIDDLE EAST

DANKWART A. RUSTOW

W · W · NORTON & COMPANY
NEW YORK   LONDON

The text of this book is composed in 10 point Times Roman, with
display type set in Peignot Bold.
Manufacturing by Haddon Craftsmen
Book design by Nancy Dale Muldoon

First Edition

Library of Congress Cataloging in Publication Data

Rustow, Dankwart A.
    Oil and turmoil

    Includes bibliographical references and index.
    1. Petroleum industry and trade—Political
aspects—United States. 2. Petroleum industry and
trade—Political aspects—Near East. 3. United
States—Foreign relations—Near East. 4. Near
East—Foreign relations—United States. 5. Organ-
ization of Petroleum Exporting Countries.
I. Title.
HD9566.R84 1982   338.2'7282'0956   82–2208
                                          AACR2

W. W. Norton & Company, Inc. 500 Fifth Avenue, New York, N. Y. 10110
W. W. Norton & Company Ltd. 37 Great Russell Street, London WC1B 3NU

1 2 3 4 5 6 7 8 9 0

ISBN 0-393-01597-1
ISBN 0-393-95233-9 PBK

CONTENTS

Contents

Preface

Early in 1971, I ventured to predict that, in most Middle Eastern countries, "nationally controlled operations [of the oil industry] would prove technically feasible . . . sometime in the 1970s. . . ." The statement caused disbelief or raised eyebrows among many readers at the time. But while my essay was in page proof, Algeria nationalized 51 percent of its oil concessions; and a year later, a leading petroleum correspondent asked how I felt about Middle Eastern governments having set a faster pace of nationalization than I had anticipated.

In the mid-1970s, there was much public speculation about the imminent or ultimate collapse of the OPEC cartel. Yet in a book I published with John F. Mugno in mid-1976, entitled *OPEC: Success and Prospects,* we stated that there is little "assurance against future rises in OPEC's world price that might go to $15, $20, or even $30 a barrel." Only two and one half years later, the oil price began its second spectacular climb, from $13 to $34 a barrel. Our book had "assumed that no group of governments comes by $100 billion a year in a fit of absentmindedness." Since 1979, OPEC's annual income has been running at two or three times that rate.

The price spiral set off by the Iranian revolution has shown once again how crucially the price of oil has come to depend on political events in the world's most turbulent region—and that any plausible analysis must pay equal heed to the economic and the political, as well as to the historical and the psychological, dimensions. The Western impact on the Middle East; the structure of the global oil market and the continuing interaction between multinational companies and OPEC governments;

10

PREFACEPREFACE

the internal political conflicts of the region; and the growing involvement of the superpowers: such will be some of the themes of the chapters that follow. We shall also trace the policies—or failures of policy—by which the United States has come to depend on risky foreign oil imports. Above all, we shall assess the opportunities for U. S. policy to restore some sense of steadiness to the world's energy scene and a measure of clam to the strife-torn Middle East.

To relieve the text of unnecessary detail, source references have been relegated to the notes at the end of the volume. A statistical appendix provides summary information on energy consumption, oil production and revenues, and the accelerating arms race in the Middle East. Two maps furnish some of the historical and geographic background. In giving the names of Middle Eastern persons and places, I have followed the usage of American newspapers and reference works. Better to offend the pedants among my colleagues by writing "Mossadegh" and "Nasser" than to perplex the unsuspecting general reader with "Muṣaddiq" and " 'Abd al-Nāṣir' ".

Financial support for much of the research here presented was generously provided by a grant from the International Relations Division of the Rockefeller Foundation. It is a pleasure to record my gratitude to its former director, Mason Willrich, who provided much encouragement, and his successor, Edwin A. Deagle, Jr. At the Graduate School of the City University of New York, my students Duncan Hutchison, Thomas Parker, Nina Hanan, and Howard Lax helped with many details of research. Throughout the project, the library staff at the Council on Foreign Relations provided unfailing support, and Cheryl J. Trench, of the Petroleum Industry Research Foudation, was generous in guiding me to statistical sources. On more specific points, Carolyn Ellman helped locate *The Little Engine That Could,* and Russell Baker, of the *New York Times,* traced the cry of MEOW. During the preparation of the book for publication it has been a pleasure to work with Donald S. Lamm and his staff at W. W. Norton & Company.Financial support for much of the research here presented was generously provided by a grant from the International Relations Division of the Rockefeller Foundation. It is a pleasure to record my gratitude to its former director, Mason Willrich, who provided much encouragement, and his successor, Edwin A. Deagle, Jr. At the Graduate School of the City University of New York, my students Duncan Hutchison, Thomas Parker, Nina Hanan, and Howard Lax helped with many details of research. Throughout the project, the library staff at the Council on Foreign Relations provided unfailing support, and Cheryl J. Trench, of the Petroleum Industry Research Foudation, was generous in guiding me to statistical sources. On more specific points, Carolyn Ellman helped locate *The Little Engine That Could,* and Russell Baker, of the *New York Times,* traced the cry of MEOW. During the preparation of the book for publication it has been a pleasure to work with Donald S. Lamm and his staff at W. W. Norton & Company.

During recent trips to Europe and the Middle East, I derived great benefit from discussing many separate aspects of the subject with Louis B. Turner and Paul H. Frankel in London; Øystein Noreng in Oslo; Lotte Salzberger in Jerusalem; Moshe Bitan in Tel Aviv; Aziz Shihadeh in Ramallah; Aydin Yalçın and Osman Okyar in Ankara; Dean Ali D. Johany, of the University of Petroleum and Minerals in Dhahran; M. Farouk Al-Husseini, of the Ministry of Petroleum, and Prince Abdullah

Faisal Turki Al Abdullah Al Saud, of the Royal Commission for Jubail and Yanbu, in Riyadh; His Excellency Dr. Boutros Ghali, of the Ministry of Foreign Affairs, in Cairo; and Fadhil J. Al-Chalabi, Adnan Al-Janabi, and Hamid Zaheri at OPEC headquarters in Vienna.

Back in New York, my good friends John H. Lichtblau, of the Petroleum Industry Research Foundation, and John F. Mugno, of the Economics Department of Citibank, critically read portions of an earlier draft and, as always, provided generous encouragement, sound advice, and frequent stimulation. Needless to say, neither they nor any of the persons or organizations mentioned earlier, should be held to account for any of my interpretations of fact or expressions of opinion.

Most of all, I am deeply grateful to my wife, Margrit Wreschner Rustow, who pours oil on the waves of my turmoil.

Dankwart A. Rustow

New York, N.Y.
February 1982

OIL
AND
TURMOIL

A VISIT FROM KUWAIT AND A SUMMIT AT VENICE

On December 17, 1968, Washington received the official visit of the ruler of Kuwait, Sheikh Abdullah al-Salim al-Sabah. Kuwait was a small desert principality, or emirate, that had lately developed into one of the Middle East's leading oil exporters. Long a British dependency, it had continued to enjoy Britain's protection after attaining independence in 1961, and it played no active international role. Still, to observe the proprieties during his last weeks in office, President Lyndon Johnson arranged for Sheikh Abdullah to meet his successor. Richard Nixon, in turn, was accompanied by Dr. Henry Kissinger, soon to be his national security adviser.

"The occasion," Kissinger was to recall a decade later, "was notable mainly for giving me my first opportunity to prepare the President-elect for a high-level meeting—a test which I flunked ingloriously. I assumed that the Arab-Israeli conflict would be at the forefront of the Amir's concern and prepared an erudite memorandum on the subject. Unfortunately, the Amir wanted, above all, to learn what plans the new Administration had for the Persian Gulf after the United Kingdom vacated the area, as it had announced it would do in 1971. What were America's intentions if, for example, Iraq attacked Kuwait? Nixon gave me the glassy look he reserved for occasions when in his view the inadequacy of his associates had placed him into an untenable position. Manfully he replied that we would have to study the matter. . . ."

15

Britain's decision to withdraw its remaining forces from "East of Suez"—specifically Kuwait and other Persian Gulf emirates—was the logical conclusion of a long series of similar, often far more agonizing, decisions. The British had relinquished their Indian empire in 1947, their Palestine mandate in 1948, their military positions throughout the Middle East in the 1950s, and most of their African colonies in the 1960s. They had failed in their attempt, under Eden's Conservative government, to reassert an imperial position on even a minor scale in the Suez War of 1956; and ever since the Second World War, they had faced a recurrent grave economic crisis. Now under Harold Wilson's Labour government, they saw little justification in continuing sizable military expenditures to hold on to a bare shred of empire in the Persian Gulf.

Seen in this immediate context, Kissinger's performance did not seem quite so inglorious. Americans in 1968 were in no mood to rush in where Britons no longer cared to tread. Vietnam had been the overriding issue of the 1968 campaign—whether to withdraw at any cost, as Eugene McCarthy and a growing chorus demanded from the left, or gradually and with honor, as proposed by Nixon and the moderate Republicans, or after drastic escalation and full victory, as imagined by a dwindling band of hawks on the far right. In Vietnam not only future relations with Russia and China but also America's own prestige and stature as a superpower were at stake—and so was the domestic tranquillity of American society itself after a decade of mounting protests.

By welcome contrast, the Middle East—except for that obstinate quarrel between Israel and her Arab neighbors—had long been quiescent. Soviet pressure on Greece, Turkey, and Iran had been successfully contained in 1947 by a combination of local opposition and firm American support. The French and British withdrawal from such colonial dependencies as Syria, Lebanon, Palestine, Egypt, Jordan, Libya, Cyprus, and Aden had placated local nationalists and helped to calm tensions within the region. Soviet attempts to vault the barrier of the "northern tier" and to woo countries such as Egypt, Iraq, and Syria with massive military and economic aid had succeeded only in part. The effort of Iranian nationalists under Mohammed Mossadegh to wrest control of the oil industry from the Western multinational companies had been thwarted, and the shah of Iran restored to his throne in 1953.

Relations of Washington and of the major oil companies with the leading oil producers, Saudi Arabia and Iran, were cordial. The most serious problem for the companies was persistent competition from Soviet oil exports and from smaller Western companies rapidly expanding their fields in Libya. The result had been a recurrent glut of oil and a slow-motion price war that both tripled the volume of oil traded in world markets in a decade and cut the price of the standard grade of Saudi crude petroleum from $2.08 a barrel in 1958 to as little as $1.30 in 1970.

In briefing his chief in 1968 for a visit from the head of one of the lesser states, Henry Kissinger thus might be forgiven for assuming that all was well with the Middle East aside from the Arab-Israeli dispute. In Vietnam the risks were enormous and urgent. In the Middle East the situation seemed stable and Western interests secure. Surely it would have taken a crisis graver and more imminent than some hypothetical skirmish between Iraq and Kuwait—admittedly two years or more in the future—to refocus the attention of Washington's top policy makers even briefly from the southeastern to the southwestern corner of Asia.

In June 1980 Nixon's second successor, Jimmy Carter, joined the leaders of Japan, West Germany, Canada, Britain, France, and Italy for a summit meeting in the ancient Italian city of Venice. The overriding issue this time was the price of oil, which in ten years had risen from $1.30 a barrel to as much as $32.00 a barrel, and the impact of that price explosion on the noncommunist economies of the world. The seven leaders pledged themselves to the "reduction of inflation," to breaking "the existing link between economic growth and consumption of oil," and to strengthening "the open world trading system." They deplored the "large oil-generated payments imbalances" and their deleterious impact "on the developing countries that have to import oil." Above all, they insisted that the world must "achieve and maintain a balance between energy supply and demand at reasonable levels and at tolerable prices"—although other parts of the declaration made it clear that such tolerable (let alone reasonable) conditions might not obtain until the 1990s.

It was easy to read between the lines of the Venice communiqué. The repeated appeals to solidarity betrayed the concern of the leaders assembled at the summit: whether or not the major capitalist economies would indeed face the economic challenges of the 1980s and 1990s in concert. Would they manage to reduce oil imports according to some predetermined schedule—or would the next round of price increases set off a scramble for supplies that, as in 1979, would drive prices up even faster? Would recession and unemployment be fought with coordinated stimuli to revive trade and investment—or be aggravated by import quotas and other measures of protectionism? The major industrial economies had been unable to reverse the oil price jump from $2 to $10 in the wake of the Arab-Israeli war of 1973, or that from $13 to $32 in the wake of the Iranian revolution; and they were still unsure how to cope with the effects of the first crisis when they were hit by the second. How, then, would they react if some future disturbance in the Middle East curtailed supplies once again and sent the price of oil spiraling to $40, $50, or more?

The future alone could tell whether everyone would muster the will to meet the economic challenge; yet once there was a will, at least, there would be a way: oil imports must be cut and economic activity maintained. But in facing some of the political challenges, there seemed to be neither will nor way.

A week before the summit meeting, the European Community's foreign ministers had also met in Venice to endorse Palestinian self-determination and negotiations with the Palestine Liberation Organization—in sharp contrast to Carter's recent Camp David approach. And just before turning to economic matters, the Venice summit itself had issued two political declarations: on the six-month-old Soviet occupation of Afghanistan and the seven-month-old detention of American diplomats in revolutionary Iran. In phrasing these statements, the seven leaders avoided the earlier bitter recriminations between those who supported and those who opposed President Carter's initiatives to boycott the Moscow Olympics and to impose various economic sanctions on Moscow and Tehran; instead, they united in a chorus of pious indignation and utopian rhetoric. Having vowed "to help create the conditions for harmonious and sustained economic growth," the leaders warned that "our efforts will only bear fruit if we can at the same time preserve a world in which the rule of law is universally obeyed, national independence respected, and world peace is kept."

Preserve rather than restore? Universal respect for law—as shown in Tehran—and for national independence—as demonstrated in Afghanistan? Peace on earth and good will to men? Surely, if these unexceptionable sentiments voiced at Venice were to be taken literally, they implied that the economic plans to be laid down from the summit would be doomed to bear fruit not in this world but in the hereafter.

Oil is the most important commodity in the world economy. Its price is set in the Middle East, which both contains most of the world's oil reserves and is its most troubled political region. In the eleven and a half years between the Kuwaiti emir's visit to Washington and the Venice summit meeting, the economic forces of the global oil market interacted with the political forces in the Middle East in such a way as to pose the greatest danger to world prosperity since the Great Depression of 1930 and the gravest threat to world peace since the Great War of 1939. In 1968 Henry Kissinger had proved oblivious to the problems of the Persian Gulf; by 1980 Jimmy Carter was to declare the Gulf a region of "vital interest" to the United States.

Oil tankers carry a larger tonnage than all other commercial shipping on the high seas. Petroleum represents about one-half of energy consumption in the noncommunist world, and its price movements affect the prices of most other forms of energy. Oil payments have become the largest periodic transfers in the international financial system. The major oil companies are the most prosperous and far-flung multinational corporations. And the oil exporting countries have been among the best customers of many other large industrial firms. Thus, every economy in the world has felt the profound impact of the recent petroleum revolution.

The specific problem, nevertheless, is different for every nation—and so are the available solutions. The impact has been most severe on the world's poorest economies; for many of these, the problem has been one of either obtaining aid or loans from increasingly reluctant donors and lenders or rescheduling massive debts without further disrupting economic activity. By contrast, Great Britain, with its rapidly growing oil industry in the North Sea, has been decreasing its dependence on foreign oil, thus becoming a net beneficiary. West Germany has looked to its reserves of lignite ("brown coal"), Canada to its oil and tar sands, and the United States to the coal and shale of its mountain states. France, however, has opted for an ambitious nuclear program. While many countries have tried to curtail oil imports, Japan and West Germany have relied mainly on the remarkable productivity of their economies to earn the monies to pay for the oil. To redress the imbalance of petroleum payments, Europeans and Japanese have competed in supplying capital equipment to oil exporting countries, whereas the United States has vastly increased its sales of arms. Washington has sent periodic missions to Riyadh to plead for Saudi moderation in setting the price of oil; yet even while engaging in an intensive peace effort at Camp David and elsewhere, it has not wavered in its basic support for Israel. By contrast, West Europeans and Japanese have issued numerous statements increasingly favorable to the Arab side—specifically to the Palestine Liberation

Organization. In sum, the oil and Middle East crises, while dramatizing the general need for unified action, also have multiplied the specific temptations for each nation to go it alone.

The same need for unity and similar divisive temptations were apparent back home in the United States. In Congress the interests of oil- and gas-producing states, such as Texas or Louisiana, clashed sharply with those of oil-importing regions, such as New England and the Mid-Atlantic. The Rocky Mountain states saw in the prospect of massive coal and shale development potential threats to their ecology and social structure. Railroads fought slurry pipeline operators for the privilege of transporting coal as yet unmined. Everyone wanted a better energy supply, but everyone preferred to foist the attendant hazards of pollution or nuclear accident off on his distant neighbor. Aptly, our recent energy debate has been likened to a new War Between the States.

The vehemence and confusion of the American debate reflected not only the diversity of our regions but also our sheer size and importance in the world at large. Americans produce about one-third of the world's gross product and consume over one-fourth of its energy. The American government, moreover, is the only one that in recent decades has at times provided leadership toward global political and economic order. Naturally enough, the shock waves emanating from global oil economics and from Middle East politics have converged with peculiar force on the United States.

But if we are more vulnerable to the economic dangers from the petroleum crisis and the political dangers from the Middle East crisis, we also have, conversely, a far greater potential impact on the economy of oil and on the politics of the Middle East than does any other single nation. More than half the arms currently stockpiled in the Middle East were made in the United States. And if somehow we Americans could wean ourselves from oil imports, we would deprive OPEC of its best customer overnight.

To resolve these conflicting pressures and to respond intelligently to the opportunities ahead, we need, above all, to know what is happening to us and what we can do about it. We need a keener awareness of the damage that events in the Middle East and on the global oil market are inflicting on our standard of living, on the value of our currency, and on our international stature. And we need a firmer grasp of what we can do —either to arrest the oil price spiral or to escape its effects; either to lower the tensions in the Middle East or to prevent their escalation into global conflict. In sum, we need to know what we can do to move the world economy away from stagnation and collapse toward renewed prosperity and to move world politics away from the brink of global war toward some semblance of peace.

This book is devoted to those efforts at clearer understanding and that search for more effective solutions.

1

THE WESTERN IMPACT ON THE MIDDLE EAST

THE MIXED CULTURAL SCENE

The Middle East today offers a sharply varied cultural scene. In parts of Turkey, Syria, and Lebanon, and in most of the cities throughout the region, life follows a Western pattern not very different from that in southern Italy, Yugoslavia, Spain, or other Mediterranean countries. The cities bustle with commercial and industrial activity. Agriculture is partly mechanized and devoted to cash crops, such as cotton, wheat, tobacco, or citrus. Almost everyone is literate, and the school system leads straight up to the coeducational universities. Women are emancipated; those of the middle class may hold office jobs or engage in the busy rounds of activity of the society matron. Movies and television are the staple entertainment; cocktails and theater, a normal part of social life. Religion for most people has become a private, family matter. The prayer call resounds five times daily from the minaret, often amplified by an electronic loudspeaker, but not many Middle Eastern Muslims in these Westernized settings perform their prayers with any regularity. Most mosques are empty, even on Friday—the Muslim Sabbath. Few keep the daytime fast for the entire holy month of Ramadan. Circumcision of boys and Islamic burial for the deceased are the only traditional rituals universally observed.

By contrast, the human and social scene in much of the Arabian peninsula, in small towns throughout most of the region, and in the rural areas of Egypt, Iran, or Iraq remains as it must have been hundreds of years ago. Bedouin follow their herds of camels or sheep. The soil is tilled by subsistence farmers or sharecroppers. In the small towns and the poorer quarters of the cities the factory has not replaced the craftsman's workshop, and commercial life continues to center around the bazaar. Literacy is the exception, but there are public scribes at street corners ready to compose a petition for a fee. Women in public cover all parts of their bodies except the hands and eyes. At prayer time all work ceases, and Islam, as a communal religion, suffuses all private and public life. But recent oil wealth has brought a culture shock even to these settings. Saudi Arabia's labor force today is largely imported from other Middle Eastern and Asian countries. A Saudi passenger riding his nation's domestic airline must ask for a glass of water in English—because the stewardess is a South Korean.

And, of course, the Middle East includes Israel, with its advanced technology and science, its entrenched party system, lively political debate, and omnipresent trade union organization—a country of immigrants, most of them having arrived from Europe in the 1930s and 1940s and from other Middle Eastern countries in the 1950s.

The close coexistence of Westernized and traditional styles of life in the Middle East and the presence of Israel at the core of the region testify to the peculiar quality of the encounter between the West and the Middle East. To Middle Easterners, Westernization did not result from a government's conscious decision to raise its nation to the highest standards of industrial economy—as it did in Japan in the late nineteenth century or in China in the late twentieth. Nor were the countries of the Middle East, with the exception of Israel, populated by migrants who brought their Western culture with them from Europe—as were North America, Australia, and much of Latin America. Rather, modern Europeans first came to the Middle East, as they had come to much of Asia and all of Africa, as imperial intruders and colonial conquerors.

The only difference was one of timing. Europe's colonial expansion had started with the voyages of discovery of the fifteenth and sixteenth centuries. In southern and southeast Asia, the colonial system was firmly established by about 1800, in tropical Africa by about 1880. By contrast, British troops did not occupy Egypt until 1882. The first treaty of protection between the government of Queen Victoria and Sheikh Mubarak of Kuwait (whose grandson Abdullah met Nixon in 1968) was signed in 1899. And it was not until 1920 and 1921 that France and Britain established their rule over Syria, Palestine, and Iraq. Other Middle Eastern countries managed to remain independent, but none escaped the imperialist pressure. Afghanistan survived as a buffer state between the Russians in Central Asia and the British in India. The same two powers twice partitioned Iran—in 1907 into "spheres of influence" and in 1941 into zones of wartime occupation. Turkey became a virtual German protectorate at the time of the First World War. Some of her armies had German generals as commanders; the others, Turkish generals with German aides-de-camp. Later, Turkish nationalists warded off the threat of being partitioned among Greece and various European colonial powers in a hard-fought war of independence in 1919–23. The Arabian peninsula (Saudi Arabia and Northern Yemen) retained its independence, but even here the British in the nineteenth century had established a belt of colonies or quasi-colonies from Aden to Kuwait all along the southeastern and northeastern coasts.

It was not remoteness or lack or earlier contact that delayed the full Western impact on the Middle East until the turn of the last century. The Middle East has been, to Europeans, always part of the "known world": unlike Japan or the Americas it did not have to be "opened up" or "discovered" by the arrival of ships at distant shores. Its location at the junction of three continents and two oceans has attracted to the Middle East would-be world conquerors from Alexander the Great to Napoleon and Stalin. Of all non-European regions, moreover, the Islamic Middle East is closest to Europe not only in geography but also in history and culture.

Islam grew out of the same ancient Middle Eastern Judaic and Hellenistic roots as did Christianity. Indeed, Mohammed (571–632 A.D.), as the "seal of the prophets," saw himself as perfecting rather than replacing the earlier great monotheistic traditions. In the orthodox Islamic view, God revealed Himself successively to Adam, Abraham, Moses, and all the other Old Testament prophets, then to Jesus, and at last to Mohammed—whose prophecy thus brought to its final climax the age-old process of transmission of the divine message. The cultural contacts between Islam, Christendom, and Judaism were particularly intense in the Middle Ages. Medieval Arab scholars learned their philosophy and science from the ancient Greeks. They developed them further, bestowing on the world such crucial innovations as the decimal system and the zero in arithmetic, "x" as the designation of the unknown in algebra (from Arabic *"al-jabr"*), as well as the standard names of many of the most visible fixed stars (from Aldebaran and Betelgeuze to Zubenel-genubi). In due course, the same Arab scholars passed their mathematics and astronomy and their knowledge of the Greek classics on to the European scholars of the early Renaissance.

While these intellectual contacts between Middle Eastern Muslims and European Christians were proliferating, the political relations were quite the reverse of what they later became. For the thousand years from 700 to 1700 A.D. the Muslim realms of caliphs and sultans proved militarily superior to Europe in encounter after encounter. A century after Mohammed, the caliphs conquered Spain, southern Italy, and southern France. Although European crusaders gained a foothold in Palestine and neighboring areas for several generations, they were at last decisively repelled. As the Christian kingdoms completed the reconquest of the Iberian peninsula, the Ottoman-Turkish sultans were advancing at the opposite end of Europe through the Balkans and into Hungary. Indeed, historians have argued that it was this powerful presence of the Ottomans in the eastern Mediterranean that deflected European expansionism westward across the Atlantic.

Thus nearly four centuries were to elapse between the arrival of Columbus in the West Indies and of British forces in Egypt in 1882. Setting out westward and circumnavigating Africa, and having conquered most parts of the inhabited world except China and Japan, the Europeans at last got around to a concentric attack on the Middle East. But by then much had changed on either side of the great Mediterranean divide.

THE LATE ENCOUNTER OF EAST AND WEST

What happened in those centuries from 1500 to 1900 in Europe has come to be called, in the shorthand of cultural history, a process of "modernization." We commonly date the beginning of "modern" history to the European age of overseas discovery. The farther reach of European navigation and the more pervasive firepower of European guns were among the practical by-products of a new cultural dynamism that in turn stemmed from a new attitude of mind. European intellectual development came to be dedicated to an avid exploration of the unknown, an appreciation of continuity in change and of unity in diversity, and a restless ambition to convert knowledge into power. Power, in turn, could be of two kinds: power over men through development of the arts of war and the skills of human organization, and power over nature through advances in technology and industry. Modernization in Europe and its overseas offshoots encompasses the entire Western intellectual and social development from the Renaissance through the age of absolutism and the baroque to the industrial revolution and the age of nationalism and imperialism. Imperialism, the anticolonial revolution, and the global rivalry between democratic and communist powers, in turn, have helped make of modernization a world-wide phenomenon. In sum, modernization may be defined as "widening control over nature through closer interaction among men."

The practical applications of knowledge to power were to make the Western impact as irresistible in the Middle East as during the intervening centuries it had proved in other continents. Nevertheless, at the time when these modern attitudes first were formed in Europe, Middle Eastern Muslims were ill prepared to perceive the change—let alone anticipate its implications for the distant future. When Europe underwent the intellectual revolutions of the Renaissance and the Reformation, the Ottoman empire stood at the very zenith of its power. The Ottoman Turks ruled over a vast realm stretching from Hungary and the Ukraine in the north to the Indian Ocean in the south, from Algiers in the west to the Caspian Sea in the east. With its six-hundred-year history, the Ottoman sultanate proved to be the most far-flung and most durable realm this side of China since the fall of Rome. Under Ottoman rule, Muslims peacefully coexisted with Christians and Jews—in sharpest contrast to the lethal sectarian struggles among Catholics, Albigensians, Bogumils, Lutherans, Calvinists, and Unitarians in the petty kingdoms and principalities of Europe. Ottoman Muslims had good reason to boast of the invincibility of their arms, trust in the justice of their laws, and rely on the evenhandedness of their administration. Indeed, they were inclined to invoke all these as so many further proofs of the truth of their religion.

In the latter Middle Ages, Christian-European and Muslim-Middle Eastern cultures had been intimately interwoven. Now, in an age of restless European expansion and Ottoman saturation and self-satisfaction, commercial and cultural contacts declined to an all-time low. When Napoleon Bonaparte's army arrived aboard French ships on the shore of Egypt in 1798, it issued an appeal to the local population invoking the affinity between the rationalist deism of the French Revolution and the austere monotheism of Islam and urging the local Arab-speaking populace to rise against the yoke of Turkish oppression. The reaction of the local Ottoman-Egyptian officials was one of consternation, haughty disdain, and sheer disbelief.

The incursion of French forces into Egypt and neighboring Palestine lasted only three years. In the near-century that was to elapse before European armies and navies returned to the attack, not only had Western military power vastly grown, but the attitude of Europeans to their own imperialism had undergone profound changes as well. The American Revolution in the 1770s and the Latin American revolutions a half-century later had triumphantly asserted the political equality of European settlers in overseas colonies with their cousins back home. The French Revolution had brought home to Europe itself the same basic message of personal rights and political self-determination. By the mid-nineteenth century, enlightened despotism in most of Europe had been replaced by elective parliamentary government, and dynastic by national loyalties. Even conservatives such as Disraeli, Napoleon III, and Bismarck now preferred to take their stand on expanded suffrage and on national solidarity.

This triumph of liberty, equality, and nationality among Europeans did not slow down the pace of their overseas expansion. Indeed, the French Revolution had demonstrated how an aroused populace could in a single sweep depose traditional tyranny at home and impose newfangled tyrannies abroad. The loss of European colonies in the Americas was made up for by fresh conquests in Asia, the Pacific, and Africa. The United States itself joined in this new wave of imperial expansion, acquiring Texas, California, and Alaska toward the middle and the Philippines and Puerto Rico toward the end of the century. Rightly the period from 1870 to 1914 is known to historians as the age of Western nationalism *and* imperialism.

Still, there was an obvious conflict between the creation of egalitarian, representative institutions at home and the imposition of foreign domination overseas. The "colonial question" became a subject of intense debate in European parliaments and election campaigns. Generally the upper classes and the commercial bourgeoisie supported or condoned imperialism; radical opinion in the lower middle class remained critical; and socialist opinion among the working class condemned it outright. Some notable imperialist setbacks, such as Britain's initial defeats at the hands of Dutch-descended settlers in the Boer War in South Africa (1899–1902) and Russia's defeat by Japan (1904–5), reinforced this mood of self-criticism. In a poem of 1899, Rudyard Kipling, the Anglo-

Indian poet, referred to colonialism as "the White Man's burden"—an apologetic sentiment that would not have occurred to Francis Drake and Walter Raleigh in the sixteenth century or Warren Hastings in the eighteenth.

In the Muslim Middle East, the same period—1770 to 1900—gave rise to second thoughts of a different sort. Napoleon's daring incursion of 1798 had been preceded by a long series of Ottoman defeats at the hands of Austria and Russia. The loss of the Crimea to Russia in 1783 was even more painful than the loss of Hungary to Austria a century earlier; in the Crimea, for the first time, a resident Muslim population had to be surrendered to Christian rulers. Just as their earlier military successes had been taken by Muslims as confirmation of the truth of their religion ("Power belongs to God, and His Apostle, and the believers"), so the latter-day setbacks caused not only a military and political but also a moral and spiritual crisis. Slowly it dawned on Middle Eastern rulers and viziers that, in the military arts at least, there was much that Muslims could—indeed much that Muslims must—learn from the once-despised infidels of the West.

A program of deliberate Westernization thus was undertaken by the sultans of Turkey, the pashas and khedives of Egypt, and, a little later and more hesitantly, the shahs of Iran. Military instructors were brought in from France or Prussia, shipbuilders from Italy or Britain, even a composer of martial brass music from Italy. Faced with the imminent threat of total military defeat, the impulse of nineteenth-century Middle Easterners was to try to borrow the "cutting edge" of modernization.

The cutting edge, it turned out, was not so easily detached. The new army and navy needed trained recruits and schooled officers, and this in turn required heavier taxation, a new system of schools in the capital and the larger cities, a tighter system of administration, revised law codes and special courts—and more schools to train tax collectors, district governors, judges, and teachers—and yet more taxes and yet more schools. It is a credit to the clearsightedness and tenacity of the late Ottoman rulers that, once embarked on their course of Westernizing reform, they were not to be deflected by temporary obstacles or setbacks. And the measure of their success was that the sultan's regime, which after the defeats of the eighteenth century was close to collapse in 1807 and again in 1839, fought an orderly retreat and survived until its final defeat in 1918.

Inevitably, as the movement of reform spread beyond military organization and administrative reform, it began to transform the outlook and ideals of the newly trained ruling class. Graduating from their European-style schools in Istanbul, Cairo, Salonica, or Beirut, or returning from their studies in France, the members of this new class of officers and civil servants began to develop the same Romantic literary tastes, the same dedication to ideals of representative government, the same patriotic and national enthusiasm that animated their contemporaries among the European educated class. For example, Ibrahim Şinasi (1826–71), a young Ottoman artillery officer, was sent to Paris for additional training but returned to Istanbul to found a Romantic school of poetry and the first private newspaper in Turkish. A few years after Şinasi's death, a group of his literary and political disciples took leading parts in the political maneuvers that led to the deposition of two sultans and the adoption of the Ottoman empire's first written parliamentary-representative constitution in the European style.

To the Middle Eastern rulers of the early nineteenth century, Western-style training for their military and civil servants had been a means of preserving their traditional, autocratic rule and of protecting their people's inherited Islamic values. But to the newly educated ruling class, Westernization soon became an end in itself—to be pursued under the sultan or, if necessary, despite the sultan or even against the sultan. The long-delayed re-encounter between West and Middle East thus pitted a reluctant and apologetic imperialism against a nascent and exuberant nationalism and liberalism. The sequence was most dramatic in Egypt and in Iran.

In Egypt in 1881, a group of progressive army officers had forced the spendthrift monarch to submit future budgets to the approval of a consultative assembly and to appoint a ministry acceptable to that assembly —the very steps toward financial control and cabinet responsibility that had been the starting point of representative government in England. But the European powers, foremost France and Great Britain, feared that an assertive, nationalist government in Cairo might repudiate the towering foreign debt that Egypt had incurred under her absolute rulers. The result was the British military landing in 1882 and an occupation that, though proclaimed "temporary," was to last, in one form or another, until 1956.

In Iran, too, there had been dissatisfaction with a monarch widely seen as ruling arbitrarily and squandering the national wealth. Protests took the form of mass rallies and—typically for modern Iran—a protest strike by bazaar merchants in Tehran and a march on the capital by the

well-disciplined nomadic tribes of the southern mountains. The result
was the imposition on the shah in 1906 of a written parliamentary
constitution, a step widely applauded by liberal opinion in Britain and
elsewhere. But it was only a year later that Britain joined tsarist Russia
in an agreement dividing Iran into two spheres of influence: a British
zone to the southeast and a Russian zone to the north—resulting in a
third, buffer zone, where both agreed to refrain from interference. Emboldened by this setback to the new Iranian regime, the shah in 1908
declared the constitution suspended.

The experience in Iran in 1907 confirmed that in Egypt in 1882.
Whatever Westerners might preach in their civics books about "no taxation without representation" or a "government of laws, not of men," they
evidently did not consider fiscal responsibility, parliamentary elections,
or national self-government suitable items for export. Faced with the
clamor of bondholders in Paris or London about the imminent repudia-
tion of Egypt's public debt, or with the strategic advice of military
planners, foreign offices were ready to set aside any respect for written
constitutions, liberal principles, or even international law—and to install
the regimes of military occupation or economic influence that suited
their momentary convenience. Britain, the mother of parliaments, had
twice decisively intervened to thwart parliamentary government in the
Middle East.

Perforce, the imperial war and foreign offices were more respectful of
parliamentary opinion at home. In 1881 the French had been even more
eager than the British to intervene in Egypt, but the activist cabinet in
Paris had been overturned by a vote in the Chamber of Deputies, and
the succeeding liberal government repudiated the earlier plans. The British, left to carry out the expedition alone, were all the more anxious to
proclaim it a temporary measure aimed at restoring Egypt to solvency.
One British historian has suggested that this limited-purpose "temporary" occupation was to prove harder to bring to a conclusion than might
an outright colonial annexation. The pretense of Egypt as a country with
a ruler and cabinet of its own had to be maintained. Although the
occupation authorities took full charge of the country's government,
they sought to justify each of their measures not as right or expedient
in itself but, rather, as likely to increase revenues, balance the budget,
and permit a resumption of the debt service—and hence to lead to a
prompt withdrawal of the occupation.

In 1914, with military considerations paramount, the British dispensed with the fiction of independence and declared Egypt their "protectorate" but promised independence after the war. In 1919, in what was to become a standard sequence in the course of imperial withdrawal, they first deported the leading Egyptian nationalist and then tried vainly to negotiate with him as prime minister about the terms of independence. In 1922 they declared Egypt to be "an independent sovereign State"— yet "absolutely reserved to [their own] discretion" such matters as communications, defense, and protection of foreign interests. Understandably, the Egyptian government rejected "independence" on such self-contradictory terms. A temporary accommodation was worked out in 1936, but the dispute was soon resumed: in 1942 British tanks surrounded the Egyptian royal palace to force replacement of a government leaning to the Axis powers with a pro-British one. In the years after the war, there was a mounting wave of violence by Egyptian nationalists and Muslim fundamentalists against British representatives and their local allies. Finally, in 1954, Britain agreed with Egypt to withdraw its last military contingents from the Suez Canal zone by 1956, thus bringing to an end seventy-four years of "temporary" occupation.

British relations with Arab nationalists in the former Ottoman empire started out more auspiciously. Nationalist sentiment in Syria, Iraq, and other Arabic-speaking regions had grown as the Ottoman government tightened its grip on the provinces, adopted a Turkish-nationalist policy, and engaged in heavy-handed repression of suspected treasonable activities during the world war. In 1916 the British had encouraged a rising in the rear of the Ottoman front, the famous "Arab Revolt" led by Sharif Hussein, guardian of the holy cities of Mecca and Medina, and celebrated in the writings of T. E. Lawrence. In October 1918, the Arab rebels led by the sharif's son Faisal made their triumphant entry into Damascus, chief Arab city in the Ottoman empire.

PUSSYFOOTING IMPERIALISM

Alas, relations were not to remain as cordial as they had been in the heat of battle and the flush of victory. In 1915 Sharif Hussein, in launching his revolt, had announced his aim of establishing an "Arab Caliphate of Islam" over the Arab-inhabited parts of the Ottoman empire, and the British had accepted this with minor reservations. But it was British armies that had defeated the Turkish and German forces, and at war's end, Palestine, Syria, and Iraq were thus left under British administration. Earlier, the London government had entered into secret agreements with its allies, including one that promised Syria (with Lebanon) to the French and one that envisaged an international administration for Palestine. In 1917 the British had issued the Balfour Declaration, which publicly committed them to support Zionist plans to establish in Palestine "a national home for the Jewish people." The United States, moreover, had made a decisive contribution to the final victory, and in announcing America's war aims in his "Fourteen Points," President Woodrow Wilson had repudiated all secret treaties and instead firmly espoused the principle of national self-determination. Specifically, Wilson's Point Twelve had demanded for the non-Turkish nationalities of the Ottoman empire "an undoubted security of life and an absolutely unmolested opportunity of development."

The war effort, with its simple, compelling imperatives, had superseded such differences and conflicts; at war's end they came to the fore with redoubled force. The Allied statesmen assembled at the Paris peace conference were preoccupied initially with questions such as Germany, the League of Nations, and the Bolshevik revolution in Russia. And in view of the conflicting commitments and pressures regarding the Middle East, it took several more years of intermittent diplomacy and occasional military action for the postwar settlement to take shape in the region. To the north, Turkish nationalists under Mustafa Kemal (the later Atatürk), in three years of tenacious fighting, frustrated Greek plans of conquest and Allied schemes of colonial partition for their country. Further to the south, three "mandates" were established: under the French in Syria (including Lebanon) and under the British in Iraq and Palestine (including what later became Jordan). Sharif Hussein, far from realizing his ambition of founding an "Arab Caliphate of Islam," had to content himself with a kingdom over the Hijaz—the region around Mecca and Medina of which he originally had been the hereditary administrator.

"Mandate" was a term adopted by the Paris conference to bridge the gulf between the practice of imperialism and the theory of national independence. As described in the Covenant of the newly formed League of Nations, mandates were to be "a sacred trust of civilisation," whereby certain "advanced nations" were to give "administrative advice and assistance" to "peoples not yet able to stand by themselves under the strenuous conditions of the modern world." In short, the mandate regimes in the Middle East were to be a program of foreign economic and technical aid designed to prepare these countries for full independence.

In practice, nonetheless, the "mandates" differed little from earlier colonial regimes. In March 1920, Sharif Hussein's son Faisal was enthusiastically proclaimed king of Syria (including Palestine) by an assembly in Damascus; but in August, French forces surrounded the city and, by a brief and fierce bombardment, ended the interlude of self-proclaimed independence. In Iraq, the British first used force to consolidate their rule and then shifted to a more conciliatory approach. Many of the officers who had joined the Arab Revolt were from Iraq, and after Faisal's ejection from Damascus the British invited him and his entourage to Baghdad, contriving a referendum in 1921 whereby 96 percent of the voters endorsed their prearranged choice of Faisal as king of Iraq. (The maneuver was described by a key British participant as "politics running on wheels greased with extremely well-melted grease.") Earlier in 1921 and without any pretense at election, the British had installed Faisal's elder brother Abdullah as ruler (emir) in the arid eastern part of their Palestine mandate, which was henceforth known as "Transjordan."

The French in their Syrian mandate set up a military and later colonial administration and, in a classic application of the "divide and rule" principle, did their best to emphasize religious and sectarian differences within the Arab population, such as those between the Sunni-Muslim majority and the Christian Arabs of Lebanon, the Shiite Muslims (Alawis) of the northern coastal region, and the Druzes in the southern mountains. The British instead applied a pattern of "indirect" rule that they had long developed in the princely states of India, around the Persian Gulf, and in parts of Africa: traditional local rulers preserved in their pomp and ceremony but ruling with the "advice" of British agents under the "protection" of British military forces—except in Iraq and Transjordan, where rulers without prior local connection had been imported by the British themselves.

In Palestine, the British labored under the added handicap of contradictory policies as stated in the Balfour Declaration and the mandate: There was to be a "national home for the Jewish people"; yet "nothing should be done which might prejudice the civil and religious rights of existing non-Jewish communities in Palestine. . . ." That over 90 percent of the population was a single Arab-Muslim community that cherished as its most precious "civil and religious right" the preservation of Palestine's Arab and Muslim character was a consideration conveniently brushed aside—which came to haunt British administrators in Palestine for the next quarter-century.

In the mandates, as in Egypt, Arab resentment and European bad conscience came to reinforce each other. The military force required to establish European rule in the Middle East made a mockery of the liberal principles embodied in the official pronouncements. To Middle Eastern nationalists, all the apologetic talk about "sacred trust," "temporary occupation," and "advice and assistance" sounded like so much hypocrisy, cant, and condescension. The admittedly temporary nature of the mandate or occupation regimes prevented both rulers and subjects from frankly and fully adjusting to the new realities. Both sides came to rely increasingly on force—of terrorism on one side and repression on the other. Indeed, in Palestine by the 1930s and 1940s, rival Arab and Zionist terrorist movements were pitted against a British mandate administration vacillating between accommodation and repression.

Western imperialists not only were late to arrive in the Middle East and apologetic about their mission; they also came all at once rather than one at a time. In more remote regions of the globe, a single European power usually established its predominance: Spain in South America and Britain in North America, Britain in India, Holland in Indonesia, Russia in Siberia, and France in northern and western Africa. Occasionally two of them would come into conflict, as when the Pope had to adjudicate between Spanish and Portuguese claims in the New World in 1493, the French and British clashed in Canada in 1759 and in the Sudan in 1898, or the Americans that same year took Puerto Rico and the Philippines from Spain. But the Middle East is near the geographic center of the inhabited world, a focal region where three continents join with branches of two oceans. Hence, in the last two centuries Russian, Austrian, British, French, German, Italian, and American imperial interests have all intersected in the Middle East at different times and in varying combinations.

At first such rivalry among the powers delayed their intrusion: the British fleet cut Napoleon off in Egypt in 1798; various agreements among the powers preserved Ottoman sovereignty in the mid-nineteenth century; and German forces helped the Ottomans fight until 1918. Yet the same powers that had first agreed to maintain a Middle Eastern state as a buffer might later spur each other on to its partition, as in Iran in 1907 or with the mandates in 1920. Later still, similar rivalries served to speed the colonialists' departure, as when Britain in 1945 held France to a wartime promise to evacuate Syria and Lebanon, or American and Soviet pressures hastened Britain's own departure from the region in the following decades.

In sum, the imperialists' half-heartedness and recurrent rivalries made of Western rule over the Middle East a briefer and more unsettled episode than it otherwise might have been. The record justifies the harsh judgment rendered by Bernard Lewis, leading Western historian of the region: "There is a case to be made for and against the imperial rule as a stage in political evolution. . . . But there is little that can be said in defense of the half-hearted, pussy-footing imperialism encountered by most of the peoples of the Middle East—an imperialism of interference without responsibility, which would neither create nor permit stable and orderly government."

Of course, Middle Easterners at times encouraged such "interference without responsibility." The temptation for them has been to profit from imperialist rivalries, encouraging the aspirations of the more remote power so as to loosen the grip of the power nearer at hand. This was the tactic of Sharif Hussein in 1916 in allying himself with the British against the Ottomans; of some Turkish and Syrian nationalists in encouraging American involvement in 1919; of a number of Arab leaders in the Second World War in cooperating with Nazi Germany against the British; and of recent Arab leaders such as Nasser, Kassem, and Qaddafi in aligning themselves with the Soviets against the West. The risks with this strategy are that it may not work—or work too well.

The strategy may fail because the foreign ally remains distant and proves unwilling to help. The United States after the First World War retreated into isolation and, having promoted the mandate idea, refused to take on any mandates of its own. In 1941 Hitler turned out to be too busy with his attack on Russia to pursue his advantage in the Middle East, and this allowed the British to suppress an anti-British coup in Iraq, whose leaders had vainly appealed for German help.

Or, the strategy may work too well in that the foreign ally moves in so close as to replace the previous foreign domination with a new one of his own. The Syrian and Iraqi nationalists who joined the sharif in 1916 soon found that they had exchanged their Ottoman for British and French masters. In Egypt after 1955, the Soviet presence became so massive that it was popularly known as the "Russian occupation"—and caused Sadat's break with Moscow to be greeted with joyous relief. The change of imperial masters, moreover, may well be for the worse: an ascendant and expansionist imperialism is likely to prove more oppressive than a tired and decadent one.

If a small country is to play successfully on the ambitions of the great powers, it has to muster enough indigenous strength to become a minor power in its own right. Thus Turkey in 1920–21 accepted some Soviet aid, then worked out a rapprochement with Britain and France, and in the Second World War preserved her neutrality while surrounded by belligerents. But Turkey had started off in 1919 by using armed force to assert her independence. As one of Sharif Faisal's associates stated at the time of his short-lived kingdom in Syria, "Complete independence is never given; it is always taken."

THE AGONIES OF NATIONALISM

The political and social divisions of the Middle East today reflect the facts of geography, the legacy of Islamic history, and the lingering effects of the Western imperial interlude.

The total area and population of the Middle East from Libya to Afghanistan and from Turkey to South Yemen are roughly equivalent to those of the United States. But the various parts of the region are separated by deserts, mountains, and branches of the sea; except along the coasts and in the major river valleys, much of it is uninhabitable. Politically, the Middle East is divided into as many as eighteen states, ranging in population from about 40 million for Turkey to about 100,000 for Qatar. And national and religious divisions occur within, or cut across, these boundaries.

The old Ottoman empire had been both multireligious and multinational. Under centuries of Ottoman rule, the sultans' Muslim, Christian, and Jewish subjects pursued their separate religious practices and, indeed, lived under their separate legal systems; moreover, Turks, Slavs, Romanians, Albanians, Greeks, Armenians, Kurds, Arabs, and many others each retained their own language. Government policy encouraged the geographic intermingling of these groups, and the economic pattern was one of an ethnic division of labor. The empire's soldiers and administrators, for example, were drawn from Balkan Christians converted to Islam and from Caucasian immigrants, the Muslim scholars *(ulama)* from the Arab population, and the merchants from Greeks, Jews, Armenians, and Arab Christians.

The Western imperial impact eroded and at length destroyed the Ottoman dynastic authority that had loosely held together this congeries of religions and nationalities. As recently as 1878, the Ottoman empire included all of the Middle East as here defined except Iran and Afghanistan in the East and the United Arab Emirates, Oman, and South Yemen in the Southeast. (See map 1 on the opposite page.) By 1920 the breakup into the present political units was complete. This fragmentation was not, of course, the result of any single imperialist master plan. Rather, it resulted partly from the encouragement given to secession among the Ottomans' subject nationalities—for example, the Greeks in the 1830s and the Arabs in the First World War. Partly it was a consequence of the gradual advance of imperial conquest: Algeria 1830, Tunisia 1881, Morocco and Libya 1912, and so forth. And on one occasion there was deliberate partition—when the mandate system was imposed on the Arab parts of the former Ottoman empire in 1921.

Within the separate colonies, or mandates, the European rulers often encouraged further divisions. The British in Iraq recruited some of the elite military force from the Assyrians, a small religious minority. In Syria the French gave local autonomy to religious splinter groups, such as the Alawis (Shiites) and Druzes—respectively, a minority within and an offshoot from Islam. Also Lebanon, which under Ottoman rule had been a small semi-autonomous district of Christian Arabs, was gerrymandered by the French into a much larger entity, with a bare Christian majority over a Muslim (Sunni and Shiite) minority. *"Divide et impera"* says the old Roman maxim; convenient as such fragmentation proved to the Western powers as they installed themselves, it correspondingly complicated their departure. In few regions of the world has religious and ethnic conflict in the postcolonial period raged as intensely as between Greeks and Turks on Cyprus, Arab Christians and Arab Muslims in Lebanon, and Israelis and Palestinians.

The presence of Israel in the Middle East is itself one of the more notable by-products of the Western imperial interlude. At the end of the First World War, there were only some 57,000 Jews in Palestine (about 9 percent of the population)—some communities continuously resident for centuries, others more recently established by Zionists. Toward the end of the mandate in 1946, the number of Jews had increased to about 600,000, or one-third of the total. When the British government in the Balfour Declaration committed itself to support of Zionism, it was thought that a pro-British population might help defend the imperial

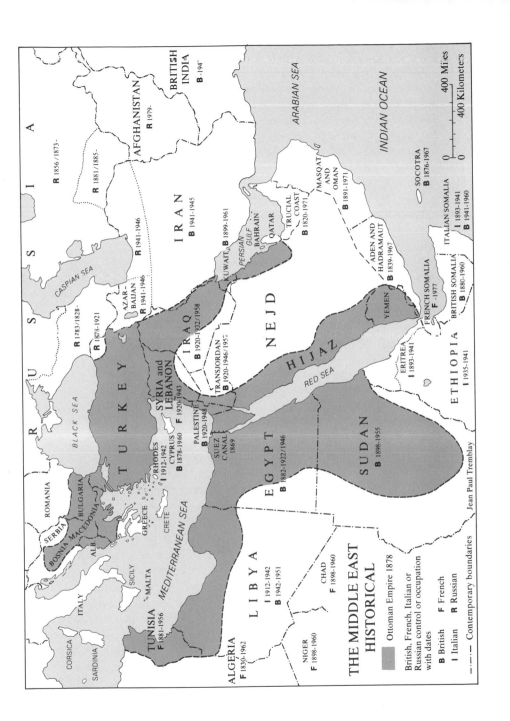

THE MIDDLE EAST
HISTORICAL

Ottoman Empire 1878

British, French, Italian or
Russian control or occupation
with dates

B British   F French
I Italian   R Russian

‐‐‐‐‐ Contemporary boundaries

Jean Paul Tremblay

S   S   I   A
R   U   S

BLACK SEA

CASPIAN SEA

AFGHANISTAN
R 1979·

BRITISH
INDIA
B 194?

ARABIAN SEA

INDIAN OCEAN

R 1856/1873-

R 1881/1885-

R 1783/1828-

R 1878-1921

R 1941-1946

R 1941-1946

AZAR-
BAIJAN

I   R   A   N
B 1941-1945

ROMANIA

SERBIA

BOSNIA

MACEDONIA

BULGARIA

ALB.

GREECE

T   U   R   K   E   Y

CRETE

RHODES
I 1912-1942

CYPRUS
B 1878-1960

MEDITERRANEAN SEA

SICILY

MALTA
B 1942-1951

ITALY

CORSICA

SARDINIA

TUNISIA
F 1881-1956

ALGERIA
F 1830-1962

NIGER
F 1898-1960

L   I   B   Y   A
I 1912-1942
B 1942-1951

CHAD
F 1898-1960

SYRIA and
LEBANON
F 1920-1943

PALESTINE
B 1920-1948

SUEZ
CANAL
1869

E   G   Y   P   T
B 1882-1922/1946

TRANSJORDAN
B 1920-1946/195?

I   R   A   Q
B 1920-1932/1958

KUWAIT
B 1899-1961

PERSIAN
GULF

BAHRAIN

QATAR

TRUCIAL
COAST
B 1820-1971

MASQAT
AND
OMAN
B 1891-1971

ADEN AND
HADRAMAUT
B 1839-1967

N   E   J   D

H I J A Z

RED SEA

YEMEN

S   U   D   A   N
B 1898-1955

ERITREA
I 1893-1941

ETHIOPIA
I 1935-1941

FRENCH SOMALIA
F -1977

BRITISH SOMALIA
B 1880-1960

ITALIAN SOMALIA
I 1893-1941
B 1941-1960

SOCOTRA
B 1876-1967

400 Miles

400 Kilometers

"lifeline" along the strategic Suez Canal and that Zionist support might swing American opinion more firmly to the Allied side in the world war. Some British leaders were impressed with the Zionists' singleminded devotion to an idealistic and seemingly unattainable goal. And Palestine, as part of the Ottoman empire, was in any case still enemy territory. But whatever the motives, Britain's commitment to Zionism had to be squared with the reality of an indigenous Palestinian population 91 percent Arab.

For the quarter-century of the mandate, British representatives steered a vacillating course that increasingly antagonized both Arabs and Jews. The exclusion of Transjordan from the mandate (and hence the provisions of the Balfour Declaration) satisfied neither side. When in 1929 and again in 1936 the British responded to violent unrest among the Arabs by granting political concessions, they encouraged future violence. The rise of Jewish immigration in the mid-1930s alarmed the nationalist Palestinians. Subsequent restrictions imposed on the flow of immigrants profoundly alienated Jewish opinion.

Both pro-Zionist and pro-Arab pressures increased with the end of the Second World War. For Jews who had lived through Hitler's holocaust, Zionism no longer represented an abstract utopia: it seemed to have become a necessity for the very survival of an entire people. The British had endorsed Zionism when it suited their imperialist convenience decades earlier; now that it had become a vital, humanitarian imperative, they turned their backs on that promise and severely restricted immigration. Having learned a lesson from the success of earlier Arab violence in exacting concessions, Jewish extremists, including the Irgun Zvai Leumi, under Menachem Begin, and the Stern group, mounted their own campaigns of terrorism.

The British, meanwhile, were eager to lighten their Middle Eastern burdens during and after the Second World War by cooperating with Arab nationalist tendencies. In 1941, Foreign Secretary Anthony Eden, in an effort to rally pro-British opinion in Iraq, Egypt, and elsewhere, had promised that Britain would give "full support to any scheme [of Arab unity] that commands general approval." This implied a further anti-Zionist commitment, for pan-Arabs would naturally consider Palestine an essential strategic link between the Asian and African halves of their wider nation and the Palestinians among the most educated and economically advanced Arabs. Furthermore, in view of the long record of Muslim-Christian-Jewish coexistence under caliphs and sultans, the transformation of Palestine from an Arab into a Jewish country was bound to seem to Arab nationalists like solving the European and Christian problem of anti-Semitism at Arab and Muslim expense. Why, at the very moment when colonial powers were withdrawing from all other parts of the Middle East, should colonialism in Palestine reappear in its most odious form? For most Arab Palestinians and for nationalist leaders in other Arab countries, Jewish statehood in Palestine and the partition of the country were anathema. Only after a lapse of three decades, after defeat in three wars and a stand-off in a fourth, could some Arab leaders begin to reconcile themselves to Israel's existence.

In the last years of the Palestine mandate, the scene was that of a civil war among Jewish, Arab, and British forces. By 1948 the British despaired of finding any solution and terminated their mandate; Israel declared its statehood; Arab-Jewish violence flared up into open warfare; and Israel's victory determined the borders of the new state for the following decades. In Israel, as earlier in Turkey, complete independence was not given but taken.

Considering the arbitrariness of the political boundaries that emerged from the interlude of Western imperialism in the Middle East, these boundaries have endured remarkably well. All eighteen states in the post-imperial Middle East are referred to, in the polite language of the United Nations and of international diplomacy, as "nations." But most of them are nations only in name, and a settled sense of national loyalty within any of these recently drawn boundaries is the exception rather than the rule.

Nations, in any region, are the product of complex historical processes. Most Western European countries (Great Britain, France, Sweden, Spain, and so forth) emerged in something like their present boundaries under hereditary monarchs three to six centuries ago. A growing bureaucracy helped the kings spread their authority throughout the regions of their realm, and linguistic and religious unity was usually the by-product of such unification from above. Later, the tighter economic and political web woven by the industrial revolution and parliamentary democracy helped transfer political loyalties from the monarch to the nation as a whole. (Nevertheless, current tensions in Northern Ireland, between Flemings and Walloons in Belgium, in the Basque region of Spain—and even in Brittany and Scotland—indicate how precarious the sense of national unity can be under even the best of circumstances.)

Germany and Italy did not achieve this early monarchic-bureaucratic unification. Instead, national unity resulted in the nineteenth century from a strong linguistic and cultural sense of identity—and from the military preponderance of one of the subnational states (Prussia in Germany and Piedmont in Italy). In Eastern Europe, in a broad belt from Finland to Bulgaria, nation-states filled the vacuum left by the collapse of dynastic (tsarist, Habsburg, and Ottoman) empires; but the *de facto,* or even *de jure,* independence of some of them proved to be brief. Finally, in some of the European colonies overseas (such as the United States, Canada, Brazil, Argentina, Australia, and New Zealand), immigration and the settlement of open spaces made for a strong sense of national cohesion on yet another—and highly durable—basis.

The European theory of nationhood and the corresponding ideology of nationalism were discovered in the Middle East by intellectuals in the late nineteenth century and by the broad masses in the mid-twentieth century—and in other non-Western regions a little earlier or later. Yet it happens that outside of Europe and Southeast Asia, there are only a few countries (such as the island nations of Japan and Madagascar) that conform to the European ideal of the nation-state as a political entity including all speakers of a given language and none other. In the Middle East, only two countries approximate this ideal: Turkey, where over 90 percent of the people speak Turkish and few Turkish speakers remain outside the national boundaries, and Israel (in its pre-1967 borders), where about 86 percent of the people speak Hebrew as their native or adopted language.

Throughout the remainder of the Middle East, linguistic and political borders do not coincide, and this discrepancy gives rise to three patterns.

• A single language is spoken in many countries: Arabic is the mother tongue of all or most of the population in a score of countries from Morocco to Oman and from Syria to South Yemen; the Kurds are a substantial linguistic group divided among Turkey, Iraq, Iran, and Syria, where they constitute from 4 to 16 percent of the population.

• Several languages are spoken in one country: in Iran only two-thirds of the people speak Persian, the remainder are divided among a dozen other languages.

• Several languages are spoken in one country and in one or more neighboring countries. In Afghanistan, about half the people speak Pushtu, which is also prevalent in Pakistan; one-third speak Persian; and the remainder, Uzbek, whose main concentration is in one of the member republics of the Soviet Union.

In Iran, the Persian-speaking majority has a strong sense of national identity with deep roots in the country's Islamic and pre-Islamic history. When Arab Muslims under the early caliphs conquered the vast region from Arabia to Spain in the West and the Indus valley in the East, the Iranians turned out to be the only subject population that retained its own language. Even the heterodox, Shiite version of Islam, which became prevalent in Iran, has served as a vehicle for national self-expression. The Shiite view of human history as an intense struggle between the forces of light and darkness harks back to earlier Iranian (Zoroastrian and Manichaean) themes, and the celebration of martyrdom and the expectation of the "Hidden Iman" who will reveal himself in the fullness of time have given recurrent hope to a long-suffering people that has seen conquerors come and go. In the eleventh to fifteenth centuries A.D., Persian literature attained its greatest flowering. And in the fifteenth to eighteenth centuries, Iran experienced a monarchic-bureaucratic unification in approximately its present boundaries—much as did the states of Western Europe.

But the Persian-speaking Iranians are surrounded by numerous minorities with different languages, including (counterclockwise from the North) Azeris, Kurds, Arabs, Qashqais, Baluchis, Turkomans, and many others. Whenever central authority has weakened or foreign pressures have mounted (as in 1906–21, 1945–53, and again since the collapse of the shah's regime in 1978–79) these divisive tendencies have come to the fore.

Arabs can look back to an equally rich and impressive cultural heritage. But Arab political unity and independence disappeared with the collapse of the early Islamic caliphate; by about 1500 most Arab populations came under Ottoman-Turkish rule, and by 1920 under European colonial rule. As the colonial powers withdrew from the region after the Second World War, the ideal of pan-Arabism—political unification of all Arabic-speaking peoples from Morocco to Oman—had a potent appeal to both the leaders and the masses. But the result has been a sequence of intense intrigues and bitter power struggles as each government, party, or individual leader tried to take advantage of this pan-Arab sentiment and establish wider unity on his or its own terms.

A certain verbalism and flamboyance are among the most engaging qualities of Middle Eastern and Arab culture. It was a Middle Easterner who two thousand years ago could write, in the opening sentence of the Gospel according to St. John, that "In the beginning there was the

Word. . . ." Alas, too often in the Middle East there is still no more than the word in the end.

More than two dozen schemes of political unification among Arab countries have been solemnly proclaimed or attempted since 1942; nearly every one has proved abortive. The major exceptions have been the short-lived United Arab Republic combining Egypt and Syria (1958–61); a number of mergers at the time of decolonization of territories divided in the colonial era (the French, Spanish, and neutral zones of Morocco, 1956; the Italian and British parts of Somalia, 1960); and the loosely structured Arab League, whose membership grew as Arab countries became independent, from seven in 1945 to twenty-two in 1977.

The first of the abortive unity moves, the "Fertile Crescent Scheme" of General Nuri Said of Iraq, was encouraged by the British in 1942, at a time when the German threat of invasion of the Middle East seemed imminent. It was rejected by Syria and Transjordan, whose counter-proposal of a "Greater Syria" found equally little support. When King Abdullah of Transjordan annexed the West Bank region of Palestine in 1949, the move was vocally denounced by Arab Palestinian nationalists, one of whom assassinated Abdullah in 1951. Although the West Bank was occupied by Israel in 1967, Abdullah's grandson Hussein has retained the title "King of Jordan."

Egypt, having defeated the various "Fertile Crescent" and "Greater Syria" schemes with its own Arab League proposal, proclaimed a joint military command with Syria and Saudi Arabia in 1951, and with Syria and Jordan in 1956—neither of them implemented. Proposals for merger or federation with the Sudan ("Unity of the Nile Valley") also proved abortive: the British in effecting their withdrawal in 1956, and on second thought the Sudanese, preferred full independence. Nasser's major political success, the United Arab Republic of Egypt and Syria of 1958, was dissolved in 1961, at the very time when economic was to follow upon political merger. Egypt retained the designation "United Arab Republic" throughout Nasser's reign; in 1971 it became the "Arab Republic of Egypt."

Nasser's merger with Syria prompted a rapprochement between Iraq and Jordan, which proclaimed an "Arab Federation" in 1958—but the violent overthrow of Iraq's monarchy prevented implementation. Republican Iraq once again became an active promoter of unity schemes. It claimed all of Kuwait's territory in 1961, but was deterred from invasion when the emir of Kuwait briefly invited British troops to return.

Following the victory of a pro-Nasser faction in Baghdad, Egypt, Iraq, and Syria proclaimed a federation in 1963, but Syria withdrew almost at once, and so did Iraq upon the discovery of an Egyptian plot against its president. Earlier, Nasser had proclaimed a federation between Egypt-Syria and Yemen ("United Arab States," 1958); instead, an inconclusive civil war in Yemen, between republican forces supported by Egypt and monarchists supported by Saudi Arabia, ended with Egypt's withdrawal in 1967.

President Qaddafi of Libya ardently wished to resume Nasser's uncompleted mission of Arab unification. A "Federation of Arab Republics" (1970) was to include Libya, Egypt, and the Sudan—or, as the Sudan withdrew, Syria. In 1972, Libya and Egypt proclaimed their "unified political leadership" and in 1973 "the birth of a new unified Arab state." But with Libya moving headlong into "cultural revolution" and Egypt under Sadat into economic liberalization the ideological and personal gulf widened. When Qaddafi sent a motorcade of twenty thousand Libyans toward Cairo to implement the union, Sadat had it stopped by force and Qaddafi responded with an abortive plot to assassinate Sadat.

The past decade has seen unimplemented unity proclamations between Yemen and South Yemen (1972), Libya and Tunisia (1974), Iraq and Syria (1979), Jordan, Syria and the PLO (1979), and Libya and Syria (1980). In 1975 Syria intervened in the protracted civil war in Lebanon among Palestinians and various Lebanese Christian and Muslim factions but was dissuaded by Israeli warnings from occupying the entire country. A nominal Lebanese government continues in Beirut but has no authority over the many armed camps into which the country is divided.

The withdrawal of British forces from the Gulf led to negotiations for a "Gulf Federation" among nine emirates, but upon the withdrawal of Qatar and Bahrain from the scheme, the remaining seven proclaimed themselves the United Arab Emirates. Rivalry between the emirs of Abu Dhabi and Dubai has kept the UAE a loose confederacy, which in its oil and foreign policies follows the lead of Saudi Arabia. Iraq's attack on Iran prompted the formation, in 1981, of a Gulf Cooperation Council, including Saudi Arabia, Kuwait, Bahrain, Qatar, the UAE, and Oman.

Almost as frequent as abortive mergers have been coups or political assassinations instigated from across the borders. When negotiations for unity break down over ideological differences or personal rivalries, often the next step is for one government to try to force the issue by plotting

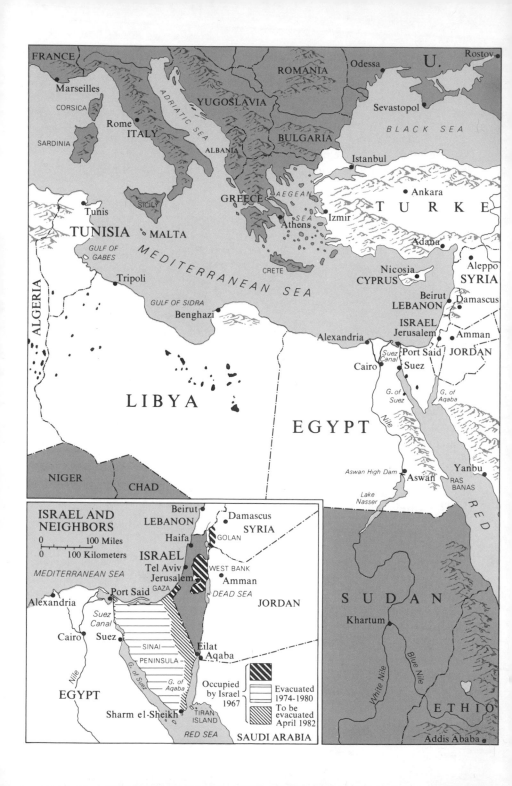

FRANCE

Marseilles

CORSICA

SARDINIA

Rome
ITALY

ADRIATIC SEA

ALBANIA

YUGOSLAVIA

ROMANIA

Odessa

U.

Rostov

Sevastopol

BLACK SEA

BULGARIA

Istanbul

Ankara

TURKE

Tunis

SICILY

TUNISIA MALTA

GULF OF
GABES

ALGERIA

Tripoli

GREECE

AEGEAN
SEA
Athens

CRETE

MEDITERRANEAN SEA

Izmir

Adana

Nicosia
CYPRUS

Aleppo
SYRIA

Beirut
LEBANON Damascus

GULF OF SIDRA

Benghazi

Alexandria

ISRAEL
Jerusalem

Amman

Suez
Canal Port Said JORDAN

LIBYA

EGYPT

Cairo Suez

G. of
Suez

G. of
Aqaba

Nile

NIGER

CHAD

Aswan High Dam

Lake
Nasser

Aswan

Yanbu

RAS
BANAS

RED

SUDAN

Khartum

ISRAEL AND
NEIGHBORS

0   100 Miles

0   100 Kilometers

MEDITERRANEAN SEA

Alexandria

Cairo

Beirut
LEBANON

Haifa

ISRAEL
Tel Aviv
Jerusalem
GAZA

Port Said

Suez
Canal

Suez

SINAI

PENINSULA

Nile

EGYPT

G. of Suez

Damascus
SYRIA

GOLAN

WEST BANK

Amman

DEAD SEA

JORDAN

G. of
Aqaba

Eilat
Aqaba

Sharm el-Sheikh

TIRAN
ISLAND

Occupied
by Israel
1967

Evacuated
1974-1980

To be
evacuated
April 1982

RED SEA

SAUDI ARABIA

White Nile

Blue Nile

ETHIO

Addis Ababa

S.   S   R.

ARAL SEA

CAUCASUS MTS

CASPIAN SEA

Tashkent

Samarkand

Batum
Tblisi
Baku

Tabriz

Kabul

Mashhad

Mosul
Kirkuk

Tehran
Qom

Herat
AFGHANISTAN

IRAN

Baghdad
I R A Q

Tigris

Euphrates

Isfahan

Z A G R O S   M T S

PAKISTAN

Basra

Abadan

KUWAIT

KHARG
ISLAND

PERSIAN GULF

Strait of
Hormuz
(OMAN)

SAUDI

Dhahran

BAHRAIN

QATAR

GULF OF OMAN

Medina

Riyadh

UNITED ARAB
EMIRATES

Abu Dhabi

Masqat

ARABIA

A R A B I A N
S E A

Jiddah
Mecca

OMAN

MASIRAH ISLAND

S
E
A

UNDEMARCATED

I N D I A N   O C E A N

SOUTH
YEMEN

THE MIDDLE EAST
TODAY

Massawa
Sanaa
YEMEN

DJIBOUTI
P I A

Djibouti

Berbera

SOMALIA

Aden

Bab el-Mandeb

GULF OF ADEN

SOCOTRA
(SOUTH YEMEN)

Oilfields

0   400 Miles

0   400 Kilometers

Jean Paul Tremblay

the overthrow of the other. (Libya under Colonel Qaddafi holds the all-time record of such alleged plots: against Morocco 1971 and 1972, Egypt 1974, Sudan 1976, Saudi Arabia 1976, Tunisia 1976 and 1977. If the allegations are true, impertinence would seem to have been matched by incompetence.) Frequent also have been border disputes leading to prolonged warfare, as between Saudi Arabia and Oman over the Buraimi oasis (1954–61) or between Algeria and Morocco over the Western Sahara (1976*ff.*), the rebellion in the Omani province of Dhofar supported by neighboring South Yemen (1965–75) or the brief war between Egypt and Libya (1972). Civil wars in one Arab country (for example, Yemen 1962–67, Lebanon 1975*ff.*) have typically resulted in military intervention by one or more others.

Many ambitious Arab political leaders, notably Gamal Abdul Nasser of Egypt (1954–70), Muammar al-Qaddafi of Libya (1969–), and Saddam Hussein of Iraq (1979–), have seen themselves as Arab equivalents of Bismarck in Germany or Cavour in Italy, bringing unity to the larger nation by a combination of politics, diplomacy, and warfare. Since all of them came to power by force, they have usually lacked the political skills that such a complex task of unification would require; nor has the recent Arab record in warfare (except in Algeria) been impressive. But behind these shortcomings, there is a more crucial difference. Prussia and Piedmont were not only the most populous and militarily the strongest in their respective group of states, but also economically the most prosperous and advanced. Among the Arab countries, Egypt has the largest population and the largest military forces—but its economic prospects are among the poorest. (Significantly, it was fear of a sharp reduction in their standard of living that prompted Syrians to oppose economic unification with Egypt in 1961 and thus to dissolve the United Arab Republic.) Without a single state that is both militarily and economically predominant, the problem of Arab unification along Bismarck-Cavour lines has remained insoluble.

For the past generation, the Arab countries of the Middle East have been in a most unhappy state of political suspense: too deeply divided in political organization to achieve effective unity; yet too close in political sentiment and aspiration to refrain from continual interference in one another's affairs.

The alternative, in sober fact, to such pan-Arab aspirations and frustrations is, of course, acceptance of national identity within the existing political boundaries. For the larger countries, this option of an Egyptian,

Iraqi, Saudi, Sudanese, or Algerian nationalism remains indeed an attractive alternative.

Egyptian developments in the past century illustrate the rival attractions of the smaller and larger national ideal. In 1881 and again in 1919, Egyptian political leaders acted as good Egyptian nationalists, concerned to secure independence for their own country. When a group of Syrian pan-Arabs appealed for help at the Paris peace conference of 1919, they received the polite reply "Our problem is an Egyptian problem and not an Arab problem." But a generation later, Egyptian leaders themselves had come to view the Egyptian problem as an Arab problem. As nationalists in Syria, Iraq, and Egypt all struggled for independence in the twilight of imperialism, the notion gained ground that inter-Arab differences were due only to the divide-and-rule tactics of the imperialists. Thus, as the foreign rulers withdrew, there was a surge of genuine enthusiasm for political unification. When Iraq promoted its Fertile Crescent scheme in the 1940s, Egypt's royal government felt obliged to respond with its own plan for the (broader but looser) Arab League. After the overthrow of the monarchy, Gamal Abdul Nasser proclaimed Arab unity to be his most cherished aspiration, and his vast popularity in Egypt and among the masses in other Arab countries was due, above all, to his championship of the pan-Arab ideal. But the dissolution of the union with Syria, the protracted and losing war in Yemen, three losing wars against Israel (in which the issues concerned mainly other Arabs, but Egypt suffered most of the casualties and the largest territorial loss), and the embarrassingly close embrace of the Soviets—all these produced a sobering effect. Under Sadat in the 1970s, there was a conscious reduction of foreign policy ambitions and a revival of pride in Egyptian (as distinct from, though not opposed to, Arab) nationality. The change of the country's official name from "United Arab Republic" to "Arab Republic of Egypt" in 1971 symbolized this transition.

In a broader historical perspective, Sadat's achievement may be compared to that of the Turkish nationalists under Atatürk—who forsook any ambition of resurrecting the Ottoman empire and instead concentrated on defending and building up a more compact and solid territory. Under Nasser as under the late Ottomans, there was a wide disparity between political-ideological ambitions and the political, military, and economic means to achieve them. Atatürk and Sadat, by contrast, insisted on bringing political ends in line with the available means. It is interesting to note that the futility of warfare in the distant mountains and deserts of Yemen (where Ottomans fought against a rebellion early in this century, and Egyptians fought a civil war in the 1960s) was a decisive motive for both leaders.

It may seem ironic that Israel and Turkey come closest to embodying in the Middle East the European ideal of the linguistic nation-state— since the vast majority of Israelis have lived in their country only for one or two generations, and since Turkish national consciousness is of equally recent origin. But Israel's national cohesion essentially derives from the same immigrant and pioneer spirit and the same power of cultural and linguistic assimilation as does that of the United States, Australia, or Brazil. These factors are reinforced in Israel by millennia of a strong Jewish religious tradition with its promise of return and redemption and by decades of a comprehensive government policy of cultural assimilation through the school system, military service for young women as well as men, and other social institutions. Israel within its pre-1967 boundaries thus became a state with a solid national majority of 86 percent. On the other hand, within the post-1967 *de facto* borders, including the West Bank, Gaza, and East Jerusalem, Jews constitute a small majority and, considering higher Arab rates of population increase, might find themselves outnumbered.

If Israel has the strong national identity of an immigrant country, Turkey, by contrast, is closer to the Western European tradition of monarchic-bureaucratic unification than surface appearances might suggest. The Westernizing sultans created an Ottoman bureaucratic and military elite comparable to those trained in France, Sweden, or Prussia one or two centuries before. The major difference was that where rising national consciousness allowed Prussia and Piedmont to expand their borders, it forced Ottoman Turks to contract theirs. For some time, the ruling class still wavered between identifying itself as "Ottoman" or as "Turkish." The nineteenth-century political opponents to the sultan were known, in their Paris or Brussels exiles, as *"Jeunes Turcs"*—but back home in Istanbul and Salonica they called themselves "New Ottomans." Following the 1908 revolution, which reimposed the written constitution on the sultan, there were debates about "Westernization," "Turkification," and "Islamization" either as major political alternatives or as joint necessities. As late as 1920, Mustafa Kemal (the later Atatürk) found it opportune to insist that the war of independence was being fought on behalf of an "Ottoman" and "Muslim," not a "Turkish" nation.

But as the First World War caused the surrender of most non-Turkish territories, and victory in the war of independence defined a territory with an overwhelming Turkish majority, the designations of "Turk," "Turkish," and "Turkey" finally won out. In the process of transition, the Turkish Republic inherited over 80 percent of the civil servants and over 90 percent of the military staff officers trained by the late Ottoman empire. The crucial asset of the Kemalists—which distinguished them from the leaders in other Ottoman successor states—was that they could draw on an army and bureaucracy that had fought an orderly retreat for a century and a half from territories two or three times as large.

POLITICS AND ISLAM

A generation later, Gamal Abdul Nasser was to define Egypt's political ambitions as bounded by three "concentric circles," Arab, Islamic, and Asian-African. Among Middle Easterners, and perhaps particularly among Arabs, the obstacle to a secure sense of national identity has been not only the territorial division of colonial and postcolonial days, but also the competition between national and religious loyalty.

"Render unto Caesar the things which are Caesar's," Jesus admonishes his disciples. In the Christian tradition, this contrast between religious and secular authority was confirmed by Christ's death on the cross, by the medieval power struggle between popes and emperors, and by the modern constitutional doctrine of separation of church and state. All these distinctions are totally alien to Islam. Whereas Christ was executed as a rebel, Mohammed, after a successful business career, became prophet, acknowledged head of a community, lawgiver, victorious battlefield commander, and founder of a state that quickly became an empire. The Koran and other Islamic sacred texts—just like the corresponding texts of Judaism—deal with the details of law, community organization, moral conduct, and personal hygiene, as much as they do with sin, redemption, and cosmology. The Muslim *ulama* (again like their Jewish counterparts) are not priests administering sacraments; rather they are learned men, trained to interpret the law and the scriptures. Muslim prayers can be performed equally well in the home as in the mosque. Since there is no priesthood, neither is there—except in the dissident "Twelver" Shiite sect prevalent in Iran and Iraq—any clerical hierarchy. In its majority Sunni version, Islam is, above all, a community religion.

Muslims expect to be rewarded not only in the hereafter but also here on earth, in accordance with the basic tenet that "Power belongs to God . . . and to the believers." But Islam, like any true religion, also shows its durability by providing solace in times of historic adversity. When Mongol and Turkish invasions during the Middle Ages destroyed most existing Muslim states, Islam survived through the growth of a network of religious orders, or brotherhoods; and before long the foreign conquerors were themselves converted to Islam. European imperialism similarly encountered its fiercest resistance from Muslim leaders and brotherhoods, including Abd al-Qadir in Algeria (1832–47), Sheikh Shamil in the northern Caucasus (1830–59), the Mahdi (or "Redeemer") in the Sudan (1885–98), and the Senussi order in Libya (1912–30). It would seem that, as a communal religion, Islam has not only been unaffected by the destruction of Muslim governmental systems, but perhaps shown a special resiliency at such times.

A fresh religious impulse under the hostile impact of the West issued from Jamal el-Din el-Afghani (1839–97), who sought both to revive and update Islam—restore it to religious fervor and prove its compatibility with modern life. His aim was to promote a spiritual and political regeneration that would enable Muslims from India to North Africa to shake off the European imperial yoke—an ideal sometimes referred to by outsiders as "pan-Islam." Afghani had many disciples among Egyptian intellectuals, for a time acted as adviser to the Ottoman sultan, and in his native Iran is credited with having engineered a nationwide boycott against a foreign tobacco monopoly as well as the assassination of a shah in 1896. Most Islamic fundamentalists of the twentieth century are Jamal el-Din's spiritual descendants. Among the most prominent has been the Muslim Brotherhood of Egypt, which developed in the 1940s as a widespread fraternal and charitable organization among the urban lower class, was responsible for several political assassinations in the late 1940s, mounted a guerrilla campaign that helped persuade the British in 1954 to evacuate the Suez zone, and periodically has constituted the only potential political challenge to the regimes of Nasser and Sadat. The austere religious fundamentalism of Libya's Colonel Muammar Qaddafi is close to the ethos of the Muslim brotherhood.

The origin of Middle Eastern nationalism can be traced back to European stimuli and influences. Yet sooner or later, it has had to come to terms with Islam—either fighting an uphill battle against religious opposition or disarming it by blending religious with nationalist themes. In limiting conscription to Muslim subjects, nineteenth-century Ottoman viziers reflected that Muslim soldiers would go into battle shouting "Allah! Allah!"—but how could Christians or Jews be expected to join? During the Turkish war of independence, a Turkish disciple of Afghani's, in a rousing poem entitled "Going into Battle," blended religious and nationalist motifs. Rhetorically the poet asks, "How can such faith be choked by that monster called Civilization with but one tooth left in its jaw?" (As Atatürk established a secular republic, the poet preferred to go into exile in Egypt; but the first, and less inflammatory, stanza of his poem still serves as the republic's national anthem.) Significantly, after the proclamation of the Turkish republic, there was never any legitimist political movement for the restoration of the sultan. The most serious resistance was a rebellion in the Kurdish regions led by a sheikh of the Naqshbandi order. In the 1950s, a quarter-century after the official banning of all Muslim orders, authorities discovered that the Tijanis, a brotherhood previously unrepresented in Turkey, had spread from North Africa—and was engaging in a concerted campaign to smash public statues (mostly of Atatürk) as violating the Muslim ban on graven images. By the 1970s, Atatürk's Republican People's party toned down the secularism of its founder sufficiently to be able to enter a government coalition with the Islamic-fundamentalist National Salvation party.

The transition from a secular toward a religious nationalism has been most striking among Arabs. At the time of the first intense cultural contacts with the West in the nineteenth century, Arab Christians in Syria and Lebanon were prominent among the early ideologues of Arab nationalism. The appeal of these early Arab nationalists was to all members of the Arab nation, regardless of religious creed or of political boundaries imposed by foreign conquerors. They could not, of course, ignore Islam. Islam, after all, is the greatest single Arab contribution to human history; and the Koran, as its first major written document, has given lasting shape to Arabic as a literary language. But the early nationalists were inclined precisely to stress the Arab-national and historical rather than the contemporary and religious aspects of Islam. As nationalism broadened its appeal from the intellectual middle class to the masses, nationalist and religious themes became increasingly intermingled. The bitter civil wars in Lebanon in 1958 and since 1975, which pitted Arab Muslims against Arab Christians, provide a clear indication of how far secular nationalism has given way to religious polarization.

In Iran, the religious element in nationalism is even more pronounced.

Shiite Islam contributed to the reassertion of a Persian sense of national identity after the Arab-Muslim conquest. The Shiites (of the "Twelver" variety prevalent in Iran and Iraq) also have—in sharp contrast to Sunnis —a steeply graded hierarchy of *mullahs, mujtahids,* and *ayatollahs* among their *ulama;* and *mullahs* have been prominent in all major spontaneous political movements, such as the tobacco boycott of the 1890s, the 1906 constitutionalist revolution, the party politics of the 1946–53 period, and the revolution of 1978–79.

WHEN CLUBS ARE TRUMPS

Thomas Hobbes, the seventeenth-century English philosopher, using a metaphor that has since gained wide currency, once likened politics to a game of cards. The players, Hobbes explained, must agree which card is to be trump—except in politics, where if no other card is turned up, clubs are trump. In most Middle Eastern countries in the past century, neither foreign imperial rule, nor indigenous national loyalties, nor religious organization have provided any reliable framework for the political process. Lack of agreement on constitutional principles, inexperience with parliamentary or electoral government, weakness of civilian bureaucracies, atrophy of political parties, all these help create an atmosphere where violence becomes the last resort—or too often the first resort—in politics. Mob demonstrations, riots, military coups, and assassinations have entered the standard repertoire of political action, and this widespread violence has propelled military officers into a central political role. The soldiers, after all, are professional experts in violence, and once clubs become trumps, it is the soldiers who hold the winning hand.

Several important historical and contemporary factors contribute to this prominence of military politics. Islam arose as a militant religion. *Jihad* (the forcible struggle to extend or defend the Muslim community) is a religious obligation; *emir al-mu'minin* (commander of the faithful) is one of the most frequent titles of the caliphs; and theology divides the world into the "House of Islam" and the "House of War." Nineteenth-century reforms in the Middle East began with the military—so that the officer corps soon emerged as the most Westernized social group. In Turkey, Egypt, and other countries, the military officers have been recruited from a broad social base, so that the army has become one of the major avenues of social mobility and merit recruitment. In Egypt in 1881; in the Ottoman Empire in 1876, 1908, 1909, and 1913; and in Iran in 1921 the modernized army overthrew the political regime under which the new officer corps had been trained.

The Western imperial interlude continued the tradition of violent politics. In Syria in 1920, French guns installed the mandate, setting aside Faisal's election as king, and in Iraq his contrived election merely completed the arrangements imposed by British force. In the 1920s and 1930s, parliamentary governments functioned intermittently in Iraq and in Egypt but, ultimately, with the support or at the sufferance of British military force. And once again it was violence—Britain's weakness as a result of the Second World War, Arab and Jewish terrorism in Palestine, and anti-British violence in Egypt—that prompted the first crucial steps toward Western withdrawal. In the larger and more advanced Middle Eastern countries (Egypt, Syria, Lebanon, Sudan, Iraq), the outgoing imperialists were careful to leave behind a set of parliamentary institutions—but these nowhere were buttressed by popularly rooted parties, an independent press, a neutral bureaucracy, or other elements of government by discussion. Within a few years after the withdrawal of Western troops (Egypt 1949–52, Syria 1946–49, Sudan 1956–58, Iraq 1955–58), the political structures they had left behind yielded to military coups. After a minimal interval to demonstrate the fragility and unpopularity of the artificially imposed civilian institutions, indigenous military rule had replaced foreign military occupation.

The Egyptian military coup ("revolution") of 1952 illustrates the almost direct transition from foreign to indigenous military rule. Until the 1930s, the Egyptian army had been commanded only by British officers; the future organizers of the 1952 coup, including Nasser, Sadat, and others, were members of the first entering class of the Egyptian military academy to which natives of Egypt were admitted. Among their most indelible impressions was the sight of British tanks surrounding the Egyptian royal palace to force a change of government in 1942. Later, as young regimental officers, they lost crucial battles in the Arab-Israeli war of 1948—defeats that they blamed on inferior equipment supplied by corrupt civilian politicians. Nasser and his friends felt that there was "a role in search of a hero"—the role of liberating Egypt and other Arab countries from foreign influence and indigenous corruption. "If the Army does not do this job," they exclaimed, "who will?"

The intoxication with the successful coup, however, quickly evaporates and, indeed, gives way to nagging headaches. The departure of the foreign rulers seems like an overwhelming achievement, but the real struggle for power and influence on a crowded international scene has only begun. A new player has been added to the old poker game of Arab unity, and the regional atmosphere thickens with new combinations and intrigues. Back home, rapid economic development, overpopulation, urbanization, the widening gap between rich and poor, and the continuing clash between Western and Islamic ideals add to the social tensions. The higher the popular expectations placed on the new regime, and the grander the ambition of the military rulers themselves, the keener will be the disappointment.

Within the junta itself and the officer corps from which it sprang, unexpected frictions arise. Aging generals will not graciously take orders from colonels who only yesterday were their subordinates but, thanks to the coup, now claim authority as chief of staff, minister of war, or head of state. As the disgruntled seniors are consigned to early retirement and replaced by junior officers, any ambitious lieutenant and captain comes to believe that he carries in his knapsack not just a marshal's baton but the ruler's scepter. Civilian politicians, meanwhile, have begun to fawn on the new military rulers, and differences of judgment or personal rivalries within the junta quickly acquire an ideological flavor. Popular dissatisfaction has long since turned against the incumbents. The stage is set for a second coup—and perhaps a third.

The sequence of events just sketched applies most strikingly to Syria and Iraq. In Syria there were no fewer than three coups in 1949: a bloodless one in March, which aligned the country with Egypt and Saudi Arabia in the current phase of inter-Arab intrigue; one in August, which produced a rapprochement with Iraq and Jordan; and one in December, which installed in power for the next four years a leadership that retreated into almost complete isolation—even while proclaiming Damascus to be the "heart of the Arab nation." There followed five years of intense parliamentary and electoral maneuvring, in which the Arab Socialist Baath party (a pan-Arab group with radical leanings), the Syrian communist party and its sympathizers, and various army factions (divided, as often as not, along sectarian lines) intensely participated. The result was the three-year union with Egypt (1958–61)—followed by another spate of coups in 1961, 1963, 1966, and 1970.

In Iraq after the proclamation of independence from the mandate in 1932, there were as many as seven coups between 1936 and 1941—followed by five years of *de facto* British military rule and a dozen years of governments selected mostly from within the circle of officers and politicians who had supported the British mandate and Faisal's monarchy in the 1920s. The game of musical chairs among these oligarchs came to an abrupt end with the military coup of 1958, the leaders of which presided over the bloody liquidation of members of the preceding regime. There followed a continual power struggle (much as in Syria earlier) between the local branch of the Baath party, the communists, and various military groups, punctuated by two military coups in 1963 and one in 1968. From 1958 to 1968, and briefly in the mid-1970s, there was also an intermittent civil war between successive Baghdad regimes dominated by Sunni Arabs and the Kurdish population of the northern mountains —at times aided with supplies from Soviet Russia or from the shah's Iran.

But variations on the staccato sequence of military coups in Syria from 1949 to 1970 and in Iraq from 1958 to 1968 also have occurred. Monarchy has continued in Jordan, Saudi Arabia, Kuwait, Oman, and the smaller gulf principalities—although Jordan's King Hussein has survived a number of attempted military coups and draws his political strength in part from his personal leadership of the armed forces, and although the Saudi regime survived one coup attempt in 1969 and the assassination of a monarch in 1975. Also, some of the rulers installed by military force have proved highly durable. The Iraqi regime of 1968 continues in power, except for a peaceful reshuffle in 1979 that replaced the retiring General Hassan el-Bakr with General Saddam Hussein. In Libya Colonel Qaddafi has been in power since he and a group of young officers overthrew the monarchy in 1969. And in Syria General Hafez el-Assad has exercised power since 1970, maneuvring skillfully on the shifting domestic, regional, and international political scene.

The besetting weakness of military rule is its patent illegitimacy. As long as the soldiers can only claim that clubs are trumps—or, as Lenin put it, that power flows from the barrel of a gun—they have issued an open invitation to any other group of soldiers to outgun them at the first opportunity. Since the new rulers are likely to have their hands on microphones (in addresses to the nation, at state dinners, or at summit meetings abroad) and not on their holsters, the opportunity will soon arise. To remove the stigma of its birth, the new regime must retain full control of the army while beginning to rely on means other than force —bureaucracy, ideology, party organization, electoral endorsement, personal charisma, or some combination of these. The soldier-rulers' ultimate political success is to transcend the military origins of their rule.

The most successful regimes by this criterion have been that in Turkey after 1920 and that in Egypt after 1952. Both of these remained in power for more than a quarter-century, and both of them registered that rare accomplishment among dictatorships—a smooth succession upon the founder's death.

In Turkey, of course, Kemal Atatürk did not come to power through any military coup; rather, he secured an assignment from the defeated government in Istanbul, which he used to organize a military and civilian movement of national resistance in the provinces. The Grand National Assembly, which he called to Ankara, represented a wide spectrum of opinion and forced his provisional government to engage in a genuine process of political give and take. At war's end, Kemal organized his People's party, with a wider network of local branches than any previous Turkish movement. He also forced his associates to make a clear choice between a political or a military career; those who remained soldiers he ordered back to the barracks with the kind of emphasis only a victorious general-turned-politician can give to such an order. Although Atatürk twice experimented with opposition parties and twice abandoned the experiment, elections were held at regular intervals, and a wide range of opinions tolerated. Under his successor Ismet İnönü (who held the presidency from 1938 to 1950), opposition parties, a free press, and free elections were at last allowed. Turkey thus embarked on the even rarer course of a peaceful transition from one-party dictatorship to multiparty democracy.

In Egypt after 1952, there was a brief internal struggle within the junta by which Nasser (the original organizer of the coup) replaced Mohammed Nagib as president. Nasser's ambitious pan-Arab policy and his success in playing on the rivalry of the superpowers greatly enhanced his popularity. Various attempts to set up a political party ended in failure; instead, the regime relied increasingly on the support of the bureaucracy.

As in Turkey, the army was once again confined to its military tasks —but the succession to Nasser in 1970 was not quite as smooth as that to Atatürk in 1938, since Anwar el-Sadat's chief rival had the full backing of the Soviet Union. Still, once in the saddle, Sadat ruled with a light hand. His abandonment of Nasser's overstrained pan-Arabism, his severance of the close ties with the Soviet Union, the partial victory in the Yom Kippur War, all these enhanced Sadat's popularity and enabled him to liberalize his regime even while pursuing his dramatic peace negotiations with Israel. Mounting criticism, by Egyptians and other

Arabs, of the actual peace treaty of 1979 gave rise to considerable discontent and an unprecedented wave of political repression. Still, following Sadat's assassination in October 1981, the new president, Hosni Mubarak, was able to revert to the earlier course of firmness and conciliation.

The role of the military furnishes another illustration of how closely domestic and international politics have become intertwined in the Middle East in recent decades. To the domestic tensions that have favored military intervention in politics have been added factors of ethnic conflict (during the Palestine mandate and in the recurrent Iraqi-Kurdish civil war), inter-Arab manipulation, and great-power rivalry. Since most Middle Eastern boundaries correspond to no deeply felt national loyalties, the dividing line between domestic and foreign policy is constantly blurred. Rival internal factions appeal for money, political support, or weapons from the outside; conversely, outside powers try to profit from internal tensions to promote their own particular designs in the region. The outside powers most profoundly interested in Middle Eastern politics since the 1950s, of course, have been the Soviet Union and the United States, and one of their favorite means of seeking to extend their influence has been the gift or sale of arms to client (or would-be client) regimes. The region's rapidly growing oil income has further accelerated that trend, which has made of the Middle East one of the world's most highly armed regions. In sum, the most callous aspect of the rivalry of the superpowers in the Middle East has been their eagerness to furnish the professional soldiers of the region, in ever more lavish quantities, the weapons with which to attack neighboring countries, overthrow existing governments, or coerce the allegiance of their countrymen.

2

AMERICA'S GROWING INVOLVEMENT

WOODROW WILSON'S EMISSARIES DISCOVER THE HITHER
EAST

Americans long stayed aloof from the European scramble for
the Middle East; indeed, the United States was the last of the world's
powers to develop any interests in the region or formulate a policy
toward it. Americans, of course, were not averse—whatever Washington's Farewell Address might have counseled to the contrary—to asserting their interests, engaging in diplomatic maneuvers, or expanding their
power; but these concerns were quite fully engaged nearer to home.
Americans were proud to have shaken off colonial rule, pleased to see
their revolution spread to South America, and determined (as President
Monroe made clear in his doctrine) to forestall a reassertion of European
colonial power on this side of the Atlantic. Meanwhile, there was half
a continent to be wrested from the Indians and opened to agriculture.
There were a vast region from Texas to California to be appropriated or
conquered from Mexico, a ferocious Civil War to be fought between
southern and northern states, a banking system to be founded, railroad
tracks to be laid, and industrial empires to be organized. A lengthy
engagement with the Barbary pirates in North Africa preoccupied
America in 1801–15. But when the impulse for imperial expansion did
seize Americans, it was directed toward Puerto Rico, Cuba, Panama,
and other localities around the Caribbean, or toward the Philippines
across the Pacific. The Middle East, so close and familiar to Europeans

from the time of the crusades to the perennial "Eastern Question" of nineteenth-century diplomats, was simply too remote to engage America's attention.

One early exception was the American Protestant missionaries, who were attracted to the Muslim Middle East, as they were to Confucian China, because it presented vast infidel regions in which to spread the gospel and save damned souls. Since Muslim rulers punished apostasy from Islam with death, the missionaries soon concentrated their efforts on other Christians—Armenian Gregorians, Orthodox Greeks, Maronites in Lebanon, Copts in Egypt—and developed a wide variety of philanthropic activities to which there was no Muslim objection: medical service, disaster relief, and above all, education. By the beginning of this century there were a dozen such American institutions—hospitals, high schools, colleges, dispensaries, along with mission stations for Christians —in cities throughout the Middle East, including Salonica, Istanbul, Izmir, Adana, Damascus, and Cairo. The oldest and for over a century the most influential was the American University of Beirut, or AUB, originally founded as Syrian Protestant College in 1866. AUB was one of the few centers of learning where Arab Christians and Arab Muslims could freely mingle; it thus became one of the first seedbeds for Arab nationalism.

America's aloofness from the Middle East came to an abrupt end in 1918. American participation in the war had expanded the European conflict into a *world* war, and preparations for the peace quickly involved the United States in the world's thorniest diplomatic and political issues —in Eastern Europe and the Middle East. The tsar's empire had collapsed in 1917; the Austro-Hungarian and Ottoman empires had shared Germany's defeat; and a dozen or more ethnic groups—Finns, Poles, Czechs, Slovaks, Croatians, Serbs, Greeks, Arabs, Zionists, Armenians, Kurds, and others—were pressing nationalist or irredentist claims. The task of redrawing the political map along a broad zone from the Baltic in the north to the Red Sea and the Persian Gulf in the south was more formidable than any that had been attempted by the world's powers since the congress of Vienna after Napoleon's defeat in 1815.

Some of those claims evoked warm sympathy among Americans. The centuries-old struggle of the Poles for national liberation had long been close to the hearts of liberals in the West, and nowhere closer than among Polish-Americans. The new nation of Czechoslovakia took shape in an agreement between Czech and Slovak exile leaders concluded in Pittsburgh in May 1918. Zionist organization was strong among American Jews, and sympathy for Zionist aspirations was even more widespread. Louis Brandeis, a brilliant lawyer and friend of Woodrow Wilson's whom the president had named as the first Jew to the Supreme Court, was a vocal spokesman for Zionism.

Wilson himself, in his Fourteen Points of January 1918 and his contributions to the Paris peace conference the next year, was eager to elevate questions of peacemaking and territorial settlement to the highest level of principle. America had no territorial or colonialist ambitions of her own, she had fought the war to "make the world safe for democracy" and would not support the vindictive impulses or expansionist desires even of her own allies. Instead of the old diplomacy with its secret treaties, there was to be a new diplomacy with open covenants openly arrived at. Peace in Europe was to be based not on the arbitrary bartering of peoples and territories that had so long been practiced by hereditary autocrats: it was to be a democratic peace, securely founded on the will of the peoples themselves. Where national allegiances were in doubt in this or that border region, a plebiscite could settle the issue democratically. And rising over this new structure of national self-determination there was to be a League of Nations to preserve the peace in the future.

Wilson's rhetoric was received with polite skepticism or pointed silence by Clemenceau, Lloyd George, and other veteran politicians enmeshed in the power struggles at Paris. It was greeted with enthusiasm among long oppressed or newly aroused peoples who, lacking any of the resources of power, were ready to set their hopes on a peace not of power but of principle. Eastern European national delegations freely invoked Wilson and the arguments for self-determination.

In the Middle East there was equal enthusiasm, and even some sentiment in favor of League of Nations "mandates," provided the United States, with its outstanding record of disinterested philanthropy in the region, agreed to be the mandatory. In the capital of the defeated Ottoman empire, a group of Turkish nationalists founded the Society for Wilson's Principles; among the members was the first woman graduate of the college established by American missionaries in Istanbul. The grand vizier lectured members of the sultan's council of state on the distinction between an "American protectorate," which he rejected as incompatible with the dignity of the defeated Ottoman empire, and an "American mandate," which he found worthy of further discussion. A few months later, at a Turkish nationalist congress he had convened,

Mustafa Kemal (Atatürk) had to tax his ingenuity to forestall any pronouncement in favor of an American mandate.

Earlier, at the Paris peace conference, Wilson himself—who had
started his career as a political science professor before launching into
actual politics—had urged the major allies "to do all [they] could to find
the most scientific basis for a settlement" and, to this end, to send a
commission of inquiry to Syria "to elucidate the state of opinion." But
the French were unwilling to appoint any members to the commission,
however scientific, and the British on second thought withdrew theirs—
which left Wilson's two appointees, Henry Churchill King and Charles
R. Crane, to steam off to Palestine and Syria by themselves.

The composition of the commission and its staff reflected America's
range of interests in the Middle East at the time and demonstrated the
approach that an administration such as Wilson's was likely to have
toward new and baffling questions of foreign policy. Dr. King was on
leave as president of Oberlin College to direct YMCA operations in the
European war theater. Crane, a plumbing manufacturer from Chicago
and regular financial contributor to presidential campaigns, had changed
his party preference from Republican to Democratic after President Taft
had first named him United States minister plenipotentiary to Peking
and then withdrawn the nomination.

A member of Wilson's staff had quipped that the president had "felt
that these two men were particularly qualified to go to Syria because they
knew nothing about it." This was a quite unfair: both men had frequently
visited the Middle East, King in pursuit of his Biblical studies and Crane
for his love of travel. The mission's senior staff member was Professor
Albert Howe Lybyer, America's leading historian of the Middle East at
the time. More recently Lybyer had joined Colonel E. M. House's "Inquiry"—that group of spirited intellectuals who undertook to supply
House's good friend Wilson with those scientific data on the ethnic,
religious, and historic divisions that he believed the peace conference to
need. The two junior staff members were Dr. George R. Montgomery,
a second-generation American missionary born in southern Turkey, and
Captain William Yale, an engineer who had served with the Standard Oil
Company of New York, as the State Department's intelligence agent in
Cairo, and as American military observer with the British forces in
Palestine and Syria.

Through Biblical studies, missionary education, petroleum engineering, and political campaign contributions, the King-Crane commission

represented most of the concerns that for many decades were to influence American policies toward the Middle East—with the conspicuous exception of Zionism. Wilson, like other presidents after him, was suspicious of the professional expertise of senior State Department officials. He preferred to seek advice from private individuals—perhaps more disinterested but certainly also less experienced. And though himself a friend of Zionism, Wilson, again like many later Americans, preferred to keep his dealings with, and sympathies for, Jews and Arabs neatly separated.

In anticipation of King's and Crane's visit, a "General Syrian Congress" had just proclaimed Sharif Faisal king of Syria and redefined a "mandate" as "equivalent to the rendering of economical and technical assistance" and thus compatible with "our complete independence." The Syrians continued, "And desiring that our country should not fall a prey to colonization and believing that the American Nation is farthest from any thought of colonization and has no political ambition in our country, we will seek the technical and economical assistance from the United States of America, provided that such assistance does not exceed 20 years."

The position of the Syrian congress was a classic instance of the Middle Eastern tactic of trying to play the far-away against the near-by foreigner. The British had let down Faisal's father in his hopes for an independent Arab kingdom; the French were ready to impose their rule in Syria by force; and Faisal had no military forces to oppose the British or the French. Only the remote hope of American assistance remained against the imminent threat of falling "prey to colonization" by the French.

King's and Crane's recommendations to the Paris peace conference were fully compatible with the Syrian resolution and, specifically, endorsed Faisal as king of Syria. The document is worth quoting at some length as an indication of the frame of mind that some Americans had in 1919, making them ready to shoulder far-reaching responsibilities in the Middle East. The purpose of the mandate should be the "education [of] citizens of a democratic state, the development of a sound national spirit," the establishment of "complete religious liberty," and the fostering of "economic development." The ideal mandatory power should be one that would "be willing to enter heartily into the spirit of the mandatory system" and eager to make "its possible gift to the world. . . . It should have a passion for democracy . . . unlimited sympathy and patience in what is practically certain to be a rather thankless task." It should be willing to provide an unprecedented example "of the self-sacrificing spirit in the relations of peoples to one another." Of course, no nation "combines all those qualifications . . . in equal degree." Yet, "From the point of view of the desires of the 'peoples concerned,' the mandate should clearly go to America"; over 60 percent of 1152 petitions received by the Commission had expressed that desire. And "America, as first choice of the [Syrian] people, probably need not fear careful testing, point by point," against all the ideal qualifications just listed. King and Crane also surmised that "No power probably would be more welcome, as a neighbor," to existing British and French interests in the Middle East; they contemplated the establishment of a second American mandate, over Turkey, where "no other Power could come . . . with hands so free to give impartial justice to all the peoples concerned."

The priorities are revealing: first, education for democratic citizenship and establishment of (unspecified) democratic institutions; then, religious liberty; then, economic development (likewise unspecified); and finally, some disingenuous speculation that Britain and France might actually "welcome" America's presence as a "neighbor" in the Middle East. The recognition that any mandate might prove to be a "thankless task" is balanced by the smug assurance that Americans "probably need not fear" to be judged by the very highest of moral standards. How mere petitions can serve to ascertain "the desires of the people" is left unexplained. No estimate is made of the financial cost that might be entailed by educational and technical assistance on such a scale. There is not even a passing mention of the need for military forces. Nor did the Commission, despite Crane's long-standing interest in electoral politics, ask itself how Wilson's administration might rally the necessary congressional and public support behind an American national commitment of such magnitude.

By the time King and Crane submitted their report in Paris, Wilson had already left for Washington; and seven months later, the Senate rejected the Treaty of Versailles with its provisions for a League of Nations, thus precluding any Middle Eastern mandates as America's "possible gift to the world." Promptly the British and the French at San Remo, finding the Middle Eastern prospects perhaps rather more "welcome" without the intrusion of any American "neighbor," allocated the mandates over Syria (including Lebanon) to France and over Iraq and Palestine (including today's Jordan) to the British. On 7 August 1920— just a year after King's and Crane's visit—French troops put an end to Faisal's short-lived kingdom in Syria.

Where the principle of national self-determination prevailed in the Middle East, it did so by virtue not of American support or encouragement but of desperate self-help within the habitual framework of power politics. As Kemal Atatürk put it in looking back on the early phases of the Turkish war of independence—with just a shade of condescension, "I confess that I also tried to define the national border somewhat according to the humanitarian purposes of Wilson's principles. But let me make clear at once: On the basis of those humanitarian principles I defended boundaries which Turkish bayonets had already defended and laid down. Poor Wilson, he did not understand that lines which are not defended by the bayonet, by force, by honor and dignity, cannot be defended by any other principle."

America's refusal to join the league, to take on mandates, or to help redraw the political map of the Middle East did not imply any lack of continuing, or even growing, interest in the region. It simply meant that, for the next two decades or more, private groups rather than deliberate government planning would set the pace in defining and developing those interests.

One group with clearcut interests was the American oil industry, which did not wish to see the British and the French monopolize the exploitation of possible petroleum resources in Iraq or elsewhere in the region. The State Department, even after the debacle of Wilson's plans for participation in the league, did not mind warning the British that any economic concessions granted should not "have the effect of placing American citizens or companies . . . at a disadvantage compared with [those] of the Mandate nation." The consequence of this insistence on an "open door" was to include two American firms in the consortium that came to hold the petroleum concessions in Iraq and other countries —which in turn tied American companies prominently into the oligopolistic network that was beginning to emerge in the global oil industry.

American private support for Zionist plans in Palestine was another Middle Eastern interest that crystallized in the period between 1920 and 1945. The Zionist sympathies of Wilson and some of his circle were among the considerations that had prompted the issuing of the Balfour Declaration in 1917. In world-wide Jewish efforts to muster financial and organizational support for Zionist settlement in Palestine, American organizations soon came to play a leading part. With the Nazi holocaust sweeping over Europe, and with Britain just then committing itself to an increasingly pro-Arab and even pan-Arab policy, the center of gravity of Zionism outside Palestine itself was fully shifting to the United States. It was thus no coincidence that the postwar program of the world Zionist movement was adopted (May 11, 1942) at a meeting of the American Zionist Organization at the Biltmore Hotel in New York. Where the Balfour Declaration a quarter-century earlier had supported the "establishment in Palestine of a national home for the Jewish people," the Biltmore program now urged that the whole of "Palestine be established as a Jewish Commonwealth integrated in the structure of the new democratic world." The goal of statehood for Israel (as earlier for Czechoslovakia) was first proclaimed on America's hospitable soil. In 1944 the United States Congress came close to voting a resolution endorsing that same aim. With the end of the war, President Truman urged the British to admit immediately one hundred thousand Jewish survivors from Europe to Palestine—a proposal subsequently endorsed by a joint Anglo-American Committee of Inquiry. In 1947 the United States (along with the Soviet Union and thirty-one other countries) voted in favor of the United Nations' partition plan for Palestine, which by then was supported by the Zionist movement and bitterly opposed by the Arab states. And a few hours after the proclamation of the state of Israel, the United States became the first government to accord it *de facto* recognition.

FRANKLIN ROOSEVELT'S VISION OF GLOBAL PEACE

As Americans went into the Second World War, they felt moral commitments as deep as had their fathers in 1917 and 1918. They were fighting for democracy and against Nazi tyranny, for a peaceful world order and against aggression, for global prosperity and against the devastations of periodic economic crisis. American leaders had learned from the bitter experience of Wilson's failure in 1920. Roosevelt and his circle were inspired by a vision of a world where the danger of war would be banished (or reduced to such dimensions that an alert fire brigade could put out the spark); where commerce could proceed freely to link all mankind in a grand division of labor; and where flows of money among stable currencies would insure the optimal use of the world's resources. Earlier, the grandiose vision of a "world safe for democracy" had been followed by the grand sulk of isolationism; now American leaders took a series of deliberate steps to bring their sturdier vision fully to life. The Bretton Woods conference, even before the end of the war, dealt with the problems of currency stabilization and set up the International Monetary Fund and the International Bank for Reconstruction and Development. With the war drawing to a close, the San Francisco conference instituted the United Nations with its Security Council as a possible executive arm. And whereas the United States a quarter-century before had been conspicuously absent from Geneva, it now became the host to the new world organization.

Reluctantly at first, but then firmly, American leaders faced the need to secure this emerging political and economic order against Russian expansionism. Communist election victories or takeovers in France and Italy were avoided. The Truman Doctrine (1947) asserted the principle of containment: American economic and military aid helped protect Turkey against overwhelming Soviet diplomatic pressure and, by 1949, insured victory in Greece over externally supported communist guerrillas. The Berlin airlift (1948–49) demonstrated that Americans meant to defend the postwar demarcation lines in Europe, however hastily or precariously drawn. NATO asserted the principle of collective self-defense among the United States, Canada, and the nations of Western Europe. The Korean "police action" (1950–53), endorsed by the United Nations through a remarkable lapse in Russian diplomatic tactics, repelled aggression by proxy in Asia.

Within this emerging political and economic world order, colonialism seemed like an embarrassing legacy of bygone days, and Americans alternately coaxed and pressured their European friends to grant independence to their colonies, just as America herself had conferred independence on the Philippines. Meanwhile, successive tariff reductions, most of them initiated by Washington, tied the world's leading trading nations more closely together. And a number of Third World countries, such as Taiwan, South Korea, Singapore, Pakistan, and Brazil, soon began to join in the global upsurge of capitalist development.

But then, some fifteen or twenty years after the Second World War, things began to go wrong. The Soviets refused to stay contained and proceeded to create their own intimate relations of foreign aid with such countries as Egypt, Iraq, and Algeria. Fidel Castro's revolution in Cuba, at first widely applauded by liberal opinion in the United States, turned out to have created a communist dictatorship only one hundred miles from the shore of the United States—and to have considerable appeal to anti-*yanqui* sentiment throughout Latin America. The Soviet Union and Communist China vied with each other in trying to establish their influence over newly independent African states. The United Nations, upon the wholesale admission of new members in the 1960s, turned out to be less and less "united," and the status of many of the new members as "nations" was just as doubtful. Increasingly its proceedings were mired in rhetoric, and on the final votes, the United States, as likely as not, found itself in the minority.

The war in Vietnam, unlike that in Korea, proved to be no simple "police action"; far from being undertaken with the United Nations' blessings, it increasingly turned world opinion against the United States. The Vietnam War lasted longer than any previous war in which America had fought, and casualties were almost as high as in the First World War. Yet it became an unwinnable war—for lack not of lives sacrificed or military means employed but of realistic definition of political goals. And no sooner had the United States painfully extricated itself from the struggle in Southeast Asia than the OPEC revolution inspired fears, in Secretary Kissinger's words, of a "collapse of the world order."

In the 1980s, Americans—who have lived through the bitter frustration of Vietnam, the lingering economic crisis of the 1970s, and the gradual erosion of our prestige and world leadership—probably need to pause for reflection before we can look back upon the full vision of world peace and prosperity of the 1940s and recognize how sweeping, how consistent, and how successful a vision it proved to be. With regard to the "first world" of democratic and economically advanced countries, a rating of "excellent" would seem to be in order. With regard to the "second world" of Marxist-Leninist regimes in Russia, China, and Eastern Europe, the rating might well be "satisfactory." Only with regard to the remaining "third world" must the verdict be one of failure.

Among the countries of the first world, West Germany and Japan emerged from their postwar occupation regimes as vigorous, full-fledged democracies and thriving, export-oriented economies; clearly, America's efforts had decisively contributed to reshaping the societies of both the former enemies in her own image. Western Europe became economically united—in the European Community of the Six and then the Nine and the Ten—to enjoy unprecedented prosperity. Americans had encouraged such economic union, even at the risk of training a formidable competitor in the world's export markets. (Perhaps no one knew just how formidable. To have extended the Marshall aid as loans rather than grants would have seemed unforgivable stinginess at the time: yet what would hard-pressed secretaries of the Treasury not have given in the 1970s to see those monies repaid with compound interest after twenty or twenty-five years!) War among the nations of Western Europe—for centuries, the tinderbox of the world—has truly become unthinkable. European unity is progressing steadily, from customs union and common agricultural policy to free movement of labor and capital, to coordinated currencies, to direct elections to a common parliament, and to occasional joint pronouncements on foreign policy.

And, indeed, the community of advanced industrial democracies, with coordinated banking and currency systems and joint discussions of long-range economic plans, extends beyond the European Economic Community to all of Western Europe, the United States, Canada, Japan, Australia, and New Zealand—in sum, the twenty-four nations included in the Organization for Economic Cooperation and Development (OECD). For all of them, the 1950s and 1960s were decades of growing economic integration and unprecedented prosperity.

COLONIALISM AND DEVELOPMENT

For the vision of global commerce, prosperity, and division of labor, the withdrawal or exclusion of the communist countries entailed no substantial loss. Neither Russia, nor China, nor the East European countries contributed more than a small fraction of the global economic product. And communist planners in all three regions sooner or later found western technology and imports, and even Western credits, to be essential for the growth of their own economies. The failure of the United Nations to provide any effective security mechanism was a major disappointment to those who had hoped to see it grow into some sort of world government. But containment of Soviet expansion and mutual deterrence among the nuclear powers provided tolerable substitutes for collective global security. Never before had the world's major powers been so terrifyingly armed, yet not since 1914 had there been as long a period of peace among them. Metternich's vision of 1815 of a Europe restored to monarchic legitimacy broke down in 1848; the European balance of power that Bismarck tried to institute in 1871 scarcely outlasted the century. In terms of time alone, the world's period of *pax Americana* since 1945 has proved more durable than most.

In regard to the Third World, the American vision of peace and prosperity was blurred by wishful thinking. Freedom for the colonies—in view of America's own national origins—seemed a moral imperative beyond question. But having few overseas colonies of her own, the United States showed little sensitivity to the problems of decolonization faced by others. In practice, in the 1940s and 1950s, those colonies that might have been most desirable to keep—because of their economic resources or strategic locations—were also the ones most insistent on early liberation: India, Indonesia, Egypt, Palestine-Israel, Indochina, Ghana. Having had to fight their way toward independence, most of them developed a sense of cohesion that lent plausibility to the notion that old colonies were ready to turn into "new nations."

Among the colonies attaining independence later, Algeria was almost the only one that went through an actual war of liberation and thus had a chance to sharpen her sense of nationhood and to establish the kinds of political organization required for independent statehood. Most of the remaining colonies in the 1960s and early 1970s were not so much freed as abandoned—when a continuation of dependency would have seemed, in the estimate of the colonial power, a needless further burden.

Americans in the 1950s and 1960s were eager to speed up this process of decolonization so as to deprive the communists of one of their more telling propaganda points against the West—and to remove what seemed to be the major cause of political friction in Asia and Africa. Americans tended to take it for granted that the ex-colonies would be infused with a sense of nationhood; that their newly designed democratic institutions would have a chance to work, unless overwhelmed by material poverty and economic despair; and that financial and technical aid from the United States and others could start them on the road of economic progress. In Europe, the Marshall Plan had strengthened democratic institutions, and cooperation among prosperous democracies had insured regional unity and peace. Why should not a well-conceived and generously supported aid plan—Truman's Point Four or Kennedy's Alliance for Progress—do as much for Asia, Africa, and Latin America? In sum, American faith in economic development as the royal road to democracy, nationhood, and peace was almost as simple and touching as had been King's and Crane's trust in education for citizenship. The elixir was assumed to be just as potent; only the label on the bottle had been fashionably updated.

Postcolonial realities turned out to be rather different. There were few economic miracles in the new states of Asia and none among those of Africa. Most "new nations" were deeply divided among linguistic, religious, or ethnic groups—only a handful of them could even boast of a single linguistic majority. In most ex-colonies, the democratic institutions bequeathed by the departing Europeans developed no indigenous roots. And in the few Third World countries where democracy did acquire some momentum, such as India, Sri Lanka (Ceylon), Turkey, and Malaysia, the going was far from smooth. In many Asian and most African "new nations," military coups or other violent upheavals broke through the electoral façade within three to five years after independence. (What was worse, even American diplomats and economic or military aid officials—not to mention intelligence agents—in practice found it easier to deal with juntas and dictators, with their simple lines of authority downward, than with governments in the complex political patterns of emerging democracies.)

The boundaries arbitrarily drawn by the colonialists, particularly in Africa, inspired little respect among the successor governments; yet there was no orderly procedure for changing them. The result all too often was violence: civil war, secession, irredentism, border clashes, annexation. Indeed, in the 1950s and 1960s, as containment and deterrence stabilized conditions in the northern regions of the globe, the Third World of Latin America, Africa, the Middle East, and south and southeast Asia became the global zone of maximum domestic and international violence.

From a hardheaded point of view of profit and loss within the global capitalist economy, the misfortunes and disappointments of the Third World had as little immediate importance as did the exclusion of communist countries. Some Third World countries were integrated into the global economy as suppliers of mineral raw materials—but none of these minerals (with one exception!) was geographically so concentrated or economically so essential as to give its producers a potential monopoly. Other Third World countries were just as closely tied into the global commercial network through their low wages for skilled labor. And naturally it was the industrial economies, with their demand both for raw materials and manufactured products, that set the pace of development for both types of Third World country. All in all, even after a quarter-century of steady expansion of trade among noncommunist countries after 1945, 95 percent of all exports still originated in, or were destined for, the industrial countries, and nearly two-thirds of total trade consisted of exports from one industrial country to another. By contrast, only 4 percent of total noncommunist trade consisted of exports from one nonindustrial country to another.

One trouble with such short-range calculations was that the difficulties of, and among, Third World countries came to play a crucial role in East-West relations. Communism had made its greatest advances at the end of the Second World War in Eastern Europe and in China. But soon the political dividing lines in Europe and the Far East hardened, and, naturally enough, the Third World began to loom larger in Soviet calculations. In Russia herself, Bolshevism had come to power through coup d'état and civil war, and these techniques turned out to have a wide range of application in locations such as Cuba (1959), South Yemen (1970), Angola (1976), and Ethiopia (1978). Here then was a ready opportunity for the Soviets—not indeed to defeat the West's "containment" strategy but simply to bypass or surmount it.

The other trouble was that the one exceptional mineral commodity turned out to be petroleum, and its cartellization by a group of Third World producers endangered the whole framework of commerce and prosperity so carefully built up among the industrial democracies.

Americans after 1945 had come to develop distinct strategies in dealing with Western Europe and Japan, with Soviet expansionism, and with decolonization and development in the Third World. But the original American vision of One World had materialized at least to the extent that those three strategies could not be pursued in isolation and failure of the third endangered each of the other two.

The Middle East borders directly on Europe, Russia, and the ex-colonial regions of Asia and Africa. The appeal of communism to developing countries, the cold war between East and West, the anti-Soviet containment policy, all either began or were soon manifested in the Middle East. The Middle East, moreover, has been at the very center of the recent petroleum revolution. In sum, no other world region has reflected as closely and continuously all the gradual trends and sudden reversals of global politics as has the Middle East.

THE TRUMAN DOCTRINE AND THE IRANIAN OIL CRISIS

In March 1947, President Harry S. Truman, in asking Congress for $400 million in aid for Greece and Turkey, insisted that the United States must "support free peoples who are resisting attempted subjugation by armed minorities or by outside pressures." In November 1947, the United Nations resolution on partition of Palestine foreshadowed the end of the British mandate and the creation of the state of Israel. Also in 1947 two more American companies joined a consortium of two others to make possible the exploitation of Saudi Arabia's enormous oil resources.

Soviet expansion, British withdrawal, Israel, and oil: all of America's major Middle Eastern concerns for the next several decades were appearing at once. In retrospect, the interconnections among the four seem obvious: Britain's departure would leave a political vacuum, which local nationalism and Soviet expansion would be vying to fill; Israel's future would depend in large measure on the interplay of these forces with Western—specifically, with American—policies; and the resulting tensions would closely affect the price and supply of oil from the Middle East to the rest of the world. But in the actual evolution of policy from crisis to crisis, some of these linkages were slow to manifest themselves.

America had no desire for an empire of its own and hence no master plan for the Middle East; instead, the region offered a field for applying policies developed or tested elsewhere. Thus the Truman Doctrine made explicit for the Middle East the need for containment of Soviet power with which Washington's strategic planners were preoccupied in Europe and the Far East. Repeatedly America tried to stimulate in the Middle East the trend toward greater unity that the Marshall Plan had done so much to foster in Europe. For a long time Israel and oil were each treated as problems quite separate from those other, region-wide themes. Support for Israel, always strong among Jews, sprang from two motives among a wider American public: first, a humanitarian anxiety for the fate of hundreds of thousands of "displaced persons" in Europe; and, later, admiration for a frontier society of immigrants with distinct resemblances to America's own past. Petroleum continued to be treated as the business of private American companies. Late in the Second World War, the U.S. government had thought about financing a pipeline to bring Saudi oil to the European front; now, Washington was reverting to its role of diplomatic support for the commercial interests of American companies—which it had played during the "open door" episode in Iraq in 1922. Whenever commercial interests began to clash with local nationalism, Washington's advice was in favor of generous accommodation.

Decolonization presented a more complex problem. In principle, Americans favored a speedy end to imperial rule, and in most conflicts their sympathies were with colonial peoples aspiring to independence. But in the Middle East, Russia's proximity and other strategic considerations often argued in favor of shoring up the old British presence or substituting a new American presence for it. Taken together, the policies or policy impulses toward Russia, Britain, Middle East nationalism, regional unity, Israel, and oil were fraught with numerous inconsistencies and latent contradictions. And the pressure of crisis or challenges from America's allies or antagonists of the moment were sure to force each of these contradictions out into the open. The successes and failures of America's Middle Eastern policies in the first postwar decade illustrate this potential for tension.

Few policies succeeded as well in their immediate context as did the Truman Doctrine of containment. The conflict with the Soviet Union had been building up as the world war drew to a close. At the Tehran, Yalta, and Potsdam conferences (1943–45) American leaders had been concerned with winning the war and planning for the United Nations—and the Soviets with carving out a geographic sphere of influence for themselves. In Europe and the Far East, which were the final theaters of war, the ultimate stakes were greatest, the lines were drawn clearly, and the eventual confrontations (over Berlin and in Korea) proved dramatic. By contrast in the Middle East, where there had been no fighting since 1942, few lines had been drawn and few details spelled out; hence there was room for Soviet maneuver, for uncertainty and confrontation —and a need for new and sweeping policy pronouncements. In postwar negotiations among the Allies, Moscow had registered an interest in the ex-Italian colonies of Libya and the Dodecanese. In Greece in 1946, the wartime coalition between royalists and communists had broken down. In the civil war (Truman's "attempted subjugation by armed minorities") that ensued, the Greek communists could count on steady supplies via Yugoslavia and Bulgaria. In Iran the Soviets violated an agreement to withdraw their occupation troops from the northern part of the country and, instead, proclaimed an "Azarbaijan People's Republic" under their protection. Against Turkey, Moscow initiated a diplomatic campaign ("attempted subjugation . . . by outside pressures"). The Soviets denounced their 1925 treaty of friendship with Turkey and as the price of resumed friendship demanded that Turkey cede to them three of her Eastern border provinces. Above all, Moscow proposed a system of "joint defense" of the Turkish Straits—a euphemism for the establishment of Soviet naval bases along the strategic waterway linking the Black Sea and the Mediterranean and potential control of Turkey's largest city, Istanbul.

The three-pronged diplomatic and military offensive against Greece, Turkey, and Iran recalled the secret Nazi-Soviet negotiations of 1940, in which Moscow had insisted "that the area south of Batum and Baku in the general direction of the Persian Gulf [be] recognized as the center of the aspirations of the Soviet Union." South of Batum were the three Turkish provinces, south of Baku was Azarbaijan: together, the two regions would have reduced Soviet air distance to the Persian Gulf from 600 to 400 miles.

But in view of Truman's firm stand, Soviet pressure abated. Russian troops withdrew from Iran in May 1946, and by December the Azarbaijan puppet regime collapsed. Turkey stood fast against all Soviet demands and modernized her armed forces with American support. Tito's break with Stalin in 1948 cut the supply lines to the Greek guerrillas, and by 1949 Athens had restored its authority throughout the country. In 1950, Turkey eagerly responded to the United Nations' call for troops in Korea. "If I do not give help today," Ankara's foreign minister explained, "how can I dare ask the United Nations for help when I am in need of it tomorrow?" By 1952 both Greece and Turkey were admitted as members of the North Atlantic Treaty Organization. The Middle Eastern frontier from Turkey to Afghanistan remained the only direction where Soviet power remained limited to the pre-1917 tsarist borders. Greece and Turkey, longtime enemies, had both joined NATO, and soon each would associate itself with the European Communities. The American policies of containment and collective security seemed fully vindicated.

Nationalization of Iran's oil constituted the second major Middle Eastern crisis of the postwar period. Before that crisis broke out, the expanded Arabian-American Oil Company (Aramco) had made Iran's neighbor, Saudi Arabia, a leading Middle East oil exporter. Demands for higher payments from King Ibn Saud resulted in a new agreement in 1950 by which the company tripled its payments per barrel and deducted the additional monies from its tax payments in the United States. Washington welcomed the agreement not only because it smoothed relations between Saudis and Americans, but also because it secured for Saudi Arabia (and later other Middle East oil countries) a financial subsidy that might have had difficulty with annual appropriations votes in the Congress. In 1951 the United States secured from Saudi Arabia an agreement for the establishment of a major air base at Dhahran, an arrangement that remained in effect until 1961.

By contrast, negotiations between the Anglo-Iranian Oil Company and the Tehran government went from deadlock to unilateral nationalization in May 1951. Britain, in response, blocked Iran's accounts in London, and her air force helped prevent the export of Iran's nationalized oil—whereas increased production in Saudi Arabia, Kuwait, and Iraq made up the shortfall for the oil companies. The economic pressure radicalized the political situation in Iran, where Premier Mossadegh and his National Front were supported by Shiite Muslim radicals and the communist Tudeh ("Masses") party in their struggle against conservatives, the military, and the shah. The United States, just having emerged victorious from the three-year battle for containment in Korea, was fearful that Mossadegh would have no choice but to throw himself into the arms of the Soviet Union. In a dramatic sequence in August 1953, Mossadegh led the political attack on the monarch, the shah fled the country, and a military coup restored the shah—with support, at some crucial moments, from the American CIA. A year later, oil production was resumed, the British concession having been converted into a multinational consortium with 40 percent American participation.

Whether this outcome in Iran is judged a success or a failure depends on one's time frame and perspective. Any danger of Soviet penetration was averted for the next decade and a half; yet if the United States had found an accommodation with Mossadegh's nationalism, such as it achieved with the conservative Ibn Saud or later sought with the radical Nasser, that danger might never have arisen. Within the Middle Eastern oil industry, Britain was forced to share her formerly exclusive concession with Americans and others, and the network of multinational oil companies was strengthened—until OPEC, in the 1960s and early 1970s drew from Mossadegh's failure the lesson for its own success. In the Middle East, the shah, despite occasional flirtations with neutralism, became a staunch supporter of Western strategic interests—as well as one of OPEC's determined "price hawks" in the 1970s. In Iran itself, the shah's position was weakened by the continuing antagonism of the nationalist, Western-educated middle class; by the social dislocations of rapid modernization; by a heavy-handed policy of political repression; and by the implacable enmity of the Shiite clergy. The shah's restored regime lasted as long as a quarter of a century, but when it collapsed in 1978/79, it did so in a political explosion of unprecedented vehemence that was to endanger Western interest in the Middle East more gravely than any event since the Second World War.

The Problem of Middle East Defense

Truman's aid program of 1947 had been prompted by Britain's announcement that, exhausted from the war, it could no longer continue its own assistance to Greece and Turkey. Further examples of United States–British cooperation in this period included

- an Anglo-American Committee on Palestine (1946), which recommended a United Nations Trusteeship under which "Palestine shall be neither a Jewish State nor an Arab State";
- a Tripartite Declaration (1950), by which the United States, Britain, and France pledged themselves to limit the supply of arms to Israel and her Arab neighbors and to intervene against aggression from either side; and
- a proposed Middle East Command (1951), under which the United States, Britain, France, and Turkey would have joined with Egypt to operate the strategic British base at Suez.

These three initiatives led to no concrete results. They overestimated the degree of political unity that could be achieved in the Middle East, or even among the Western powers with regard to it; and they vastly underestimated the depth of Middle Eastern resentment against colonial powers that had only recently begun withdrawing from the region. Turkey, Greece, and Iran in 1946/47 were countries with long traditions of jealously guarded independence; the Soviet threat for them was imminent; and they welcomed all outside help. Egypt in 1951 had asked for no help and felt threatened by no one—except Britain, which had recently ended its sixty-seven years of occupation. To make things worse, the Middle East Command proposal repeated verbatim the crucial passages of the 1936 Anglo-Egyptian Treaty, which Egypt had just denounced—except that it now gave to four outside powers the right to station forces in Egypt. Rejection of the proposal by Egypt (October 1951) was followed by an unprecedented outbreak of anti-Western violence (January 1952) and the overthrow of the royal regime that had so long cooperated with the British in a radical military coup under Nagib and Nasser (July 1952).

A few years later, Washington worked hard behind the scenes to bring about the pact concluded at Baghdad in 1955 by which Turkey, Iraq, Great Britain, Pakistan, and Iran agreed to "co-operate for their security and defense" in ways to be specified by further agreements. But few such specifics were ever agreed upon; the United States never became a formal member; and the arrangements went little beyond existing provisions for American military aid to Turkey, Iran, and Pakistan.

The inclusion of Iraq and Britain had been championed by General Nuri Said, the most pro-British of Iraq's small circle of leaders since 1921, who wished to avoid the debacle that had overtaken Anglo-Egyptian relations in 1951 and to catapult Iraq and himself into a position of leadership toward Arab unity in competition with Egypt. But the first attempt to solicit another Arab member backfired. King Hussein's flirtation with the pact ran into strong anti-Western sentiment in Jordan; and, far from joining, the astute young monarch found it advisable to dismiss the British officers who had commanded his army. In Iraq, the pact similarly polarized sentiment. In 1958 a military coup overthrew the monarchy, killing the royal family, Nuri, and others and freeing (as the victorious colonels put it) "our beloved country from the corrupt clique installed by imperialism." In 1959 Iraq officially withdrew from the Baghdad Pact, which was renamed Central Treaty Organization (CENTO). In the Arab world at large, the Baghdad Pact served to reinforce anti-American, pro-Russian sentiment and to strengthen the hand of Nuri's archrival, Gamal Abdul Nasser of Egypt, in exploiting those attitudes.

Washington's original conception of what eventually became the Baghdad Pact had been sketched in a speech of John Foster Dulles, Eisenhower's secretary of state, in mid-1953. "A Middle East Defense Organization," such as attempted in 1951, Dulles found, "is a future rather than an immediate possibility. Many of the Arab League countries are so engrossed with their quarrels with Israel or with Great Britain or France that they pay little heed to the menace of Soviet Communism. However, there is more concern where the Soviet Union is near. In general, the northern tier of nations shows awareness of the danger. There is a vague desire to have a collective security system. But no such system can be imposed from without. It should be designed and grow from within out of of a sense of common destiny and common danger."

Of the four Middle Eastern Baghdad Pact members, Turkey belonged also to NATO, and Pakistan to SEATO—the South East Asia Treaty Organization inaugurated by Dulles in 1954. The global conception was that of a *cordon sanitaire* around the Russian and Chinese perimeter from Norway to the Philippines. It was a rigid, mechanical extension of the principle of collective security, which had worked so well in Western Europe and in Greece and Turkey, to regions that lacked the necessary preconditions. The SEATO pact was part of the same misapplication of the containment principle that got us embroiled in the disastrous war in Vietnam; by contrast, the Baghdad-CENTO pact simply lingered for two decades and then quietly expired.

With regard to the Middle East, Dulles had learned the lesson of 1951: no regional defense scheme could be "imposed from without." He was also right in asserting that most Arabs were more conscious of the past threat from Europe and the present threat from Israel. There was, as he claimed, more awareness of the future danger from Russia in countries such as Turkey and Iran; but unlike the Western Europeans, or even the Arabs with their common language and persistent dreams of unity, Dulles's "northern tier" was a miscellany of countries with no "sense of common destiny" whatever. Nor was the mechanical combination of three American military aid agreements (Turkey, Iran, Pakistan) with one revised British base arrangement (Iraq) capable of conjuring up such a "sense of destiny." To its staunchest supporter, Nuri Said, Western support of the Baghdad Pact became (almost literally) the kiss of death. And Dulles's nightmare of "the menace of Soviet communism" to the Middle East was likely to become a self-fulfilling prophecy.

DULLES VERSUS NASSER AND THE DEBACLE AT SUEZ

Just as Middle East geography links oceans and continents, so Middle East diplomacy is likely to link diverse issues— including some that the diplomats would prefer to keep separate. Dulles's "northern tier" conception of 1953 had addressed only the problem of regional defense against Russia. In developing the Baghdad Pact, the British and Iraqi governments had injected the decolonization issue, hoping to work out an orderly transition from a quasi-colonial relationship to a new partnership among allies. But this meant that several more issues inevitably got entangled: inter-Arab rivalry, the Arab-Israeli conflict, Washington's relations with its NATO allies, Russian relations with the Middle East and with Washington, and even the security of oil supplies from the Middle East.

Relations between Washington and Cairo were crucial to the drama set off by the Baghdad Pact. America had showed much sympathy for the colonels' junta that in 1952 deposed the corrupt regime of King Farouk, and the State Department discreetly had pressured London into composing its differences with Cairo over Suez. The Eisenhower administration was also receptive to Egyptian aid requests, notably for the High Dam at Aswan that had come to symbolize the new regime's development ambitions. Nasser on his part, though refusing to join any Western-sponsored alliances, had emphasized that "left alone, the Arabs will naturally turn toward the West to ask it for arms and assistance."

Dulles, of course, had not left things "alone." By encouraging the Baghdad Pact he may have hoped to make Nasser jealous and thus to accelerate his predicted "turn toward the West." Similarly, Washington's refusal to join the pact as a member was meant to reassure both Egypt and Israel. Nasser, however, felt neither jealous nor reassured but provoked and slighted in his claims to Arab leadership. He therefore turned to Moscow for the arms he now felt he needed more than ever —although the actual arms agreement was disguised as a deal with Czechoslovakia. Washington kept alive the Aswan aid offer, hinting that Egypt must show its devotion to economic development by not procuring communist arms. The Egyptian press denounced such strictures as interference with Egypt's sovereign rights, and Nasser vainly applied to Russia for the Aswan aid as well. (He obtained it only two years later.) When Nasser was ready to accept Washington's aid package, Dulles withdrew it—publicly, in the most humiliating fashion. Not to be outdone, Nasser a week later proclaimed the nationalization of the Suez Canal.

The canal company, registered in Paris, had British and French stockholders, and earlier in 1956 Britain had evacuated the Suez base under the 1954 agreement. Both London and Paris protested sharply in the name of freedom of navigation and the sanctity of international agreements; both inclined to strong countermeasures, not excluding force. Washington joined in the protests but shrank from any use of force, and soon distrust was as great between the United States and its leading Western allies as between any one of them and Egypt.

Israel, meanwhile, had been understandably concerned about Western support for the Baghdad Pact (which Iraq had been quick to advertise as implied support of Arabs against Israel); she was alarmed at the rapid flow of advanced Soviet weapons to Egypt. Hence, Israel was willing to cooperate fully with French and British plans for military intervention. On October 29, 1956, Israel launched its lightning attack on Sinai, capturing much Soviet weaponry that the Egyptians had had no time to learn to use. The next day, Britain and France, ostensibly still concerned about the freedom of navigation, issued an ultimatum ordering both belligerents to withdraw ten miles from either shore of the canal. Israel (to which the ultimatum by implication guaranteed its first one hundred miles of conquest) readily accepted; Egypt, predictably, rejected it; and the British and French forces began their own military operation against the canal zone.

At the United Nations, Russia was in the rare position of voting with the United States for a resolution vetoed by Britain and France. The Soviets, above all, welcomed the diversion of world attention from their own invasion of Hungary the week before. Noisily, Nikita Khrushchev warned Britain and France of possible rocket attacks on their capitals unless they withdrew from Egypt. More discreetly, but also more effectively, Washington warned that United States oil exports would not make up for any cutoff of Middle Eastern supplies to Britain or France unless their troops were withdrawn— apparently the first effective political use of an "oil weapon."

For Egypt, the Anglo-French landing at Port Said added little to the military defeat already inflicted by Israel's occupation of the whole Sinai peninsula; instead, it helped turn military defeat into a diplomatic and propaganda victory. On the diplomatic scene, world reaction against the British and French landings (with the transparent hypocrisy of the preceding ultimatum) was much sharper than against the original Israeli attack; and subsequently, Britain and France proved more sensitive than Israel to United Nations and United States pressures for immediate withdrawal. Meanwhile, Nasser's propaganda could readily imply that he would have beaten the Israelis—if only Britain and France, the heinous old colonialists, had not stabbed him in the back. Indeed, he went on to claim the British-French withdrawal as his own victory.

The Suez crisis had begun with Dulles's attempt to teach Nasser a lesson by withdrawing the offer of aid for Aswan; it escalated with Nasser's reverse "lesson" of nationalizing the canal. Its net effect was an enormous boost to Nasser's prestige and to his regional pan-Arab ambitions—and a major advance for the Soviet Union, which had managed simply to leap over Dulles's "northern tier" barrier and establish itself as a major diplomatic force in the Middle East in alliance with Arab, anti-Western tendencies.

Alarmed at how far things had gotten out of hand, Washington went to the counterattack with the Eisenhower Doctrine, proposed by the president in January 1957 and enacted by both houses of Congress in March. It pledged "the employment of the armed forces of the United

States to secure and protect the territorial integrity and political independence of . . . nations [in the Middle East] requesting such aid against overt armed aggression from any nation controlled by international communism."

There were some ambiguities in the statement. "Overt armed aggression" would be easy enough to identify, but the crucial danger was that of subversion by coup, intrigue, or perhaps armed uprising. Similarly, a military attack by the Soviet Union itself would be obvious enough—but unlikely. At what point would some other nation be judged to be "controlled by international communism"? The realistic danger, after all, came from Nasser's Egypt and the radical pan-Arab regime in Syria, which were armed and supported by the Soviet Union but hardly "controlled" by it. And of course, a few months earlier, the United States itself had vigorously opposed any "employment of armed forces" against Nasser.

Above all, would the United States be able to bring timely military help to beleaguered regimes? There were some American units in Turkey and under military aid programs in Iran, an American base at Dhahran in Saudi Arabia (recently extended until 1961), and plans for other bases in Ethiopia. But again: air force units would be ideal for intercepting an airborne or seaborne attack from Russia herself, whereas the likelier danger of subversion or insurrection would require ready land forces—or else a long-term political rather than a short-term military resolution.

Reaction to Washington's new policy announcement was mixed. Of the fourteen countries between Libya and Pakistan, the United States was already committed to the defense of Turkey, Iran, Pakistan, and (indirectly) Iraq. Four other countries also readily accepted the protection offered: cosmopolitan Lebanon and the monarchies of Libya, Saudi Arabia, and Afghanistan. Israel, in view of the fresh experience of the Suez-Sinai War, was not inclined to place much reliance on America's protection and early in 1957 yielded only reluctantly to Washington's pressure to evacuate the Gulf of Aqaba and the Gaza Strip; but on second thought the Israeli parliament did endorse the doctrine in June. Jordan cautiously avoided official endorsement, as did the Sudan; Yemen specifically rejected the doctrine. The remaining two countries, Egypt and Syria, were the recipients of massive Soviet military aid and, hence, the likeliest "direct or indirect" aggressors.

Like Dulles's "northern tier" policy of 1953, the Eisenhower Doctrine served further to polarize the Middle East. Washington's early gains were a marked westward shift in Saudi Arabia and Jordan. The first test came in the fall of 1957, when pressures from Nasser's followers and from Soviet-armed Syria converged on Jordan; in response, American arms were airlifted to Jordan, and Turkey massed its troops on Syria's opposite, northern frontier. In Syria itself, an intense power struggle developed between factions supported by Moscow and Cairo, respectively; but the surprise announcement of Syria's merger with Egypt in the United Arab Republic under Nasser's presidency threw the victory to the pro-Cairo group. The second test came in the summer of 1958, as the victorious Nasserites mounted an armed insurrection in Lebanon and prepared to overthrow the Jordanian and Iraqi monarchies. This time American troops landing in Lebanon and British troops flown to Jordan restored or preserved the pro-Western regimes; but in Baghdad, Colonel Kassem's radical coup swept away the Iraqi monarchy the day before American units arrived over five hundred miles away in Beirut.

Washington's policy, it might be claimed, contributed indirectly to thwarting a possible Soviet takeover in Syria—but, if so, the price was immeasurably to advance Nasser's claims to pan-Arab leadership and to precipitate the downfall of the Iraqi monarchy—the one Arab regime that had openly espoused Dulles's conception of collective defense for the Middle East. Since 1956 Washington had been increasingly alarmed at massive Soviet arms shipments to Egypt and then to Syria; by 1958 Iraq and Yemen had joined the list of recipients of such Soviet arms aid —followed by Algeria in 1964, the Sudan in 1967, Southern Yemen in 1967, and Libya in 1969. Washington, in turn, sped up military deliveries to Turkey, Iran, Pakistan, Jordan, and Saudi Arabia. The 1956 crisis above all had immeasurably escalated the arms race in the Middle East. Soon critics in the United States complained that it would have been far cheaper to grant Nasser his Aswan aid than to take on the military commitments made under the Eisenhower Doctrine.

The Legacy of Imperialism

In less than ten years, America's Middle Eastern policy had gone from the striking success of the Truman Doctrine to the futility of the Middle East Command and the Baghdad Pact, to the fiasco at Suez, and to the patent inadequacy of the Eisenhower Doctrine. Washington's major concern had been to unify the region against the threat from Russia; Britain's abandonment of its hegemonial position in the region only added urgency to that concern—but also posed a dilemma.

Most of the region, as Dulles had recognized in 1953, was far more anxious to hasten the British departure than to delay or prevent the Russian arrival. Furthermore, the end of British hegemony brought into the open the many internal divisions in the region that had been both accentuated and repressed by a quarter-century of colonialism. How could America's quest for regional unity and the divisiveness of the Middle East itself be reconciled in a single viable policy?

The British in their own day had followed the simple, intuitive logic of imperial power politics: encourage unity against others; discourage or prevent it against yourself. In 1915 Britain had supported Sharif Hussein's dream of Arab unity and his revolt against the Ottoman empire, Britain's enemy. In consolidating their power in the 1920s and 1930s, the British had preferred to see the Arab East divided into Iraq, Syria, Lebanon, Palestine, Transjordan, and a dozen principalities on the Arabian peninsula—not to mention the North African colonies and protectorates from Egypt to Morocco. Twice more, the British offered support for Arab unity: in 1941–42 under the imminent threat of Nazi invasion and in 1954 under the pressure of their own departure. (Both times their chosen instrument for leadership toward Arab unity happened to be Nuri Said, with whom they had closely cooperated since 1916.) But the hard facts of decolonization are that the departing rulers take with them the external unity that they used to impose (for example, through such London agencies as the colonial office, the India office, and the imperial general staff) and leave behind the internal divisions, rivalries, and animosities that had existed before their arrival and had been allowed to proliferate under their administration. No last-minute shift of policy can undo these effects of decades of colonial rule. The Fertile Crescent unity scheme of 1942 and the Baghdad Pact of 1954 thus remained doomed as much as were Britain's belated efforts to create unity between Hindus and Muslims in India in the 1940s or between Greeks and Turks on Cyprus in the 1950s, or Britain's plans for various confederations in East Africa (Tanganyika-Kenya-Uganda; Nyasaland-Southern and Northern Rhodesia) or among various groups of Caribbean islands.

After independence, where there is natural affinity of language and culture, as among Arabs, the quest for unity may be resumed—as it was under Nasser—with resentment of the departing colonialists providing an added impetus. But the basic political reality left behind by imperialism—whether in the Middle East or Africa in the 1960s or in the belt of successor states from Finland to Turkey in 1918—is a checkerboard pattern, where each state is at odds with its immediate neighbors and courts its neighbors-once-removed. Since the map never lines up in tidy rows and columns, however, the pattern is more complex than that of a checkerboard; there is a restless thrashing of alignment and realignment in what has been aptly described as the "Arab cold war." Significantly, the one limited and temporary success of Arab unity came between Egypt and Syria, which shared no common frontier—only a common Israeli enemy.

Americans in the 1950s had no inclination whatever to follow Kipling's advice to "take up the White Man's burden," in the Middle East or anywhere else. But short of imposing a new form of empire on the Middle East, there was little the United States could do to rally the region to a common defense. To associate with Britain and France and with Turkey, as in 1951, made matters worse, since this meant cooperating with not only the most recent but the two most recent sets of imperial rulers. Even among Turkey, Iran, and Pakistan there was no "sense of common destiny"—only separate, parallel fears of Russia. And as the history of the Balkans and of East Central Europe earlier in this century had shown, such parallel fears can lead to joint defense arrangements in the beginning but to separate, competitive accommodations with the aggressor later.

At times, Americans chose the opposite horn of the dilemma—to support the unification plans not of the departing British but of the vocal anticolonialists, such as Nasser. But this would expose them to the Middle Easterners' old ploy of playing foreigner against foreigner, in this case Moscow against Washington; and the abrupt shift from one policy to another (for example, pro-British to pro-Nasser) would, of course, undermine the credibility of each.

Given this unfavorable constellation, American efforts in the Middle East were likely not just to remain futile but to backfire. The harder Washington pushed for unity, the more it was likely to bring the latent divisions out into the open. The more it tried to force Middle Easterners to opt for the West, the more likely some of them (for example, Nasser and Kassem) were to opt for Moscow. The more Washington talked about containment, the more the Soviets felt encircled and compelled to break out. In sum, each of Washington's moves only provided so many more occasions for Moscow to play the full checkerboard, as with its aid programs in Egypt, Syria, and Iraq in the late 1950s and in the 1960s.

There remained, from an American point of view, several consolations. As the British completed their evacuation—by 1958 from the larger countries, by 1971 from most of the rest—memories of Western imperialism were bound to fade; and the more favorable impressions created by America's technology, educational opportunities, and foreign aid likely to become more prominent. Even the presence of Israel, so long resented by Arabs as imperialism's most odious legacy to the Middle East, would become more palatable, at least to some Arabs, after three decades and four vain attempts to force a military decision.

Conversely, the Russians, as they arrived in growing numbers, managed to make themselves more unpopular—probably at a much faster rate than had the Europeans some generations earlier. (The Egyptians, we already noted, came to speak sarcastically of the Soviet "occupation" of their country, and Iraqis in the 1970s found Russian oil technology to be no match for that of the departing Western multinationals.) Inevitably, too, as the Soviets extended their influence, they themselves became victims of the checkerboard syndrome and found themselves saddled with the regional quarrels of their several clients and protégés. Above all, throughout the 1960s and 1970s, Turkey and Iran continued to interpose a physical barrier between Soviets and Arabs; and this left governments in Baghdad, Damascus, and Cairo free to align and realign themselves for or against Moscow, without fear of seeing Soviet forces march in, as in Budapest in 1956, Prague in 1968, or Kabul in 1979. And, naturally, every Soviet setback was a corresponding opportunity for the United States or other Western powers.

Meanwhile, the 1960s brought something of a lull to the Middle Eastern international tensions, as both superpowers came to be preoccupied outside the Middle East: the Soviets absorbed in their deadly quarrel with the Chinese for supremacy within the world communist movement, the Americans ever more deeply mired in their disastrous venture in Vietnam.

Yet when the Middle East, in the 1970s and 1980s, once again became the major focus of the global conflict between Washington and Moscow, the risks and the stakes had become far greater. The Russians had learned from their disappointing experience in countries like Egypt and Iraq; they had begun to concentrate their efforts on smaller, more backward countries—more easily dominated and readily accessible to them by sea or land—such as South Yemen, Somalia, Ethiopia, and Afghanistan. Their shift, in midwar, from a pro-Somali to a pro-Ethiopian alignment must, by all odds, be considered a brilliant maneuver. And by 1979 the Iranian revolution had created a power vacuum in the very part of the region most readily accessible to the Soviets.

Above all, the stakes in the Middle East had been increased by the petroleum revolution of the 1960s and 1970s—the process whereby the global noncommunist economy had increasingly come to depend on imported petroleum as its major fuel, whereby the price of petroleum on the world market had come to be set by a handful of Middle Eastern governments, and whereby, in brief, any minor political crisis in the Middle East might come to translate into a major economic crisis for the rest of the world.

3

THE RISE OF MIDDLE EAST OIL

In 1882 the British expedition to Egypt opened a new and painful chapter in the age-old encounter between Europe and the Middle East. That same year Gottlieb Daimler, a German engineer, founded his experimental workshop in Canstatt, where in 1883 he constructed the world's first internal combustion engine. Over the next century, Daimler's invention was to revolutionize all transport by land, sea, and even air; shrink weeks of travel into hours; knit together the world's economies more tightly than ever before; and extend the sweep of wars clear around the globe. Meanwhile, the European imperial presence in the Middle East set the framework for the discovery and exploitation of petroleum resources of staggering magnitude, the displacement of coal by oil as the industrial world's prime fuel, and the abject dependence of most of the global economy on the price of oil as set by the postimperial governments of the Middle East.

Neither Daimler tinkering in his workshop near Stuttgart nor the British commanders about to disembark at Alexandria could, of course, foresee these joint and distant consequences of their actions. It was not the quest for oil that had brought the British to the Middle East. Economic concessions of all sorts, to be sure, were a normal adjunct of Europe's imperial penetration; but the specific economic motive of the expedition, it will be recalled, was the protection of bondholders in Paris and London caught in the boom-and-bust cycle of this concession economy. Also, since the boring of the first oil well in Pennsylvania in 1859, petroleum had been used ever more widely, mostly in lamps as a substitute for whale oil; but America and tsarist Russia for many decades remained the leading producers. In the Middle East, oil was not discovered in marketable quantities until the present century: Egypt 1909, Iran 1913, Iraq 1927, Saudi Arabia 1936, Kuwait 1946, and Libya 1961.

The early economic concessions in the Middle East concerned mostly transport and communications, and rivalry among the powers played its part. A French company opened the Suez canal in 1869. A British subject persuaded the shah of Iran to allow him to build railways and telegraphs, mine for minerals, and establish banks. A consortium headed by the Deutsche Bank received a railroad concession from the Ottoman sultan—and the kaiser himself arrived to inaugurate the massive terminal station on the Asian shore opposite Istanbul.

The presence of petroleum in underground reservoirs here and there in the Middle East had long been suspected. The Biblical tale of the three men in the "burning fiery furnace" (Daniel 3:25) appears to refer to oil and natural gas seepages in the Iraqi mountains. Yet exploration for petroleum remained in the hands of Western companies long after Middle Eastern entrepreneurs or governments had taken over railways, telegraphs, banks, and shipping lines. Drilling technique and geological knowledge were becoming ever more specialized. Companies such as John D. Rockefeller's Standard Oil Trust and the Royal Dutch-Shell group were establishing their predominance in the burgeoning global oil trade. Only companies with sizable resources and far-flung operations could face the large financial risks of prospecting and exploration. Middle Eastern petroleum development has depended wholly on Western technology, Western capital, and the prospect of Western markets.

The typical pattern in the Middle East and other Third World regions until the middle of this century remained for a Western company to be given exclusive rights to prospect and produce oil throughout all or most of a country's territory. A handsome initial payment induced the sultan, shah, or emir to grant the concession; if oil was found and production started, the government was promised a royalty (literally, the "king's fee") fixed either in gold or as a share of the sales price—typically one-eighth or one-sixth of the profits. Frequently, several Western oil companies would obtain a concession jointly, either to resolve conflicting political or commercial claims or to reduce the risks in what were thought to be venturesome explorations. The Kuwait concession in 1934 came to be shared between a British and an American company; that in Bahrain (1929) between two, and that in Saudi Arabia (1947) among four, American companies.

Western governments, too, showed an active interest. In 1913, as the Royal Navy was rapidly converting its boilers from coal to oil, the British Treasury acquired a majority interest in the petroleum concession earlier obtained by an Australian in Iran. In the peace settlement of 1919, the British agreed to transfer the German one-quarter share in the concession covering Iraq to the French; and in 1922, in response to State Department pressure for an "open door" to Americans, a further one-quarter to two United States oil companies.

Since the days of the First World War, the petroleum industry has advanced rapidly. The global automobile fleet increased sixteenfold from 1924 to 1978. In the First World War, battleships began to run on oil, and planes and tanks made their debut. In the Second World War, planes and tanks proved decisive, so that for Hitler the Romanian and Caucasian (and for Japan, the Indonesian) oil fields became important objectives; but United States petroleum production helped insure the Allied victory. Postwar recovery in Europe and Japan was fueled largely by petroleum, which was beginning to replace coal in such uses as residential heating and electricity generation and to be used as a raw material in the chemical industry. All in all, between 1880 and 1970, the world's petroleum consumption doubled approximately every ten years.

For most of this period, Middle Eastern oil made a very modest contribution to the over-all trend. As late as 1946, Iran was the only sizable producing country; the region's total exports (9 percent of world consumption) were dwarfed by those of Venezuela (12 percent)—and both alike by production in the United States (62 percent of the world total). But already Middle Eastern petroleum reserves were known to be enormous and of superior quality. Furthermore, most Middle Eastern oil, once drilled, flowed freely under its own pressure. This eliminated the need for pumping and kept production costs to a minimum: between $0.10 and $0.22 a barrel in the Middle East as against $0.39 in Venezuela and as much as $1.51 in the United States. Yet the greatest significance of the Middle Eastern concessions in this period was their impact not on costs but on the economic structure of the global oil industry.

Oil, the flammable liquid, is hard to store but easy to transport by tanker or pipe. The giants among the early oil companies achieved their preeminence by rationalizing transport—Rockefeller's Standard Oil by negotiating bulk contracts with the railroads, Marcus Samuels' Shell Transport and Trading Company by assembling a whole fleet of ocean-going tankers. Control of cheap and orderly transport enabled them to lure the owners of producing wells with regular collections, and the wholesale or retail dealers in petroleum products with dependable supplies. But the growing dependence of dealers and producers on the middleman also gave him a potential stranglehold. Before long, Standard Oil and Shell were able to buy out firm after firm at both ends of their transport links, thus establishing a pattern of "vertical integration."

"Vertical integration" to the business economist denotes a condition where a single company or its affiliates are active in each of the many phases of a particular industry, from mining through processing and manufacturing to distribution to, ultimately, the consumer; in few industries has this pattern become as entrenched or widespread as in oil. Vertical integration, of course, eliminates the open market at the intervening stages, and this has two specific advantages. First, the more vertically integrated an industry, the harder it will prove for new competitors to gain a foothold. In the oil industry, for instance, they may find themselves having to drill wells, build refineries, charter tankers, and set up a chain of filling stations—all before they can make even a single sale. Second, if a vertically integrated firm operates across state lines or national borders, it can freely allocate its profits and losses to operations in various jurisdictions—and gain an edge over its more localized competitors by reducing its taxes. As Professor Adelman succinctly states: "Transfer prices from one to another division of the same corporate entity"—say, those paid by a refining to a producing subsidiary for a given amount of crude oil—"are simply bookkeeping notations to permit the corporation to minimize its tax bill." The Supreme Court's decision in 1911 breaking up Rockefeller's empire into Exxon, Mobil, Socal, and other regional constituents was the largest antitrust case in judicial history; yet it did little to alter the industry's vertical integration from wellhead to gas pump and nothing to prevent each of the newly spun off companies from growing far beyond the size of Rockefeller's original conglomerate.

Even before the development of Middle Eastern oil, it would have been difficult for newcomers to challenge the entrenched position of the large multinational companies. But once the Middle Eastern oil concessions tied the companies into a single network, competition among them was inevitably reduced. For joint ownership of a concession meant, as a matter of course, a single sales price to outsiders. Interlocking concessions meant uniform prices throughout the Middle East, established not by open competition but by joint policy of the seven companies. More importantly perhaps, the companies had to coordinate long-range estimates of market demand for their products so as to be able to decide at which rates to develop known fields in the Middle East and when to explore promising new areas. Elsewhere in the world, the companies might continue to compete in aggressive marketing drives. Yet their long-range production plans, which under truly competitive conditions would have remained the most closely guarded of business secrets, were made not only with one another's full knowledge, but by joint agreement among their instructed delegates.

Adam Smith, the Scots moral philosopher who first formulated the science of economics, once observed that "People of the same trade seldom meet together even for merriment and diversion, but the conversation ends in conspiracy against the public, or in some contrivance to raise prices." The net of oil concessions that Western imperial governments and multinational companies had so deftly cast over the vast oil resources of the Middle East relieved the world's oil executives from any need for furtive conversation over tea or cocktails. Instead, they could calmly state their points in speaking to the agenda at the board meetings of Aramco or the Iraq Petroleum Company.

Whenever long-range plans were on those agendas, the companies, needless to say, would hope to preserve, or perhaps slowly raise, existing levels of price and profit—ambitions that their memoranda were likely to express in such bland catch phrases as "market stability" or "orderly development." Specifically, the companies operating in the Middle East were eager to protect the system whereby "From the earliest days of the industry, oil sold in world markets" had been "priced as if it had originated in Texas." This implied that the enormous benefits of cheaper production costs in the Middle East would not be passed on to consumers but accrue to the companies themselves as added profit. Given their dominant position in the world oil market at the time, the seven companies in the Middle East network had little difficulty in enforcing their pricing decisions or realizing their planned growth rates. Together, they controlled 65 percent of petroleum reserves outside the communist countries, 55 percent of the production of crude petroleum, 57 percent of refinery capacity and major pipelines, and, through ownership or long-term leases, 67 percent or more of all privately owned tanker space.

It was this interlocking pattern of concessions, first in Iraq, Kuwait, and Saudi Arabia and then in Iran, that caused the major international oil companies to become popularly known as the "Seven Sisters." Three of the seven (Exxon, Socal, and Mobil) were successors to Rockefeller's Standard Oil; two others (Gulf and Texaco) also were American-based; and the remaining two (BP—formerly Anglo-Iranian—and Shell) were British or British-Dutch.

MOSSADEGH BATTLES THE COMPANIES

The postwar pattern of concessions was completed in 1947 with the entry of Exxon and Mobil into Aramco (Arabian-American Oil Company), the group producing oil in Saudi Arabia. Within a few years, this network of Middle Eastern subsidiaries was to demonstrate its outstanding value to the seven parent companies—not only by alleviating competitive pressures world-wide, but also in confronting nationalist challenges from disgruntled governments in the Middle East.

In Iran the British Petroleum Company (BP) had been producing oil since 1913, and before long exports from Iran were second only to those from Venezuela. As in other petroleum exporting countries, oil revenues soon came to account for a major share of government income; yet unlike other Middle East countries, Iran was not a mandate or protectorate but an independent nation that had been trying to fight off imperial pressures for most of a century. It was only logical, therefore, that the first major conflict in the Middle East between a nationalist government and a foreign oil company should be coming to a head in Iran.

Iran's oil resources had time and again become an issue in the country's tenacious fight against British and Russian encroachments. In deference to Russia, the concession in which the British Treasury came to hold a majority interest was, from the start, limited to the country's southern regions. The 1907 partition into Russian and British spheres was followed, in 1915–18, by *de facto* occupation by British, Russian, and German forces. In 1919 the Iranian parliament refused to ratify an agreement that would have made the country a virtual British protectorate; in 1920 a new oil agreement was signed with BP; and in 1921 Reza Khan (later Reza Shah) established, through a military coup, a more assertive nationalist regime.

Under the 1920 agreement, Iran's oil revenues depended less on the amount of oil produced than on complex details of the company's internal accounting. For example, oil production rose steadily through most of the 1920s, quadrupling over the decade. Yet payments to the Tehran government fluctuated wildly: after tripling between 1924 and 1927, they dropped back to near their previous levels—mainly because the company had chosen to reduce its dividend on ordinary shares from 12.5 to 7.5 percent. Noting belatedly that a British adviser had represented Iran in the 1920 negotiations, Reza Shah's government declared the agreement void. It took five years, including a formal dispute before the Council of the League of Nations, before a new agreement was concluded in 1933. Iran this time was guaranteed a minimum payment for each ton of oil produced, and the payment was set in gold so as to safeguard against further currency devaluations, such as the British pound had undergone in 1931. Even so, the parties for several more years disputed whether those payments should be calculated according to the English "long ton" of 2,240 pounds, or the 2,200-pound "short ton."

During the British-Russian occupation of Iran in the Second World War, the Soviets vainly sought a far-reaching concession to explore for oil throughout the northern part of the country. (Since no major petroleum deposits have ever been discovered in northern Iran, one may wonder whether the Soviets at the time were planning to exploit the geological or the strategic and political prospects.) Instead, the Iranian parliament, on motion of Dr. Mohammed Mossadegh, passed a law forbidding the government from negotiating, let alone signing, any new oil concession without specific authorization from the parliament. The issue was revived in the 1946–47 Azarbaijan crisis. This time, the Iranian premier, Ahmad Ghavam, developed an intricate legal argument to persuade the Russians to postpone their demand for the oil concession until they had withdrawn their troops—and when they had done so, refused it. Soon Dr. Mossadegh pressed a campaign in parliament for nationalization of the existing British oil concession. An offer by the company for higher payments was rejected, Mossadegh's National Front swept into power on a high tide of popularity, and in September 1951 Iranian troops shut the company's British technicians out of the oil installations they had run for four decades.

The Iranian oil nationalization dispute dragged on for over two years. The World Bank, a diplomatic mission from the United States, the United Nations Security Council, and the International Court of Justice, all tried to intervene or received appeals—but in vain. The British government seized Iran's sterling deposits in London and sent the battleship *Mauritius* to waters near Iran—just in case. But Mossadegh's government was adamant. He had earned his doctorate in international law at the University of Lausanne four decades earlier, and under international law a sovereign government's right to nationalize foreign property, by legal procedure and with fair compensation, was beyond question. Replacing the departed British technicians with other foreigners, Mossadegh's National Iranian Oil Company resumed production at a trickle. But to ship any oil at all to foreign buyers, tankers had to be found that were not controlled by BP or its six sister companies—transport, as in the days of Rockefeller and Samuels, still was one of the choke points in the oil trade. Some tankers made it safely to Japan or Italy; others were forced by units of Britain's Royal Air Force into port at Aden (then still a British crown colony), where BP's lawyers stood by to have the cargoes impounded. In 1952 and 1953, Iran's marketed production was a mere 3 percent of what it had been before nationalization.

The companies' most effective weapon in the showdown with Mossadegh was not the colonial courts, or warplanes buzzing overhead, or financial retaliation in London, but their network of Middle Eastern concessions. BP, in addition to the entire concession in Iran, owned a half share in Kuwait and a quarter share in Iraq. Pressed to honor its commitments to supply crude oil to refiners and products to dealers, BP, with the concurrence of its partners, stepped up production in both these neighboring countries. Kuwaiti output in 1950–53 increased two and one-half times, Iraq's quadrupled. (It was not customary for governments to take any part in decisions on amounts of production; and, in any case, Kuwait and Iraq were pleased to see their production, and hence oil royalties, rise.) For good measure, Aramco's output in Saudi Arabia also increased by half. The net result was that, despite the Iranian shutdown, oil production for the Middle East as a whole increased 11 percent in 1951, 8 percent in 1952, and 16 percent in 1953. Meanwhile, an intensive exploration program launched by the companies in Kuwait, Saudi Arabia, and elsewhere added more petroleum to their inventory of "proven reserves" in three years than had been extracted from Iran in four decades.

The lesson that the companies were trying to convey to Mossadegh, and other nationalist governments that might rashly attempt nationalization, was loud and clear. No government had any ultimate leverage over the terms of a concession. The companies (and the world at large) could get along indefinitely without oil from any given country. Nationalization meant seizure of a worthless asset.

Did Mossadegh succeed or fail? The answer, once again, depends on the viewpoint and the time frame. By 1953 his immediate political hopes were shattered, he himself was on trial for his life, and his archenemy the shah was imposing a regime even more authoritarian than that of his father Reza Shah in 1921–41. Nothing came of the dream of Mossadegh's National Front of a national regeneration at home and full independence abroad based on Iran's management of its own oil resources. Western companies soon were handling the oil once again, and the mounting revenues helped finance the pomp, the militarism, the "white revolution" from above, the moral corruption, and thus perhaps the ultimate collapse, of the shah's regime. Internationally, too, the shah's Iran was closely aligned with the Western imperial interests that had helped restore him to his throne.

But even Mossadegh's bitterest enemies were forced to pay him grudging respect. The shah's courts tried him for high treason but imposed a sentence of no more than three years of solitary prison, allowing him to spend his remaining days in quiet retirement. No one dared revoke his oil nationalization law or dissolve his National Iranian Oil Company. Oil production was resumed in 1954 on the legal fiction that the oil itself remained nationalized and that the new concession awarded to the Western companies concerned only its production. (In 1975, on Persian new year's day, the shah went one better by "nationalizing" the production as well, while guaranteeing the foreign consortium its customary role in the management and share in the output; only with the Khomeini revolution of 1979 did foreign managment of Iran's oil come to an end and "nationalization" become a fact.) In deference to Iranian sensibilities, BP was limited to a 40 percent share in the new consortium—and compensation for the nationalized properties fixed at a modest sum payable over ten years. Above all, even though the multinational companies might have gotten along well enough without Iran, political pressures on them were such as to restore Iran (along with Saudi Arabia and Kuwait) to a leading position in Middle East oil.

In relations between Middle Eastern governments and Western companies for the next decade or so, the Iranian crisis of 1949–53 resulted in something of a standoff—or rather an accommodation with benefits to both sides. In facing down Mossadegh, the companies had demonstrated the futility of outright nationalization. In the next two decades, there were few challenges to their right to determine rates of oil exploration or levels of production, and none to their discretion over prices.

Conversely, the Iranian crisis had impressed on the companies the need to pay substantially higher sums to Middle Eastern governments for the privilege of operating a highly profitable oil industry from their subsoil. For the next two decades there were sizable increases in company payments to governments per barrel and even steeper increases in total amounts paid.

On the companies, these added payments imposed no serious hardship —the increase being covered by tax credits at home and by increased sales. Resumed production in Iran might have been a drawback for the companies—if Europe's and Japan's postwar recovery had not boosted market demand far beyond any previous levels. The 1954 Iranian consortium arrangement, moreover, served to weave even more tightly the companies' web of joint concessions: where once BP had been the sole concessionaire in Iran, now all seven major companies held a share, as did a number of their minor potential competitors. And in persuading the large American companies to help resolve the Iranian situation, the government in Washington agreed to drop a major antitrust suit that it had been preparing against them.

For Middle Eastern governments, the immediate advantage of rising payments was obvious—a seventeenfold increase between 1950 and 1970 for the Persian Gulf oil producers as a group. This implied a further advantage that would become apparent later: mounting oil revenues were likely to mean accumulating foreign exchange reserves, and this in turn would mean a much stronger bargaining position in any subsequent disagreement with the companies. But to maximize this bargaining potential, the oil countries would have to coordinate their tactics. The most important lesson of the Mossadegh crisis was that, in any dispute between companies and governments, victory must go to the side that established the greater unity in its ranks. In 1951 the companies had defeated Mossadegh by maintaining a solid front against a divided group of governments. Two decades later, the governments would show as much or more cohesion than the companies. In this dialectic fashion, Mossadegh's failure in the 1950s laid the groundwork for OPEC's successes of the 1970s.

THE COMPANIES SETTLE—AND UNCLE SAM PAYS

The oil concession arrangements of the 1950s benefitted companies as well as governments—the chief benefit to the companies being that they could increase payments to host governments at no cost to themselves. This was the result of an accommodation between American companies and Arab governments. In 1949 while BP began its fruitless parlays in Iran, Aramco pursued a different tack in Saudi Arabia, and the resulting "fifty-fifty" agreement of December 1950 soon was to become the norm throughout the Middle East. The details followed a precedent established in 1948 in Venezuela. Profits from the oil producing concession were to be shared between company and government, implying a tripling or quadrupling of government receipts per barrel. But the difference between the old 12½ or 16⅔ percent royalty and the new 50 percent rate would take the form not of royalty but of a corporate income tax. This meant that, under applicable United States law, these payments would become a tax credit and could be subtracted dollar for dollar from the companies' corporate income tax payments back home. Thus "the shift to 50:50 represented largely a transfer of tax revenue from the American and the British treasuries to those of the Middle East. The companies became the channel for this transfer. . . ."

The United States government, despite the certain loss in tax revenue, actively encouraged the arrangement. In view of the volatile political situation in the Middle East, the State Department was eager to have American companies not get involved in the kind of drag-out fight in which the British had become embroiled in Iran. Generally, Washington was anxious to cement relations with the Arab countries as they moved to greater independence. But American support for Israel was a liability, and Washington's habitual way of demonstrating friendship through foreign aid would have meant prolonged congressional hearings and strong opposition from pro-Israeli circles. By contrast, the tax credits had been on the statute books since 1921 and required neither legislation nor annual appropriations. In brief, the fifty-fifty arrangements provided "a seductive alternative for a more politically controversial direct foreign aid program." The same Saudi fifty-fifty pattern was followed in Kuwait (1951), Iraq (1952), and Iran (1954, on conclusion of the consortium agreement).

Throughout the 1950s the oil companies had to adjust to a rapidly shifting situation. Nasser, who came into power two years before the 1954 settlement in Iran, concluded his Soviet arms deal in September 1955 and nationalization of the Suez Canal in July 1956. And the resulting Suez-Sinai War closed the canal from November 1956 to March 1957 —the route by which 43 percent of all Persian Gulf oil reached its markets. Disruption of this major artery meant that tankers had to make a voyage more than twice as long around Africa, which sent tanker rates and quotations on the spot market for petroleum soaring.

Beyond this immediate effect, the canal dispute had profound symbolic significance. The Suez Canal, built in 1869, was a visible legacy of imperialist days—the oldest foreign economic concession in continuous operation anywhere in the Middle East. In the escalating diplomatic dispute that preceded the Suez War, the British government of Anthony Eden had insisted that maintenance of the canal and navigation through it were technical matters far too complex to be entrusted to Egyptians. Hence, for the sake of global freedom of navigation, it was imperative that the canal be restored to international control, if necessary by force. Yet, in the event, it was the military action mounted by Britain and France that prompted Egypt to close the canal; soon after its reopening under Egyptian management, the volume of traffic handled exceeded all previous records. Egyptians took understandable pride in this outcome —as well as in their own management of an engineering project as complex as the Aswan Dam (completed in 1970). In view of such achievements, it was not difficult to foresee that "Growing Middle Eastern expertise will contribute to the governments' ability eventually to assume full direction of petroleum production in their countries."

The Suez crisis compared to that in Iran demonstrates two important facts about the oil trade: that the global market is as sensitive to disruptions of transport as it is to curtailments of production, and that man-made transport facilities, such as pipelines and canals (and, presumably, port facilities), are more vulnerable to such disruption than are production facilities. Reductions of supply can be readily counteracted, as in 1951–53, if there is unused production potential elsewhere. By contrast, the acute temporary shortages caused by transport interruptions can be made up only if there is adequate storage.

The industry's response to the Suez crisis explored all available short- and long-term remedies. Tankers already in service were at once rerouted around Africa, causing an interruption of deliveries to Europe for several weeks, but part of the shortfall was made up by exports from the United States. Plans for a major pipeline that would carry Persian Gulf oil via Iran and Turkey to the Mediterranean were abandoned as offering no improvement in economic cost or political safety. Instead, the oil companies and shipping concerns began to develop a fleet of "supertankers"— larger than any previously routed through Suez—thus reducing the time and unit cost of shipment from the Persian Gulf to Europe or North

America. As a result, the size of newly built tankers had doubled by 1965 and increased tenfold by 1975, greatly reducing the cost advantage of the Suez route. In fact, the newer tankers were too large to make the passage through Suez. Even with the expansion program, begun after the canal's reopening in 1975, only half the tanker fleet could sail through the canal in the early 1980s.

The most successful response, in the medium term, was the stepping up of exploration in promising regions west of the Suez bottleneck. Thus major new discoveries were made in Algeria and Nigeria in 1958 and in Libya in 1961.

A Whiff of Competition

Despite the Mossadegh crisis and the Suez scare, the 1950s turned out to be excellent years for the major oil companies. Europe's industrial recovery stimulated a demand for energy in amounts that the ancient coal mines in Lancashire or the Ruhr area could no longer handle. The mines were showing signs of depletion; postwar wage levels were rising, with the politically powerful miners setting the pace; and still there were prolonged strikes and recurrent shortages. With European coal prices rising steadily, coal imports from Poland and even the United States and oil imports from the Middle East became a profitable alternative. Middle East oil prices remained stable, increasing only slightly after the 1956 Suez crisis, and the companies' handsome rate of profit on each barrel of Middle East oil remained unchanged—thanks to the fifty-fifty agreements and the tax credits. Yet Western Europe's oil consumption roughly tripled between 1950 and 1960—and so did the companies' exports from the Middle East.

Many of these trends continued through the 1960s. As domestic American oil prices continued to rise, it soon became cheaper to import Middle Eastern oil, despite the substantial freight charges across the Atlantic. The response in the United States, however, was the protection-ist program of "oil import quotas," which for more than a decade virtually excluded Persian Gulf oil from the United States market. There remained, as the companies' major outlets, Western Europe, where demand continued to grow briskly; and Japan, where energy expansion and the shift from coal to oil started late but proceeded faster. From 1960 to 1970, the companies' total exports from the Middle East tripled once again.

But meanwhile a number of unforeseen developments combined to give the international oil market its first whiff of competition in memory. There had been world-wide rivalry in the early days of John D. Rockefeller and Marcus Samuels. There had been a brief period of cut-throat competition among small oil operators who suddenly hit it big in Texas in the 1920s—while Rockefeller's and Samuels's successors were settling into a comfortable pattern of vertical integration, interlocking concessions, and stable oligopoly. But now a new set of competitors jostled their way in, lured by the promising market in Europe and the lucrative resources of the Middle East and North Africa. And soon the governments of the oil-producing countries would band together in OPEC—the Organization of the Petroleum Exporting Countries. And taking advantage of this new climate of competition among companies, OPEC began to challenge the companies' power as it had not been challenged since the beginning of the oil industry a century before.

Foremost among the new competitors were the Italian state oil company Ente Nazionale Idrocarburi (ENI), headed by Enrico Mattei, and a number of small or middle-sized American companies, such as Getty, Occidental, Marathon, and Atlantic-Richfield. In the background there was the Soviet Union, which found in its growing oil exports to Europe since the mid-1950s one of its few reliable sources of foreign currency.

Mattei was the spirited giant-killer who had pinned on the goliaths of the oil industry the mock-affectionate label *le sette sorelle*—"The Seven Sisters." His country was one of Europe's leading energy consumers; but unlike Britain, France, or Germany, which could count on domestic coal resources or supplies from multinational oil companies of their own, one-half (or by 1970, three-fourths) of Italy's energy came from foreign oil companies that insisted on payment in dollars or sterling. As head of Italy's largest indigenous oil concern, Mattei had every reason to welcome the Soviets as an alternative supplier; and during the crucial early years of the Russian export drive, he became their best customer.

The smaller American companies, in the current jargon of the trade, were known as "independents": they remained outside any of the large petroleum conglomerates, being mostly refiners, or refiners and distributors, with few or no oil wells of their own. This, of course, meant that they were heavily *dependent*—their volume of turnover depending largely on the variable surpluses of the producers. As the Middle East emerged as one of the world's major oil regions, the "independents" were naturally attracted to that region, in hopes both of securing steady independent supplies of crude oil and of sharing in the bonanza previously reserved to the majors. Not surprisingly, therefore, on the rare occasions when a small concession still was available, the "independents" were willing to snatch it up at terms far more favorable to the government than were customary with the majors. For example, in 1948 and 1949, the rulers of Kuwait and Saudi Arabia disposed each of his half-interest in oil in the "Neutral Zone"—a small strip of desert right between the two countries' oil fields and formerly disputed between them. After much canvassing and haggling, the successful bids were entered by two separate consortia of "independents," which offered a royalty of $0.33 to $0.55 a barrel respectively, as against the $0.22 then paid by Aramco, and gave the Middle Eastern ruler the right to acquire a sizable bloc of shares in the newly formed enterprise.

However generous the terms of the "independents," their Middle Eastern prospects were circumscribed by the lack of hopeful oil territory not preempted by the majors. Thus it had been the fluke of a belatedly settled boundary dispute between Kuwait and Saudi Arabia that gave them their first Middle Eastern foothold and Neutral Zone production through the 1960s never exceeded 4 percent of the Middle East total. In 1955 the "independents," with some help from the antitrust lawyers of the Department of Justice, scored another minor victory: a 5 percent share in the newly formed Iranian consortium. But their real opportunity came when the 1956 Suez War shifted the focus of oil prospecting westward to Libya.

The royal Libyan government, established in 1951 at the end of a period of U.N. trusteeship, sought advice from competent European oil experts and, in planning its oil development, broke with a number of established precedents.

It would not have been difficult to get one of the major oil companies, or a consortium of them, to bid for a concession covering the entire country. But in view of the companies' abundant Persian Gulf resources, Libya's bargaining position would have been weak, and concession terms at best would have matched those elsewhere. Besides, if the major companies were put in charge, what was to prevent them from using Libyan oil merely as a stopgap to compensate for temporary interruptions, such as in Iran or at Suez? Worse, might the companies not acquire a concession as a preemptive move—not to produce Libyan oil at all but merely to keep others from doing so?

Libya therefore decided to divide the more promising oil areas into dozens of separate parcels and to put each of those up for world-wide auction to any qualified bidders. The strategy proved singularly effective. The successful bidders included a dozen American "independents"; Mattei's ENI; several European companies from Germany, France, and Spain; as well as six of the seven majors. Soon more than a score of companies were moving their drilling rigs up and down Libya's rolling sand dunes. Exploration started in 1955 and intensified after 1956. The first finds came in 1959, and commercial production began in 1961. If any company's rate of finding oil lagged behind those in adjoining parcels, the company's officials had to be ready with a good explanation for skeptical and irascible Libyan officials. Payments per barrel to Libya were somewhat higher than in the Middle East, reflecting the good quality (especially the low sulfur content) of the oil; as well as the "Suez premium"—Libya's proximity to European (and later American) markets and immunity from any canal closures.

Production, once started, increased by leaps and bounds. Firms such as ENI, Occidental, and Marathon were eager to move into the rich markets once reserved to the seven majors, and the majors were determined to hold their own. Within two years, by 1963, Libya was producing as much oil as Iran in pre-Mossadegh days. By 1967 the renewed closing of the Suez Canal (until 1975, it turned out) prompted even more rapid development. By 1968 Libya was outproducing Kuwait. Libya now was the world's fourth largest exporter, after Venezuela, Iran, and Saudi Arabia. Its revenues grew proportionately—to as much as $1.1 billion in 1970. Also in 1970 Libya had accumulated financial reserves of $1.6 billion, equivalent to nearly three times annual imports.

There is an obvious strategy by which a new seller forces his way into an established market—whether that seller is Soviet Russia or ENI in the mid-1950s, or the independents and Libya in the early 1960s, or, for that matter, the owner of a new supermarket as he announces "grand opening day." He cuts prices a little or offers a bonus—the logical bonus for a seller from Libya being the lower transportation cost. If the challenge persists, the established sellers have no choice but to shave their prices by as much, or a little more, so as to maintain or restore their market share. Again, the newcomers may retaliate—and the price war is on. Step by step, prices will be cut, and the quantities offered for sale will increase —to the joy of the lucky consumers. Left to itself, such a price war comes to a logical conclusion when production facilities are strained to the maximum; or when the price cuts have wiped out all profits, and the competitors, one by one, start going bankrupt; or when the players (by tacit or explicit agreement) decide to stop the game as suicidal for them all.

The late 1950s and 1960s saw such a price war proceeding in slow motion on the international oil market. The reopening of Suez and expanding supplies from Russia prompted a steady series of price cuts by the major companies in the Persian Gulf region between 1957 and 1960. And the entry of Libya into the market after 1961 accelerated that same downward trend, until prices by the late 1960s had been cut by as much as one-half.

The effect of the slow, steady decline of prices was dramatic. World consumption of oil tripled between 1955 and 1971, and oil in international trade increased nearly fivefold. Libya and the Persian Gulf furnished most of the added flow of oil; and with the American market restricted by the import quotas, its major destinations were Europe and Japan. Since Persian Gulf production increased apace with Libya's, the major companies retained the lion's share of the vastly expanded market, limiting the American "independents" and other newcomers to one-sixth or less. It was in those years that more than half the tonnage carried by ships on the high seas came to be petroleum (1961), the value of the petroleum trade began to exceed that in all other mineral raw materials combined, and petroleum surpassed coal as the world's principal fuel (1967).

These were also the years when Americans moved to the suburbs, when the size of the automobile fleet of all other countries combined began to surpass that in the United States (1967), when the airplane became the standard mode of intercontinental travel, when Western Europe and Japan made their most spectacular economic advances, and when world commerce reached an unprecedented intensity. Rapid economic growth came to be widely viewed as the cureall for the political problems and tensions of the postcolonial world. Per capita energy consumption was taken as a ready indicator of economic advancement and of human welfare. In short, energy, as incrementally supplied by petroleum from the Middle East and elsewhere, was assumed to be freely available in almost any quantity desired. Needless to say, most citizens of the industrial world felt well disposed toward the multinational oil companies, large or small, that were the bearers of such gifts of bounty and saw little need to regulate their activities or to interfere in their relations with the governments of oil-producing countries.

The age of petroleum dawned on the world of the 1950s and 1960s as a time of unprecedented prosperity, apparent harmony of interests, and unbounded optimism.

OPEC's Trial and Error

Elation over declining oil prices was widespread but not universal. One group that had cause for early alarm were the governments whose income, under the fifty-fifty formula, was tied to that price. Aggregate revenues of the leading export countries (Venezuela, Kuwait, Saudi Arabia, Iran, and Iraq) had quadrupled between 1950 and 1960, from $560 million to $2.2 billion. But toward the end of the decade, as the companies started cutting prices, per-barrel incomes began to decline; some countries even saw their incomes decreasing absolutely. Middle East governments once again became keenly conscious that their financial fortunes depended on commercial decisions over which they had no control.

A decade earlier, there had been halfhearted attempts at coordinating policies among the oil exporting countries. As Venezuelans began to implement their 1948 tax law guaranteeing the government a 50 percent share in the companies' production revenues, they worried that inexperienced Middle Easterners might let the companies continue on more generous terms, that production might rapidly shift to the Middle East, and that Venezuelan tax coffers might remain empty. In 1949 Venezuela therefore initiated discussions with six Middle Eastern governments about a possible association of oil-producing countries. Nothing came of this, and soon the Mossadegh crisis showed just how little solidarity there was among oil governments in the Middle East. Still, Venezuela's mission helped spread the "fifty-fifty" idea to that region.

Now, after an entire decade, the desert soil proved more fertile. Historians of the French Revolution, ever since Alexis de Tocqueville, have discovered that people are likely to rebel not when their misery is extreme, but when a long, steady improvement of conditions is threatened by a sudden reversal. The steadily growing oil incomes of the 1950s and the sudden price cuts late in the decade created such a revolutionary situation in miniature. The First Arab Petroleum Conference in the spring of 1959 insisted that the companies should not reduce prices unilaterally. In May 1960, Venezuela sent another mission to the Middle East, and a joint Venezuelan-Saudi statement called for a "common petroleum policy" among major producing countries. Yet the companies, by a further round of price cuts in August 1960, made it clear that they had no intention of consulting on their pricing decisions or other commercial policy. This time the response was a meeting in Baghdad, where Venezuela, Saudi Arabia, Kuwait, Iraq, and Iran agreed to found the "Organization of the Petroleum Exporting Countries" on September 14, 1960. The event was ignored by the oil industry and went virtually unreported in the international press. The price cuts that so alarmed the founders of OPEC had been due, as we saw, to the entry of new companies into the oil market. Some years were to pass before OPEC learned to turn this competition between large and small companies to its own advantage. When it did so, the constellation of the oil market was changed beyond recognition.

To some of OPEC's founders the obvious purpose of collective action was formation of a producers' cartel, and the classic cartel strategy had always been to drive up prices by keeping down production. But this would have meant choosing an over-all production ceiling, allocating shares to each country, and enforcing those decisions on the companies —three tasks any one of which would have daunted the new organization. How much of a production cut would it take to maintain prices at any desired level? On what principle should production be allocated— what, for instance, if Venezuela insisted on its customary one-third share of world exports and Middle Eastern producers on maintaining their recent rates of relative growth? How could production limits of any sort be imposed on the companies? And even if the companies could somehow be brought to comply, what was to prevent them from recouping the missing oil elsewhere? After all, they had beaten Mossadegh with Arab oil, and their price-cutting spree of the late 1950s and 1960s had been made possible by the advent first of Soviet and then of Libyan oil.

The very attempt at formulating a cartel strategy would have been sure to bewilder OPEC's economists, to set member government against member government, and to shatter the unity of the infant organization. But OPEC's founders set themselves far more modest and safer aims for a start.

Luckily for OPEC, all the major oil discoveries of the 1950s and 1960s were made in Third World countries—where multinational companies had found the concession terms to be easy, but where the idea of a joint front against them now was likely to catch on quickly. One of OPEC's first concerns became to extend its organization: Libya and Indonesia joined in 1962, Abu Dhabi (largest of the United Arab Emirates) in 1967,

Algeria in 1969, and Nigeria in 1971. With its membership roster thus periodically updated, OPEC proceeded not to grandiose cartel schemes but to comparing notes on government-company relations, especially on the details of bookkeeping on production, prices, royalties, and taxes. OPEC began to look closely into the pesky legal and financial details that over the years had caused so much bad feeling between British Petroleum and successive governments in Iran and at last driven Mossadegh to his ill-starred attempt at nationalization.

In the guerrilla war among the chartered accountants that ensued, OPEC's first major victory came about very quietly—and consisted in making member governments' income independent of continuing price fluctuations. Ever since the 1940s, the companies had established at the Persian Gulf a system of "posted prices," which at the time simply meant the actual price at which the crude oil was offered for sale. By the 1950s, royalty percentages and the 50 percent income tax had come to be based on these posted prices (less production costs); it was their reduction by as much as 16 percent from 1958 to 1960 that had called OPEC to life. OPEC's resolution of 1962 demanding a rollback to 1959 price levels seemed to fall on deaf ears; yet it turned out that the companies had taken note, after all. Actual sales prices continued their steady decline as Libyan oil flooded the market, but the companies now deemed it wise to leave the posted price intact and give a discount, which, of course, had to be absorbed in their share of the fifty-fifty split. The "posted price" from this time onward became a mere tax-reference price for royalty and tax accounting purposes. For example, the standard grade of Saudi oil remained "posted" at $1.80 a barrel throughout the 1960s, even though actual sales early in 1969 were made at close to $1.00 a barrel.

Just as significant was another resolution adopted by OPEC in 1962 that, on the basis of alleged ambiguities in the wording of the most recent concessions, demanded that the royalty (16⅔ percent in Venezuela and 12½ percent elsewhere) be calculated separately, rather than as part of, the 50 percent income tax. Faced with uniform pressure from all OPEC members, the companies agreed to this system—which, in effect, abandoned the fifty-fifty principle by bringing their payments closer to 60 percent. The governments, in turn, agreed to phase in this increase over a number of years, from 1963 to 1967.

Emboldened by these initial successes, and with much time for reflection on strategy, OPEC in 1968 came up with a Declaratory Statement of Petroleum Policy in Member Countries, its chief author, apparently, being Saudi Arabia's youthful petroleum minister, Sheikh Ahmad Zaki Yamani.

The declaration concerned itself wholly with government-company relations, and it spelled out only procedural rules, not substantive policies. OPEC would not waste its time trying to fix production quotas or even draw up a common list of demands on the companies. Rather, each member or group of members would remain free to press its particular producing companies for a better price, or tax rate, or participation in share holding, or training program for its nationals, or whatever. But all contracts would remain subject to renegotiation in "changing circumstances" (Art. 1.3), and all OPEC members would insist that any renegotiated contract should conform to the "best of current practices" (art. 10) —that is, give the government the benefit of whatever any companies might have conceded to anyone else. The most revolutionary proposition was OPEC's demand that the tax-reference prices not be negotiated but determined unilaterally by the government.

Within these stringent conditions, which would have seemed inconceivable only a few years earlier, the declaration envisaged for the companies a continuing positive role in exploration, investment in oil facilities, management of production, and world-wide distribution and sales —in short, as OPEC's junior partners or hired technical agents. Or, as the opening paragraph (art. 1.1) of the declaration states in dry legalistic language: "Member Governments shall endeavour, as far as feasible, to explore for and develop their hydrocarbon resources directly. The capital, specialists and the promotion of marketing outlets required for such direct development may be complemented when necessary from alternate sources on a commercial basis."

Yamani's major contribution to OPEC's long-range strategy was to convince his colleagues that the major companies need not be OPEC's sworn enemies, that government and company interests need not be irreconcilable. And, indeed, it would become clear over the years that the companies' old idea of "market stability"—and the global sales organization that enables them actually to "stabilize" the market—would be crucial in protecting OPEC from the kind of mutual suspicion and rivalry that could have brought the OPEC cartel down in a general price war.

The future reversal in government-company relationships was summed up in the laconic statement that the "tax reference price . . . shall be determined by the Government" (art. 4). OPEC meant to set tax rates unilaterally and wrest from the companies their privilege of setting prices. To make the companies surrender on this central point, OPEC in the next few years was to develop two additional tactical principles. First, a company that in a dispute with any member government found itself faced with the threat of a shutdown would not be allowed to increase production in any other OPEC country—there was to be no repetition of the early fifties when companies had turned on the valves in Kuwait and Saudi Arabia so as to defeat Iran's nationalization. Second, and worse, such a company might find itself (as an OPEC resolution of 1971 was to state) subject to a "total embargo" in all member countries.

In the first decade of OPEC's existence, from 1960 to 1970, the aggregate income of its members had gone up from $2.2 to $7.3 billion yearly. Not only was OPEC determined to see this upward trend continue, the organization also meant to put its hands firmly on the levers that determined the relevant trends. OPEC's strategy for the 1970s was neatly summed up by one shrewd observer: "After cash must come control." The actual tactics have turned out to be even more resourceful: more cash, more control, then more cash and yet more control, and then still more cash.

THE COMPANIES IN RETREAT

The late 1950s and 1960s continued the pattern of rapid growth for the world oil industry and of unprecedented prosperity for the major companies. But behind that splendid façade, the companies were coping with two separate but interrelated attacks: from smaller companies such as ENI and the "independents" for a larger share of the market; and from nationalist governments in the Third World banded together in OPEC for a larger share in the income—and eventually a decisive say in the management.

Responding pragmatically to each threat as it arose, the companies had hit on two major devices that enabled them to hold their own in the face of both attacks. The first were the tax credits, which enabled them to keep ahead of the governments' appetite for additional monies at no expense to themselves. The other was the spectacular expansion of their markets in Europe and Japan, which made it possible to satisfy independents, majors, governments, customers, and their own shareholders alike. In the 1950s the companies had clashed head on, first with Mossadegh and then with the "independents," in a zero-sum game in which each side's gain was the other's loss. Now the companies' strategy for the 1960s had deflected the head-on collisions and converted the play into a positive-sum game in which no one stood to lose.

The multinational oil companies, and later OPEC, have dominated that portion of the world's petroleum that flows in international trade— about one-third of the total in 1950 and one-half or more after 1960. In 1950, net revenues from this oil production for international trade were in the neighborhood of $2.7 billion, and these were divided about 83:17 in the companies' favor. By 1970 the volume of this trade had increased sevenfold; the price—and hence net revenues per barrel—had dropped by one-half; and the division of revenues was 73:27 in the governments' favor. Total net revenues were approximately $11 billion, of which $7.3 billion went to OPEC governments, $2.7 billion to the major companies, and somewhat over $1 billion to the minor oil companies or non-OPEC exporters, such as the Soviet Union. The government and company shares had been almost exactly reversed; but with a far larger pie to share, everyone's piece was much bigger.

OPEC countries obviously did better than anyone else at this reslicing —the crucial steps being the fifty-fifty agreements at the beginning of the period and the added royalty of the mid-1960s. Consumers throughout the world used about twice as much oil in the mid-1960s than they had a decade earlier but paid only a slightly larger total. Even the coal miners and mine operators lost only in relative, not absolute terms: while coal's share in energy declined, total world energy consumption had tripled in twenty years and coal consumption had increased by one-half.

Tax credits and market expansion had kept the major companies ahead of the game for nearly two decades—but could not do so forever. The trouble was that no company can claim credit for more than 100 percent of its tax bill and no customer can shift from coal to oil for more than 100 percent of his energy needs. In the late 1960s, the companies had run into the first of these limits and were approaching the second.

When the fifty-fifty agreements were first applied, it will be recalled, the companies in most Middle Eastern countries paid a royalty of 12½ percent and (royalties being counted toward the tax) a corporate income tax of 37½ percent, which they could credit in full against their corporate income tax in the United States. For example, Aramco in 1950 had paid a total tax bill of $106 million, $50 million to the United States and $56 million to Saudi Arabia. In 1951 the payments were $6 million to the United States and $110 million to Saudi Arabia for a total of $116 million.

That picture was basically changed when OPEC began to impose its new rule that royalties could no longer be counted toward the tax but must be paid in addition. The full 50 percent tax, of course, exceeded the 48 percent U.S. corporate income tax, which meant that companies owed no U.S. income tax on their earnings in OPEC countries, but also that they accumulated excess tax credits. This was only another way of saying that some portion of the companies' tax payments to OPEC governments was beginning to come out of the companies' own pockets. And that portion would increase substantially as OPEC countries raised their tax rates from 50 to 55 percent in 1971 and 60 percent or more later.

Still, the companies did well as long as price cuts insured a steady market expansion. Their earnings per barrel might decline from $0.54 in 1960 to $0.38 in 1970, but with the volume of world imports nearly tripled, their total earnings from foreign production also rose—from $1.6 billion to $2.7 billion in the decade. The open question was how long this expansion could continue. In Western Europe, petroleum consumption between 1950 and 1970 had increased from 9.4 to 57.3 percent of total energy; in Japan the increase had been even more dramatic—from 3.1 to 69.3 percent. How much more oil would the market absorb and what further price cuts might it take to overcome increasing buyer resistance?

Here the companies ran into their most serious difficulty. Their combined tax and royalty payments in the Middle East had increased from 50 to 56 percent, and they had allowed those percentages to be calculated on a fictitiously high "posted price." This meant that they were absorbing all price cuts, as well as any tax increases, out of their share of the original fifty-fifty arrangement. At prices of $1.30 or less reached early in 1970, their net production profit was down to about $0.24 a barrel. (See the accompanying table.) Any further price cut or any increase in the tax rate to 55 or 60 percent would convert that profit into a net loss —except for the tax credit that U.S. companies could claim and the possible "downstream" profits, say on refining. And those two compensations also had diminished—the companies had been accumulating "excess tax credits," and competition from the "independents" had cut into refinery returns.

No company can operate at a loss more than briefly—and the obvious, indeed the compelling, escape from such a price-and-tax squeeze is to raise the price. This is, indeed, what the companies started doing in the

Persian Gulf Oil: Government and Company Revenues 1960–1970

	1960	*1970*
Posted price per barrel	$1.80	$1.80
Less: Discount	--	.50
Production cost	.10	.10
Royalty*	.21	.21
Income tax**	.64	.75
Subtotal	.95	1.56
Company net revenue	.85	.24

*Royalty is calculated as posted price, less production cost, divided by eight.
**Income tax in 1960 is calculated as posted price, minus production cost, divided by two, minus royalty. Income tax in 1970 is calculated as posted price, minus production cost, minus royalty, divided by two.

early 1970s, even before their profits had disappeared; and since they all made more or less the same price response to OPEC's identical pressure, no one company's competitive position was impaired. But OPEC's share already represented three-fourths of the price. If the companies passed OPEC's future tax raises on to the customers, they would stop the spectacular market expansion of the 1960s. Worse, they would risk abdicating their crucial decisions on price and volume of business for good. Where once they had been sovereign commercial agents, they might wind up being no more than a vast "tax collecting agency" for OPEC—as the chairman of BP once vividly put it. OPEC's master plan of 1968 had imagined the companies in the humble function of adequately remunerated technicians and sales agents—temporary hired help. To allow OPEC to control the companies' prices might reduce them to such a menial position all too quickly.

OPEC for its part was sure to step up the pressure. For years the companies had been generous in responding to OPEC's financial demands, first at the expense of Western taxpayers, and then by virtue of expanding sales. Now such generosity had come to haunt the companies: plainly, it had engendered not gratitude but greed. *L'appétit vient en mangeant,* says a French proverb, and few appetites are so insatiable as that for money. In OPEC's case, the very act of eating increased not only the craving but also the ability to satisfy it. In 1952 and 1953, the blocking of Iran's deposits in London and the lack of oil income had helped undermine Mossadegh and precipitate his downfall. But in the years since, every statesmanlike, generous settlement between the companies and OPEC had increased the financial reserves of the governments and thereby their ability to hold out in any future contest. Between companies that habitually stored no more than a few days' (or at most a few weeks') worth of oil, and governments whose financial reserves amounted to several months or even years of their countries' total imports there could be no fair contest. The storage of oil is costly—whereas the storage of money yields a handsome dividend.

The largest financial reserves in relation to the size of the country's economy had accumulated in Libya. Libya already was the country where major companies and "independents" were directly in competition. A change of regime in that country, together with a favorable international constellation, would soon ensure that Libya would use precisely those financial reserves in the service of precisely those insatiable appetites. And whatever concessions Libya extracted from the companies, other countries would be ready to claim under OPEC's "best of current practices" doctrine. The international petroleum scene was all set for its most dramatic and momentous reversal.

4

OIL, THE UNITED STATES, AND THE MIDDLE EAST: THE KNOT IS TIED

"DRAIN AMERICA FIRST"

The first three chapters of this book have dealt with the Middle East and its politics in the twilight of imperialism; with the United States and its gradual involvement in Middle East diplomacy; and with oil and its rise to the status of the world's leading fuel. In the early 1970s a number of separate trends all gathered momentum so as to transform the relationship of those three elements beyond recognition. America came to depend increasingly on foreign oil. Control over the international petroleum market was shifting from the large oil companies to Middle Eastern governments. And Middle Eastern political attitudes toward the United States were turning increasingly critical or hostile. All at once, the United States became both a tempting and a vulnerable target for an "oil weapon" that Middle Easterners were just getting ready to wield.

The proclamation of the Arab oil embargo in October 1973, and the gasoline queues of the following winter, helped create a crisis atmosphere that convinced many American citizens of the need for drastic government action. The Nixon administration's "Project Independence"—though neither coherent enough to be a "project" nor purposeful enough to reduce our dependence on foreign energy—accurately captured the mood of public impatience. Yet few Americans were aware that the federal government had had an oil policy, and specifically a policy relating to foreign oil, for many years—and that the crisis that hit us in 1973 had been seriously aggravated by the effects of that policy.

The United States has always been the world's leading petroleum consumer and was, from the beginning of this century until the 1970s, also the leading producer. American exports dominated the world trade in the 1920s and 1930s, and during the Second World War, oil from American wells propelled Allied planes, ships, and tanks to their victories over Germany and Japan. As late as 1948, the "Galveston basing point" still provided the method for calculating the price of Middle Eastern oil exports to Europe. After the war, domestic consumption rose even faster, as Americans moved to the suburbs, made the automobile their favorite means of transport, and generally enjoyed a rising, energy-intensive standard of living. Per-capita energy consumption in the United States, always the world's highest, rose a further 40 percent between 1937 and 1962; and within that growing total of energy consumed, the share of oil rose from one-quarter to three-eighths.

But in oil production, America was gradually losing its dominant position. Meeting a rapidly growing demand for many decades, some of the old fields in Texas, Oklahoma, Louisiana, and California were beginning to show signs of strain. For a time, exploration and drilling activity kept ahead of rising demand. The crucial ratio of "proven reserves" to production—which Professor M. A. Adelman has referred to as the "ready-shelf inventory" of the oil companies—for many years remained around twelve to thirteen years, which would seem to be the industry's favorite "shelf" size. Soon however, there came a time in the 1960s when, despite expanded drilling activity, the annual additions to "proven reserves" were less than the amounts withdrawn from those reserves by current production. This, of course, meant that the reserves/production ratio declined—from about twelve years in the mid-1950s to ten years in 1966 and eight years in 1971. It would only be a matter of time before production itself would decline, which, indeed, it did after hitting a peak of 11.3 million barrels a day in 1970.

Foreign production increased rapidly just as American production began to slow down and decline. Kuwait and Saudi Arabia started full-scale production in 1952 and the flow of oil from Iran resumed in 1955. The Suez crisis of 1956 and the busy activities of the "independents" started the North African oil boom. By 1952, the United States only accounted for half of the world's oil production, and by 1968 for only one-fourth. By the mid-1950s, Middle Eastern oil underbid oil from

Texas and Louisiana in the New England and mid-Atlantic markets. The center of world petroleum had shifted from Galveston, Texas, to Ras Tanura, Saudi Arabia.

As production costs from America's aging wells kept climbing, competition between Middle Eastern and African producers reduced prices steadily in foreign markets. How soon would the burst of competition that had revolutionized the energy economy of Europe and Japan spread across the Atlantic? And what would be the response to such competitive pressures?

The first rounds of price cuts by the multinational oil companies called into action the governments of oil exporting nations, who were eager to protect the income they had enjoyed at the higher price levels. But it took OPEC the better part of a decade to devise an effective strategy to this end. American domestic oil producers were just as alert to the danger that the new flood of cheap oil from the Middle East and North Africa posed for their own higher-priced production. And they knew themselves to be far more vulnerable to any process of vigorous, cut-throat competition—for in the foreign markets the network of large interlocking concessions could be counted on as a restraining influence, whereas in the United States oil production was scattered among many smaller companies, and even the majors had no interlocking network. Yet if the dangers of competition were great, protectionist measures by a single government in Washington offered a tempting and effective remedy.

The natural result of the two opposite trends—toward scarcity and higher prices in the United States and toward ample supplies and successive price reductions abroad—would of course have been a growing stream of imports. This inflow of oil would have brought American prices down to prevailing world levels, stimulated production in the Middle East and North Africa even faster, and presumably caused the more expensive wells in the United States to shut down—at least temporarily, until such time as world prices might once again be rising. The net effect, it has been estimated, would have been a pattern whereby all oil consumed East of the Mississippi would have been imported from Venezuela or the Middle East, leaving to American domestic production the market west of Texas and across the Rockies. The blow to some of the smaller and less efficient producers would have been severe. Some of the multinational oil companies with production wells both here and abroad (for example, Exxon, Gulf, and Shell) were divided in their reaction: a rising domestic price would boost the profits of their Ameri-

120

can affililiates; a free market for imported oil would allow their international subsidiaries to conquer a growing share of the lucrative American market.

Naturally, the lead in the political battle for import restrictions came to be taken by the domestic producers. Although individually smaller than the multinational oil companies, they were spread collectively across a number of large states, such as Texas, California, Louisiana, and Oklahoma, and this gave them considerable influence in Washington. The arguments invoked—as usual in battles for economic subsidy or against foreign competition—were not from private or commercial but from public interest, specifically from national security and defense. Oil, the protectionists warned, was essential to military operations and to industrial production in time of war—the Korean War of 1950–52 once again had demonstrated that. The recent shutdown in Iran and the interruption of the Suez Canal showed how unreliable foreign supplies might be. If the United States allowed its oil industry to be ravaged by cheap foreign competition now, it might find itself without any domestic oil industry at a time of dire need in the future.

The lack of logic in such arguments is glaring. The spokesmen for the high-priced domestic oil producers blithely transferred to a natural resource a line of reasoning more familiar to manufacturing. The difference, of course, is that manufacturing is labor intensive and dependent on skills that are developed over a lifetime and maintained by continued use. Thus it has been argued—inaccurately perhaps, but at any rate plausibly—that a protective tariff on cheap watches from Switzerland or Hong Kong is needed in peacetime to preserve the skill of the American watchmakers who may build the control panel for a jet bomber in time of war. By contrast, petroleum is a consumable commodity: any gallon of it that is drawn from American wells to be burnt up today will not be available tomorrow to fuel a tank or jet plane for use in war or for any other purpose.

Only a decade earlier, there had been a spirited debate about oil and national security when a major war was in actual progress. In 1943 and 1944, Harold Ickes, secretary of interior and petroleum administrator for war, had expressed anxiety that dwindling American supplies of oil might be insufficient to fuel both the war machine and the industrial economy. He therefore developed a plan to acquire the Saudi Arabian oil concession from the two private companies then owning it; or, failing that, to have the American government finance a pipeline that could bring Saudi oil to the Mediterranean and hence to the European theater of war. At that time, too, oil industry reaction had followed predictable lines of self-interest. The companies owning the Saudi concession were cool to any U.S. government takeover but enthusiastic about a pipeline to be built at U.S. government expense. Their competitors were strongly opposed to any such government subsidy to bring Saudi oil to the outside market. But no one questioned Ickes's premise that foreign production would help conserve American resources. Indeed, a spokesman for the antipipeline faction sought to reassure the public by asserting that American oil resources would be "sufficient to supply our needs at the present rate for more than a thousand years." Others cautioned (rightly as it turned out) that the war would be over before the pipeline could be built. (It was built in 1948–51, with private funds.)

In the 1940s and 1950s, a more accurate logic of national security might have counseled in favor of encouraging a maximum of imports in peacetime, combined perhaps with a modest surcharge to finance some form of emergency stockpiling. Stockpiling, in turn, might have taken the form either of the Naval Petroleum Reserve, established in 1920, which keeps idle wells in operating condition on a standby basis, or of the Strategic Petroleum Reserve of 1979, which stores oil in underground caverns for future emergency use. Instead, the protectionist pressures of the late 1950s prompted the adoption of a program of oil import quotas, imposed by a directive of President Eisenhower's National Security Council in 1959 and maintained in one form or another until the spring of 1973. The details of the program were readjusted a number of times; the over-all effect was to limit imports of overseas petroleum (that is, from anywhere but Canada) to 10 percent, and later to 12.2 percent, of America's domestic production.

The import quotas were only the latest in a series of policies by which Washington had, from time to time, intervened in the world petroleum market. Each measure, like the quotas of 1959, had been adopted in response to specific commercial or political pressures; and their effects, were often contradictory. By encouraging the entry of American oil companies into Iraq in the 1920s and into the Iranian consortium in 1954, Washington had strengthened the pattern of interlocking concessions that had enabled the major oil companies to keep prices at ten times or more their cost of production in the Middle East. For good measure, the government in 1954 had also dropped its major antitrust suit against the international oil industry. By contrast, the U.S. Economic Cooperation Administration, directing the Marshall Plan purchases of petroleum for Western Europe, had been the first, as early as 1948, to challenge Middle East oil prices derived from the "Galveston basing point." And the allocation of a small share in the Iranian consortium to the "independents" gave some limited stimulus to competition.

Just as pervasive were the effects of the tax credits that enabled American oil companies to settle their financial differences with Middle Eastern governments at U.S. Treasury expense. With their tax payments refunded, the companies could afford to charge less for their Middle Eastern oil than they otherwise might have; in this way, the tax credits contributed indirectly to the downward price spiral in the world oil market—and to the protectionist response in America itself. And with a generous flow of revenues assured jointly by Washington and the companies, Middle Eastern governments accumulated funds for their showdown with the oil companies. Hence the tax credits contributed indirectly to OPEC's meteoric rise in the 1970s.

The oil import quota program of 1959–73 similarly had direct and indirect effects. Its direct effect was to allow the American domestic oil price to remain about 70 percent above world levels. This represented an added charge to the American consumer, and an added gain for the domestic oil producer, that has been estimated at well over $50 billion for the full period—"probably the largest subsidy to any single industry in U.S. history." And with American producers and consumers thus "protected," the benefits of price competition in the world oil market accrued to the consumers in Europe and Japan.

In the United States, the import quotas mandated the use of domestic oil where buyers would have preferred oil from abroad—and thus led indirectly to more rapid depletion of wells that might have been shut down or added to the Naval Petroleum Reserve. In short, the indirect effects of the import quotas made a mockery of the national security argument on which supposedly they were based. Sarcastically but aptly, S. David Freeman has referred to the quotas as a "Drain America First Policy." The import quotas were keeping Middle Eastern oil off the American market at a time when its importation would have been cheap and free of political strings. Conversely, they forced us to rely on Middle East imports at a later time, when their price was rising sharply and political strings were assiduously being attached. In making this retrospective assessment, it is important to keep in mind the relative orders of magnitude. The six months of the Arab oil embargo of 1973–74 were preceded by fourteen years of an American boycott of Middle East oil. The American boycott every year probably kept as much or more oil off the American market than Arab countries withheld in 1973/74. The cost to the American consumer of mounting an adequate storage program would have come to a small fraction of the cost of the import quotas.

By the early 1970s, American oil was showing the obvious signs of having been "drained first." Coincidentally, the power shift from international oil companies to Middle Eastern governments was causing a gradual, steady rise in the world price of oil. Hence the earlier pressures for protectionism abated, and the quota program was phased out and ended in April 1973.

ISRAELIS AND ARABS

American policy in the Middle East had been highly active in the 1950s but unable to reconcile the divergent requirements of orderly decolonization and regional unity in face of the Soviet threat. The shah was back on his throne, and oil from Iran was flowing again; but nothing had been salvaged from the British positions in Egypt, Iraq, Jordan, or the Sudan. Despite all the exertions of the Truman and Eisenhower administrations, there was no allied Middle East Command, and there was no Middle East Defense Organization. The Baghdad Pact had crumbled before it was effectively organized; far from rallying moderate Arabs to the West, it had scared them off or undermined their position. The major military action of the period, at Suez in 1956, had turned into a confrontation not between East and West but between Washington and its major European allies. By converting Nasser's military defeat into a political triumph, the United States had earned no gratitude in Cairo; instead, it had driven Egypt further into Moscow's arms. The Eisenhower Doctrine, proclaimed in hopes of limiting the damage and once again setting limits to "international communism," had only encouraged Moscow's radical and pan-Arab allies of the day.

The lull that followed in American–Middle Eastern relations in the 1960s was a natural sequel to those overexertions and frustrations. Soon also the Cuban missile crisis (1962) and the conflict in Southeast Asia shifted the focus of the East-West struggle to other regions. By the late 1960s, the war in Vietnam had come to engage America's most strenuous military and diplomatic efforts and to dominate even the domestic debate. Thus, during the crucial decade when America's domestic oil was being "drained first" and when OPEC was cautiously perfecting its organization, Washington paid no more than sporadic attention to developments in the Middle East.

Soviet-American rivalry in the region in the 1960s took the form mainly of competitive programs of foreign economic and military aid. In the Muslim Middle East and North Africa, the Soviet Union became the major arms supplier for Egypt (1955), Syria (1956), North Yemen (1957), Algeria (1964), the Sudan (1967), South Yemen (1968), Libya (1969), Somalia (1969), and Afghanistan (1973). Ever-increasing quantities of American arms went to Turkey, Iran, and Pakistan; by 1969, the United States also replaced France as Israel's major weapons supplier. Turkey and Israel were the major recipients in the Middle East of American economic aid, supplemented in Israel with a growing stream of private donations. American economic support for countries such as Saudi Arabia, Kuwait, Iran, and Iraq took the form not of foreign aid but of hidden subsidies under the "fifty-fifty" agreements between those countries and the multinational oil companies.

The heavy flow of weapons into the region from both East and West (see table 5 in the Appendix) had a number of obvious consequences. For one, it tended to enhance the role of the military in the domestic politics of the recipient countries. By the 1960s, military coups had become the normal method for changing governments in Syria, Iraq, and many other Middle Eastern countries. On most of the Arabian peninsula, traditional rulers retained their thrones, but some of the more recently instituted monarchies, such as in Jordan and Iran, survived only in close alliance with their armed forces. Even in Turkey a promising, vigorous democratic development was interrupted by interludes of military rule (1960–61 and beginning in 1980) or indirect military intervention (1971–73). And in Israel a growing proportion of the governmental leadership came to be recruited from among generals who, after early retirement, had taken leading positions in one or another political party.

Even more directly, the inflow of arms made of the Middle East one of the major testing grounds for the latest in American and Soviet weaponry—the whole deadly arsenal of tanks, rockets, missiles, and supersonic planes.

In Europe, of course, the arms buildup was more massive, but no actual armed clashes occurred for over three decades; there was room for deterrence first, and later even for détente. But aside from Korea (1950–53) and Vietnam (1964–72), the Middle East, with its periodic

Arab-Israeli confrontations, was the one region where such weapons were likely to be put to actual use and, between successive rounds of war, to exacerbate the efforts of diplomacy.

There remained the nagging question of what political purposes—of either the donors or the recipients—this lavish flow of arms was likely to serve. Perhaps the question arose in its most emphatic form for Israel after the war of June 1967.

From a military viewpoint, the Six-Day War, which Israel fought mostly with weapons obtained from France in the previous decade, was a brilliant success. There had been ample Arab provocation. Nasser, responding to taunts from Arab rivals that his anti-Israel stand was all talk and no action, had announced (but not enforced) a blockade of shipping bound for Israel through the Gulf of Aqaba. Above all, he had requested the withdrawal of the United Nations peacekeeping force stationed on the Egyptian side of the armistice line around the Gaza Strip and had thus undone the arrangement under which Israel had agreed to withdraw from Sinai and Gaza in 1957. Israel responded with a lightning preemptive strike against first Egypt and then Syria and Jordan, which in line with earlier commitments had joined the war on Egypt's side.

As a result of the Six-Day War, Israel traded the precarious 1948 boundaries for new lines that offered all that a military planner could wish. Earlier, the ten-mile waist between the Jordanian-held West Bank and the Mediterranean and the thirty miles of barbed wire along the Gaza Strip had made Israel vulnerable to bisection in any military offensive and to constant guerrilla infiltration even in times of alleged peace. Now the Dead Sea, the Jordan river, the Golan Heights, and the Suez Canal provided a set of ideal defenses, whether against infantry, tanks, or nighttime guerrillas. Above all, Israeli occupation of the Sinai peninsula put Egyptian jet planes over one hundred miles farther from targets in Israel—and, conversely, Israeli planes at half their previous distance from Cairo or Alexandria.

But none of this helped much in the long-term political balance. Within the 1967 de facto boundaries, including the West Bank, the Gaza Strip, and East Jerusalem, the Arab-speaking residents under Israeli jurisdiction had increased from 300,000 to as much as 1.4 million, or 37 percent of the total population. Since Jewish immigration in the late 1960s had virtually halted, and Arab Palestinian population-increase rates are among the world's highest, this suggested the prospect of an Arab majority well before the end of the century. No matter how desirable, therefore, the 1967 lines in the view of the military planners, they threatened the Jewishness and the egalitarianism of Israel—in sum, the two central ideals of Zionism for which the state of Israel had been founded to begin with.

Outside the 1967 lines, the war increased the number of Palestinian refugees, from 1.3 million to 1.5 million—the largest group of them in Jordan and since 1970 in Lebanon. It hardened the resolve of the Palestinian political organizations in exile (loosely coordinated since 1964 in the Palestine Liberation Organization) not just to harass but, if possible, to destroy Israel. Gamal Abdul Nasser, in defeat, remained unshaken in his popularity at home and became more closely beholden to the Soviet Union abroad. Israel's victory had gained her not acceptance in the Middle East but implacable hostility. And world opinion beyond the immediate region, which in 1948 and 1956 had tended to side with Israel as the underdog, began to shift in its sympathies to the Arab and more specifically the Palestinian side. For example, within a few days of the June War, President de Gaulle, whose country had been Israel's largest arms supplier, cut off all aid and explicitly blamed the Israelis for starting the war.

The 1967 war thus emphasized the wide gap of perception within and outside of Israel. Israelis no doubt had been sincere in thinking of the June War as preemptive and defensive. Surrounded by Arab countries that refused to acknowledge her existence and deprived of contact with those neighbors, except for bellicose tirades from Radio Cairo or fedayeen raids from the Gaza Strip, Israel had much reason to feel defensive. But in fact Israel had proven her military superiority twice before and starting from far less favorable positions than the lines reached in 1967. Arab fears of Israeli expansion were grounded in the reality of three defeats; and the transfer to Israeli rule or renewed flight of one and a half million Palestinians could only deepen those fears. The results of the 1967 war were thus bound to sharpen the Arab hostility, and the Israeli sense of being beleaguered, that had originally precipitated the war.

Such perspective puts in question even the strategic value of the new lines from Golan to Suez. In 1967 Israel's planes or tanks could easily have reached Damascus, Amman, or Cairo; but her military and demographic resources remained unequal to any military occupation even of these nearest Arab capitals. Distance had been Russia's most strategic asset in the wars launched by Napoleon and Hitler, and Arabs could count on that asset against Israel many times over. No matter how many battles Israel's valiant forces might win, there would always be Arabs—all the more embittered by defeat—beyond the armistice lines. There could be no lasting military solution in Israel's favor, because 3 million Israelis would not be able to force their will on over 100 million Arabs. The true challenge to Israel was not to win wars but to win peace. And if future generations of Israelis were to live in peace, it was with Arabs that they would have to start making peace.

The balance of political gains and losses from the headlong militarization of the region looked no more favorable on the Arab side. Despite the massive influx of Soviet weapons and despite the tough talk by Nasser and others, the Arabs in 1967 had proved no match for the Israelis. And this time there was no explaining away the defeat. In 1956 the Soviet weapons had only just arrived; this time the Egyptians had had a decade for training. Then, Israel had joined Britain and France in invading Egypt; now, Israel had singlehandedly beaten Egypt, Syria, and Jordan. Then, the Israelis had been pressured to withdraw; now, they meant to stay.

Between the two wars, in 1961, Nasser had seen the United Arab Republic, his most visible achievement, dissolve at the very moment when formal union with Syria was to be followed by complete integration. And for five years prior to the war of 1967, Egypt's armed forces had been embroiled in what came to be known as Nasser's Vietnam—an inconclusive fight on the side of the republicans in the Yemen civil war. Far from being welcomed as liberators, they met fierce resistance from the royalists and their Saudi allies. Now, as a result of Israel's lightning strike, Egypt had lost her Russian-built air force, her Sinai province, and control of the Suez Canal that Nasser had so proudly nationalized in 1956. When Nasser in the spring of 1969 denounced the 1967 cease-fire to begin the so-called war of attrition, Israeli planes began to roam far over Egypt, and Nasser was soon reduced to asking for Soviet antiaircraft weapons—complete with Soviet personnel. When Gamal Abdul Nasser died in September 1970 at the age of fifty-two, his dream of Arab unity under Egyptian leadership and his pretensions as the spokesman for the Third World against Western imperialism lay hopelessly shattered.

The disaster of complete Israeli occupation of Palestine heightened the activism and the militancy of the Palestinian political movement. Whereas the defeated Arab states emphasized the demand of return of occupied territories, the PLO's avowed purpose now became the destruction of Israel itself—or, as the Palestine National Covenant of June 1968 put it, "to liquidate the Zionist presence in Palestine."

In the year between the 1967 war and that statement, Yassir Arafat, head of both Fatah and the PLO, had endeavored to organize a resistance movement in the Arab-inhabited Israeli-occupied territories—the earlier success of the Algerian guerrilla war serving as the major inspiration. But in Palestine, the guerrilla efforts, in view of the vigilance, ruthlessness, and flexibility of the Israeli authorities, ended in complete failure. The PLO's center of gravity therefore shifted first to Jordan and then to Lebanon. Soon there developed a steady pattern of guerrilla incursions into Israel or Israeli-held territory and of Israeli reprisals against PLO bases in the host countries. The more radical groups among the Palestinian exiles concentrated on spectacular acts of terrorism, such as the highjacking of two international airliners flown to Jordan in 1970 and an Israeli airliner flown to Entebbe, Uganda, in 1976; the murder of Israeli athletes at the Munich olympics in 1974; and the attack on civilians on the shore road south of Haifa in 1978, which claimed thirty-seven dead and eighty-two wounded.

Spectacular as were these acts in their daring and cruelty, they had no effect whatever in loosening Israel's grip on the occupied territories, let alone in weakening Israel's resolve. The militants, in pursuing their "Algerian" strategy, had become victims of their own false analogy. The French colons in Algeria, after years of civil war with nine-tenths of the population potentially against them, came to view their continued stay as an expensive luxury. The Israelis, whether original Zionists, survivors of the holocaust, refugees from Arab countries after 1956, or native born descendants, had no other place to go. They were defending their one and only home—indeed, their national existence.

The PLO guerrilla raids from Jordan or Lebanon provided the excuse for massive Israeli counterraids and, on balance, weakened the PLO and its host states far more than Israel. The terrorist acts far from the scene, such as at Munich or Entebbe, were an obvious admission of impotence on what was to have been the primary battleground in Israel-Palestine itself. The mixed effect of a decade of Palestinian militancy was thus a series of failures in battling Israel; a complete rout in a brief civil war and bid to take over Jordan in the "Black September" of 1970; the destruction of Lebanon as a political entity in the civil war of 1975–76; and a series of triumphs of diplomatic recognition. In 1974 the Arab League declared the PLO the "sole legitimate representative" of the

Palestinian people, and subsequently the United Nations gave the PLO observer status at the General Assembly.

WASHINGTON, MOSCOW, AND THE MIDEAST POWER VACUUM

The massive infusion of arms, it is clear, had brought matters no closer to a decision in favor of either Arabs or Israelis. The conflict had not been a "zero-sum game," where one side gains what the other loses, but a "negative-sum game," where each side stands to lose. If Arabs and Israelis had fought only with indigenous weapons or at a lower level of arms imports, their conflict might have ended as did many protracted quarrels in Latin America, say, the Andean War of 1879–84 or the Chaco conflict of 1928–35; after exhausting both sides, the conflict would have petered out in an accommodation roughly reflecting the resources and determination of each side. The massive supplies of MIGs, Mirages, Phantom jets, tanks, and rockets only protracted the conflict and raised the level of destructiveness, magnifying the total losses in the negative-sum game.

The steady inflow of arms, moreover, was likely to tempt Egypt, Israel, and even Syria to try to play the game with Moscow's or Washington's chips in addition to their own. They might want to take a major diplomatic or military risk in the hope that the allied superpower would have little choice but to redeem it. For the superpowers, there was the frustration that past weapons deliveries gave no control over present policies —as the Nixon administration found out in trying to get Golda Meir's government in Israel to agree to the peace plan formulated by Secretary of State Rogers in 1969 and 1970. But even the withholding of future deliveries may give no such control, if the client prefers to do without them or feels free to break the relationship—as the Soviets found out in dealing with Sadat in 1971 and 1972. At any time, moreover, both superpowers face the risk that a local Middle Eastern conflict, started without their approval or even knowledge, might escalate into a nuclear confrontation between both—as in the messages from Washington to Moscow in October 1973, which, in President Nixon's words, "left little to the imagination."

For Washington there was also the recurrent temptation to try to settle the Arab-Israeli conflict with Moscow's help, or in the context of a broader East-West agreement. This remained a theme of Washington's diplomacy from the time of Security Council Resolution 242 of November 1967 and the Rogers Plan of 1969, to the brief Geneva conference of 1973 and the Soviet-American joint memorandum on the Middle East of October 1977. Yet it remained a false hope: first, because of the difficulty each superpower was likely to have in imposing a solution on an unwilling client; second, because the other items on the Washington-Moscow agenda were more likely to delay rather than expedite a Middle East agreement; and third, and above all, because there was no evidence that the Soviets, after all their diplomatic gains from the Arab-Israeli conflict and after such strenuous efforts to unsettle the Middle East, had any interest in settling it.

Between the two superpowers, the balance sheet of their massive involvement in the Middle East from 1955 to 1970 seemed to favor the Soviets. The number of countries receiving their military or economic aid increased steadily. So did their naval bases and landing facilities along the coasts of the Southern Mediterranean (Algeria, Egypt, Syria), the Red Sea, and the Indian Ocean (Sudan, North and South Yemen, Somalia, and beyond).

But Moscow's hopes of seizing internal control in any of the larger Arab countries were repeatedly frustrated. In Iraq the local communists were in an inconclusive political struggle with General Abdel-Karim Kassem from 1959 to 1963, until both were ousted by a coup of the Baath party. In 1971 Aly Sabry, Moscow's candidate for Nasser's succession, lost to Anwar el-Sadat; and a communist coup in the Sudan, after initial success, was suppressed by the army. The prevailing forces in the major Arab countries inclined to a course of neutralism and independence and the playing off of one foreigner against another, as so often before. And as long as Turkey and Iran, as Western allies, were firmly wedged between the Soviet Union and the Arab countries, no temporary political victory could be consolidated by Soviet military occupation, as in Budapest in 1956, in Prague in 1968, or in Kabul in 1979. Hence the most durable foothold the Soviets gained in the Arab Middle East turned out to be in South Yemen—accessible by sea and in a superb strategic location—and small and backward enough to be dominated with a relatively modest political, economic, and military effort.

Still, as long as the Soviet aim in the region was to hasten the departure of British power while preventing the establishment of a new American hegemony, such setbacks as in Egypt and Iraq were not decisive. Throughout the 1960s and early 1970s, the Soviets remained the major arms suppliers of Arab countries against Israel; and even repeated defeats would make the Arabs only more dependent on Moscow. In sum, a protracted Arab-Israeli conflict resulting in a stalemate, or even recurrent Arab defeats, admirably suited the Soviet aim of destabilizing, as distinct from dominating, the region.

For the United States, which had no desire to dominate the region to begin with, this twilight situation was tolerable. The shift of nuclear strategy from bombers to intercontinental missiles now made obsolete Dulles's conception of 1953 of a Soviet-Chinese perimeter ringed with airfields for American B-52 bombers; and when there was pressure to withdraw them, Washington showed little hesitation in obliging. Thus Saudi Arabia in 1961 declined to renew the agreement for an American air base at Dhahran, and a newly installed radical regime in Libya insisted on the closing in 1970 of the Wheelus air base, which had been used mainly to train young NATO fliers in Libya's ever-blue skies.

The low military profile that the United States kept throughout the Middle East in the years of Britain's departure from the region (and of the Vietnam war) implied that Washington tended to place heavy political reliance on allies such as Turkey, Iran, and Israel. Such dependence, of course, had its own costs and risks. The close connection with Israel was bound to strain relations with most Arab countries. From the mid-1960s, the Cyprus conflict led to sharp tensions between Greece and Turkey, with the United States as often as not caught in the middle between its two allies. And the shah's close cooperation with the United States—it became evident later—contributed to undermining his domestic position and embittering subsequent Iranian attitudes to the United States.

Cyprus had been one of the last British crown colonies in the region, until a prolonged guerrilla war, supported by its Greek inhabitants, made the British position untenable. But instead of yielding to the desire of the Greek majority for *enosis* (union with Greece), the departing British in 1960 granted independence to the island under a complex constitution of checks, balances, and concurrent powers for the four-fifths majority of Greeks and the one-fifth minority of Turks. A treaty of guarantee signed by Britain, Greece, and Turkey gave each power the right to station some military contingents and, if necessary, to intervene to protect the delicate arrangement. When Turkey in 1964 prepared to intervene militarily on behalf of her oppressed co-nationals, a blunt letter from President Johnson persuaded Ankara to call off the invasion at the last moment. But the American warning was deeply resented, and a decade later (July-August 1974), in another flare-up of ethnic tension on the island, Turkey landed her forces and occupied the northern two-fifths of the island without consulting Washington. This time, Greece felt aggrieved enough to suspend active membership in NATO; and to bring pressure on Turkey, the U.S. Congress suspended American military shipments to Turkey. Turkey, instead of becoming more accommodating on Cyprus, responded by closing American (but not NATO) bases on her soil. In 1978-79 a new base agreement was negotiated, but Turkish-American relations were not soon likely to be as cordial as before 1964.

Dependence on allies seemed to work more smoothly elsewhere in the region. Thus the shah's Iran intermittently (1964-75) supported a Kurdish rebellion against the Soviet-armed regime in Iraq and, conversely, gave decisive help to the regime of the sultan of Oman against rebels supported by communist South Yemen (1973-76). In Jordan in the "Black September" crisis of 1970, Israeli mobilization deterred Soviet-armed Syria from full-scale intervention in the Jordanian conflict and thus became crucial to King Hussein's victory in his deadly fight with the PLO.

A well-informed observer of America's Middle Eastern policy in the 1960s and 1970s, William B. Quandt has suggested that the success of this indirect intervention in Jordan tended "to breed a sense of complacency." Further, he adds that ". . . Israel, Jordan, and Iran were emerging in official Washington's view as regional peacekeepers. Aid and arms to these United States partners would serve as a substitute for a costly American presence in the region or unpopular military intervention."

With the evacuation of Dhahran and Wheelus, the United States, far from replacing Britain, had begun to join in its withdrawal. However insignificant in the strategic balance with Russia, such military positions could serve secondary purposes in the vicinity: for example, the protection of oil interests, as indicated by the use of British naval and air units in 1951-53; or the protection of friendly regimes, as when British forces returned to Jordan in 1958 and to Kuwait in 1961. But this time the British were determined to complete their withdrawal from East of Suez by evacuating their small forces from the Persian Gulf by December 1971.

The alarm felt by the sheikh of Kuwait has already been described. The emir of Dubai (in what is now one of the United Arab Emirates) mused plaintively to the correspondent of the London *Times:* "Who asked them to leave?" Suggestions that the local rulers pay for the continued British presence, or that it be replaced by American units, fell on deaf ears.

Britain's eagerness to withdraw, America's reluctance to enter, and Russia's difficulties in countries such as Egypt and Iraq created in the Middle East a power vacuum in which forces of local nationalism, toward the end of the 1960s and the beginning of the 1970s, found themselves with unprecedented room for maneuver. But the aims that such nationalist forces could effectively pursue were limited. Any frontal attack against the few remaining Western military positions (for example, the NATO base on Cyprus or the British military advisers in Oman) might produce a strong reaction and undo the delicate balance. Any ambitious scheme of pan-Arab unification would be stalemated by local rivalries and tensions—as Nasser's experience had shown. One of the few spheres where nationalist interests could be asserted with impunity—and would tend to unify rather than divide the region—was that of petroleum. The Middle Eastern countries were now fully sovereign, and a country's sovereign right to control its economic resources was beyond legal challenge. In addition, the Western oil companies had reached, by the end of the 1960s, a point where they would be more vulnerable than ever to financial pressure from governments of the oil countries.

By the intersecting of two separate lines of development, the Middle East (and notably its oil regions in Libya and around the Persian Gulf) was becoming politically fully independent of the West at the very time when the leading Western countries, including the United States, were becoming economically dependent on oil from the Middle East.

QADDAFI: VERBOSE, MOROSE, AND SLEEPWALKING

In September 1969, an army officers' conspiracy deposed the aging King Idris of Libya. Its leader, Colonel Muammar Qaddafi was, at twenty-six, by far the youngest head of any military junta to have seized power in the Middle East—Iraq's Kassem had been forty-four in 1958, Egypt's Nasser thirty-four in 1952, and Enver Pasha, the Young Turkish leader had been thirty-two when he began the series of twentieth-century Middle Eastern coups in 1913.

By ideological orientation Qaddafi was a pan-Arab and an austere Muslim fundamentalist. In temperament he was diffident, brooding, and by turns morose and verbose. His style of political leadership came to alternate between rambling monologues—delivered at rallies, on television, or to individual listeners for hours at a time—and periods of solitary meditation for days and nights in a tent in the desert. Qaddafi's hero was Gamal Abdul Nasser, and his consuming ambition after Nasser's death became to assume the mantle of his leadership as unifier of the Arab-Muslim nation and champion of the Third World against its erstwhile oppressors. Qaddafi's bad luck was to have been born in Libya, one of the smallest Arab countries in population and one of the least economically developed. His good luck was that, in the years of his rapid rise through the military ranks, Libya had become one of the world's major oil exporters.

An Italian colony before the Second World War, Libya had briefly become a U.N. Trusteeship and had then been declared independent under King Idris el-Senussi, whose family had begun as hereditary sheikhs of a Muslim monastic order in a desert oasis and had then led the resistance against Italian colonization after 1911. Britain had been the trustee power until 1951, and British influence continued strong throughout the monarchic period. It was on the expert and disinterested advice of British consultants that Libya invited a score of Western oil companies by competitive bid to develop its oil resources.

Once in power, Qaddafi's first objective was to secure the departure of the hated imperialists. The British agreed to evacuate their bases by March 1970; the Americans left Wheelus Field in June of that year. The French government, which had recently broken with Israel and now had high hopes of reestablishing some influence in the Muslim Middle East by supporting various radical movements, offered to have French technicians run the bases and to sell Libya a squadron of Mirage jets.

Qaddafi's next targets were the foreign oil companies, yet his aims were more limited than Mossadegh's had been two decades earlier in Iran. Few Libyans were well enough educated to attempt to run the country's oil industry, and its small population and lack of arable land offered few opportunities for large-scale economic development. Even the comparatively modest oil revenues of the 1960s had resulted in mounting financial surpluses. By 1970, Libya's foreign exchange reserves exceeded those of Brazil, or India, or all of Tropical Africa and would have been sufficient to finance as much as three years' worth of Libyan imports. Qaddafi's true aim was neither Libyan control of oil nor ambitious economic development, but the simple assertion of power. Throughout the young colonel's life, Western unbelievers had dominated his country and its God-given resources. Here was a rare chance to redress the balance. In deposing the ailing king, in securing the closing of foreign bases, and in dealing with the multinational oil companies, Qaddafi proved as sure-footed as a sleepwalker.

The timing could not have been more favorable. When Qaddafi seized power, world oil transport was slowly recovering from the closing since 1967 of the Suez Canal: the large supertankers that would make the Canal dispensable were still being built and only a few of them were beginning to ply the circuitous route around Africa. Most of Iraq's and one-fifth of Saudi Arabia's oil was flowing to the Mediterranean by pipeline and thence by short tanker trip to Europe. But the TAP-line from the Saudi fields had been damaged in Syria in May 1970, and the Damascus government, in a dispute over transit fees, refused to allow repairs for several months. The inevitable result was that world tanker rates soared to all time highs—rising by as much as 66 percent from January to December 1970. Oil from Libya and Algeria, with the shortest tanker runs to Europe, was at a premium.

Fully conscious of the extraordinary bargaining opportunity, Qaddafi in June 1970 put pressure on the oil companies one by one, starting with the "independents," such as Occidental, which had no alternative sources of petroleum production. The pretext was the need for conservation of underground petroleum so as to achieve optimum geological management of the company's field. The demand was an increase from 50 to 55 percent in the tax rate, and an increase of $0.30 in the "posted price," by which tax and royalty were calculated. The implicit threat was to close down the Libyan operations of any company that refused to comply.

The companies anxiously conferred but failed to come up with a common plan. The "independents" appealed for support from the "majors," or Seven Sisters, whose world-wide operations gave them the best chance to ride out the storm. But the majors bore a deep grudge against the independents and other interlopers. After all, it had been companies such as ENI and Occidental that had perversely insisted on paying more to the governments and charging less to the customers; time and again they had stepped up their Libyan production and foisted on the seven major companies the price war of the 1960s. When Armand Hammer of Occidental offered to hold out against Qaddafi's threat of shutdown as long as Exxon would sell him the missing oil at cost, Exxon, with stiff politeness, offered to sell any amount of oil at standard third-party prices.

And the difference between production cost and third-party prices was, of course, precisely the profit margin on which Occidental or any other company would depend for their continued existence. Rather than risk becoming an Exxon subsidiary, Hammer preferred to give in to Qaddafi's demand.

Quickly the same pressure was on all the other companies operating in Libya, majors and minors alike. The crucial questions, during the next several months, would be, first, whether the companies could resist the Libyan attack by increasing their production in other locations, such as the Persian Gulf, Venezuela, or Nigeria, and, second, whether perhaps Washington would be willing to bring political pressure to bear.

The answer was no and no. Washington was preoccupied with Vietnam, the Jordan crisis, and Russian submarines in Cuba. Rather than getting directly involved in the Middle East, the Nixon administration just then had preferred to let Israel take the lead in warding off the Syrian threat to Jordan. The United States itself, under the import quotas, was supplying no more than 2 percent of its oil from Middle Eastern countries. What seemed to be at stake, therefore, was nothing more than the commercial interests of American and other companies. Had there been discrimination against American companies, Washington would gladly have taken up the challenge; but where a foreign government changed the terms on which any foreign companies did business, Washington's instincts invariably were in favor of accommodation. This, at any rate, was the lesson of the State Department's earlier role in encouraging the fifty-fifty oil agreements with their tax credit provisions. At the very time of the Qaddafi round of negotiations with the oil companies, moreover, the State Department's petroleum expert, James E. Akins, had given a speech in the neighboring OPEC capital of Algiers, complaining that the price of oil was too low. Clearly it would have been unrealistic for the companies to expect any help from that quarter.

The other OPEC members, far from undercutting Qaddafi, scented their opportunity to do as well or better. Persian Gulf countries, such as Iran and Kuwait, joined in the demands for higher prices and for the 55 percent tax. OPEC as a whole, at a meeting of ministers in Caracas in December, declared 55 percent to be the minimum tax in all member countries. Venezuela at once raised its own tax rate to 60 percent, made the increase retroactive to January 1970, and henceforth claimed the right to set tax-reference prices unilaterally—in line with OPEC's program of 1968. Nigeria, where production had started in the mid-1960s, and which, like any new seller, had offered some initial rebates, joined

OPEC in the midst of the ensuing negotiations and insisted on the same premiums as exacted by Libya. The oil-producing countries, in sum, were breaking ranks only to see how fast they could overtake one another in forcing concessions from the companies.

The most dramatic negotiations took place two months later in Tehran, where twenty-three companies were confronting the oil governments of the Persian Gulf and where over two-thirds of OPEC's production was at stake. The companies, wary of Qaddafi's earlier tactic of picking them off one by one, had insisted on negotiating as a single group, but so had the governments. When conversations deadlocked, OPEC's ministers reconvened to threaten a total embargo against any oil company that would fail to accept the 55 percent tax rate. After one final consultation with the State Department, the companies accepted the 55 percent rate, an immediate increase in posted prices of $0.27 a barrel, and successive further increases spread out over the next four years. As a result, for the Gulf countries, the average government revenue per barrel of crude oil rose from $0.87 in 1970 to $1.25 in 1971. Even without further price rises or increases in production, the Tehran agreement was designed to raise their annual income from about $4 billion to $6 billion at once, and to $7.5 billion by 1975.

The financial terms negotiated at Tehran were comparable to those extracted by Libya the previous autumn. But Qaddafi was not content to remain first among equals. Relying on the low sulfur content of Libya's crude and its proximity to major European markets, he insisted on a premium of nearly $1 above the posted prices set at Tehran. Similar markups were obtained by Saudi Arabia and Iraq for the oil sold via their Mediterranean pipelines, and by Algeria and Nigeria.

Optimistic observers proclaimed that there had been tough negotiations and generous accommodation and the accords signed at Tehran and Tripoli would bring stability to the oil industry for the next five years. In actual fact, the "agreements" of February and April 1971 were the beginning of a landslide—and were superseded many times over in the five years they were supposed to run. Ten days after the Tehran agreement, Algeria nationalized 51 percent of its French oil concessions. In July, Saudi Arabia joined with other Arab producers of the Gulf region in a campaign for government "participation" in the oil concessions—nationalization on the installment plan. That same month, Venezuela—always proud to be OPEC's founder and chief innovator—passed legislation requiring foreign oil companies to surrender "unexploited concession areas" by 1974 and "all their residual assets" by 1983.

138

In September 1971, OPEC's ministers insisted on a revision of the agreements signed just a few months before so as to take account of the declining value of the dollar; the companies agreed to raise Persian Gulf "posted prices" by 8.5 percent in January 1972 and by another 5.7 percent in April 1973. In March and June 1972, OPEC backed Iraq in its protracted dispute with IPC—the oldest surviving concessionaire company—with a warning that no company whose interests might be nationalized in that country would be allowed to increase its production in any other OPEC country. Meanwhile, Qaddafi had nationalized 50 percent of British Petroleum's Libyan concession in December 1971 and 50 percent of ENI's in September 1972—the pretext for the first measure being alleged "collusion" by the British, as they evacuated their forces from the Persian (as Qaddafi would insist, "Arab") Gulf, in allowing Iran to occupy three uninhabited islands in the strategic Strait of Hormuz. 1971 and 1972 turned out to be busy and rewarding years for OPEC.

OPEC's "Best of Practices": Competition for Monopoly

Qaddafi's Libya holds the all-time record among Arab governments for abortive plots and unconsummated merger schemes. And Qaddafi's indignation at the British over the three islands is a good reminder that, even in oil economics, not every scheme hatched in the youthful colonel's fevered brain was likely to succeed. His major measure of retaliation against perfidious Albion was to have been the sudden transfer of Libya's huge foreign exchange reserves from Britain to Switzerland. The effect was that the Swiss bankers, responding to an acute shortage of funds in London and an equally acute surplus in Zurich, retransferred the money almost at once—collecting not only their own usual service charge (negative interest) from Libya but also the normal interest payable in London. The net loss was Libya's, the net gain that of the Swiss, with the British totally unhurt.

But in launching his attack on the oil companies' interests in the Middle East, Qaddafi happened to stumble upon an economic configuration of truly revolutionary potential—a potential that only someone with his thirst for power and deep resentment of the West, his ruthlessness and daring, indeed his ascetic's contempt for money and what money buys, would be likely to exploit to the hilt.

The seller of petroleum or any other commodity can increase his revenue by raising either his price or the quantity of his sales. And this means that a host government can increase its oil revenues in one of three ways: by an increase in price, by an expansion of sales, or by a larger share of net revenues going to the government instead of to the companies. The overriding concern of the governments, since the days of Mossadegh and before, had been with this last point—the share of the price that companies must pass on to them in the form of royalty or tax; from 1950 to 1970, the countries had succeeded in reversing the ratio by which the proceeds had been divided between companies and governments. But the governments had been just as anxious to increase amounts of production. Iraq's major complaint since the 1930s had been that the company consortium deliberately failed to open up promising new oil fields, and the shah's major worry after 1954 had been that the oil industry might not resume Iranian production fast enough to assure his government a steady income. Libya under King Idris had been just as obsessed with the danger of deliberate underproduction and, for that very reason, had dealt with many different companies and spurred them on to greeater competition. Only in this way had Libya in less than a decade risen to the front rank of exporters.

Changes in volume, such as the Middle Eastern governments were trying to bring about, are related to price by the basic economic law of supply and demand. A falling price tends to increase, a rising price to reduce, the demand for a product, and hence the volume of sales. The seller's revenue may rise either way provided that sales increase faster than the price decreases—or fall off more slowly than the price rises. OPEC's pressures for greater revenues had forced the companies to cut prices, but sales had expanded rapidly. All in all, OPEC's pressure for more production and a higher share of revenues had paid off handsomely indeed: it had tripled OPEC's revenues in a decade.

For a while OPEC had flirted with the opposite tactic—imposing production cuts so as to force up the price; but this had led nowhere. Qaddafi's tactic amounted to a vast improvement on that earlier scheme; it also tended to curtail supplies, but by individual improvisation rather than common agreement. Where Idris's ministers had bargained with twenty companies so as to *increase* production, Qaddafi exploited the same bargaining situation to threaten them with selective shutdowns— with *decreases* in the flow of oil.

But Qaddafi's tactic went beyond reversing Libya's own policy; it set

140

off a reverse spiral among the leading OPEC members. Where once Iran, Saudi Arabia, Libya, Nigeria, and others had pressured companies to increase their production, they now vied with each other in limiting it —whether through higher taxes, raised prices, cancelled concessions, or alleged measures of conservation. And this new strategy paid off more handsomely yet: where OPEC's revenues had tripled in a decade between 1950 and 1960 and once again between 1960 and 1970, they quadrupled in only three years, between 1970 and 1973. (In 1973/74, of course, they were to quadruple once more in a single year.)

Where agreed production limits would have set OPEC member against member, the series of individual initiatives first launched by Qaddafi—combined with OPEC's "best of current practices" rule of 1968—resulted in a game at which anyone could play, with no risk to himself and for the benefit of all. If one particular gambit should fail, the government that had tried it could simply abandon it and be no worse off than before. If it succeeded, all the other governments in OPEC would imitate it and thus join in the advance. The "best" practice, in OPEC's view, of course, was that which yielded more control and, above all, more cash.

OPEC in this crucial period derived much strength from sticking singlemindedly to its original design—a limited-purpose alliance among sovereign governments bent on maximizing the monetary returns from the exploitation of their petroleum resources. This turned out to be a potent common denominator to simplify any set of complex fractions. There were deeply engrained differences in political attitude, at times even bitter political quarrels, between such countries as democratic Venezuela, traditionalist Saudi Arabia, radical Iraq, Islamic-fundamentalist Libya, and the shah's repressive dictatorship in Iran. No matter: a common desire for more revenue from oil was the one aim in which they could all readily concur. In the mid-1970s a writer for *Fortune,* after a visit to OPEC headquarters in Vienna and several member capitals, exclaimed with evident surprise: "practically the only action they ever fully agree on is raising the price of crude oil." OPEC, that is to say, was nothing more and nothing less than a successful cartel.

But let us remember that the desire for more money is a very common phenomenon: among the thirteen oil-producing countries included in OPEC; among other Third World countries producing oil, such as Mexico, Malaysia, and Trinidad; among oil producing Western democracies, such as Canada, Norway, and Great Britain. All of these countries have followed OPEC's price lead since the early 1970s. The same desire, of course, animates the international oil companies that lost the battles at Tripoli and Tehran but soon found their own lucrative adjustment to the OPEC revolution. Indeed, the predilection for monetary gain is so widespread that textbooks on economics since Adam Smith have taken it to be the impelling motive of economic man.

No organization in history has been as spectacularly successful in satisfying this universal craving for monetary gain as has OPEC. And perhaps the secret has been that OPEC's pattern—of individual initiatives emulated by other members appealed to another deep-seated instinct in economic man. OPEC's tactic left the fullest play for individual temperament; it left room for exploitation of the most diverse circumstances; it allowed for the testing of divergent hypotheses. In sum, OPEC managed to put competition itself in the service of monopoly!

Examples of this versatility, in the crucial years from 1970 to 1973, abound. A closed canal, a pipeline in disrepair, allegations of bribery, a slide in the value of the dollar, an Arab-Israeli war—these and many others could become so many occasions for OPEC members to flex their muscles. Libya might take advantage of its proximity to Europe and the low sulfur content of its oil; the Persian Gulf countries could rely on their huge production potential; Venezuela could bank on its ready access to the American market and safe distance from Middle Eastern wars. Libya might raise the tax rate, others the posted price, and Venezuela insist on raising both. Venezuela, Iraq, and Libya might threaten nationalization; the Saudis, protesting loudly their devotion to private enterprise, might opt for "participation" instead. Qaddafi might indulge his penchant for fire-breathing harangues to inspire fear in the companies; the shah might insist on being rewarded for his reasonableness and long record of friendship with the West; and Sheikh Yamani might beguile the companies with his subtle understanding of their problems. But the refrain was always that the companies—and if necessary their customers—must pay more, more, and yet more.

And the customers in importing countries did begin to pay; indeed, the companies had little choice but to pass along the OPEC increases of the early 1970s. Their profit margin had dropped to about $0.24 a barrel in 1970, and the increases in government revenue agreed to at Tehran amounted to $0.27 a barrel. The discounts off the "posted price" that had been applied throughout the 1960s were quickly phased out: Adelman calculates that the price at the Persian Gulf rose from $1.27 in 1969 to

$2.01 at the end of 1970. In 1971 the posted price rose to $2.18, in 1972 to $2.48, and in June 1973 to $2.90—a 128 percent increase in three and one-half years.

The open question, both for OPEC countries and for the oil companies, was the effect that such price increases would have on sales. If sales fluctuate sharply in response to price changes, the demand for the product in question is said to be "elastic"; if the fluctuations are slight, the demand is said to be "inelastic." Whenever the change in demand will exactly offset a given change in price (for example, a 10 percent price increase drives away 10 percent of the customers), the price elasticity of demand is said to be equal to 1. This level of "unit elasticity" is, of course, a monopolist's preferred price: it shows him that "he's gone about as far as he can go."

Experience of the previous decade had indicated that the demand for petroleum was relatively elastic: a cut of the price by one-third had tripled the volume of sales in the global market of petroleum exports. It might thus have seemed reasonable that a sharp price increase would have the opposite effect of reducing sales—the only question being How much?

If such were the expectations, then the reaction of the world oil market to the price changes of the early 1970s was quite abnormal: regardless of price increases, world oil consumption, and with it the amounts traded between countries, rose year by year. Thus total world oil imports rose 10 percent in 1971, 7 percent in 1972, and 13 percent in 1973. The reasons were not far to seek. After the wholesale conversion from coal to oil in Europe and Japan in the 1950s and 1960s, even a relatively sharp increase in oil prices would not be enough to justify the long-term capital expenditures of reopening obsolete coal mines or converting boilers and engines. The demand for oil had become quite inelastic in its response to price at least in the short run; indeed, the major variation in levels of oil consumption through most of the 1970s turned out to be in response not to price but to the general business cycle of prosperity and recession.

But there was an additional reason for the steady upsurge in demand for oil on the world market and particularly in the Middle East: the gradual phasing out, and by the spring of 1973 the lifting, of the American oil import quota program. United States imports rose by 8 percent in 1970, 15 percent in 1971, 21 percent in 1972, and 32 percent in 1973, doubling almost exactly in the four years from 1969 to 1973—to the point where, early in 1973, the United States overtook Japan as the world's single largest oil importer.

Most of the additional imports to the United States and other industrial countries came from the member countries of OPEC, which collectively maintained—and even increased—their share of 82 percent to 86 percent of world oil exports. The surge in demand, however, was affecting individual OPEC countries somewhat differently. Thus, Venezuela, which had intensively produced oil for more than half a century, was beginning to feel the strain on some of its older fields. Rather than engage in an expensive program of drilling to explore and develop new fields, the Caracas government preferred to husband its production. If this tended to raise prices, or help Venezuela earn more money from less oil, or increase the value of each barrel kept underground for the future, then so much the better. In Libya, where competing companies had rapidly expanded production in the 1960s, there were similar signs of strained fields, and Qaddafi's aggressive policy of bullying the companies and keeping the Libyan price above the OPEC level also tended to reduce output. From 1970 to September 1973, Venezuelan output fell by 9 percent and Libya's by as much as 31 percent. This left countries such as Nigeria, Indonesia, and above all the producers on the Persian Gulf to furnish the bulk of the additional supplies. The greatest expansion occurred in Iran, where production from 1970 to September 1973 increased by 52 percent, and Saudi Arabia, where the increase was as much as 129 percent.

Saudi Arabia's youthful oil minister Ahmad Zaki Yamani had been the chief author of OPEC's bold program of 1968, which claimed for member governments the right fully to manage their hydrocarbon resources, and the departure of Western military units from the Persian Gulf had removed any direct threat of outside political interference with such claims to self-management. In charting their own oil policy in these crucial years, the Saudis probably paid little attention to broad circumstances of price inelasticity of the demand for oil or to the marginal productivity of fields in other OPEC countries. The fact of immediate and overwhelming relevance to them was that, in three and one half years, their revenues per barrel had nearly doubled (from $0.99 in 1970 to $1.80 in September 1973) and their sales abroad had more than doubled as well. There could be no clearer indication that Saudi Arabia was not charging for its oil what the traffic would bear. Just as Libya, with its bulging foreign exchange reserves, had become the leader in OPEC's push of 1970–71, it was now Saudi Arabia's turn with its expanding and lucrative production.

5

THE YOM KIPPUR WAR
AND THE OIL EMBARGO

THE DRAMA OF OCTOBER 1973

The climax of the high drama of oil and Middle East politics opens in the autumn of 1973. On the morning of October 6—the Day of Atonement, or Yom Kippur, for observant Jews—Egyptian forces attack across the Suez Canal and Syrian forces across the crest of the Golan Heights. The Israelis, clearly caught by surprise, throw their available forces against the Syrian front, only ten to fifteen miles from the thickly settled Hula plain in Israel. In a few days, with their mobilization complete, they turn about to push the rapidly advancing Egyptians back across the Sinai desert. Losses, particularly in disabled tanks and other matériel, are enormous on all sides. Responding to urgent Egyptian and Israeli appeals, the Soviet Union and the United States each carry out large-scale air and sea lifts of new war equipment, the U.S. arms being delivered directly to the Sinai front at the Israeli-occupied town of el-Arish. The Israelis once again reach the Suez Canal, and some units cross to its west side. President Sadat, declaring that he is not ready to fight the United States, agrees to a cease-fire, which is set for October 22. Some hours after the armistice, the Israelis resume their encirclement of the Egyptian third army at Suez. The cease-fire is restored on October 24, and by November 14, Egyptian and Israeli commanders, meeting in the no-man's land, formalize the arrangement that returns everyone's forces to the October 22 positions. From the time the Israeli forces have regained the east bank of the canal, they are clearly under heavy American pressure to halt their advance. In announcing the Israeli government's acceptance of the cease-fire to his fellow citizens, Defense Minister Dayan explains, "I'm not sure the soldiers know it, but the shells they are firing today were not in their possession a week ago." By January 18, 1974, Henry Kissinger, shuttling between Egypt and Israel, brings about a first disengagement agreement, under which Israel withdraws its troops about a dozen miles from the canal.

On the third day of the Yom Kippur War, OPEC's ministerial committee, representing the Arab producers of the Gulf region and Iran, at a previously scheduled meeting with oil company representatives in Vienna, demands a price increase from $3.01 to $5.12 a barrel; the companies refuse. As the meeting adjourns, Sheikh Yamani informs the industry representatives airily that they will hear the next development on the news wires. On October 16, the oil ministers reconvene at Kuwait and announce the 70 percent price increase to $5.12 unilaterally. The next day, the five Arab ministers meet separately to announce a set of production cuts, which, on November 5, are specified as 25 percent immediately and 5 percent for every month until Israel evacuates the territories occupied since 1967.

Almost from the beginning of the war, Arab countries one by one announce a halt in oil shipments to the United States: Iraq does so on October 7, Libya follows on October 19, Saudi Arabia announces its decision on October 20, and the smaller Arab principalities of the Gulf —Kuwait, Qatar, Dubai, and Bahrain—follow suit on October 21. The embargo is subsequently extended to the Netherlands, Portugal, Rhodesia, and South Africa. There is major confusion on the global oil market. Many West European countries ban Sunday driving, and in the United States, particularly in East Coast cities, motorists are caught in lengthening gasoline queues. Meanwhile, on December 25, following the first cease-fire at the canal and a ceremonial meeting of a Geneva peace conference, the Arab ministers announce the reversal of the production cuts. The embargo is officially lifted on March 18, 1974.

In December 1973 Iran holds an auction, where oil sells for as much as $17.00 a barrel. On December 22 the ministers of the Persian Gulf oil countries—the Arab oil producers minus Algeria and Libya plus Iran— meet at Tehran and, on the shah's proposal, raise the posted price to $11.65, which implies a jump in government revenues from $3.00 to $7.00 a barrel. Finally, in June 1974 Saudi Arabia announces an increase in its rate of "participation," or part ownership, of the Aramco oil concession from 25 percent to 60 percent retroactive to January 1, 1974; this implies a further increase in government revenues to $9.27.

On each occasion, the raised revenue rates decreed—by the Gulf ministers in October 1973, at the shah's meeting in December, and by Saudi Arabia's "participation" in June 1974—are matched by OPEC and non-OPEC oil exporters throughout the world. Whereas the revenue increases of 1970 and 1971 still were achieved through negotiation and pressure on the companies, the OPEC revolution of 1973/74 is imposed by unilateral decree. OPEC's aggregate oil revenues, which had been $14 billion in 1972, soar to $23 billion for 1973 and to as much as $96 billion in 1974.

Numerous aspects of the Yom Kippur War remain intensely controversial after all these years. Why was Israel caught so completely off its guard? Understandably, this has given rise to much political recrimination among Israeli politicians. What was the precise content of the messages exchanged between Washington and Moscow in late October that, in Nixon's words, "left little to the imagination"? Was there a Soviet threat to land troops to drive the Israelis back from Egypt? Was there an American nuclear threat? Was either side bluffing? Who was responsible for the magnitude of the American airlift to the Israeli front? Nixon and Kissinger both have claimed credit and implied that the other was reluctant; both seem to agree that the decision was a welcome relief from Watergate troubles. What was the relation of strengths between Israeli and Egyptian forces west of the canal after October 22? Each side has boasted that it could handily have beaten the other—the Israelis by encircling the Egyptian third army, the Egyptians by cutting off the Israelis at the canal—if only the cease-fire had not been proclaimed or reimposed.

Happily, such details can be left to future military and diplomatic historians. For our own analysis, a number of broader questions are crucial: What motives prompted Sadat to launch the October War, and other Arab governments to apply the "oil weapon"? And what was the impact, actual and perceived, of the oil embargo on the United States?

SADAT MAKES WAR TO PREPARE FOR PEACE

In retrospect, President Anwar el-Sadat's policy, leading to his break with Moscow, the October War of 1973, his dramatic visit to

Jerusalem, the peace treaty with Israel, and his close cooperation with the United States, seems remarkably consistent. Yet there were many twists, turns, and apparent contradictions along the way; even his own conception of that policy crystallized only gradually.

Almost from the time of his accession to the presidency in September 1970, Sadat was determined to move Egypt toward peace and away from its abject dependence on Moscow. The two moves, of course, were closely related: Nasser's inordinate foreign policy ambition and lack of realistic appraisal of Egypt's power potential had precipitated two military defeats at the hands of Israel in 1956 and 1967 and a third in the "war of attrition" of 1969–70. Each defeat, in turn, had made Egypt more dependent on Soviet weapons and, by 1970, even on Soviet military personnel.

In a major public speech on February 4, 1971, Sadat declared himself eager to end the state of belligerency with Israel in return for evacuation of the occupied territories. Ultimately he envisaged formal peace; in the meantime he proposed arrangements for reopening the Suez Canal—a plan that years later became the basis for the second disengagement agreement negotiated by Kissinger in 1975. Within a few days after Sadat's speech, Ambassador Gunnar Jarring, who had been acting as the United Nations mediator, probed the readiness of Egypt and Israel to proceed to serious negotiations on the basis of Security Council Resolution 242. The answer from Cairo was a qualified yes; from Mrs. Golda Meir's government in Israel, a brusque no.

There were many reasons why Sadat's initiative of 1971 fell on deaf ears in Jerusalem. Resolution 242, which envisaged peace in return for occupied territories, was bound to be more attractive to the Arabs as the losers of the 1967 war than to the Israelis as the winners. Israel at the time countered with a proposal of withdrawal of *both* sets of forces from the Suez Canal—an echo of the 1956 Anglo-French ultimatum that was, of course, totally unacceptable to Egypt.

Nor was it clear, in February 1971, why *any* proposal from Sadat should be taken seriously. He had gained the presidency only four months earlier because he happened to hold the vice-presidency at the time of Nasser's death. His record under Nasser had been that of a colorless yes man, and his earlier political career had been marked by impulsiveness and ineptitude.

In sixteen years of dealing with Nasser, moreover, the world had grown used to a wide gap between Egyptian rhetoric and Egyptian performance. Only gradually did it become clear that Sadat meant what he said and was ready to reverse Nasser's entire political style and ideology as well as his foreign policy: instead of high-strung pan-Arab ambitions, a sober Egyptian nationalism; instead of a socialist police state, a return to private enterprise and some measure of political freedom. But back in February 1971 there was as yet no indication to reassure the skeptic of Sadat's willingness or ability to reverse Nasser's aggressive and unrealistic policies. And Israel's experience with its Arab neighbors had taught her to be skeptical.

The deliberate ambiguity of Sadat's tactics was bound to reinforce the existing doubts. With his peace overture rejected, his alternative was to launch a war that would either regain the canal and the Sinai by force, or at least dissipate the myth of Israeli invincibility and thus create a more genuine basis for negotiation. And for this he needed Russian arms —and a more warlike rhetorical stance.

Moscow repeatedly rebuffed Sadat's appeals for massive new weapons for such a war and thus made a mockery of Sadat's boast that 1971 would be his "year of decision." Moscow's rejection should, perhaps, have come as no surprise. Sadat, after all, had defeated the Soviets' chosen candidate for Nasser's succession, and in his conversations in Moscow he left no doubt that he meant to be in full control of any weapons furnished. Friction increased steadily, with Sadat becoming more insistent in his demands for weapons and Moscow evidently hoping that internal pressures would lead to his overturn. Thus began the rift that culminated in July 1972 in Sadat's ouster of fifteen thousand Soviet technicians and his insistence that the Soviets take back to Russia any weapons, such as advanced antiaircraft missiles, that they would not turn over to the Egyptians.

The break with Moscow implied a decision to undertake the war with the Soviet equipment in hand—on the basis of purely Egyptian training and planning. Although the details of the war plan, of course, remained secret, there was no attempt to disguise the basic intention. Quite the contrary, the earlier talk of 1971 as the "year of decision," a series of press interviews in the spring of 1973, and two practice mobilizations of Egyptian military forces in May and August 1973 constituted a pattern of perfect deception that ensured the surprise of the October 6 attack.

The first of the false alarms was preceded by a media campaign during which Sadat, in an interview with Arnaud de Borchgrave of *Newsweek*, quite candidly stated his paradoxical theme: a war to hasten a settlement of the long-smouldering conflict with Israel. A "resumption of the battle" was "undesirable." Yet diplomacy must "continue before, during and after the battle," and the result would be "a rosy future in the area for all parties if we have peace based on justice. . . ."

In fact there was little diplomatic activity before October 1973, yet the activity during and after the war indeed was intense. The United States, and Secretary of State Kissinger personally, came to play a central role in that diplomacy. Three and a half years earlier—almost exactly a year before Sadat's initiative of 1971—Kissinger himself had shrewdly predicted "that the Arabs will come to realize that it is the U.S. and not the USSR that holds the key to what they want." And, on another occasion, he expressed the hope that "At some point it will become apparent that time is not working for the Soviets. If they cannot get Arab territory back, the Arabs may well come to us." For nearly two decades, the Arabs had received from the Soviets the weapons with which they had gone down to defeat and territorial losses. From the United States, through its influence in Israel, they might get the necessary diplomatic support to regain those lost lands. Moscow could help the Arabs make war; only Washington could help them make peace.

For half a century and more, the impotence of Middle Eastern states in the face of Western imperialism had given rise to a recurrent desire to play off the distant foreigner against the nearby foreigner: the British against the Turks in 1915, the Germans against the British in 1941, the Russians against the British and Americans in the 1950s. Nasser's alliance with Moscow had been the biggest and most desperate gamble in this series of attempts to manipulate the powers by remote control. The danger, as always, was that the distant foreigner would come too close and the gambler would not gain independence but trade mere dependence for an even worse state of subjection.

Nasser manifested a second tendency common to leaders of weak states, in the Middle East and elsewhere, that might be called the politics of compensatory fantasy. Thus Italy's Mussolini, smarting at his country's alleged mistreatment after the First World War, indulged in visions of a new Roman empire but proved unable to overcome even the valiant Greek forces in 1940. Thus the Young Turks of the declining Ottoman empire, having lost Libya in 1911 and their Balkan provinces in 1913, cherished political dreams of Panturkism and Panislam. Enver Pasha, having led the empire to defeat and enemy occupation of its capital in 1918, lost his life in a quixotic quest for one of those dreams in Central Asia. And thus Nasser, still struggling to induce the British to evacuate

Suez and unable to defeat Israel, dreamt of Egypt's leadership in the Arab nation, the world of Islam, and the Afro-Asian world.

It is realism and self-limitation, not grandiose fantasy, that are the mark of the true statesman. The defeated Ottoman Turks were fortunate in finding, in Kemal Atatürk, a political leader who was willing to abandon the Young Turks' delusions and to help them defend and rebuild their homeland in the smaller Turkish Republic. And Egypt was equally fortunate to find in Anwar el-Sadat a leader who could persuade his fellow citizens to renounce Nasser's fantasies of Panarabism and Third World leadership—as well as the grim reality of subjection to Russia—for the more modest and realistic aim of peace with Israel and national independence. Alone among recent Arab leaders, Sadat showed the statesmanship of measuring his ends to the available means; alone he mustered the courage to end the negative-sum game into which war with Israel and arms from Russia had plunged his country. It is perhaps not surprising that Sadat's strategy took some years to crystallize in his own mind and some more years to be recognized by others and to come to fruition. As Kissinger observed in looking back on his first direct diplomatic exchanges with Sadat in 1972, "It was all, as I would come to realize, vintage Sadat. His negotiating tactic was never to haggle over detail but to create an atmosphere that made disagreement psychologically difficult. He . . . laid stress on a philosophical understanding, recognizing that . . . agreements between sovereign states cannot be enforced. . . . I cannot say that I fully understood Sadat's insight then. Great men are so rare that they take some getting used to."

The full implications of Sadat's strategy, from his peace initiative of 1971 to the treaty with Israel of 1979, took eight years to unfold. The attack launched on Israel in 1973, together with the supply and then interruption of American weapons to Israel, created a military standoff that cleared the ground for diplomacy—a situation in which the leading Arab country, as Kissinger had predicted, was ready to "come to us." This standoff, in turn, made possible Kissinger's shuttle diplomacy of 1973–75, the disengagement agreements between Israel and Egypt (and then Syria), Sadat's Jerusalem visit of 1977, the Camp David accords of 1978, and the de facto American-Egyptian alliance since 1979. The shift from Nasser's hankering for war to Sadat's desire for peace, and the consequent reversal of alliances, was as momentous a Middle Eastern gain for the United States as had been Nasser's original arms deal of 1955 for the Soviet Union.

Most Americans have been far slower than Henry Kissinger to appreciate these ultimate implications of Sadat's new course. And the greatest obstacle to such appreciation, no doubt, was the far more immediate impact, psychological and political, of the Arab oil embargo.

YAMANI CAUTIOUSLY UNSHEATHES THE "OIL WEAPON"

As petroleum began to fuel the ships, planes, and tanks of war, the world's military planners became concerned about the security of its supply. The British admiralty prompted the treasury to buy into the Iranian oil concession in 1913. A generation later, the Japanese conquered the oil fields of Sumatra, Hitler conquered those of Romania and the Caucasus, and German scientists developed synthetic gasoline. And, for almost as long, diplomats have sought to use the denial of oil as a means of pressure on belligerents. Thus the League of Nations in 1935 responded to Italy's attack on Ethiopia by imposing sanctions—ineffectual, as it turned out—that were to include an embargo on weapons, financial credit, and, above all, petroleum. With oil becoming the chief civilian fuel as well, the temptation to use it as a diplomatic weapon increased. Thus the Eisenhower administration in 1956 had refused to pool oil supplies with Britain and France until those powers withdrew from Suez. It was not unnatural, therefore, that Arab countries, as they rose to the status of major petroleum exporters, should feel tempted to use oil as a weapon in their protracted struggle against Israel and against Western imperial powers supporting the Zionist state.

The major pipeline that carried Iraqi oil to the refinery at Haifa on the Mediterranean was closed in 1948, never to be reopened. Israel, of course, had no difficulty in obtaining oil from other sources—during the sixties and seventies mainly from Iran and since then from Mexico, Egypt, and the European spot market. The 1956 invasion of the Suez canal zone resulted in an interruption of normal tanker traffic and a temporary oil shortage in Europe: hence, the relevance of the threat from Washington. During the Six-Day War of June 1967, Iraq, Saudi Arabia, and other Arab oil-producing countries decided to interrupt oil shipments to Britain and the United States. But Radio Cairo's allegation that those countries had joined in air strikes on Egypt proved to be false. The embargo was not formalized until the fighting had ended, and Israeli forces obviously fought the war with supplies that had been in hand before the outbreak of hostilities. For the United States in 1967, moreover, oil from Arab sources constituted no more than one-eighth of all imports, or as little as 2 percent of total oil supplies. In a world oil market where producing countries were still vigorously competing for shares of the market, it quickly became clear that any interruption of shipments would hurt the exporters rather than the importers, let alone Israel; and the attempt at embargo was soon abandoned as a failure.

The question acquired a rather different aspect as Arab oil production, from 1967 to 1973, doubled; as OPEC perfected its solidarity and wrested control over prices and production levels from the companies; as the departure of Western military garrisons from the Middle East ruled out instant retaliation against embargoes or other acts of economic warfare; and as the United States lifted its oil import quotas in the spring of 1973. Since tankers can be easily rerouted on the high seas, it would, of course, be difficult to aim the embargo at specific consumer countries. Still, the effects of disruptions in transport or curtailments of supply on all consumer economies might be severe. As talk about a new round of war in the Middle East intensified in 1972 and 1973, there was increasing speculation about the prospective use of an Arab "oil weapon."

The tactics of this oil diplomacy, indeed, closely paralleled those of the diplomacy of peace and war. Just as President Sadat had preceded his preparations for the October 1973 War with his peace initiative of 1971, so the Arab oil embargo against the United States was preceded by the proposal of a United States–Saudi alliance based on complementary oil interests. The suggestion came during oil minister Ahmad Zaki Yamani's visit to the United States in the autumn of 1972, in which he pursued the first round of negotiations for Saudi "participation" in the Aramco concession. In a lecture to a private group of Middle Eastern specialists in Washington on September 30, 1972, Yamani cited the upward trend in American oil imports and estimates then current of American oil import needs of 8 to 10 million barrels a day by 1980. Only Saudi Arabia, with more than one-third of the world's proven reserves, would be able to satisfy America's growing thirst for foreign oil. Earlier in 1972, Aramco, in consultation with the Saudi government, had announced a long-range expansion of Saudi production capacity from its current 8 million barrels per day to as much as 20 million by 1980, thus lending plausibility to Yamani's implied offer. The *quid pro quo* suggested was both a privileged status for the huge investments that Saudi oil money could bring to the United States and a basic modification of American policy toward Israel. The suggestion, like

Sadat's peace offensive a year and a half before, fell on deaf ears. When their tactic shifted to implied threats, the Saudis found a much more receptive audience in the United States. Hints about the possible use of an Arab "oil weapon" multiplied from the time of Sadat's *Newsweek* interview of April 1973. That same month, the prestigious quarterly *Foreign Affairs* featured an article by James E. Akins, chief energy specialist in the State Department on loan to the White House, entitled "The Oil Crisis: This Time the Wolf Is Here." It gave a comprehensive analysis of the recent forces in the global oil market: declining American production and mounting imports, vast Saudi oil reserves, growing OPEC solidarity, and the need for concerted action by consumer governments to halt the price spiral and develop alternative sources of energy. Akins also speculated on the likelihood of Arab countries imposing an oil "boycott" if the Arab-Israeli problem was "not solved" by the late 1970s and went on to sketch a grim picture of the "difficult and limited choices" with which this would leave the United States: "we could try to break the boycott through military means, i.e. war; we could accede to the wishes of the oil suppliers; or we could accept what would surely be severe damage to our economy, possibly amounting to collapse." On two different occasions in May 1973, King Faisal of Saudi Arabia personally met with Aramco executives to impress on them that "time is running out with regard to U.S. interests in the Middle East, as well as the Saudi position in the Arab world." He warned them that "You will lose everything," but he also explained that "a simple disavowal of Israeli policies and actions" by Washington "would go a long way toward overcoming the current anti-American feeling." On May 15, the twenty-fifth anniversary (by the Gregorian calendar) of Israel's independence, oil workers in Libya, Iraq, Algeria, and Kuwait protested by cutting the flow of oil for part of the day. That same month, Qaddafi abruptly halted the Libyan production of one American company because the United States deserved (as he chose to put it) "a good hard slap on its insolent face." Aramco's parent companies took pains to relay the king's warnings both to Washington and to the American public. Mobil took out an ad in the *New York Times* on June 21 warning that "political considerations" might dominate future Saudi decisions on oil and the time therefore had come "for the world to insist on a settlement in the Middle East." The chairman of Standard of California, Otto N. Miller, on August 2 went to the length of sending a letter to the company's three hundred thousand stockholders and employees, stressing America's growing future dependence on Arab oil imports and appealing for "understanding on our part of the aspirations of the Arab people and more positive support of their efforts toward peace in the Middle East." Later that month, Sheikh Yamani warned Aramco more specifically that its November production might be held to 7 rather than 9 million barrels a day.

The mass media took up the cue. An article in the *New York Times Magazine* entitled "Can the Arabs Really Blackmail Us?" referred to the widespread view that "the United States will soon have to choose between having an adequate oil supply and continuing its support for Israel." And a cover story of *Newsweek* on "The Arab Oil Squeeze" depicted a bearded, smirking young man in bedouin garb in front of an American filling station pump, the gasoline hose clutched to his midriff in a gesture of stingy denial. President Nixon, to be sure, in a televised press conference, reminded his audience that "Oil without a market, as Mr. Mossadegh learned many, many years ago, doesn't do a country much good. We and Europe are the market." His jaunty remark, however, drew a rebuke from an analyst for the *New York Times,* who reminded the president that in the 1970s "The problem is not whether oil will find markets, but whether markets will find oil."

James Akins as early as April had shrewdly surmised that an oil embargo might be imposed for a combination of "political or economic" reasons, and the economics of the oil market had indeed changed profoundly since Mossadegh's day. In the Tripoli-Tehran rounds of negotiation of 1970–71, the OPEC countries had mustered far greater solidarity than had the companies. Meanwhile, OPEC's income per barrel and production levels both had risen sharply—those of Saudi Arabia doubled in the two and a half years before the embargo. In contrast to the 1950s, when the companies could handily replace Iranian oil with oil from Kuwait or Saudi Arabia, there now was little spare capacity—except in the Arab countries. If OPEC stuck together, the world price of oil could be raised substantially, and a temporary curtailment of the flow of oil would be the surest means of effecting such a further rise.

The intense round of conferences among oil-producing countries in the fall of 1973, significantly, was set off three weeks before the Yom Kippur War, on September 15, when OPEC insisted on renegotiation of the 1971 Tehran agreement. This was the purpose of the October 8 meeting, at which OPEC's "Gulf committee" (five Arab countries plus Iran) confronted the company representatives with their demand for a 70 percent price increase. On October 16 in Kuwait, the ministers announced the increase unilaterally, and the next day the Arab oil ministers decided on production cutbacks. The exact formula for the cutbacks and the specifics of the embargo were announced by individual countries over the following days and weeks in a process bearing all the earmarks of improvisation. The sequence of events would seem to reflect the priorities: first, a price increase, not negotiated with the companies but imposed by the governments, Arab and non-Arab alike; second, the Arab production cutbacks, which supported the raised prices by reducing the oil available in the global export market by about 13 percent between October and December 1973; and third, the embargo against the United States, the Netherlands, and various other countries. Note that the Saudis took the lead on the first two measures but were among the last to proclaim an embargo.

For the oil-exporting countries, in sum, the Arab-Israeli war of 1973 provided a golden opportunity to assert the potential market power they had acquired since 1970. It allowed them, once and for all, to establish their control over prices and production and, by a sudden tightening of supplies, to quintuple their income. In this setting of acute shortage, the Arab political demands associated with the embargo were in the nature of a nonmonetary side payment at a time when price alone did not clear the market.

The priorities once again became apparent when the Saudis and others decided, on March 18, 1974, to lift their selective ban on oil shipments. The demand for Israeli withdrawal from the occupied territories remained unfulfilled; the "Palestinian rights," which had been the other major concern expressed in October, had not even been discussed. But the fourfold price increase had been enforced, and OPEC's control over prices and production had gone unchallenged. It was against this background that the Arab ministers were content to call off the embargo. In their statement they were, of course, too delicate to mention anything as crass as monetary gain. But they did dwell on the political aspect of the embargo—and in doing so, probably revealed their true strategy more accurately than they had in the blustering declaration of October. The embargo's "main objective," the ministers explained in retrospect, had been to "draw attention of the world to the Arab cause in order to create the suitable political climate for the implementation of Security Council Resolution 338, which calls for the restoration of the legitimate rights of the Palestinian people." The "oil weapon," in the meantime, had "made world public opinion aware of the importance of the Arab world for the welfare of [the] world economy." As an instance of such new awareness, the ministers specifically noted "the signs which began to appear in various American circles calling (in various degrees) for the need of an even-handed policy vis-à-vis the Middle East and the Arab world." In sum, the aim had been not actual pressure but mere atmospherics.

For Saudi Arabia, the decision to use the "oil weapon" marked both an economic and a political turning point. The desert kingdom's international financial reserves jumped from $3.9 billion in 1973 to $14.3 billion in 1974 and $49.6 billion at the end of 1976. Along the way, Saudi accumulations of foreign exchange, gold, and other international reserves overtook those of Japan later in 1974, those of the United States early in 1975, and those of West Germany—previously the world's largest—by the middle of that year. At the end of 1976 those reserves amounted to more than one-fourth of the world's total. Politically, the events of 1973 propelled Saudi Arabia from the sidelines to the very center of the Arab and global diplomatic stage.

Today's Saudi Arabia is the ancient home not only of Islam but also of the Arabic language. Aspirations to Arab and Islamic leadership have never been far from the minds of Saudi rulers ever since King Ibn Saud consolidated his rule over the holy towns of Mecca and Medina in 1926. Even in the conflict with Israel, the Saudis have tended to emphasize the need to restore to Arab rule the old city of Jerusalem with its Mosque of Omar, the holiest of Muslim shrines outside their domain. Yet the radical and pan-Arab propaganda emanating from Nasser's Egypt and more recently from Baghdad and Tripoli denigrated the Saudi regime as the quintessence of feudal backwardness, as hopelessly beholden to Western imperialism and its commercial emissaries, the oil companies. The growing influx of foreign workers and technicians into Saudi Arabia, including Yemenis, Egyptians, and Palestinians, only sharpened the sting of such criticism.

The Saudi leadership, conversely, was deeply troubled about the flow of Soviet weapons to other Arab countries and the growth of Moscow's influence in Cairo, Baghdad, and Damascus. Far from accepting the Soviet Union as an ally against Israel, Saudi leaders had always considered it an additional threat: the late King Faisal, against all empirical evidence, professed to see no difference between Zionism and communism as parts of one single global conspiracy. Sadat's break with Moscow

—and continued enmity toward Israel—thus was a development even more welcome in Riyadh than in Washington; and Saudi financial aid began to flow generously to Cairo. Sadat's decision to fight Israel with such Soviet weapons as remained under Egyptian control promised to make the 1973 conflict more nearly a purely Arab war. Rather than stand aside and suffer once again the obloquy of Arab radicals, why should not the Saudis seize the initiative? And what better way to seize the initiative and to demonstrate their devotion to the Arab anti-Zionist, anti-imperialist cause than to wield their very own "oil weapon"? A decade earlier, Saudi and Egyptian forces had been deadlocked in supporting monarchists and republicans in the Yemen civil war; now Egyptian armies and Saudi oil would be allied in fighting for the same cause.

The oil revolution of 1973 was also a personal triumph for Saudi Arabia's oil minister Ahmad Zaki Yamani. In 1967 Arab countries had vainly sought to impose an oil embargo on Western powers presumed to be supporting Israel. In the aftermath of that demonstrative and ineffectual gesture, Yamani had developed his long-range oil strategy, enshrined in OPEC's declaration of 1968. There was to be partnership between Western oil companies and governments in the Middle East, with control shifting as rapidly as possible to the governments; this was the essence of OPEC's "best of current practices" doctrine. Since then, Qaddafi's aggressive tactics, a tightening of the global oil market, and America's growing need for imports had vastly enhanced the oil countries' bargaining power. The alacrity with which the American officials of Aramco in October 1973 chose to implement the letter and the spirit of the embargo, imposed against their own home country, is a measure of the success of Yamani's strategy of 1968. As Aramco's president was to testify later, the company judged that its "only alternative was not to ship the oil at all. . . . obviously it was in the best interest of the United States to move 5, 6, 7 million barrels a day to our friends around the world rather than to have that cut off."

In Washington, of course, the announcement of the embargo was taken with less equanimity. Yet, whatever the considerations that prompted Nixon's and Kissinger's policy in October 1973, the fact remained that, after having supplied Israel during the second phase of the October War, the United States cut off those supplies and pressured Israel for an armistice—concluded, as it happened, only two days after the Saudis' announcement of their embargo.

The Saudis' new-found diplomatic prominence lasted throughout the

1970s. Earlier, their aloofness had exposed them to contempt and criticism from pan-Arabs and Third World radicals; now they were everyone's hero. Evidently hatred of Israel and its American backers was as potent a rallying force among Arabs as was the love of money among the producers of oil. In the fall of 1976, the Saudis played host at a meeting in Riyadh to settle the Lebanese civil war and develop a joint strategy among Syria, Egypt, and Jordan in moving the Arab-Israeli conflict toward resolution. Once, at an indiscreet moment in an interview with Oriana Fallaci, Yamani had boasted that "To ruin the other countries of the OPEC, all we have to do is to produce to our full capacity; to ruin the consumer countries, we only have to reduce our production." Early in 1977, the Saudis demonstrated this ascendancy over the oil scene—not indeed by ruining their fellow OPEC members, but by slowing down the price rise on which eleven of the other twelve were agreed. Already the post-embargo announcement of March 1974 had distinguished between the use of the oil weapon in a "positive" and a "negative manner"—as reward and as punishment. In the battle with his fellow OPEC ministers in December 1976, Yamani again showed his knack for trying to get political mileage out of Saudi economic policies: the United States, Yamani hoped, would show its "appreciation" of Saudi price moderation by expediting an acceptable Arab-Israeli settlement.

Nonetheless, there were occasional reminders of the fragility of this sudden power and prosperity. The assassination of King Faisal in 1975 by a disgruntled relative and the attack on the mosque in Mecca by a group of Muslim fanatics in 1979 were indications of the internal vulnerability of the regime. The massive inflow of foreigners made it impossible to isolate the kingdom from the social and political currents of the outside world. Sadat's visit to Jerusalem in 1977 moved the issue of peace between Arabs and Israelis into directions that the Saudis could not—or dared not—approve. Since they had failed to undertake any substantial expansion of their oil installations, their spare production capacity by 1979 could no longer compensate for the virtual shutdown of Iran's oil industry; Saudi Arabia, in sum, had lost, at least temporarily, its ability to "ruin"—or even effectively to restrain—its fellow OPEC members. Above all, the shah's fall in 1979 showed how precarious any one-sided reliance on the United States could be; yet more than ever it emphasized the need for American military protection from dangers that might lurk from Iran, Iraq, or Russia. By the end of the 1970s, Saudi diplomacy in the Middle East and the world at large reverted to the cautious, soft-spoken, behind-the-scenes activity that had been the hall-mark of Riyadh's inter-Arab policy of the 1950s and 1960s.

BLACKMAIL OR CONVENIENT ARRANGEMENT?

If Egyptian and Saudi policies leading to the Yom Kippur and oil wars seem ambiguous, the American response to those events is profoundly puzzling. The Arab moves were subtle and dialectical: Sadat was following the Latin maxim, *Si vis pacem, para bellum* ("If you want peace, make war"). The Saudis, similarly, tried to apply the oil weapon first in a "positive" and then in a "negative" manner—as carrot and as stick. Sadat was determined to disprove the myth of Israeli invincibility; the Saudis were eager to raise their oil income and diplomatic stature. But why, since the embargo's impact on the United States turned out to be so slight, did American opinion react so strongly?

There is a widespread interpretation that the airlift of American arms to Israel's Sinai front on October 14 "directly provoked the Arab states to cut back production and embargo the United States"; that the United States, compelled "to choose between . . . an adequate oil supply and . . . support for Israel," forced Israel to accept the cease-fire; and that the gasoline queues of the following winter prompted Kissinger to work out the subsequent disengagements. This chain of inferences is almost certainly wrong.

The timing on the Arab side, for one thing, does not bear out the notion of American "provocation." The most daring oil move—the sharp price increase—was planned at least as far back as September and announced unilaterally on October 8, several days before the weapons airlift. The cutbacks, imposed between October 16 and November 5, were needed to make those new prices stick. And the embargo, an-nounced piecemeal by individual Arab countries between October 7 and 21, had been talked about *ad nauseam* for six months. At most, the American airlift and President Nixon's request for $2 billion of weapons to Israel came as a convenient justification for Arab moves previously planned.

Nor does the timing on the American side support the hypothesis of oil blackmail. It takes a month or more for a tanker from the Persian Gulf to reach the American coast. October and November 1973 were months of record oil imports; a mild reduction of imports occurred in December—but the full impact of the shortage was not felt until February and March 1974. If American policy changed in October, at most it changed in anticipation of, rather than in response to, any impact of the embargo.

But *did* the October War change Nixon's and Kissinger's policy in the Middle East? The crucial steps—emergency supplies of arms when Israel seemed on the verge of defeat, and their denial when Egypt's defeat in turn seemed imminent—fit in so well with Nixon's prior policy and Kissinger's earlier analysis as to require little further explanation. When Sadat in 1971 proposed peace based on step-by-step evacuation of occupied territories, Kissinger objected to this not as undesirable but as inconsistent with Egypt's 1967 defeat, and hence not likely to be palatable to Israel. He also surmised that the Arabs, having gone to Moscow for arms for many years, might "come to us" for peace and to regain their territories. Indeed, as early as 1969, Kissinger had anticipated that "in a stalemate Soviet standing in the Arab world was bound to deteriorate." Kissinger, in other words, was hoping for a deadlock that would make Egyptians and Israelis dependent on the United States and allow Washington to nudge them both toward a settlement. Only in this way would the United States have a chance to close the gigantic political opening that a quarter-century of Arab-Israeli hostility had provided for the Soviets throughout the Middle East. American actions in October 1973 helped bring about the stalemate for which Kissinger had been hoping.

The Arab-Israeli conflict was the first foreign policy issue that the Nixon administration chose to tackle prior to inauguration—even though (or just because) the Vietnam War had dominated the 1968 campaign. Having selected Kissinger as national security adviser on November 26, the president-elect in early December dispatched William Scranton as his special emissary to the Middle East. The visit caused a public furor among American supporters of Israel when Scranton advocated that the United States should pursue an "even-handed" policy as between Arabs and Israelis. Note that those remarks, delivered after crossing the Allenby bridge from Jordan into the Israeli-occupied West Bank, came only eight days before Nixon's conversation with the ruler of Kuwait—for which Kissinger mistakenly briefed his chief not on the British departure from the Persian Gulf but on the Arab-Israeli conflict.

The Nixon administration's first major effort in the Middle East dispute—the Rogers Plan of December 1969—accords well with Scranton's earlier formula but proved vastly premature. It was only the military stalemate of 1973, to which the United States so decisively contributed, that first laid the foundation for an "even-handed" approach. The word "even-handed" itself had by then, of course, long been discredited; but the adjective accurately enough describes both Kissinger's shuttle diplomacy of 1973–75 and Carter's subsequent efforts at Camp David in 1978.

The conclusion thus suggests itself that, for key American as well as Arab policy makers, the events of October 1973 provided a convenient setting—perhaps a welcome pretext—for doing what they had long wished to do in any case.

Questions of timing and motive aside, the image of an "Arab oil squeeze" exaggerates the role of oil imports in the United States in the early 1970s. Above all, it lays the stress on physical availability rather than quantity of flow—and thus attributes unwarranted importance to the embargo as distinct from the production cutbacks and price rises. Petroleum is a "fungible" commodity: any barrel of it can be used interchangeably—except for minor differences in sulfur content or gravity that might temporarily strain refinery equipment. Its method of transportation across the world's high seas is ideally flexible: tankers can be rerouted at any point in their voyages. For all these reasons, the embargo might create "a logistical headache of major proportions" for the transport divisions of the multinational oil companies. Yet as long as U.S. imports did not exceed total non-Arab exports, there could be logistical snarls and minor delays en route but no physical shortage in America; and in 1973 U.S. imports corresponded to less than half of Arab production. Even combined with the production curtailments, which alone gave the oil weapon its cutting edge, the embargo did not "deprive" the United States of oil on any serious scale—in fact, deprived it less than it did most West European countries.

This result may seem surprising; yet it was a natural outcome of the activities of the multinational oil companies. The companies during the 1973/74 crisis strove to reconcile two imperatives: to abide by the rules of the embargo so as not to jeopardize their access to the large amounts of Arab oil still produced; and to reroute non-Arab oil in such amounts as to spread the shortage evenly among the customers. At the depth of the cutbacks in December 1973, Arab countries were producing 24 percent less oil than in September; but they controlled less than half of global exports, and part of the shortfall was made up by increased production in Iran, Nigeria, and elsewhere. Global exports dropped only about 13 percent, and total world oil supplies about 7 percent; it was this shortage that the companies, by rerouting tankers and swapping cargoes, had to try to spread.

Of course there were imperfections in the system of rerouting and reallocation that the companies hastily contrived; but, if anything, the countries with the largest imports came out a little better—a merchant with dwindling supplies will set some of them aside for his best customers. During the first quarter of 1974, when the embargo and cutbacks were felt most sharply at transatlantic destinations, American oil imports were 16 percent below the 1973 average. Professor Stobaugh, taking into account increases in demand projected before the embargo, calculates that American oil supplies, domestic and imported, were 11 percent below normal—as against 3 percent in Japan and 19 percent in Western Europe. If energy sources other than oil—mainly coal and natural gas —are considered, the differences narrow somewhat: total energy short-fall in Japan was 2 percent, in the United States 5 percent, and in Western Europe as much as 12 percent, and among all importing countries, the United States and Japan were, of course, the companies' largest customers.

The one impact that all importing countries felt at once was the price jump, from $3.01 to $5.12 in mid-October and to $11.65 in January 1974 —and up to $17.00 for small amounts in panic buying on the spot market; but even here the differences were significant. The price explosion obviously affected each major economy in proportion to its dependence on imports for oil, and on oil for total consumption of energy. In this respect the United States clearly fared better than all other major industrial countries. For Japan, petroleum constituted more than three-fourths of all energy consumption; and virtually all of that was imported, making for an energy dependence on imports of 76 percent. The countries of the European Common Market relied on oil for three-fifths of their energy, and imported most of that, resulting in an import dependence of 59 percent. By contrast, petroleum constituted less than half of America's energy consumption, the remainder being mostly domestic coal and natural gas. Only 37 percent of that oil was imported, which meant an energy import dependence of only 17 percent.

Although the cost of American oil imports, both crude and refined, nearly quadrupled between 1973 and 1974, from $7.7 billion to $26.3 billion, that price jump affected only one-sixth of all energy consumed. The contrast of this differential impact on America, Europe, and Japan is so striking that, in an article written in the summer of 1974, I asked "Who Won the Yom Kippur and Oil Wars?" and suggested that it was the United States which did. For West Europeans and Japanese this effect was particularly galling: the United States, because of its growing and wasteful energy consumption was beginning to compete for their traditional energy supplies from the Middle East; and United States policies toward Israel were providing the excuse for sharply raising the price for everyone. One notable effect of the oil embargo was to strain the previous pattern of political and economic cooperation between the United States and its allies in Europe and Japan.

But if the impact of the embargo, cutbacks, and price jumps on the United States was relatively mild and occurred well after the October War, the question becomes all the more insistent: Why was there such widespread fear of an Arab oil squeeze well in advance of the event, and such confusion and panic when the embargo was announced?

There were, to begin with, two specific sets of interests that were glad to see the American media dramatize the prospect of an Arab oil weapon threatening the United States. One was the group of Middle Eastern experts in the State Department and the foreign service loosely known as the "Arabists," who had long been persuaded of the justice of the Arab case against Israel, of the need to make peace on the basis of resolution 242, and of the danger that our association with Israel would jeopardize American interests throughout the region. During the years of the Jarring mission and the Rogers Plan, these experts had vainly tried to pressure Israel into yielding territories and making peace. Now they could cry out, with James Akins, that "this time the wolf is here."

The other group eager to alert the American public to the impending Middle East oil crisis were the major oil companies. In the past, the protectionist wall erected by the import quotas had clearly separated the American and international petroleum markets. The companies might win their battle against Mossadegh in the 1950s, confront the independents in Libya in the 1960s, or close ranks in their retreat at Tehran in 1971. Those events affected the companies' overseas profits, and hence indirectly the American balance of payments; but they had no impact on the supplies received by refiners, or the gasoline prices paid by drivers, in the United States itself.

All this had changed by 1973. The wave of nationalizations that was beginning to surge from Algeria and Libya eastward was threatening to undermine the whole structure of Middle Eastern oil concessions on which the companies' control of the global market had rested for the past half century. If the companies were forced to retreat abroad, their future profits would depend largely or wholly on their domestic American operations. At the same time, the phasing out of the import quotas meant that rising global oil prices would henceforth reach directly into the pocketbook of every American consumer. In the past the State Department had rarely gone to battle for the oil companies; instead it had helped them work out a successful strategy of retreat in their confrontations with nationalists and money-hungry governments. Now that the showdown fight for the overseas concessions was approaching it was no more than prudent and patriotic for the companies to alert the American government and the public at large. Defeat in the battle for the concessions would mean not only lower profits for the companies but also higher prices for the consumers. Had not King Faisal himself, the most conservative of monarchs, personally warned that all might be lost unless there was some "simple disavowal of Israeli policies"? Company executives such as Otto Miller felt an obvious sense of urgency in relaying this timely warning to their employees and stockholders.

Oil prices in the United States, indeed, were bound to rise whether the companies won or lost their battle for the concessions overseas, and no matter what the future mix between domestic and imported oil. With the center of the companies' operations likely to shift to the home market, it seemed, once again, no more than prudent and patriotic to alert the consuming public that the days of cheap energy were at an end. The clearest message came in a series of advertisements taken out by Mobil opposite the editorial page of the *New York Times* and in other newspapers from May 1972 to April 1973. A few excerpts will convey the gist of the message. "*The gap.* No one can be sure how the U.S. will be able to get the additional energy needed." "*To have and have not.* . . . a critical gap between energy supply and demand . . . will widen dangerously . . . painful as the idea may be, petroleum product prices are going to have to rise." ". . . we have made it through another summer and fall. No major fuel shortages, no freezeouts or widespread blackouts. . . . Now all we have to worry about are the coming winter, spring and next summer . . . the energy crisis is one winter nearer." "If . . . cold weather prevails, . . . 25 percent of the workers in parts of Illinois will be laid off. . . . The price of gas ought to be raised." "*Q: A gasoline shortage? A: Yes. Sad, but true.* Q: Is it critical? A: Not yet, but it can become so . . . service stations . . . may run out. . . . Unlikely, though, that all stations . . . will run out at the same time. . . ."

When else in the history of institutional advertising did a major corporation choose to spend hundreds of thousands of dollars to inform the public not of the availability and attractiveness but of the imminent disappearance of its major product?

The State Department's eagerness for a compromise settlement in the Middle East and the oil industry's fear of imminent nationalization may explain why the American media provided such a convenient megaphone to Saudi Arabia's advance rattling of the oil weapon. The receptiveness of the American public to the same message was heightened by a number of broader and unrelated developments.

AMERICA PUTS A WOLF IN ITS TANK

The threat of the embargo came at a time when America's position in the world, and specifically America's energy economy, were in a period of fundamental change. The Vietnam War, terminated in January 1973, had been the first major defeat in the country's two-hundred-year history; it had been costlier in lives and wounds than any war except the Second World War; but it was a sacrifice the need or justification of which few Americans understood. Earlier, in August 1971, the Smithsonian Agreement had ended the dollar's historic role as the world's reserve currency, and the United States had quickly yielded its leading position in trade and finance to such rivals as West Germany, Japan, and Switzerland. The effects of draining America's oil first became apparent in those same years: domestic production began its decline in 1971, and President Nixon saw himself forced to terminate the fourteen-year program of import restrictions on 18 April 1973—the very month when President Sadat chose to start publicizing the Arab "oil weapon."

The lifting of the oil import quotas was an abrupt reversal of policy that had vaster implications than most observers appreciated at the time. For the oil industry itself, of course, the matter was simple enough. Growing demand and the drawing down of domestic oil resources had caused prices to rise steadily: those for domestic crude oil rose 15 percent between 1968 and 1971, and another 15 percent between 1972 and 1973. But the Qaddafi phase of OPEC's revolution had set foreign prices rising even faster, until by early 1973 they had caught up with prices in the United States. OPEC's price increases of January 1972 and April 1973 in response to the falling value of the dollar and the approaching threat of nationalization meant that, in the foreseeable future, prices abroad would keep rising well ahead of domestic prices. Gone, therefore, was the need to "protect" Americans from a flood of cheap imports. On the contrary, there was now much to be said, from the industry's viewpoint, for letting a rising tide of expensive imports sweep up future prices at home.

If the end of the import controls was a boon to the oil industry, it put consumers in double jeopardy. The protectionist barriers for over a decade had kept domestic petroleum prices from falling in current dollar terms; but with production on the rise, the prices had at least not risen either. Indeed, in inflation-adjusted, "real dollar" terms, fuel prices had declined throughout most of the 1950s and 1960s—coal reaching its lowest level in 1968, domestic crude oil in 1970, and natural gas in 1972. Now, at the very moment when domestic oil was beginning to rise in price, it was about to be supplemented with oil imports whose prices were rising even faster. And since in petroleum, as in other markets, prices are normally set by replacement costs at the margin, this meant that, in the absence of price controls, domestic oil would now keep pace with any further increases imposed by OPEC.

The transition from stable or falling to sharply rising energy prices posed a direct threat to the life style of Americans as it had evolved since the end of the Second World War. There are few families who, as car owners or users of heating oil, are not directly affected by petroleum prices. Together with prices for natural gas, coal, electricity, and energy-intensive industrial products (such as aluminum and steel), they affect everyone. When those prices were declining, Americans freely indulged their taste for mobility, for living in gracious surroundings in one-family homes in the suburbs rather than in city apartments, and for a growing array of comforts and labor-saving devices. Between 1950 and 1970, the number of registered automobiles more than doubled, and the number of homes heated with natural gas nearly tripled. Inside those homes, in the 1960s alone, the number of freezers nearly doubled, clothes driers tripled, air conditioners quadrupled, and automatic dishwashers increased four and a half times. And all these upward trends continued in the 1970s.

The 1960s and early 1970s also mark the beginning of a self-conscious and organized environmental movement—for which the publication of Rachel Carson's *Silent Spring* in 1962 and Barry Commoner's *Closing Circle* in 1972 may serve as convenient landmarks. While environmentalism did not reduce our voracious appetite for energy consumption, it did complicate the choice among sources of energy and the location of facilities for its processing. Could the nation allow the strip-mining of coal to convert vast tracts of land into moonscapes? Could we afford to live with the hazards of accidents in nuclear power plants and the unresolved problems of nuclear waste disposal? Could we allow electric utilities to foul the air with soot from coal or sulfur from coal and fuel oil? Everyone liked to enjoy the comforts of dependable electric power and of abundant gasoline, but few people wanted power stations or refineries built in their neighborhood or their favorite stretch of ocean beach ruined by construction of a tanker port. The consumer movement (Ralph Nader's *Unsafe at Any Speed* was published in 1965) added new caveats—and similarly mounting costs—to the long-range planning of America's industrial economy.

In the 1940s and 1950s, the municipal radio station in the nation's largest city used a proud slogan as its station identification: "This is New York, the city of opportunity, where seven [or later: "eight"] million people live in peace and harmony and enjoy the benefits of democracy." In the 1960s, the jingle was quietly dropped; by the 1970s it would have sounded like bitter sarcasm. The defeat in Vietnam, the antiwar protests and student riots, the environmental and consumer movements, all added up to a loss of innocence and self-confidence. The starkly Malthusian report entitled *Limits to Growth,* by Dennis Meadows and others at MIT, appeared in 1972. America no longer seemed the land of open spaces and bountiful resources, no longer the unquestioned leader among the free nations of the world. Economic opportunities seemed more constricted and democracy less beneficent. Sharply rising energy costs accentuated the malaise of a nation long proud of its unlimited mobility and profoundly addicted to machinery and gadgetry. For distant and unsavory foreigners to clamp their hands on the very nozzle of America's gasoline hose conjured up a frightening nightmare of abject servitude, of loss of power and sapped vitality.

Earlier, when the economy was expanding steadily and energy seemed to be available in limitless quantities, many problems of economic and social policy could be readily solved or deftly evaded. In the political struggle over a growing economic pie, it was possible to give to each without taking from any. In an economy of higher wages and shorter hours, the heavy and tedious work could be turned over to labor-saving (and energy-consuming) machines. Now that America's energy pie seemed to have expanded to the very rim of the plate and beyond, many age-old political struggles acquired a more intense, a more ominous—

and a more confused—aspect. And in a stagnant or shrinking economy, it would no longer be possible to give to Peter without robbing Paul.

Specifically, the end of our energy isolationism in the spring of 1973 was bound to have a profound impact on the alignment of economic interests. Earlier, since the days of the railroad magnates and Rockefeller's Standard Oil Trust, there had been continual battles between transporters and refiners, small and large companies, railroads and truckers, producers and consumers. Regulation of commerce, transportation, and public utilities, tax legislation and labor relations, all had been among the stakes in the continuing contest. Now, upon these ancient alignments were superimposed new divisions between "snowbelt" and "sunbelt" states with their different energy appetites; among the southwestern states and Alaska as producers of oil, the mountain states as reservoirs of coal and shale, and the northeastern states as chief importers of oil; between energy producers and environmentalists; between companies eager to increase their profits, politicians determined to tax them away, and a myriad of special interests clamoring for subsidies or tax relief. Few political battles since the Great Depression of the 1930s have so intensely transformed the quality of our political debate as has the Energy Crisis of the 1970s. During the depression, nonetheless, the new battle lines soon emerged clearly enough—between farmers, workers, and industrialists, and a government forced to choose or compromise among them. By contrast, the recent energy battle has remained confused, and the public's concern vastly out of proportion with its level of information.

For that wider public, the most puzzling aspect, both during the depression and now with the energy crisis, has been the forced end of isolationism. Just as a bank crash in Vienna could have remote but inexorable consequences for our economy in the 1930s, so could a meeting of oil ministers in Kuwait, Caracas, or Vienna in the 1970s. The most vociferous battles were all fought at home, between the oil companies and their critics, between environmentalists and champions of nuclear power, between energy surplus and energy deficit states. Similarly, the remedies closest at hand all were domestic: price controls, regulation of refineries and filling stations, performance standards for automobiles, speed limits on highways, taxation of oil companies, subsidies for home insulation or perhaps for the producers of oil from coal and shale. Yet the real problem had long since escaped overseas, far beyond the three-mile limit of national jurisdiction. No amount of taxes levied on the oil companies' profits could force OPEC to roll back its prices. The U.S. government in the past had had a spotty record in using the available legal means to fight petroleum cartels at home. Now, a monopolistic price had been imposed by a cartel of sovereign producer governments, most of them located in the politically most explosive region of the globe, and this time there were no legal means available—no antitrust division to prosecute them, no Sherman Act to invoke against them, and no court before which to haul the culprits.

No wonder then that few of the measures taken by the federal executive or enacted by the Congress helped to forestall or remedy the problem when it suddenly confronted us. A disingenuous clamor about national security had induced Americans to forego Middle Eastern oil when it was cheap and available without political strings and, instead, to drain their domestic oil first. Now that Middle Eastern oil prices were rising by leaps and bounds, when the attempt was made to use oil as a political weapon—in sum, when oil and national security were for once genuinely connected—we had no emergency storage, no standby rationing system, no bureaucracy practiced in the art of energy regulation, and not even a uniform and comprehensive system of government statistics to inform us of existing levels of oil reserves, production, refining, or inventories.

The oil import quota regulations of 1959 were a major contributing factor to the problem as it arose in 1973. Government price controls, imposed on parts of the national economy in August 1971 and applied to petroleum by the Cost of Living Council since early 1973, introduced rigidities into the process of partial changeover from domestic to imported oil. And environmental battles delayed the necessary construction of tanker ports and refineries to handle the growing flow of imports.

In the 1950s and 1960s, there had been lively price wars throughout most of the country between the established filling station chains of the major oil companies and the "private branders"—individual stations or small chains with such alluring names as "Olé" and "U-Filler-Up"— which took advantage of the population shift to the suburbs, the spreading highway net, and self-service techniques to bring "to gasoline retailing the economies of modern mass merchandising." But as the economy shifted from domestic to imported oil, the major companies turned out to have far better access to foreign sources and to be less affected by the growing shortage of refinery capacity. Naturally enough they used these competitive advantages to squeeze out the independent operators. The local shortages of fuel oil in the Middle West in the winter of 1972/73 and of gasoline during the summer of 1973 were due mainly to this combination of declining production, price controls, and commercial warfare between the majors and the "private branders."

Yet for the public at large, such local shortages constituted the essential background noise that attuned newspaper readers and television watchers to the ever more frequent talk about the "energy crisis" and the impending "oil squeeze." Thus one leading oil expert, John H. Lichtblau, had to reassure a sophisticated audience four weeks before the embargo that no Arab oil weapon had yet been applied: "Since no oil exporting country has taken special steps to withhold oil just from the United States, the reason for the shortage is obviously internal. We need look no further than our domestic refining capacity."

Anwar el-Sadat's continual talk of war had served as superb camouflage for his surprise attack on Israel. In America, the advance publicity about an "Arab oil squeeze"—the cries of wolf from State Department officials and oil executives—had a similar effect: there was a state of vague apprehension that heightened rather than lessened the shock of the embargo.

When the embargo came, the Federal Energy Office, which was set up in Washington early in December 1973 to cope with the crisis, and the automobile driving public each overreacted, with cumulative effect, and together caused much needless inconvenience. The FEO tended to credit early estimates that the embargo would leave the United States short by 2.7 to 4.0 million barrels of oil per day. The higher figures were based on the absurd anticipation that almost the entire amount of Arab production cutbacks would show up as a shortage here—absurd, because this presupposed that curtailed Arab shipments to such destinations as the Netherlands would be made up by diverting normal non-Arab imports away from the United States. The lower estimates, to which the FEO shifted by January 1974, corresponded to the total of American pre-embargo imports from Arab sources, including Arab crude oil refined en route in the Caribbean. This still was a vast overestimate, for it ignored the efforts of the oil companies to spread the pain evenly by rerouting some European and Japanese imports from Iran, Nigeria, and Indonesia to American ports. In fact, total American imports of crude and refined oil in the first three months of 1974 only were 1.2 million barrels a day below those of the previous quarter: less than half the shortage for which the FEO was preparing.

Washington bureaucrats hastily assigned to new and complex tasks should perhaps not be judged too harshly for miscalculating the exact workings of the embargo, for digging in for a long siege, for anticipating a colder winter than in fact came—in sum, for trying to prepare for the worst. Yet the FEO could have saved itself and the public much anguish if it had defined its task as one of managing not import shortfalls but inventory levels. As a result of FEO's overcautious policies, American stocks of crude oil, gasoline, fuel oil, and other products actually *increased* during the embargo—whereas a moderate drawing down of inventories might have fully alleviated the shortage of consumer products. It has been estimated that the FEO's policies in restricting consumption and increasing storage aggravated the shortages by as much as 60 percent.

The public's reaction was almost the exact reverse of the FEO's, making the combined effect that much worse. The citizenry managed the ample supplies of heating oil prudently, discovering quickly that their leaders' advice to lower the thermostat helped everyone save on mounting fuel bills. But the same prudent homeowner panicked as soon as he took to the wheel of his car, stubbornly insisting on changing not his driving habits but his purchasing pattern. Throughout December, the nation's drivers, amply forewarned of a gasoline shortage, took to "topping out" their tanks with purchases of a few gallons at a time. This made for additional customers at the filling stations and caused the short queues to lengthen rapidly as passing drivers panicked in turn. The gasoline stations were caught in the middle between FEO's overly severe measures, which created bulging inventories at the refineries, and the nation's motorists who laid in additional inventories in the tank of each car. In a grim satire on Exxon's advertising slogan, Americans put a wolf in their tank, and this time the wolf was here.

The FEO had little choice but to enforce policies that lengthened those queues even further. Gasoline allocation rules had been applied by presidential directive since the spring of 1973 and then by congressional legislation introduced at the time but finally passed under the pressure of the approaching crisis in October. Unfortunately the allocation rules were meant to do justice not among individual drivers but among filling stations and for privileged groups such as truckers, farmers, and government agencies; in short, they were enshrined in a patchwork of special-interest legislation so typical of the American political scene. The major rule was that each wholesaler must allocate gasoline to its filling-station clients in the same ratio as during the same month of the preceding year.

The purpose was to protect the independent stations, or "private brand-ers," from the kind of discrimination by the major chains that had become rampant in 1972.

The effects were counterproductive in several ways. The priority allo-cations to truckers, farmers, and government offices vastly added to the general hoarding and, inevitably, diminished supplies for everyone else. The allocation rule itself was unrealistic: many gasoline stations had closed since 1972, before the law tried to come to their rescue; others had expanded, either because of population shifts or because of the disappear-ance of competitors. The new national pastime of "topping out" meant a further substantial shift of demand from areas of pleasure driving to places of work or residence and from remote to accessible filling stations. Under the existing rules, there was no way of compensating for these shifting patterns of demand. Prices were controlled; filling stations were unable to switch to other suppliers; wholesalers were rigidly held to outdated patterns of distribution; and the FEO, wisely, shrank from the daunting task of coupon rationing. Inevitably—and by default—length-ening gas lines remained the only available means of sub-allocating the gasoline stations' finite supply among harried and panicky drivers. How inadequate the allocation scheme turned out to be became clear when the amounts of gasoline available in each state in February 1974 were com-pared with local needs, as projected by the FEO itself. Half the states received between 78 and 91 percent of that projected need, but the range was from as much as 122 percent for Wyoming down to 63 percent for New Hampshire and Virginia.

Nonetheless, it should be noted that the self-inflicted inconvenience of the American gasoline lines during the winter of 1973/74 was probably less than that of the drastic expedient to which European countries were resorting to at the time: a ban on weekend gasoline sales.

DOOMSDAY OR BUSINESS AS USUAL?

At home there had been first the scare talk of the oil squeeze and energy crisis, then special-interest legislation and bureaucratic bungling, and at last the major annoyance of the gas lines. Abroad there was the unprecedented spectacle of a sovereign cartel levying its $100 billion tax on the global economy—the most gigantic international reallocation of income in history. Soon there were also the many painful problems of readjustment that this forced transfer caused among the world's richest and poorest nations and in the international banking and currency systems. In the Middle East, there was the growing diplomatic stature of Arab oil producing countries and their pressure for a settlement with Israel on Arab terms. The American reaction, from the political leaders and technical experts to the mass media and the common citizenry, was a babble of conflicting voices that was not to subside for some years. Diagnoses of the problem ranged from near-fatal disease to mild indisposition to rampant hypochondria; prescriptions ranged from drastic surgery through a number of patent medicines to nothing more than conscientious dieting or fresh air and regular exercise.

Among the most pessimistic assessments were those offered early by the nation's highest leadership. Dr. Kissinger sounded a general alarm at the Washington Energy Conference of oil-importing states in February 1974: Unless urgent measures were taken at once, the world would face "a vicious cycle of competition, autarchy, rivalry, and depression such as led to the collapse of the world order in the thirties." Half a year later, President Ford himself avowed that it was "difficult to discuss the energy problem without lapsing into doomsday language." And by the end of the decade, Walter J. Levy, who had been one of Kissinger's expert advisers, spoke gravely about "Oil and the Decline of the West." Specifically, there were fears that international banking would be caught in a squeeze between the short-term deposits of their *nouveaux riches* OPEC customers and the long-term borrowing needs of oil importing countries faced with vastly raised energy costs; or—as economist C. Fred Bergsten of Brookings warned—that OPEC's example would be followed by a whole procession of Third World mineral cartels.

Yet there was little agreement on the precise dimensions of the problem. Specialists in petroleum or world finance, in a period of only six months, published forecasts that estimated OPEC's unspent financial surplus by 1980 at anywhere from $22 billion to over $510 billion. And in contrast to Ford's and Kissinger's doomsday visions, a World Bank official calculated the tax that OPEC was levying on industrial countries as proportionately no larger than that which the United States voluntarily had imposed on itself by the Marshall Plan.

Nor was there agreement on the antecedents of the crisis, or even its "reality." "Is the Oil Shortage Real?" Professor Adelman of MIT had asked as early as 1972—and pointed out that the global problem was not one of sudden physical exhaustion of petroleum resources, but of price manipulation by OPEC. But others suspected the oil companies, and their suspicions were fed by Mobil's advertising campaign and some of the companies' handsome profit statements of the mid- and late 1970s. "The American people want to know," Senator Henry Jackson thundered, "why oil companies are making soaring profits. . . . The American people want to know if this so-called energy crisis is only a pretext. . . ." Finger pointing became almost as popular a pastime in 1974 and 1975 as had been "topping out" in the winter of 1973. One of the more bizarre theories had it that Henry Kissinger himself had encouraged his good friend the shah to raise the price of oil so that, flush with money, he would step up his arms purchases from the United States. One would be inclined to assign this hypothesis to the realm of fantasy if it had not been publicized by such prominent figures as James Akins, U. S. ambassador to Saudi Arabia in 1973–75, and William E. Simon, who as secretary of the treasury from 1974 to 1977 served with Kissinger in the Nixon and Ford Cabinets.

The proposed remedies covered an equally wide range. Kissinger in February 1974 was eager to form a solid front of oil importing countries —a measure proposed earlier by Levy and later carried out on a more modest scale in the International Energy Agency. There was some public speculation about possible counter-embargoes, perhaps of food exports ("No crude, no food" was the message of a popular bumper sticker) or of oil-drilling equipment. By the end of the year, Kissinger was openly hinting at the "use of force" if future actions by the oil countries should result in "some actual strangulation of the industrial world." On balance, however, both Walter Levy and Henry Kissinger emphasized that a common front of consumer countries would be intended to avoid rather than provoke confrontation with OPEC.

The obvious alternative was negotiation, and a lengthy and fruitless process of negotiation was begun in the so-called North-South dialogue between industrial and developing nations (the latter including both producers and non-producers of oil) in Paris from 1975 to 1977. A more elaborate agreement was envisaged by Øystein Noreng, a Norwegian political economist: OPEC countries would restrict themselves to modest price rises now, in return for being given a major financial stake in the industrial countries' substitute energy sources in the future.

But there were also hopes for more direct negotiations, or for special relationships between the United States and oil producing countries such as Iran or Saudi Arabia. Shortly after the ceremonial opening of the Geneva Peace Conference in December 1973 the Arab countries had decided not to cut production any further. And following the first Egyptian-Israeli disengagement agreement, negotiated by Kissinger in January 1974, they had called off the embargo. For many years, the State Department and the White House continued to believe that special favors done to Saudi Arabia or pressure on Israel for a settlement would be the best American *quid pro quo* for keeping the price of oil from rising —or from rising too fast. The theme was sounded most uncompromisingly by John Connally in his abortive campaign for the Republican presidential nomination early in 1980, when he asserted that oil imports were essential to the United States but support of Israel was not.

While statesmen oscillated between nightmares of doomsday and visions of clever deals by which they would solve the problem, some respected oil experts believed that the problem would solve itself. "Every cartel," Professor Adelman insisted, "has in time been destroyed by one, then some members chiselling and cheating. . . ." If necessary, this process of OPEC's crumbling could be accelerated by changing the procedures under which the United States imported foreign oil: for example, by auctioning off import tickets to anonymous bidders. Others hoped that the problem would disappear, if not through a price war within OPEC, then through a glut caused by normal market swings or by new oil finds in the North Sea, Alaska, Mexico, or perhaps China.

One of the subtler diagnoses was that the oil shortage was not then "real" but soon would have been, if a doubling of world consumption every eight or ten years had been allowed to exhaust finite supplies. By inhibiting our avid thirst for oil, OPEC was unwittingly doing us a favor, forcing us to pay attention to the development of substitutes while there was time. This theory of OPEC as our secret benefactor was popular in segments of the oil industry and in OPEC circles—in both of which it served as a convenient rationalization for high prices. Thus the shah of Iran used to wring his hands and, with a sweet-sour smile, lecture Western visitors on their nations' habits of "wasting this precious liquid," which by rights ought never to be burnt but rather saved for nobler, petrochemical uses.

But since the assumption was that OPEC was doing us a favor despite itself, there remained a lingering fear that the favor might be suddenly withdrawn. Proponents of the shortage theory argued that the industrial countries must respond to OPEC by making investments in energy alternatives such as oil from coal or shale—estimated at $75 billion in the summer of 1973 and as "in the trillion dollar range" a year later. But what if OPEC, at the very time such astronomical sums were committed and had begun to repay the investment, decided to lower its price so as to retain its market and thus pulled the rug out from under this burgeoning, expensive industry of substitute fuels? The obvious answer was for the participating industrial countries to protect their investment by agreeing in advance on a permanent *floor price,* both for petroleum and for the substitutes produced by those trillion-dollar investments.

It all sounded quite unlikely—except that the chief proponent of the theory was Thomas O. Enders, who as assistant secretary of state was sent around numerous Western capitals to negotiate just such a floor price of $7 to $8 a barrel, just a year after his chief, Henry Kissinger, had seen in that same price as set by OPEC an ominous portent of another great depression and of the collapse of democracy.

In sum, if OPEC was the author of the price revolution, the choice was between fighting it, waiting for it to collapse, making a deal, or (if OPEC was doing us an unwitting favor) making sure that it would continue to do so. If, on the other hand (as Jackson and much of the American public suspected), the oil companies were the real culprits, a number of retaliatory actions suggested themselves. One was simply the indignity of congressional investigation, applied by Senator Jackson and by Senator Frank Church and his committee in the well-publicized hearings on multinational corporations. Another was the proposal of "divestiture"— forcing the vertically integrated companies to separate out their production, transportation, refining, and distributing activities, a proposal espoused by Senator Edward M. Kennedy. A third was to set up a rival, federal company (to be known as FOGCO, or Federal Oil and Gas Company), as conceived by their colleague Adlai Stevenson of Illinois. And finally, there was the possibility of a special tax levy, or windfall profits tax, to relieve the companies of what were presumed to be their ill-gotten gains. This measure, proposed by President Carter, proved highly popular in Congress, where it was at last adopted in 1979. Investigations, divestiture, partial nationalization of the industry, and special taxation—whatever the merits of these measures, they had one common drawback. None of them would have the slightest effect on OPEC or on the world price of oil as set by its members and passed along by the companies. Whatever the role of the companies in facilitating OPEC's ascent, to move against them now was to close the barn door after the horse had been stolen.

Finally, there was the notion that the real trouble was not with

OPEC's price gouging, or with the companies' profiteering, but with the profligate energy consumption habits of the American public. This was a notion congenial to environmentalists and spelled out in the Ford Foundation's Energy Policy Project, as well as (in more detail) in a number of studies financed by the foundation and carried out by Resources for the Future. This was the self-critical notion that underlay President Carter's energy policy proposal of 1977, which he proclaimed to be the "Moral Equivalent of War" but which found little resonance in Congress. In due course it was abandoned for the more popular scheme of a "windfall profits" tax on the oil companies—combined with a huge subsidy to those same companies' investments in synthetic production of oil from coal or shale.

The accuracy of these various explanations of the energy crisis, and the merits of the major remedies proposed will be reviewed in the following chapters in the context of an analysis of the world oil market in the 1970s and 1980s and of the United States' energy policies. In concluding the present assessment of the impact of the Yom Kippur War and the oil embargo on the United States, it is relevant to note that almost all the themes just listed made their appearance in the American media of information in the mid-1970s. The two notable exceptions were the oversubtle floor-price scheme and the call for an end to the waste of energy as the Moral Equivalent of War, which could hardly become popular at a time when even environmentalists glorified nature with megawatt hi-fi music. How well the remaining notions were represented will appear from the following listing of slogans, culled from titles of articles in popular and specialized magazines mostly in 1973–75.

First the chilly doomsday perspectives: "Farewell to Oil?" "Shutting Off the World's Oil." "Energy Crunch: Who'll Get Hurt?" "Facing Up to Cold Reality: Down Go the Thermostats." "Fuel: Button Up Your Overcoat." "Arabs' Oil Squeeze: Dimouts, Slowdowns, Chills." "Energy Crisis: Worse Than Before the Arab Embargo." "How Hard Will OPEC Push?" "This Time the Wolf Is Here." "Oil and the Decline of the West."

And now for the silver lining on the horizon: "Is the World Oil Scarcity Now Becoming A Surplus?" "Welcome Optimism on Oil Imports." "Oil Prices Start To Droop." "Glut Worsens." "OPEC Tries to Tackle a World Oil Surplus." "Our Vast Hidden Oil Resources." "OPEC Is Starting to Feel the Pressure."

Now let's see what's behind it all: "Oil: America's Huge Stake in

Mideast Fighting." "Blackmail by Oil." "Over the Mideast Oil Barrel." "Can the Arabs Really Blackmail Us?" "Have We Put Ourselves at the Mercy of the Arabs?" "Arabs' Final Weapon" "Our Arab Masters." *But can it really be true?* "Arabian Fantasy." "Is the Oil Shortage Real?" "Gas Shortage: Fact or Fiction." "Oil Shortage: Real or Contrived?" (This latter was a speech given by James K. Jamieson, head of Exxon—a clear indication that the question must have been on the public's mind.) "Is the Big Oil Shortage Just Gas?"

It's high time we found the culprits: "Who's to Blame for the Crisis?" "Oil Hoax." "Shortage Scenario: Big Oil's Latest Gimmick." "Did the Oil Companies Create the Gas Shortage." "OPEC and Big Oil: The Malign Cooperation." "Energy: No Shortage of Suspicions."

And finally, what is to be done about it? "Calling OPEC's Bluff: How to Break the Cartel." "Seizing Arab Oil: Proposed Invasion of Arab Oil Fields." "Can We Crack the Oil Cartel?" "Can the Arab Stranglehold Be Broken?" "Living With OPEC."

The media's clamor—and presumably the fitful thoughts of the public —broadly mirrored the confusion and cross-purposes of the leaders and the experts. There was a substantial body of opinion that resignedly asked the doomsday question Must we all freeze in the dark?; there was a frequent impulse simply to wish the problem away; and there was an occasional outburst of anger bent on lashing out. According to the fatalists, there was nothing that could be done; according to the wishful thinkers, nothing needed to be done. Meanwhile those filled with angry frustration spun out drastic but unrealistic fantasies of what might be done. There was only one thing that all three attitudes had in common: they prevented American leaders and citizens from exploring the modest but fruitful ground of concrete action in the world of reality.

While the United States was caught in its confusion and conflicting impulses of action and inaction, our oil imports nearly doubled between 1972 and 1977; and OPEC prepared for its second major round of price increases, which, from December 1978 to December 1980, was to raise the cost of those imports from $13 to $32 or more per barrel.

6

OPEC'S SECOND REVOLUTION

Throughout the summer of 1978, political tensions mounted in the cities of Iran. By late July, there were riots in thirteen cities. By autumn, the shah promised reforms in his autocratic regime, but also ordered his troops to disperse the demonstrations in the capital by force. Yet the crowds refused to be intimidated: each political concession by the regime, and each desperate show of force, was seen as an additional sign of weakness. At length the conscript soldiers refused to fire on their fellow citizens, and disloyalty spread to some of the elite military units. The shah himself lapsed into deep depression.

The American journalist Joseph Kraft, who interviewed the shah in the autumn, found him monosyllabic. What had made him so "sombre"? "Events," was the reply. What might happen in the future? " 'I don't know.' " What did his advisers think would happen? " 'Many things,' he said with a bitter laugh, and he rose indicating that was all he had to say." On December 29, the shah appointed Shahpur Bakhtiar, one of his more moderate opponents, to head a caretaker government. On January 16, 1979, he fled his country.

Shah Mohammed Riza Pahlevi also had fled his country a quarter-century earlier, in August 1953, when Prime Minister Mohammed Mossadegh, flushed from his nationalization of the Anglo-Iranian Oil Company and supported by a wave of revolutionary enthusiasm, had ordered him deposed. But a royalist coup, assisted at a crucial moment by the

U.S. Central Intelligence Agency, had nipped the Mossadegh revolution in the bud and restored the shah to his throne. Since then he had been ruling with a firm hand, ruthlessly suppressing all overt opposition, but also using the regime's growing oil wealth to launch a "white revolution" —that is, to lure the aspiring middle class to the side of the regime. In his foreign policy, the shah had steered an independent course, cultivating friendly relations with both the United States and the neighboring Soviet Union; continuing to supply petroleum to Israel yet vying with the Arab countries in hastening the OPEC revolution.

Successive Washington administrations had sent a growing stream of modern weapons to Iran. Nixon and Kissinger had made it a principle to honor any of Iran's requests for weapons without any detailed assessment of need or purpose. Carter's security adviser, Zbigniew Brzezinski, thought of the shah's Iran as a "regional policeman" to help preserve order in the Gulf region. The shah, in return, had supported the Kurdish rebellion against the Soviet-leaning regime in Iraq; and he had helped Oman suppress a rebellion in its province of Dhufar, instigated by the Russian-installed regime in neighboring South Yemen.

But within Iran, oil wealth and militarization only served to accentuate social tensions and to alienate the masses from the hollow pomp of the shah's repressive regime. By 1978 the opposition had crystallized around three groups: liberals continuing the tradition of Mossadegh's National Front; left-wing groups including the underground and Soviet-controlled Tudeh ("Masses") party; and the clergy of the Shiite denomination of Islam, which is the faith of the Persian-speaking majority of Iran. As the struggle sharpened over the months, the Shiite priests, or *mullahs*, became ever more prominent within the opposition. Their mosques and seminaries provided them with a measure of sanctuary, and their clerical hierarchy gave them something of a command structure and hence of tactical cohesion. Their religious symbolism had more appeal to the common masses than did the self-abnegating principles of Westernized liberal intellectuals. Above all, in Ayatollah Ruhollah Khomeini, the radical Shiite clergy found a respected and uncompromising leader who, by telephoned or tape recorded messages from his exile near Paris, soon managed to coordinate the revolutionary effort. On February 1, 1979, the ayatollah made his triumphant return to Iran, where the crowds hailed him as the *imam,* or reincarnation of the spiritual-temporal leaders of the earliest days of Shiite Islam.

The disturbances of the fall of 1978 had quickly spread to the southern province of Khuzistan, which produces virtually all of Iran's oil and where communist trade unions were strong among the petroleum workers. Self-appointed revolutionary committees had demanded the departure of foreign technicians, and soon the management of Iran's oil fields was in complete disarray. Production dropped to less than half of normal by December 1978 and was virtually halted by a strike in the oil fields from late December to mid-March 1979.

The effect on the world oil market was electric. There had been no major OPEC price rise since mid-1974. The "marker" price had inched up from $10.46 to $12.70 by 1978 but had declined in "real," or inflation-adjusted, terms. This was precisely the intention of the Saudis, who wished the price to lag behind inflation so as to help the world economy recover from the recession of 1974/75, to which OPEC's earlier price explosion had so markedly contributed. And in OPEC's mini price war of 1977, the Saudis had proven that they held the whip-hand in the organization.

As Iranian production declined in the closing months of 1978, this Saudi-dominated OPEC structure held intact. The Saudis and other OPEC members raised their production to make up for the shortfall in Iran. And at its price-setting meeting in December, OPEC decided to raise prices by 5 percent—to about the level that the hawks in the organization had wished to see established in mid-1977.

But then things got out of hand. In January and February 1979, with the Iranian workers on strike, there was a sharp temporary dip in total OPEC output. The Saudis found that they could not sustain their record production levels of December, and most other OPEC countries were already producing near their capacities. The total drop in OPEC production, of 3.6 million barrels daily between September 1978 and January 1979, was smaller than the 4.2 million drop at the time of the embargo in 1973. But this time the effect on the global oil market and on prices was worse.

The impact was felt most acutely on the "spot market," that set of transactions in Rotterdam and other major ports where odd lots of oil are traded that do not stay within a single integrated oil company and are not covered by long-term purchasing arrangements, at prices fluctuating somewhat above or below the official "contract" prices. Between January and March 1979, at the time of the Iranian strike, those spot-market prices rose by more than 40 percent. The Saudis inadvertently aggravated the situation by reducing their production as soon as the

Iranian workers called off their strike—and while the earlier production shortfall was still working its way through the global distribution system. And although Iranian production from late March on averaged about two-thirds of normal levels, the situation in Tehran turned increasingly chaotic, and no one could tell when there might be another oil shutdown in Khuzistan.

Thus in the spring and summer of 1979, the world oil market bustled with unwonted activity. Anxious buyers and hopeful speculators, expecting that the shortage would send prices soaring, bought whatever oil they could get their hands on and paid whatever price was asked. The effect was that of a self-fulfilling prophecy. The frantic buying aggravated the shortage, speculation drove up prices and attracted additional speculators, and rising prices caused yet more panic. As the exiled shah made his way from Egypt to Morocco and Mexico, spot prices doubled and tripled. OPEC's "marker crude" had long been the light grade of Saudi Arabian oil, which throughout 1978 had sold at $12.70 a barrel, its official price rising to $13.34 in January 1979 and to $14.55 in April. But its spot price rose from $16 in January to $22.50 in February and to $35 in June. By the time the shah arrived for his surgery in New York City in November and Iranian militants occupied the American embassy in Tehran, Saudi Arabian Light was trading at $41 a barrel.

Ironically, total OPEC production by July 1979 was back near the record levels of the previous September—but at prices 50 percent higher in the contract market and up to 200 percent higher in the spot market. The panic and hoarding each time quickly reopened the gap that higher production was beginning to close. In 1973 and 1974, the rigidities of U.S. price controls and allocations had caused local shortages of gasoline, and lengthening queues at the filling station had caused growing panic among drivers bent on topping off their tanks. Just so, the panic on the international oil market spread by example throughout 1979—this time the world market had put a wolf in its tanker.

Because of its excessive fear of shortage, it turned out that the world oil industry in 1979 built up an unprecedented surplus. Since the world tanker fleet had been rebuilt in the 1960s and early 1970s in the expectation of a steadily growing market, idle tankers now made ideal storage facilities. And by mid-1979 all such facilities were beginning to bulge with amounts far beyond normal working inventories. By mid-1980 these above-normal stocks were approximately twice as large as the total amount of oil by which the Iranian oil strike had reduced supplies the year before. The bulging oil stocks of 1980 brought with them one minor consolation. When Iraq's ruthless and ambitious dictator Saddam Hussein launched his invasion against Iran in September 1980, land and air attacks from both sides quickly brought Iranian and Iraqi oil exports to a complete halt. The drop in production this time was 3.5 million barrels a day, virtually as large as at the time of the Iranian strike. But with storage facilities brimful, the shortfall did not lead to a second buying spree, and hence there was no panic or price rise. The consolation, then, is that a Middle Eastern political crisis may occasionally curtail the flow of oil as often as once a year, but the world oil market cannot throw itself into a price-driving panic more often than every two or three years.

HAVE RATCHET, WILL TRAVEL

The Iranian revolution helped bring out the latent political and economic rivalries within OPEC. Of course there had never been much political harmony among the organization's thirteen member states. The shah, as already noted, supported Israel with oil and Kurdish rebels in Iraq with weapons. From time to time Iraq would press a territorial claim to all of neighboring Kuwait—the threat to which the Kuwaiti emir had tried to alert Nixon and Kissinger in 1968. Throughout most of the 1970s, Iran and Saudi Arabia used much of their new oil wealth to indulge in a multibillion-dollar arms race across the Persian—or, as Arabs would insist, "Arabian"—Gulf. Libya's mercurial president Qaddafi is considered a political menace by most conservative Arab regimes. And on one occasion, Qaddafi even forbade Libyans to make the Muslim pilgrimage to Mecca—on the rather farfetched grounds that Saudi Arabia, including its holy cities, was under military occupation by American infidels.

None of these threats or insults, however, could compare to OPEC's predicament as the organization entered its third decade. For months, OPEC had been publicizing the ceremonial meeting that would be held at Baghdad to celebrate the organization's twentieth anniversary. Instead, a few days before the twenty years were completed, Iraq attacked Iran, and the celebration was quietly canceled. At OPEC's regular business meetings, new, nonalphabetical seating arrangements had to be devised to prevent a physical clash between the delegates from Iran and

Iraq. On one occasion, the Iranian representative bitterly complained that his country's oil minister, who would normally have attended, was instead a prisoner of the Iraqi forces. Throughout 1980, the monthly issues of the *OPEC Bulletin* published by its Vienna headquarters proudly bore a design of the member countries highlighted on a world map. The map was festooned with the inscription (in English) "1960 OPEC 1980—20th anniversary" and encircled by two stylized olive branches below and the motto "Progress Through Solidarity" above. The spectacle of OPEC's meetings during this twentieth-anniversary season made a mockery of the artist's brave conception of solidarity and olive branches.

Nor was this all. In earlier years, no matter how bitter feelings had run among OPEC's members, the thirteen countries had still managed to perform their central function as a price-setting cartel. Even the mild price war of 1977, when the Saudis had refused to match the full increase voted by most other members, had ended in an all-round truce after no more than six months. But now the price structure, too, was in disarray. The Libyans and other price hawks tried to cash in on the gains of the spot market by running up their contract prices from $13 to $23 to $30 to $40 a barrel. Saudi Arabia vainly tried to restore unity by matching each of the earlier increases some months later, going from $14.55 to $18 in June 1979, to $24 in November, to $26 in January 1980, to $28 in April, to $30 in August, and to $32 in November. But each time the hawks foiled such attempts at reunifying the price by raising their prices yet again. Although total OPEC production declined almost month by month throughout 1980, prices thus kept climbing rapidly. The Saudis' game of catch-up quickly deteriorated into a game of tag, with a good deal of bitterness and nose-thumbing along the way. In the spring of 1981, Saudi Arabia's Sheikh Yamani truculently announced that his country had kept production at maximum levels for the past year or so so as to contrive an oil glut that would force other OPEC members into line. And still the hawks held out for much of 1981.

Nonetheless, despite all these signs of confusion, friction, and disarray, the events of 1979 and 1980 provided a clear indication of OPEC's inherent strength. From the time of its founding in 1960, OPEC had followed the dual aim of "cash and control." It had started as a limited-purpose association of newly sovereign governments determined to tighten their control over their countries' petroleum production and to increase the profits from its export. The cartel's spectacular rise in the 1970s resulted not from the elaborate conception or rigid implementation of some single master plan. Rather it was made possible by the discovery, after much trial and error, of an effective and flexible strategy, summed up in the so-called best-of-practices doctrine. This meant quite simply that, whatever device any member country had adopted, or stumbled upon, in adding to its cash or extending its control, all other members would henceforth claim that same device as their right. As soon as one of them had gone a step or two ahead, all the others would cry, Me too! Me too! In this way OPEC, as we noted, had managed to put competition itself into the service of monopoly.

Specifically in 1970–71 and again in 1973–74, OPEC had developed a three-phased process of price manipulation; and the crisis of 1979 and 1980 followed the same basic pattern.

- The process is launched by some political event that sharply curtails the flow of oil. This may be deliberate, as at the time of the embargo in 1973. Or it may be the accidental by-product of other political events, such as the workers' strike during the Iranian revolution. Or else it may be a combination of deliberate and accidental events, as in 1970 when a broken pipeline in Syria prompted Qaddafi to threaten a shutdown in Libya.
- Next, the resulting price increase is accelerated by panic buying on the spot market. This phase was very important in 1973 and 1979, for it provided OPEC strategists with a crucial empirical test of what the traffic would bear, at least at the moment.
- Finally, in the third phase, OPEC members apply their most important device, which turns out to be a portable ratchet. As shortage and panic subside, they cash in on most of the resulting increase by refusing to sell at lower prices and by allowing production to decline instead.

Note that the three-step tactic works to OPEC's benefit because the decline in demand in phase three does not match the increase in price in phase two. Or to put it in technical economic language, the short-run price elasticity of demand for OPEC's oil remains well below 1.0. Thus OPEC in 1974 sold as much oil on a base price of $10 as it had the year before on a price of $3, and in 1975 its sales declined only about 12 percent. Similarly, OPEC's production increased by 3 percent from 1978 to 1979 and declined by 13 percent in 1980 and another 14 percent in 1981—while its base price jumped from $13 to $34. All in all, OPEC's oil income grew rapidly from $124 billion in 1978 to $188 billion in 1979 and $272 billion in 1980, declining only slightly to $265 billion in 1981.

The Iraq-Iran war of the fall of 1980 only served to confirm this over-all picture. By attacking each other's oil installations, the belligerents caused another sharp drop in production. Since inventories were still bulging, this caused no panic; yet it delayed any approaching glut and continued to strengthen the hand of OPEC's price hawks in their contest with the more moderate Saudis. Nearly a year would pass before producers such as Nigeria and Libya had to confront the difficult choice between seeing their production decline to one-half or less or reducing their prices from the all-time highs of 1980.

In sum, the 1979 experience amounted to a further perfection of the basic OPEC process. When the member governments function and are in agreement, they agree on raising the price of oil. When one of the governments is paralyzed by revolution, or when two of them are at war, the price rises even more steeply—all by itself in response to market pressures. OPEC had put into the service of monopoly not only the competition but even the deadly quarrels among its members. And it follows that OPEC's twentieth anniversary was indeed a joke, but the joke, for the time being, was on OPEC's customers. There were no olive branches and no solidarity, but there was progress toward higher and higher prices—and the customers kept paying.

How long will OPEC be able to wield its ratchet? The price elasticity of demand for its oil remains below 1.0 in the short run. But what of the longer run? Will another oil-curtailing war or revolution give OPEC's hawks a chance to drive the price to $50, $80, or $100 a barrel, or is there a limit where the customers will refuse to pay? Or has OPEC perhaps overdone it already? Is the time coming when customers will no longer scramble for OPEC oil, but when OPEC's members will have to cut prices to scramble for customers?

These are crucial questions for the oil market and the world economy of the 1980s and 1990s; indirectly, they may become crucial questions for war and peace in the Middle East and the world at large. Before attempting any answers, it will be well to dispel certain myths spread by OPEC's own apologists and by some of the OPEC watchers in the West; to take a closer look at the nature of the division between price hawks and price doves within the organization; and to take a look in particular at the oil policies of the kingdom of Saudi Arabia, which has long been OPEC's most influential member.

The two myths dear to OPEC's official spokesmen are that "OPEC is not to blame"—as an article in the monthly *OPEC Bulletin* put it at the height of the 1979–80 price rise—and that OPEC countries are doing their customers a favor by producing oil beyond their own financial "requirements." The first myth gains some superficial plausibility from phase two of the three-phase process just analyzed. In this second phase, buyers in the world oil market, and particularly in the oversensitive spot market, respond to the politically caused shortage of phase one, thus allowing OPEC members to gauge what the traffic will bear. It is an important phase, because OPEC in itself is not strong or cohesive or prescient enough to devise and implement any major price-driving scheme without such an interim market response. And it is true that during such a tight seller's market, it is the eager buyers who are setting the pace. But OPEC *is* responsible, for it has repeatedly shown itself capable of taking advantage of this tight market by applying the ratchet in phase three. Without OPEC's cartel structure, loose as it is, the seller's market would quickly be followed by a buyers' market as glut followed upon shortage, and the oil price, after going up from $13 to $41 would take a nose dive back to $13 or less.

The high tide of prices in the wake of the Iranian revolution flooded most OPEC countries with revenues far beyond their previous expectations. OPEC's total revenues more than doubled between 1978 and 1980. And this sudden affluence seems to justify the other favorite cliché of OPEC's ideologues, that their countries are producing oil far beyond their "national requirements." Out of the goodness of their hearts, one gathers, they are doing their customers a big favor. The plain truth, of course, is that OPEC countries produce certain amounts of petroleum, and sell them at certain prices, for one reason alone: to make money. And it turns out that the financial requirements of OPEC countries are extremely variable—at least in the upward direction. As table 3 in the Appendix indicates, OPEC countries have built up growing financial reserves since the 1970s, yet the relative size of those reserves has declined from seven months' oil income in 1973 to four months' income in 1980—a clear indication that OPEC governments have had little difficulty in learning to spend the larger sums they receive—and of course they are getting much help from eager consultants, suppliers, and industrial and arms manufacturers in the West.

It is of course true, as long as demand remains relatively inelastic, that each price rise will yield for the exporters an income beyond their previous "requirements." As long as the world remains addicted to OPEC oil, the less OPEC produces, the more the world will pay. And any attempt by OPEC countries to limit their incomes by cutting production would have the very opposite effect of *adding* to their income—a situation that I have described as "King Midas' dilemma."

Once again, the economists have a more technical term for this: such a mechanism is called a "backward-bending supply curve" and is considered one of the bugaboos of economic theory, for it plays havoc with all normal supply and demand relationships. As the price rises, supply does not increase as it would in normal markets; on the contrary, it diminishes —the supply curve "slopes backward." While this condition prevails, the official OPEC argument about income "beyond requirements" amounts to a thinly veiled prescription for unlimited price escalation. If OPEC members really wished to do their customers a favor and really were eager to limit their incomes—if the Midases of this world really wanted to stop having all they touch turn into gold—why, all they would have to do is to cut their prices and increase production. But then there would be no more OPEC.

Although both OPEC myths are transparently self-serving, each contains a kernel of truth. OPEC is not alone to blame. The Western world's colossal carelessness in allowing itself to become economically dependent on Middle Eastern oil just as the Middle East was becoming politically independent of the West must share in the blame. So must American policies in the 1970s that encouraged rising oil imports into the world's largest economy. And although OPEC countries have had little difficulty in spending or overspending their rising incomes, those incomes for most countries have indeed gone far beyond the optimum required for balanced economic or political growth. Without the rapidly rising oil incomes of the 1970s, it is unlikely that there would have been an Iranian revolution.

The myth dearest to optimistic Western observers is that any slowdown or temporary reversal in OPEC's fast-rising price curve might herald the beginning of the end. The glut on the world oil market that began with the buildup of stocks in 1979 and 1980, so the optimists insisted, would continue throughout the 1980s. The bickering at OPEC's meetings in May and August 1981, at which the Saudis vainly tried to unify the price, were only the early symptoms of impending trouble. Energy conservation in the industrial countries, development of non-OPEC oil resources, and substitution of coal and other fuels for petroleum were cutting severely into OPEC's sales. Soon some OPEC members might be unable to quench their growing thirst for foreign exchange from dwindling oil exports and have trouble financing their ambitious development programs. The result might be a price war, which would further undermine OPEC's position. By the end of the decade, the world's dependence on OPEC oil and the high prices of the 1970s and 1980s would all have passed like a bad dream. Indeed, the United States and other industrial countries might see themselves forced to impose tariffs so as to protect their carefully developed synthetic fuels and other petroleum substitutes from the flood of cheap oil that OPEC would be tempted to dump on the world market. As Professor S. Fred Singer, one of the more amiable spokesmen for this glut-and-gloat school of OPEC watchers, put it in an op-ed piece in the *New York Times,* world oil demand might drop by as much as two-thirds by the 1990s. "Clearly, the

Organization of Petroleum Exporting Countries must take a cut, and Persian Gulf production could drop all the way to zero. But if OPEC members insisted on producing they would have to cut prices in order to sell their oil."

Such hopeful speculation about OPEC's imminent demise was at least premature. In October 1981, when the Saudis finally restored unity around their preferred price of $34, the cartel's exports had dropped to only two-thirds of their 1978 level, but its aggregate income was still running at about twice the 1978 rate. OPEC had taken two steps forward and one step back to consolidate its second and most drastic price revolution. The danger—indeed the folly—of the wishful thinking about OPEC's early collapse was that it might stop or slow down the measures of conservation and investment in alternative energy sources, which are the industrial world's only means of protecting itself against a third or fourth OPEC price revolution.

Nevertheless, here too there was a kernel of truth in the legend. The world oil market goes through a ceaseless ebb and flow of glut and shortage. In 1981, the selling off of excess inventories and the Saudi maximum production of which Yamani had boasted—along with price decontrol in the United States, sharply rising oil prices, and global recession—had exaggerated such a temporary glut. The result had been an unprecedented strain between OPEC's doves and hawks: some of the latter did not heed the Saudis' call for unity until their production had dropped to less than half. The open question was whether a more severe glut next time might indeed weaken or perhaps break the cartel.

Minor fluctuations in supply and demand are inherent in the structure of the world oil market and exert almost constant upward and downward pressure on prices. It takes several weeks for the typical supertanker to make its voyage from an export terminal in the Persian-Arabian Gulf around the Cape of Good Hope to one of the major tanker ports in North America or Europe, or across the Strait of Malacca to Japan. It takes another few weeks for the oil to be processed in a refinery and delivered in refined form to a filling station, power plant, or fuel oil company. There, at the ultimate point of sale, demand is subject to much seasonal variation: more gasoline is used in the summer, more fuel oil in the winter, and the use of each fluctuates with warm or cold weather. Swings in the business cycle, and hence over-all levels of economic activity, and consumer resistance to spiraling prices add further variations to that seasonal pattern. It is virtually impossible for the oil companies that handle this global flow of oil to predict the cumulative effect of such variations with any precision three or four months ahead.

Some of the inevitable disparities can be corrected by buying or selling small amounts of oil from or to other companies that may have made the opposite miscalculation; this, indeed, is the normal, non-panic-stricken function of the spot market. Another method of correction is to adjust the product mix or level of refinery utilization—the technical decisions by which a daily amount of refinery "throughput" is converted from this much crude oil into that much gasoline, diesel fuel, kerosine, heating oil, naphtha, and so forth. The ability of oil companies to change the speed or destination of their tankers and to build up or draw down their stocks both of crude oil and petroleum products provides a third adjustment mechanism. But the flexibility of refineries and the capacity of storage tanks are limited, and the spot market is oversensitive. The net result at best is still some slight imbalance in the world market—a constant but rather unpredictable ebb and flow of shortage and glut.

Indeed, the sensitivity of the world oil market to such fluctuations was further sharpened by the events of 1979–81. In the seller's market following the Iranian revolution, OPEC's price hawks loosened many of their long-term contract relationships with the multinational companies, diverting a maximum of oil to eager old and new buyers in the lucrative spot market. In the glut of 1981, the major companies applied the same tactic in reverse, invoking any cancellation or *force majeure* clauses that their contracts with Libya, Algeria, or Nigeria might provide. As one American oil executive recalled in mid–1981, "The Mexicans told us in the negotiations that a barrel we suspend now is a barrel they won't sell us when the market gets short. But what can they do? They can't blacklist us all. Whom will they sell to?"

With much of Iraqi and Iranian production shut down in 1980/81 and most other OPEC members driving their advantage to the hilt in the shortage of 1979/80, Saudi Arabia was almost the only OPEC country that carefully preserved its long-standing contract relationships with the oil multinationals. And indeed it was that relationship with the four Aramco partners—Exxon, Socal, Texaco, and Mobil—that enabled the Saudis to place on the world market the additional oil they were producing in 1980/81.

Elsewhere in the OPEC market, arms-length relationships between governments and multinational oil companies were becoming the rule. And the effect of this change was to make the world oil market even more sensitive to the changes in supply and demand that had played such a decisive role in the crisis of 1979. The net result might well be to make the movement of supply, demand, and prices in the 1980s more erratic and less predictable than ever.

What will remain more predictable is the disparity or asymmetry between the relevant changes in supply and in demand. A glut due to seasonal variation in consumption, the usual imperfections of the companies' foreknowledge of the market, or consumer resistance to higher prices is not likely to be as severe or as sudden as a shortage due to political interruptions of the flow of oil. Recent increases in Saudi output have not run higher than 1 million barrels daily from one month to the next. In contrast, the Iranian oil workers' strike—and again Iraq's attack on Iran—almost overnight deprived the world market of more than 3 million barrels daily in supplies. A reduction in consumption of roughly equal size did not occur until a year later—after prices had more than doubled. And the building up and drawing down of excess inventories in 1980 and 1981 occurred just as gradually.

Even more distant are the effects of additions to non-OPEC energy supplies, such as new U.S. offshore fields, synthetic fuels, expanded nuclear power, or new solar energy technologies—far too remote to remedy any short-term imbalance such as that caused by a Middle Eastern war or revolution. More than anything else, it was this major contrast between mini-gluts and maxi-shortages that, throughout the 1970s, kept tipping the world oil balance in OPEC's favor.

OPEC HAWKS VERSUS DOVES

When OPEC members agree, they meet periodically to raise the price of oil. And market forces assisted by OPEC's ratchet raise the price when member nations are racked by revolution or are at war with each other. There has also been another type of intra-OPEC dispute, about price itself; unfortunately for the customers, this kind of dispute typically has been not about raising the price, but only about raising it by how much and how soon.

In the first half of 1977, for example, the Saudis insisted on a 5 percent increase above 1976 prices, and most other OPEC members on an increase of 10 percent. By the middle of 1977, the two sides negotiated a truce in their mini price war: the Saudis matched the 10 percent increase of the others, and they in turn abandoned plans to raise the price by 15 percent. A similar scenario was reenacted several times in 1979 and 1980 —except that the price jumps were bigger and the Saudis' tactic of arresting the upward price spiral did not work. From December 1976 to July 1977, the Saudi price rose by 10 percent and from mid-1979 to late 1980 by as much as 120 percent, to $32. At last this bitterest of OPEC price disputes ended not in a net reduction but in a compromise: as the Saudis late in 1981 raised their price once again from $32 to $34; and the hawks, such as Libya and Venezuela, cut theirs by an average of $2 a barrel. Note that throughout this period the Saudis never once suggested, let alone implemented, an actual cut in their own price.

Indeed, there was little mystery about the Saudis' preferred price strategy: they were opposed to steep, sudden, or unpredictable price rises and instead preferred gradual and predictable ones. And there was equally little mystery about the determination of other OPEC members, such as Libya, Algeria, Nigeria, and Venezuela to charge what the traffic would bear. These contrasting attitudes stem from a number of basic economic factors, with just a dash of politics added for spice. And those factors are well worth examining in detail, for our over-all estimate of OPEC's viability and, hence, of the likely price structure of the world oil market for the remainder of this century must heavily depend on them.

The crucial economic factors are the size of a country's oil reserves and of its population. The petroleum of countries such as Algeria, Venezuela, and Nigeria is almost certain to run out in the next several decades unless production is reduced drastically or new methods of "enhanced recovery" are applied. By contrast, oil reserves around the Persian-Arabian Gulf are certain to last—at present rates of production—through much of the twenty-first century. It happens that the distribution of population is almost the exact reverse. Saudi Arabia's population in 1980 was estimated at 8 million, Kuwait's at 1.4 million, and that of the United Arab Emirates at only 800,000—as against 14 million for Venezuela and 19 million for Algeria. Nigeria alone, with 77 million, has a larger population than the entire Gulf region, including Iran and Iraq; and there are 152 million Indonesians—more than the inhabitants of Nigeria and the Gulf region combined.

Governments with large populations atop small oil reservoirs apply a short time perspective. They have pressing financial needs for economic development, and their wells will run dry before the world has completed its shift from petroleum to other fuels. If rapidly rising prices should reduce production and stretch out the dwindling reserves over another decade or two, so much the better. The major concern of those governments is to make all the money they can from current oil production and to invest it for the benefit of future generations. (The inefficiency and corruption that accompanies development efforts in such countries as Nigeria and Indonesia increase rather than lessen the financial pressure.) Indonesia, Nigeria, Algeria, Venezuela—along with the more oil rich but populous Iraq and Iran—are known in the jargon of current OPEC watchers as "high absorbers" of oil income, and in the price controversies of 1977 and 1979–81 they were all among the hawks. Even Sheikh Yamani conceded that if he were an Algerian he would wish to see the price of oil rise to $100 a barrel.

The "low absorbers" are the countries with small populations atop huge petroleum deposits, and naturally they must take a longer perspective. They enthusiastically participated in the first two phases of the OPEC revolution in 1970–71 and 1973–74, but since then they have preferred slower or more gradual price rises. Their oil is already securing for them both a lavish current income and a growing foreign exchange reserve—in 1980 that income was around $13,000 and that reserve around $3,000 for every Saudi and Kuwaiti resident. To pursue a hawkish price policy of maximizing present income by exploiting short-term inelasticities would only magnify the risks inherent in their economic situation.

Already the Arab Gulf states are heavily dependent on foreign experts, technicians, and workers to implement current development plans, to the point where the indigenous population is a minority in some of the states. An even faster accumulation of oil income would enhance not the economic opportunities at home but only the financial assets abroad. And for the longer run, such a price policy might mean economic suicide.

For all OPEC countries, sharply rising prices would mean lower sales now, more oil underground, and a powerful incentive for the customers in the industrial world to speed their transition from petroleum to coal, synthetics, fusion, or other forms of energy. OPEC's hawkish high absorbers have little to fear from such a prospect: their oil will have been sold and their wells will have run dry long before oil becomes obsolete even under the most ambitious crash-program for Western energy independence. But for the oil-rich Gulf countries, the risks would be enormous. The world, forced by wildly escalating oil prices to spend hundreds of billions on conservation and on alternative energy forms, would be unlikely to switch back to petroleum on a massive scale, even if the price were brought back down belatedly to competitive levels. To drive too hard a bargain now risks scaring off the customers for good; to overplay OPEC's hand might make the remaining oil under the sands worthless for all future. Nor are the Saudis and other oil-rich "low absorbers" interested in provoking the industrial countries into such desperate countermeasures as a military invasion of oil fields—as envisaged in Kissinger's "actual strangulation" scenario of December 1974 —since they presumably would be the most tempting target for such an operation. Here is one of several political calculations that serves to reinforce the commitment of Saudi Arabia and others to a moderate price policy.

Political considerations of an opposite sort have influenced Libya's policy. The country's oil reserves are of an intermediate order, about three times those of Algeria but only one-third of Kuwait's and one-seventh of Saudi Arabia's. But President Qaddafi's conduct over the years has been marked by Islamic fundamentalism, a profound resentment of the Western world, mounting arms purchases from the Soviet Union, and cooperation with its Middle Eastern protégés such as Syria, South Yemen, and Ethiopia. Over the years, Qaddafi has been a major supporter of the more extremist affiliates within the Palestine Liberation Organization. Allegedly, he has been financing terrorists as far away as Ireland and the Philippines. He has plotted invasions or coup d'états against almost every one of Libya's neighbors—Egypt, Sudan, Chad, and Tunisia—and was involved in an abortive attempt to restore to power Uganda's deposed dictator Idi Amin. Preoccupied with his present activist and often destructive policies, Qaddafi is not inclined to worry about the welfare of future generations of Libyans. Fanatically opposed to the existing global economic and political order, he cares little for the prospects of international economic stability. No doubt Muammar Qaddafi also remembers with pride that it was he who in 1970, at the age of only twenty-seven, threatened to shut down one by one the Western oil companies in Libya—and thereby launched OPEC on its meteoric rise to wealth and global influence. No one, it seems, can amass and expend money with such sovereign disdain as can a fiery-eyed and power-hungry ascetic. Political attitudes such as these have made of Libya the leading price hawk, where considerations of a purely economic nature might have counseled a more moderate price policy not unlike Saudi Arabia's.

SAUDI ARABIA: THE KEYS OF THE KINGDOM

At the opposite end of the Arab political spectrum stands Saudi Arabia, and here the long-term economic arguments for a dovish price policy are reinforced by more immediate political and psychological considerations. The Saudi kingdom remains, by all odds and despite its sudden oil wealth, the Middle East's most traditional regime. The Muslim creed is inscribed on its flag: "There is no god but God, and Mohammed is His prophet." The Koran is considered its written constitution. Women are veiled in public, the shops close their shutters at prayer time, there is no drinking of liquor in public, and non-Muslims are not allowed into the holy city of Mecca. Two centuries ago the family of Saud, in alliance with the fundamentalist Wahhabi sect of Islam, set out to purify the way of life of the bedouin, and to conquer one by one the regions of the Arabian peninsula. Today, Saudi Arabia is ruled as a family oligarchy, by a king and a crown prince selected from among their peers by a family council of some three thousand princes of the royal house. King Abdul Aziz Ibn Saud, who reigned from 1897 to 1953, considered Zionism and atheist communism the chief enemies of Islam and hence of Saudi Arabia. The sudden inflow of billions of oil money into the country since the days of King Abdul Aziz has reinforced this anti-communist, pro-capitalist bias of the regime. On a more personal level, most princes and other members of the ruling clan have by now accumulated sizable personal investments—in real estate, business, and banking—in the United States or Western Europe.

All this is to say that the effect of oil prices on the health of the global economy is a matter of genuine concern to members of the Saudi government. Specifically, any sudden increase in oil price that would plunge the Western economies into recession and unemployment prompts a twofold apprehension. First, recession means reduced energy consumption, and as the world's swing producers of petroleum, the Saudis have felt such drops more keenly than others. For example, the recession years of 1975 reduced oil demand in noncommunist industrial countries by 8 percent, OPEC production by 10 percent, and Saudi exports by as much as 17 percent. And of course any such sudden drop can upset the most careful economic planning.

Second, a global recession inspires in Saudi minds a vaguer, but no less genuine, fear of a possible rise of communism in Western Europe and of a weakening or ultimate collapse of global capitalism. The Saudi rulers are not unlike a rich family who has just purchased the penthouse of a luxury apartment: they are not about to wreck the building while moving to the top floor.

Political considerations relating to the Arab-Israeli conflict, contrary to a widespread opinion, seem to have had little if any influence on Saudi oil policy. The 1973 war offered a convenient political opportunity to take advantage of Saudi Arabia's unused economic, oil-price-setting potential. As the communiqué ending the embargo said, its purpose was "to draw attention to the Arab cause" and to make "world public opinion aware of the importance of the Arab world for the welfare of [the] world economy." Since the mid-1970s, the Saudis more than ever have seen themselves as the natural leaders of that Arab world. They identify with the Palestinians as fellow Arabs; but they are particularly alarmed by the continuing Arab-Israeli conflict because it places their pro-Western and pro-American economic commitments at odds with their Arab political aspirations. Similarly, the Saudis objected to Sadat's Jerusalem visit because it was made without any prior inter-Arab consultation and to Camp David because they saw it as leading to a separate peace, to Egyptian defection from the Arab alignment, and to a hardening of Israeli positions on other matters. Hence they joined the meeting of rejectionist Arab governments at Baghdad following the Washington treaty, broke diplomatic relations with Cairo, and canceled plans for further financial aid to Egypt. But they maintained their previous financial commitments and did not even consider curtailing the large flow of Egyptian workers to Saudi Arabia—or of their Saudi earnings back to Egypt. And they seem to have quietly welcomed the establishment of American military facilities in Egypt following the Camp David agreement.

Saudi production levels varied significantly in the three years following the Camp David meeting. In the final months of 1978, their production was stepped up month by month, reaching an all-time high of 10.4 million barrels daily (mb/d) in December. In the first quarter of 1979, Saudi oil continued to flow at the high rate of 9.8 mb/d; for the second quarter (April-June 1979), it was cut back to 8.8 mb/d; for the third quarter it was back at 9.8 mb/d; and in October 1980 it was raised once again to 10.3 mb/d. The major controlling factor throughout this period would appear to have been the situation on the world oil market and the Saudis' desire to prevent a wild escalation of prices. Production rates were raised to a maximum in the months immediately following Camp

David—when the approaching revolution in Iran severely curtailed exports from that country—and maintained at a high level through March 1979, that is, for the duration of the Iranian oil workers' strike.

The only decision whose motivation remains unclear is the 1 mb/d production cut for the second quarter of 1979. One interpretation is that the motive was economic: the Saudis reduced output as soon as the Iranian strike was settled and misjudged the continuing panic that the earlier shortage was causing on the spot market. The other interpretation holds that the Saudis reduced production "perhaps to show their displeasure with the Egyptian-Israeli peace treaty" just signed. In any case, they restored the earlier high production level in July 1979, when the wild price jumps on the spot market had become apparent and shortly after their break of diplomatic relations with Egypt. And in October 1980, at the time of the Iraq-Iran war, they resumed their program of maximum production, which, a year later, enabled them to force the OPEC price hawks back into line. Use of oil as a "political weapon" obviously would have required the Saudis to cut their production throughout this period when the Camp David agreement was being negotiated and implemented and to join Libya and other hawks in charging $40 a barrel or more.

The Saudis' oil policy, instead, has been based mainly or wholly on economic motives of long-range self-interest and on their concern to maintain or reestablish their ascendancy within OPEC. Oil revenues are the kingdom's only economic asset; without oil, Saudi Arabia might quickly revert to the desert economy from which it emerged a generation ago; hence, the price of oil is far too important to be used as an instrument in short-term political maneuvers.

None of this, to be sure, has prevented the Saudis from trying to get additional political mileage out of a policy that is dictated by their economic interest. In 1972, when Aramco was making plans for doubling its oil production capacity, Sheikh Yamani visited Washington to propose a long-term Saudi-American economic partnership and a suitable modification of Washington's Middle East policy. In 1973, having seen both their unit revenue and their export volume grow steadily for two years, they implemented a dramatic price increase—and accompanied it with a well-advertised demand for Israeli withdrawal to the 1967 lines. Five months later, before any significant withdrawal but after general acceptance of the new price, they quietly dropped the demand. Soon after their victory in OPEC's mini price war of 1977, they proposed to Washington the purchase of a major consignment of F-15 fighter jets. And when their production was at a maximum in 1980/81 they proposed, even more insistently, the sale of five Airborne Warning and Control System (AWACS) planes and of additional equipment for the F-15s.

The broad goal of Saudi oil policy since 1974 has remained a slow and steady rise in the world oil price, ahead of the global rate of inflation at times of prosperity and lagging behind that rate, and thus declining in real terms, at times of recession. The policy worked superbly until the end of 1978. The mini price war of 1977 showed that no OPEC country could successfully raise prices beyond the Saudis' preferred levels. During the period of divided prices early in 1977 their own production rose 2 percent and their price 5 percent, for a total gain in revenue of 7 percent, whereas elsewhere around the Gulf, a 10 percent price increase was wiped out by declines in sales of 12 to 19 percent. The Saudis' spare capacity throughout this period was larger than the spare capacity of any other OPEC member and, indeed, larger than the total production of any but one of their twelve associates. Therefore, if any member had tried to flood the market so as to break the common OPEC price, Saudi Arabia could have outflooded it; and if anyone had tried to drive up the price by cutting production, Saudi Arabia could readily have replaced the missing output.

Anyone's missing output, that is, except Iran's, whose normal pre-1978 production was almost twice as large as Saudi Arabia's spare capacity. This posed little danger during the shah's reign, when Iran consistently sided with the price hawks but also consistently kept production at maximum levels. But when the revolution of 1978/79 first reduced and then paralyzed Iranian production, the Saudis' controlling position and OPEC's orderly price structure of the 1970s temporarily broke down.

Some months before the Iranian revolution, OPEC had appointed a "ministerial committee on long-term strategy." The move had been suggested by Saudi Arabia, and Sheikh Yamani's staff played the key role in formulating the committee's first major report submitted in February 1980. The strategy proposed was an indexing system whereby the price of oil would be adjusted quarterly in the light of three factors: global inflation, variations in the value of the dollar against other currencies, and the rate of economic growth in industrial countries. Such a formula would have prevented the 13 percent decline in the "real," inflation-adjusted price of oil that occurred between 1975 and the end of 1978, and instead would have secured a "real" increase of about 3 percent a year in line with economic growth rates in Europe, America, and Japan. Considering global inflation as well as economic growth, the authors of the report themselves estimate that the triple indexing formula, in any typical time period, would bring about a doubling of the current-dollar price of oil every seven years. If the formula had been applied from 1974 onward, this would have brought the price of oil to about $20 a barrel in 1981 and to $40 in 1988.

The report—perhaps in deference to the sensibilities of the more hawkish OPEC members—glosses over several other implications. The triple indexing scheme ties OPEC incomes not only to the global business cycle but also to trends in demand. In a deep and prolonged global recession, not only would OPEC's sales volume decline, but so would its "real" price per barrel until recovery set in—hastened, presumably, by OPEC's forbearance. At other times, if demand for OPEC's oil declined slowly—whether because of new oil finds elsewhere, consumer resistance to high prices, or massive switching to other fuels—OPEC's real income might hold steady. But in any prolonged and severe decline in demand, OPEC's income would inevitably go down as well. The saving grace, from an OPEC point of view, is that, just as the "long-term strategy" envisaged no more than small and orderly increases when OPEC's market power was strong, so it envisages only small and orderly decreases whenever OPEC's grip on the market should weaken.

When OPEC's experts first unveiled their strategy, the Saudis and the price hawks were fully absorbed in their game of catch-me-up and thumb-your-nose. And when the Saudis won their hard-fought victory in October 1981, the new unified price was at $34—a level the strategists had originally envisaged only for 1986 or 1987. Not surprisingly Sheikh Yamani declared in September 1981 that "the so-called OPEC formula for prices is now in the deep freeze."

The sequence of events since 1978 points to the basic flaw in the indexing scheme, which with admirable evenhandedness would restrain both wild price rises and sharp drops in price. The flaw is quite simply that the formula, at any given moment, is likely to suit either the hawks or the doves but not both. When shortage and panic create a strong seller's market, as in 1979 and 1980, the price hawks will blithely disregard any formula and instead drive their advantage to the hilt; when prices are unified at a level above the formula, as in the fall of 1981, the Saudis want it consigned to the "deep freeze." The crucial question was what economic and political pressures there would be on the oil market of the mid- and late 1980s and beyond. Would the weak market of 1981 last for most of the remainder of the decade? If so, would OPEC's money-hungry "high absorbers" start fighting each other for shrinking market shares—that is, indulge in a general price war that would tear down the entire cartel structure? Or would the Saudis and the chastened hawks at last get together on some indexing forrmula like that of February 1980 so as to minimize the infighting and delay OPEC's gradual decline? Or else, would a new, politically caused shortage send the oil market on another price driving binge like that of 1979 and 1980?

ECONOMIC PRESSURES, POLITICAL RISKS

The economic portents for the 1980s, on balance, pointed to a gradual shrinking of OPEC's market, to Saudi Arabia's growing ascendancy within the organization—and hence presumably to the eventual adoption of some indexing formula.

When the Saudis forced the reunification of the price in the fall of 1981, OPEC's production, at 20.4 million barrels daily, was lower than it had been at any time in the 1970s. For the year 1981, OPEC production remained 17 percent below 1980 and 27 percent below 1979. Some temporary factors contributed to this result, such as the unloading of excess stocks left from the panic buying of 1979 and 1980 and a deepening recession in some of the major industrial countries. Other factors were the early signs of longer-range, structural changes: the gradual increase in production from the North Sea, Mexico, and other locations, the shift from oil back to coal, the shift of American car buyers from larger to smaller models—in sum, the long-term elasticity and substitution effects of the price jumps of 1973 and 1979. As OPEC production recovers from its temporary slump of mid-1981, it might be headed for a long period of stagnant or slowly eroding demand throughout the 1980s.

The next crisis for OPEC might come as soon as Iraq and Iran decide to call off the lingering war in Khuzistan that began in the fall of 1980. In the immediate postwar period, each country is likely to push production to the maximum—and within a year or less this might throw an additional 3 or 4 million barrels daily onto that same sluggish world market. The lower the total demand for OPEC oil by then, the more painful it would be for the eleven other members to preserve the existing price structure by letting the market allocate the necessary production cuts among them. And the greater the pain, the greater the temptation for OPEC's hawks to fight each other for shrinking market shares by hidden or open discounts—that is, by indulging in the "chiselling and cheating" that, according to Professor Adelman, will be the downfall of OPEC and of any other cartel.

The question thus was essentially whether OPEC, on its wild price binge of 1979/80, had not overdone it already. At 1981 price levels, the cost of coal per unit of energy was less than half the cost of oil. Since enormous investments in industrial plant and infrastructure are required to effect the shift from oil, those elasticity and substitution effects would be delayed by many years, but once they came they would come inexorably. OPEC might not find out that it had overreached itself until it was too late. Its loose structure served the cartel admirably when it could take advantage of the seller's market of the 1970s—and so did the loosening of long-term supply relationships with the companies in the price spiral of 1979/80. But would they serve equally well in a buyer's market of the late 1980s or 1990s? In cartel economics as in mountain climbing, a false step on the way up merely delays your progress; a false step on the way down is likely to prove fatal.

The answer, in terms of cartel economics, is that OPEC may have had a close escape but the chisel-and-cheat or cliff-hanging scenarios are rather unlikely. The same forces that would shrink OPEC's market will automatically confirm and enhance Saudi Arabia's predominance in the organization, and the Saudi stage directors have no intention of letting those scenarios be enacted. OPEC's hawks, in effect, will be faced with a squeeze play between falling demand in industrial countries, which will cut down their sales, and Saudi Arabia's growing spare capacity, which will keep a lid on their prices. Remember that it was in the fall of 1981, when OPEC's production had dropped to its lowest point in a decade, that Saudi Arabia's position within the cartel was strongest.

At the time of the embargo of 1973, the Saudis were producing just over one-fourth of OPEC's total; by mid-1981 their share had grown close to one-half. What will be even more decisive in future intra-OPEC battles is spare capacity. Since the painful lesson of the Iranian crisis, when their reserve production capacity was unequal to replace all of Iran's missing production, the Saudis have quietly expanded existing oil installations and explored several promising new fields. Their total installed capacity thus may well go from its 1981 level of 11.3 million barrels daily to 12 or 13 million by the mid-1980s. Let us assume that a declining market and peak production in Iran and Iraq will have reduced Saudi Arabia's normal production to 6 million barrels daily: this would automatically put them in a position to double their output at one stroke. Their position thus would be far stronger than in the mid-1970s, when they could raise production by no more than one-third or one-half. If any other OPEC members were tempted to break the price by flooding the market, the Saudis could readily outflood them. In any all-out price war, only the Saudis would emerge as the ultimate winners. Thus there might be some painful confrontations, and even some temporary confusion in the world market—but in the end the Saudis would have less difficulty in restoring price unity on their terms than they did in 1980/81. Indeed, the ideal time for adoption of the Saudis' indexing scheme might be just after the Saudis had nipped an incipient price war in the bud.

Aside from strengthening their hand in a possible future price war, the expansion of the Saudi oil fields also guards against the very real danger of a sudden, politically caused shortage like that of 1979. And this insurance coverage provided by Saudi Arabia's spare capacity will also be enhanced automatically as OPEC's market and the production of individual members continue to shrink. In 1979, the Saudis were able to replace only about half of Iran's production. In the mid-1980s scenario just given, their spare capacity of 5 to 6 million barrels daily could replace, almost or fully, the combined production of Iran and Iraq even after those countries had resumed their position as OPEC's second- and third-ranking producers. Similarly, Saudi Arabia could by then compensate for production cuts due to simultaneous political difficulties in two or three of OPEC's lesser producers, such as Libya, Nigeria, or Venezuela.

The political insurance motive is even more readily evident in another part of the recent Saudi petroleum expansion program. A 750-mile pipeline was completed in 1981 from the northeastern oil fields clear across the desert to the newly bustling port city of Yanbu on the Red Sea. In a few years the pipeline will be able to carry from one-third to one-half of Saudi Arabia's production. Major oil storage facilities, and a second pipeline from Iraq's oil fields, are also being planned. The Yanbu development is clearly designed to make Saudi exports immune, at least in part, to any disruption of the major sealane, from the Persian Gulf via the Strait of Hormuz. From Yanbu the Indian Ocean can be reached via the Bab el-Mandeb at the southern end of the Red Sea; for oil exports to Europe and the United States, the route via an enlarged Suez Canal is even more convenient.

The pipeline from Iraq would diversify that country's oil outlets—and incidentally tie its restless regime more closely to the Saudis. Significantly, too, the new port at Yanbu is only 140 miles across the Red Sea from Ras Banas in Egypt, where, in the wake of the Camp David treaty, major military and air facilities have become available to U.S. forces. The shipment of major quantities of Saudi oil via Yanbu and Suez will also serve to strengthen Saudi-Egyptian relations.

The Yanbu facilities, nonetheless, offer no more than partial protection against just some of the risks that might threaten the flow of Middle Eastern oil in the 1980s and 1990s. The oil shocks of the 1970s were set off by political curtailments, deliberate in 1973 and accidental in 1979, and the Middle East in the late twentieth century remains an arena replete with deliberate enmities and possibilities of accident.

There is continual friction between Qaddafi's Libya and most of its neighbors. Lebanon is divided into half a dozen armed camps. The unresolved Palestinian question continues to fester. President Sadat's assassination in October 1981 indicates the potential of unrest in even the stablest of Middle Eastern regimes. The Soviet occupation of Afghanistan, and Soviet ascendancy in South Yemen and Ethiopia, present a latent threat to the entire region. The assassination of Saudi Arabia's King Faisal in 1975 and the occupation of the holy mosque in Mecca in 1979 illustrate some of the internal tensions that Saudi Arabia has to withstand. The delicate mission of U.S. Ambassador Philip C. Habib in preventing open hostilities between Israel and Syria in Lebanon in 1981, the announcement of plans for "strategic cooperation" between Israel and the United States on the occasion of Prime Minister Menachem Begin's visit to Washington in September 1981, and the passage of the AWACS sale to Saudi Arabia by a single vote in the Senate a month later —all these illustrate the difficulties that the United States may have in manuevering amidst such deep-seated tensions and suspicions. The aerial incident between American and Soviet-built Libyan planes in the fall of 1981 over the Gulf of Sirte is a reminder of how easily Middle Eastern tensions might escalate into superpower confrontation.

Looking more closely at the Middle Eastern political scene, it is possible to distinguish between political tensions that will have little or no effect on oil; upheavals that may interrupt the flow from one or another of the smaller oil-producing countries; events that might place at risk the whole oil flow from the Gulf region; and developments that might change Saudi Arabia's role as the balancer, or insurer of last resort, of the industrial world's imports of oil.

Political upheavals in, or conflicts among, some of the Middle East's non–oil-producing countries are largely irrelevant to the future of the world oil market. The Greek-Turkish dispute over Cyprus, a military coup in the Sudan, rioting in the Israeli-occupied West Bank, a war between the two Yemens, a clash between Jordan and Syria—none of these would curtail the production or flow of oil. Nor does the long-standing Greek-Turkish dispute over oil as yet unexplored in the Aegean Sea affect the price of oil already in world trade. Some of these conflicts might influence the situation very indirectly—by weakening the ties of the United States with friendly countries and thus reducing America's potential as a stabilizing force in the Middle East; by conversely promoting Soviet or Libyan influence and encouraging the forces of instability; or by otherwise setting off shock waves affecting the internal stability of oil-producing countries.

A political upheaval in one of the lesser oil counties—say, Kuwait, the United Arab Emirates, or Libya—would not affect global oil supplies as long as the Saudis could, and would, turn on their excess capacity. Similarly, the Saudis would be able to compensate for a future war disrupting oil production in one oil country—say, an Egyptian-Libyan clash—or even in two—say, Iraq and Iran. Furthermore, most internal conflicts even in oil-producing countries do not affect the flow of oil at all. Since the 1930s, Iraq has experienced a dozen or more military coups —with successive governments ever more determined to increase the country's oil exports. Even the recurrent Kurdish conflict, in the immediate vicinity of the Kirkuk oil fields in Northern Iraq, at no time disrupted the flow of oil. It takes an internal upheaval as serious as the Nigerian civil war of the 1960s or of the Iranian revolution, or direct military attacks on oil fields or export terminals as in the Iraq-Iran war, to shut off a country's production—and, in the future, to create a situation even to *test* the Saudis' standby production and other political insurance measures.

The most critical political dangers would be a prolonged disruption of traffic through the Strait of Hormuz, a Soviet takeover in Iran, or a political upheaval in Saudi Arabia itself.

Oil export routes are more vulnerable than oil fields, since the fields are compact and easily guarded, whereas the transport routes are necessarily strung out and hence subject to interruption by governmental fiat, military action, or sabotage at many points. The closing of the Iraqi pipeline to Haifa in 1948 and of the Suez Canal in 1956 created minor problems, since Middle East oil at the time accounted for only a small fraction of Western energy. But the closure of the canal after 1967, together with the broken pipeline from Saudi Arabia to the Mediterranean, gave Qaddafi his opportunity in his fight with the companies in 1970.

By far the most serious supply disruption would be one at the Strait of Hormuz. It is a wide enough channel not to be blocked by the sinking of one or two tankers, and its southern shore is part of the sultanate of Oman, which has been more receptive than most Middle Eastern countries to strategic cooperation with the United States. But on the strait's northern shore is Iran, some three hundred miles farther north is Afghanistan, and in the strait itself is a small cluster of islands that the British allowed Iran to occupy when they withdrew from the United Arab Emirates in 1971. In the fall of 1980, Iraq threatened to occupy those islands but was dissuaded by Saudi pressure, and perhaps the presence of American AWACS planes assigned to Saudi airspace. Yet the mere threat of naval warfare in the strait temporarily sent insurance rates soaring and for a time delayed the normal tanker traffic through Hormuz.

Even if a shrinking oil market in the 1980s and expansion of Saudi facilities at Yanbu should cut oil traffic through Hormuz far below its maximum of the late 1970s, a closure of the strait would create a sudden oil shortage of at least twice the dimensions of that caused by the Iranian upheaval of 1979—with consequences many times more disruptive.

A Soviet takeover in Iran is not a likely immediate outcome of the revolutionary turmoil in that country, but it remains a distinct possibility in the years ahead. The danger is not an unprovoked military invasion —something the cautious Soviets have not attempted since their abortive attack on Finland in 1939. Rather, there may be a prolonged power struggle in the wake of Khomeini's death, either between various military or civilian factions in Tehran or between guerrilla groups in several civil wars along the non-Persian periphery inhabited by Azeris, Kurds, Turkomans, Baluchis, and others. In the jockeying among coalitions in Tehran, the Soviet-controlled Tudeh party and its allies might gradually gain ascendancy—much as did the Czech communist party in Prague in 1945–48. In any local civil war, the side with better access to outside—

that is, Soviet—supplies would be certain to win. Once a Soviet-backed regime were installed in one of the provincial capitals or Tehran itself, any attempt to oust it would be likely to call into the field Soviet troops —as in Budapest in 1956, Prague in 1968, and Kabul in 1979. Iran, with a tradition several centuries long of centralized government, might be easier to control by military occupation than was Afghanistan, with its remote valleys and anarchic traditions. And any Soviet presence along Iran's one-thousand-mile Gulf coast would bring all of the Middle East's oil, from Basra, Kuwait, and Ras Tanura to Abu Dhabi and Hormuz, under an ever-present threat of Soviet disruption.

A fundamental change in the present regime of Saudi Arabia would also seem to be a remote contingency, yet its effects on world oil might be even more disastrous. The fearful analogies that some Western observers drew between the fall of the shah and the likelihood of a Saudi revolution are ill-informed and misleading. Saudi Arabia is a Sunni, not a Shiite, Muslim country. There is far more wealth than in Iran, and it trickles down more effectively to a smaller population. The kingdom's working class consists of migrants from North Yemen, Pakistan, the Sudan, and other impoverished countries of the surrounding region. The managerial middle class contains a growing proportion of Egyptians, Lebanese, and other foreigners. There is little historic precedent for such a diverse group of migrants being attracted by the higher wages of a booming economy and then caught up in either a bourgeois or a proletarian revolution. Should things begin to seem intolerable, repatriation rather than revolution would be the obvious alternative.

Above all, the Saudi regime has shown its resiliency after the assassination of King Feisal, and the occupation of the Mecca mosque. Unlike the shah's personal tyranny, the Saudi regime is a far-flung oligarchy of several thousand princes supported by a growing number of technocrats, among whom Sheikh Yamani has become the best known. There is safety in numbers. Even a temporary sharp division or confrontation within the ruling family, or a palace coup replacing one ruler with another, would not be likely to disrupt Saudi oil production or deflect Saudi oil policy: both sides presumably would be interested in maintaining the kingdom's petroleum wealth, which, after all, would be the major stake in the contest.

A more fundamental upheaval, might take the form of a military coup —perhaps a coup led by officers appealing to the ethos of Wahhabi fundamentalism on which the kingdom once was founded and supported by a wave of revulsion at the spread of personal and financial corruption. And an austere leadership combining modern technology with religious fundamentalism might care little about the subtle workings of the world oil market, the personal wealth that petroleum has brought to members of the preceding regime, or the stability of Western capitalism. A Saudi military dictatorship might in no sense be a replica of Qaddafi's. But geology and international politics have assigned to the Saudi government a crucial role in managing the world oil market for the next generation or two: the role of keeping in check the OPEC hawks and of compensating for the effects of political upheavals or disruptions in other oil-producing countries. Hence, even a slight shift in Saudi oil policy—a more hawkish attitude on price, a linking of oil production to the diplomacy of the conflict with Israel, or a temporary disruption of the oil fields —might drastically alter the entire global oil constellation.

In sum, the economic prospects of the 1980s—of growing Saudi preponderance in a shrinking world oil market—seem sturdy enough to survive a number of minor political crises. But they are unlikely to survive a prolonged blocking of the Strait of Hormuz; a Soviet presence in Iran that would make all of Middle East oil a pawn in cold war diplomacy; or a collapse of the Saudi monarchy. The probability of each of these political events may be only slight, but the consequences of any one of them would be extremely grave. How soon or in what precise form a major oil crisis might arise is thus impossible to tell. Yet if the crisis came before the Western world had attained its independence from Middle East oil, it might well throw the global market into the sort of chaos of which the Yom Kippur War of 1973 or the Iranian crisis of 1979/80 would have given the merest foretaste. The effects of a further tripling or quadrupling of the world oil price above its 1981 level of $34 a barrel might come close to resulting in the "actual strangulation" of which Kissinger warned in 1974. And the political tensions might well be such that any precipitous move could plunge humanity into a Third, thermonuclear World War.

THE GLOBAL TREADMILL

A glance at the economic scene of the 1970s and 1980s shows how badly the world as a whole has been coping with the effects of even the previous oil crises. The impact of the price jumps of 1973 and 1979 were felt quite differently in different parts of the global economy. The added burden of higher energy costs has placed the greatest strain on the weaker economies—those already hit by recession, unemployment, lack of industrial development, or severe international payments problems. Stronger economies have felt the burden also, but were much better able to carry it; indeed, because of the greater weakness of the others, their competitive position has been strengthened. Thus the 1973 oil shock aggravated the existing economic problems of industrial countries such as Denmark, Italy, and the United Kingdom (before the development of its own North Sea oil) but strengthened the relative position of West Germany, Japan, and the United States. The 1979/80 oil shock deepened an ongoing recession in West Germany, aggravated inflation in the United States, enhanced the relative competitive position of Japan—but threatened to bring into play protectionist pressures that might counteract that Japanese advantage.

The effects of the oil crises of the 1970s were particularly grave in some of the countries caught in the problems of early and uneven industrialization. Thus Peru, Zaire, Turkey, and others found themselves unable to meet their foreign-payments burdens until painfully rescued by the International Monetary Fund, or consortia of multinational banks, or Western governments. And the effects of OPEC's successive revolutions were nothing short of disastrous in countries where population pressure or lack of resources have prevented any sort of rapid economic development —notably Bangladesh and the countries of the Sahel, or drought belt, of West Africa.

OPEC governments might feel that their escalation of oil prices were a measure of sweet revenge against ex-colonialists who had callously exploited their underground resources in bygone days. Yet the cruellest blows of OPEC continued to rain on the weakest and most defenseless countries in the Third World itself. And although OPEC as an organization and its individual member countries rapidly expanded their foreign-aid programs throughout the 1970s, those programs remained highly selective—favoring, typically, fellow Middle Eastern or Muslim nations —and woefully inadequate to the growing need.

In the United States and other industrial economies, inflation and recession were already persistent problems before 1973, and OPEC's impact aggravated both tendencies. In theory, oil-importing countries could absorb the higher prices either by using less oil more efficiently or by increasing exports to pay for the higher cost. But in practice, raising

212   OIL AND TURMOIL

levels of efficiency takes time and concerted effort, and meanwhile recession solves the conservation problem by default. Thus, demand for
OPEC oil remained steady from 1973 to 1975 but declined sharply in the
recession year of 1975.

Similarly, increasing a country's exports takes time and effort, and all
industrial economies cannot increase their export surpluses at once—
somebody's surplus must be someone else's deficit. The alternative by
default is to pay the higher oil price in inflated currency. It happens that
OPEC's preliminary revolution of 1970/71 coincided with the loosening
of the international monetary system from its gold-standard and Bretton
Woods moorings. The Tehran agreement of February 1971, from which
optimists expected a five-year period of oil price stability, was renegotiated only eleven months later to compensate for an 8.5 percent drop
in the value of the dollar. And since 1973 each major OPEC price
increase has accelerated global tendencies toward both recession and
inflation. To what extent the world has paid its oil bill in inflated currencies is indicated by table 3 in the Appendix: Although OPEC's export
income in current-dollar terms jumped from $23 billion in 1973 to $91
billion in 1974 and $272 billion in 1980, its share of total world financial
reserves since 1974 has remained fairly constant. Instead, the annual
increase in the world's consumer price index, as calculated by the International Monetary Fund, has ranged from 9.3 to 15.5 percent since 1973
—as against 4.0 to 6.0 percent in the previous decade.

These inflationary effects of the oil shocks might be likened to a global
treadmill. This particular treadmill was already in motion before the
OPEC passengers climbed aboard, but as they started running forward
with their oil price, everyone else was forced to run faster so as to stay
in place or get ahead. As the treadmill picks up speed so do the individual
runners, as best they can. The healthiest runners do get ahead, others
barely hold their own. The weaker ones get hopelessly overtaken, and the
weakest ones collapse from the exertion and fall off.

For the remainder of this century, the world oil market will operate
under the shadow of political crisis in or around the Persian Gulf. There
is a glaring disproportion between the economic probability of a slowly
growing glut that will enable the Saudi kingdom to reassert its moderate
price leadership and the political possibility of a sudden and even greater
shortage that might send the price of oil to $60 or $100 and precipitate
global economic and political disaster.

This small risk of a major catastrophe makes it imperative that the industrial oil-consuming nations reduce their vulnerability to any future oil shocks and restore a measure of political calm to the troubled Middle East. And both within the global oil market and on the Middle Eastern diplomatic scene this imposes a special responsibility on the United States, which for a century has consumed more oil than any other nation and for a generation has sought to bring peace and stability to the Middle East.

7

ENERGY FOR AMERICA

In the decades before the OPEC revolution, the world still took for granted the availability of petroleum in limitless quantities and at constant or falling prices. Energy consumption was rising rapidly as Western Europe and Japan rebuilt their postwar economies and as the United States attained unprecedented levels of prosperity. Ships and railroads burned diesel fuel instead of coal. Hundreds of electric power plants replaced their coal furnaces with oil burners, and so did millions of individual homeowners. The American and European middle classes moved from the cities to the suburbs and rode to work or to the super-market in ever more powerful automobiles. In America first, and in Europe later, refrigerators and washing machines, television sets and hi-fi equipment, even deep freezes and air conditioners became standard ac-cessories in city apartments or suburban homes. And the neon lights flickered all night to advertise the glittering, high-energy way of life of the affluent consumer society. In the 1960's alone, the world used up as much petroleum as had flowed from all its wells in the preceding century —and by 1970, oil consumption ran at twice the 1960 rate. The world's consumer countries were burning up petroleum as if there were no tomorrow.

Suddenly it turned out that there might be no tomorrow—or at least that tomorrow would be quite different from any of our yesteryears. From its founding in 1960, OPEC had managed to raise the oil income

215

of its member governments tenfold by 1973, then a hundredfold by 1980. Although the price explosion of 1973 slowed down the pace of world oil imports, the bill kept going up, from $125 billion in 1974 to well over $300 billion in 1980.

Oil consumption grew faster in the 1960s in Europe and Japan, but the United States remained the leading petroleum power. American engineers had drilled the first modern well at Titusville, Pennsylvania, in 1859, and Henry Ford had turned the automobile into the vehicle of the masses. The United States remained the leading exporter of oil until overtaken by Venezuela in 1938, and its leading producer until surpassed by the Soviet Union and Saudi Arabia in 1975 and 1976, respectively. To this day, the United States consumes more petroleum than any other country—more than one-fourth of the global total.

This avid thirst for oil meant that the United States soon became the world's most thoroughly explored petroleum province. The strong gushers and large fields were soon exhausted, and new deposits of oil were discovered in ever smaller or deeper pockets. Although the number of wells drilled increased substantially after 1973, no new discoveries were made that were anywhere near comparable to that on the North Slope of Alaska in the late 1960s. Typically, the amounts of oil added to America's "proven reserves" in any given year were less than half the amount of oil produced from domestic wells during the same year. And the ratio of reserves to annual production (Professor Adelman's "ready-shelf inventory") declined from 11.1 years in 1970 to 8.3 years in 1979.

Even before the decline in oil reserves set in, American production costs began to rise. Once the giant new fields of the Middle East started flowing after the Second World War, it became cheaper to produce oil at the Persian Gulf and to ship it across two oceans to Galveston, Texas, than to produce it at home. There followed a quarter-century of policies designed to protect high domestic prices with various import restrictions —and of "draining America first." But having kept foreign oil out when it was cheap and free from political complications, we soon became obliged to import it when it was becoming ever more expensive and attempts were being made to use it as a political weapon. No sooner were import restrictions lifted in the spring of 1973 than the United States became almost overnight the world's leading oil importer, thus vastly adding to the total volume of international oil trade and to OPEC's opportunities. For the United States, the cost of those foreign oil imports amounted to $7.1 billion in 1973, or 10 percent of the total value of our merchandise imports. In 1980, oil imports were only fractionally larger, but the price tag had gone up more than tenfold, to $79 billion; oil now constituted nearly one-third of the cost of all imports.

If the world price of oil had reached its 1974 level of $10 or its 1980 level of $32 as early as the 1960s—or indeed if such steep rises had been foreseen—those railways and power plants would never have installed their diesel engines, those cars might have remained trim and compact, and those successful career people might never have moved to the suburbs. Even our lawmakers in Washington might have grasped that the real threat to our economic security came not from cheap but from expensive foreign oil. All this might have been, but things have turned out differently. The ways of the affluent energy-guzzling society cannot be quickly or easily reversed. The average American automobile is six years old, electric power plants are designed to serve for several decades, apartment buildings and suburban homes are built for half a century, and it will take more than a quadrupling of the price of gasoline or fuel oil to make the suburbanites, or their children, move back to the city. Industrial societies are not, of course, as helpless as the heroin user who takes to the drug when he buys it cheaply and finds himself addicted as the dealer raises the price at will. Still the high-energy habit is easier to acquire than to overcome, and the energy habit that the world has acquired furnishes OPEC with its only oil weapon.

When our petroleum consumption reached its peak in 1978, Americans were using 28 percent of the world's commercial energy and 29 percent of its petroleum and bought 24 percent of the petroleum sold in international trade. The sheer size of our country and its economy, and the intensity of our consumption, make American energy policies crucial not just for ourselves but for the world economy. Our 1978 oil imports were equivalent to the entire output of Saudi Arabia; the *increase* in our imports between 1973 and 1977 was as much as the total oil consumption of all of France; and the reduction in our imports in just a single year, from 1979 to 1980, was equivalent to the oil industry having discovered another North Sea or another Alaska. Too often our political leaders have badgered us with dire predictions and moral exhortations as we have become ever more deeply entangled in the complexities of our high-energy way of life. Perhaps it is time for us to look ahead a bit more confidently at how much we can do to solve our own energy problems with just a little ingenuity and persistence—and at how richly those efforts will be rewarded as they contribute to solving the energy problem for the world at large.

SLICING THE TWO-TRILLION-DOLLAR PIE

America's response to the OPEC revolution, the Arab embargo, and the gasoline queues of 1973 was a confusion of attitudes among the public and a welter of conflicting regulations from Washington. In their moods of foreboding, Americans expected the collapse or the inexorable decline of the good society and the orderly world that they had so long taken for granted. In their spells of wishful thinking, they anticipated the instant collapse of OPEC, or a flood of new oil discoveries that would wash away their energy troubles. In their fits of anger, they fantasized about dropping batallions of paratroopers on distant oil fields or starving OPEC nations into humble submission. Above all, in their moments of curiosity and suspicion, they wondered about the hidden operations of the oil industry. In Washington, the subcommittee on multinational corporations of the Senate Committee on Foreign Relations, under the charimanship of Frank Church, mounted an elaborate investigation of the foreign operations of the U.S. oil industry that began around the time the first long gasoline queues formed in January 1974 and made the headlines on and off throughout the year.

The White House, rising above such confusion in a posture of wise leadership, came forth with a succession of reassuring slogans. In April 1974, on the heels of the oil embargo, President Nixon announced "Project Independence"—a set of non-policies supposedly designed to make us independent of oil imports within a decade. Three years later, President Carter pitched in with characteristic fervor and declared a "Moral Equivalent of War" against the energy crisis.

Meanwhile, most legislation already on the statute books, or newly enacted under the impact of the crisis, did not help reduce our dependence on foreign oil but, on the contrary, aggravated it. Foremost among these policies were price controls. Price controls on gasoline allowed the consumer to live in a fool's paradise of cheap energy and to use oil at such rates that more and more had to be imported at OPEC's vastly higher prices. For, naturally, the price controls did not apply to OPEC; nor, as we shall see, did they serve to limit the oil companies' mounting profits.

The companies were affected more directly by the price controls on domestic crude oil, which were introduced in 1974, frequently redefined over the years, and at last phased out between 1979 and 1981. Those controls created a rather bewildering set of categories. "Old oil," later known as "lower tier oil," which had been in production before 1973, was controlled at about 30 percent above the precrisis level, its price rising from about $5 to $6 by 1979. "New oil," later called "upper tier oil," discovered since 1973 or coming from wells with expanding production, was controlled at a level slightly below that of foreign imports. And "stripper oil," from wells producing ten barrels a day or less, was exempt from controls, its price rising from $12 in 1976 to $23 in 1979.

The purpose of price controls is, of course, to prohibit sales at higher prices at which there still would be willing sellers—and buyers. By setting the price below that natural market level, the controls create demand in excess of supply. In the retail gasoline market of 1973 and 1974, this discrepancy between supply and demand had been overcome by two rather clumsy rationing devices: allocation of wholesale supplies to retailers in proportion to past sales and suballocation of retail gasoline to customers willing to wait their turn in lengthening lines. Many a harried driver would have preferred to avoid the long wait by paying a bit more for his gas; but the law, in effect, mandated rationing not by price but by queue.

Price controls on crude oil would have created similar problems among the customers for crude oil: the country's refineries. Faced with differential price controls, all refineries would have made a beeline for the strictly limited supplies of inexpensive "old oil." They would have shunned the "new oil" and "stripper oil"—and the imported crude oil, which was of course beyond the reach of any of Washington's elaborate price controls. The result would have been a perennial and acute shortage and an imperative need for extensive measures of rationing, by queue, coupon, or some other device.

Instead of devising such a rationing system, Washington's regulators decided to take with one hand what they had given with the other. Having elaborately decreed a set of price regulations that created a two-to-one spread between the more expensive and cheaper categories of crude oil, they then devised a Crude Oil Entitlements Program, which reestablished a uniform price and thus enabled any refinery to buy old or new, domestic or foreign oil at will, without incurring any price penalty or competitive disadvantage.

To give a simplified example, assume that, in a given period of 1977, refinery A had been processing 100,000 barrels a day of domestic oil acquired at $9.50 a barrel and refinery B had the same amount of daily "throughput" of 100,000 barrels of imported oil costing $14.50. The entitlements program would impose a payment of $2.50 a barrel on A, "entitle" B to receive a similar payment, and thus bring both their crude oil acquisition costs to $12 a barrel—or rather, after addition of a slight bureaucratic service charge by the U.S. Department of Energy, to $12.10.

Over the years of its existence, the entitlements program was modified numerous times, usually to create a financial bias in favor of the country's smaller (and hence, usually, less efficient) refineries. The small-refinery bias diminished somewhat over time, as a growing number of "teapot refineries," built in response to the opportunity thus offered, took advantage of it in the mid- or late 1970s. As the entitlements program was phased out in 1980 and 1981, a whole group of "teapot refineries" faced bankruptcy and were shut down.

On a nationwide basis, the price controls and entitlements kept the average cost of crude oil to refiners (and hence indirectly of refined products to consumers) below the world market replacement cost. The spread in "refiner acquisition cost" for domestic and foreign oil, was $5.36 a barrel in 1974, dropped to $3.96 a barrel in 1978, and rose to as much as $9.66 in 1980.

This artificial lowering of domestic crude-oil prices below world market replacement levels meant, of course, that Americans were encouraged to consume considerable amounts of additional oil every year. Internationally, this put additional buyer's pressure on the world oil market—at a time in the mid-1970s when sagging demand in Europe and Japan made it difficult for OPEC to maintain its $11 to $13 price level. Our friends abroad had often suspected that American oil companies had had some direct or indirect part in encouraging the OPEC revolution; now they were sure that America's price controls and oil-import subsidies added to the world price of oil that they were forced to pay.

The story of the crude-oil price controls, entitlements, and "teapot refineries". is typical of Washington's fitful attempts at regulating the oil crisis in the 1970s. There were gasoline price controls to protect automobile drivers from added expense; there were allocation rules to protect filling-station operators from the whims of gasoline wholesalers; there were entitlements to protect refiners from unfair competition. But there was no program to protect the nation as a whole from the impact of

OPEC's revolution—no program to reduce oil imports, to limit the drain on our balance of payments, or to help reduce global oil prices. Indeed, measured by such criteria, the programs were downright counterproductive. The retail price controls encouraged oil consumption far beyond America's domestic production, and the entitlements subsidized the resulting imports.

All this meant that the nation in the mid-1970s was left to rely, by default, on the worst possible means of restraining its thirst for oil imports: economic recession. The 1973/74 oil shock happened to coincide with a prolonged business downturn, and oil price increases deepened that slump. But any slowdown in economic activity automatically reduces energy consumption: unemployed workers do not commute to their jobs and idle factories burn no oil. Hence, in the recession years of 1974 and 1975 our oil imports remained at 6.1 million barrels daily, compared to 6.3 million in 1973. But then, as recovery set in, they took off as never before: 7.3 million barrels daily imported in 1976, 8.8 million in 1977, with a temporary peak of 10.0 million reached in February of that year. Full-scale oil operations on Alaska's North Slope brought about the first increases in domestic production in 1977 and 1978—after a steady decline since 1970. But our oil imports from 1969 to 1977 increased by 158 percent. One oil analyst suggested that, just to keep our oil imports steady, "we would have to discover another . . . Alaska every two or three years."

Two months after that import peak of 10 million barrels daily, President Carter transmitted to Congress his ambitious energy program, which he declared to be a Moral Equivalent of War. But still, American oil consumption continued to climb, reaching an all-time high of 20.4 million barrels daily early in 1979, and imports remained virtually unchanged: 8.5 million barrels daily in 1977, 7.9 million in 1979. Soon Russell Baker, the *New York Times'* gentle satirist, discovered that the acronym for that program spelled MEOW—and before long, most of Carter's proposals were rejected by Congress.

Numerous reasons can be adduced to account for this sorry record of our energy policy in the 1970s. Historically, the open frontier had been the nation's formative experience; there had been no precedent in two centuries for dealing with major constraints on a basic raw material and none since the Great Depression for coping with economic problems transmitted from overseas. More immediately, each president had to place the continuing energy problem into his political context of the moment. Nixon tended to see in the Arab-Israeli War of 1973 and in Project Independence welcome distractions from his Watergate troubles. Jimmy Carter, whom the electorate had sent to Washington as a rank outsider, correctly diagnosed that the energy crisis was the foremost problem confronting Americans in the late twentieth century. And he wrongly concluded—with characteristic rectitude and naïveté,—that the energy problem should therefore be the very first on his administration's agenda: before his political team had gained any experience in controlling the bureaucracy or shepherding legislation through Congress.

Beyond such past and present factors, there was a changing economic reality that was bound to transform all relevant future perspectives. The OPEC revolution, by sending oil prices spiraling upward, was adding immensely to the potential value of any barrel of America's oil and any cubic foot of America's natural gas still left underground. Robert Stobaugh and Daniel Yergin have calculated that "In early 1973 the value of domestic U.S. oil and gas reserves was $200 billion at then current world prices. On January 1, 1980, the value of those reserves (even allowing for depletion) had increased, at OPEC prices, to more than two trillion dollars—a tenfold increase. How this increase in value should be divided among consumers, producers and the government has been at the core of the political struggle over price decontrol and the windfall tax." And indeed it was at the core of much of our energy-policy formulation throughout the 1970s.

Two trillion dollars, any way you look at it, is a huge amount of money. If you were a statistician, you might compare it to the size of America's gross domestic product, which in 1980 was 2.6 trillion, and reflect that OPEC's revolution had secured nine months' free income to every man, woman, and child in the United States. If you were a Washington lobbyist, of course, you would realize that this bonanza was not for everyone, but only for those authorized by the appropriate legislation to share in it. And if you were a congressman presiding at interminable hearings on oil price control and decontrol, entitlements and allocations, windfall profits, and taxes and subsidies for synthetic fuels—why, you might get a dawning sense of having been appointed umpire in the biggest sweepstakes of the century.

No wonder that so few of our laws and regulations in the 1970s had any effect in reducing our foreign-oil dependence or in helping to roll back the global price of oil. There was no time to try to shrink the two-trillion-dollar pie when everyone was busy figuring out how to slice it. Consumer advocates and automobile associations championed price controls that would rebate all or most of that two trillion dollars to gasoline and fuel-oil users. Oil companies, on the contrary, wished those controls to be lifted and to keep the two trillion as their established right and as a prime asset for their future. A legal battle raged between the governments of oil states, such as Alaska and Louisiana, which wished to tax the oil at the wellhead, and federal authorities which insisted that the oil, being destined for interstate commerce, be subject only to federal taxation. And of course any new source of potential tax revenue, whether in Juneau, Baton Rouge, Albany, or Washington, sends myriad special interests rushing into the arena which insist on spending it, almost before it is collected, for the worthiest of purposes: more Medicaid and Social Security, better schools, improved mass transit, support for the arts and humanities, a stronger global defense against communism, subsidies for the production of oil from shale or coal, a bailout for Detroit's ailing automobile industry, or urgently needed tax relief for the poorest taxpayers—or indeed for the wealthiest and, hence, presumably most productive.

A HOMECOMING FOR THE OIL COMPANIES

Few Americans had occasion to reflect that as a result of price controls, their gasoline prices only doubled in 1973–74 while world oil prices quadrupled or that Europeans were paying three times as much for *their* gasoline. Instead, American drivers and homeowners grumbled freely about rising prices at the pump and about mounting fuel bills, and they were only too ready to blame the oil industry. All the talk about "energy crisis," they were inclined to suspect, was no more than a smokescreen for the companies' mounting profits. If OPEC had any part in the alleged crisis, who could tell whether or not the companies had put those Arabs up to it? There was strong popular support for price controls as the most obvious way of restraining the companies' appetite for profit—until it became embarrassingly clear in the course of the 1970s that the controls had no such restraining effect.

Regardless of the price controls on gasoline and old crude oil, the crisis of 1973/74 increased profits for the oil companies—as indeed any scarcity or rising price is likely to do. A group of thirty petroleum companies analyzed by the Chase Bank's financial experts saw its total revenues rise by 130 percent between 1972 and 1974 and their net income by 138 percent. In 1974 Exxon for the first time replaced General Motors at the top of *Fortune*'s list of the 500 largest American corporations, and by 1979 nine out of the top fifteen on that list were oil companies. Nonetheless, the reasons for this affluence were far more complex than the man-in-the-street—or rather in the gasoline queue—tended to suspect.

The oil companies, far from encouraging OPEC, had first ignored it and then fought it—and lost. Among the many factors that combined to bring about the oil shock of 1973 were OPEC's newly gained resiliency from its 1968 "best of practices" doctrine; the British departure from the Middle East and Qaddafi's aggressive dealings with the companies in Libya; the end of American import quotas and the sharp rises in world demand; Sadat's pressure for Saudi support in the war of 1973, and the Saudis' expectation that a production cut would make prices and revenues soar.

The companies' contribution to this train of events was indirect and incidental. They had created the network of "vertical integration" in the world oil industry—from wells in Venezuela and the Middle East through tankers and refineries to gas pumps in Europe, Japan, and America—of which OPEC was now trying to take advantage. By yielding to the Middle Eastern governments' financial demands in the 1950s and 1960s, the companies had strengthened the bargaining position of the Qaddafis and Yamanis in the 1970s. As prices of foreign oil rose above those in the United States, the companies had advocated the lifting of import restrictions; Mobil had advertised the "energy crisis" to prepare the public for higher prices. And in 1973 oil executives had urged Washington to adopt a more pro-Arab policy for fear that their lucrative Middle Eastern concessions might be held to ransom in the next Arab-Israeli conflict.

Nonetheless, the climax of October 1973 caught the companies unprepared, and it turned out to be a defeat of strategic dimensions. In Libya in 1970 and at Tehran in 1971, the companies still had been able to bargain—tenaciously, if at times ineffectually or with divided ranks. On October 16, 1973, they were faced with a unilateral *diktat.* Arab governments were now claiming the right to set prices, amounts of production, and destinations of exports; and the higher prices were quickly emulated throughout OPEC. Nationalization of the concessions in most countries did not officially come until the mid- or late 1970s. But after October 1973 there was little left to expropriate. For an oil concessionaire who is no longer allowed to set prices and production levels or to choose his customers no longer has effective property rights over the oil; he has been downgraded to the status of a paid technician—perhaps a profit-sharing technician—in charge of pumping the oil and shipping it overseas.

If the value of America's underground oil reserves in the 1970s increased to $2 trillion, so OPEC's control of two-thirds of the world's petroleum reserves was worth at least $1.5 trillion in 1973 and more than $15 trillion in 1980. Nonetheless, there was no serious discussion between OPEC governments and companies in the 1970s about compensation for such astronomic assets. The companies had long since recouped their original investments in Venezuelan or Persian Gulf oil; and the governments claimed the underground oil as theirs by sovereign right. Moreover, it was OPEC that had catapulted the value of the oil to the $15 trillion level and, therefore, meant to reap that full benefit—just as its members bore the full risk if OPEC's price structure should collapse. Discussions between governments and multinational companies at the time of nationalization centered on two secondary questions: the companies' continued "access" to most of the oil produced in a given country and the size of the discount from the price charged to other buyers, which they would receive in return for their continuing technical services. Sheikh Yamani, for one, was in favor of preserving that "access" —that is, of guaranteeing the companies' position as bulk buyers—and of allowing them a discount of no more than $0.30 a barrel, or about 3 percent at 1974 price levels. Until the crisis of 1979 few OPEC nations departed from that pattern of "access," and the discount remained at a level of about $0.30 to $0.40 even as prices rose sharply in 1979.

The pattern of nationalization, in the sense of technical management of the oil fields by the country's own citizens, varied widely. Venezuela had large enough cadres of technicians to handle most of the production and refining of its oil. Libya continued to deal with both major and minor, American and European, companies throughout the 1970s. In Saudi Arabia, Aramco continued to provide its full range of technical services under the direction of Saudi officials. Iraq for some years tried to rely on its own and on Russian technicians until, somewhat contritely, it came back to deal with the more experienced Western companies

This continuing role of the large companies as wholesale buyers of OPEC oil was an arrangement to mutual advantage. It allowed OPEC to set the global price of oil, and the companies to help allocate the production quotas among the cartel's members and to collect OPEC's "tax" from the ultimate consumers. It also gave the companies an opportunity to stock up more than the required minimum of working inventories at times when they saw an OPEC price rise in the offing. Such extraordinary inventory profits largely account for the steep rise in the net foreign earnings of oil companies in 1974, 1979, and 1980.

A further benefit of OPEC's revolution accrued to those companies with domestic American production: it was, as it were, their current slice of the two-trillion-dollar pie. American companies had been operating their domestic wells at a profit in 1973, when the price of crude oil averaged $3.89 per barrel at the wellhead. But in 1974, even the most tightly price-controlled "old oil" could be sold at an average of $5.03; and "new oil," for which exploration costs were likely to be somewhat higher than in the past, could be sold at double that price for $10.13. All in all, the domestic oil industry since 1973 has produced an amount of crude oil averaging 8.6 million barrels daily (not considering natural gas liquids), but the average price per barrel went up from $3.89 in 1973 to $21.59 in 1980. Hence, annual gross revenues at the wellhead jumped from $13 billion to $22 billion in 1973/4 and from $39 billion to $68 billion in 1979/80—a fivefold increase in only seven years.

The combined effect of those indirect benefits of the OPEC price revolution for the American oil industry are well documented for the major segment of that industry analyzed by the Chase Manhattan Bank. Its net income from foreign sources reached a peak in 1974 and again in 1979/80, but declined in intervening years, whereas net income in the United States showed a continuously upward trend. From 1975 through 1978, domestic income exceeded income from foreign sources.

"Chase Group" of Oil Companies: Net Income 1972–1980

	U.S.	*($ billion)* Foreign	*Total*
1972	3.7	3.2	6.9
1973	4.1	7.5	11.7
1974	6.4	10.0	16.4
1975	6.0	5.5	11.5
1976	7.5	5.6	13.1
1977	7.8	6.6	14.4
1978	8.3	6.7	15.0
1979	12.8	18.7	31.5
1980	15.6	19.6	35.2

The 1979/80 oil shock thus provided a second bonanza for the oil companies, both at home and abroad. Yet it also implied some risks for their international situation in the future. Saudi Arabia and a few other countries kept intact their long-term supply arrangements with the multinationals. But other governments, foremost Libya, freely diverted exports to the fast-rising spot market; and by 1981 the companies in their turn became reluctant to buy Libya's and Nigeria's overpriced crudes. In November 1981, Exxon became the first major American oil company to announce its withdrawal from Libya.

The *de facto* expropriation of company interests that had begun in the early 1970s thus was largely complete by the early 1980s. The future might see companies and OPEC governments increasingly in "arms-length" relationships of buyers and sellers for short-term contracts. The net result was increased competition—among companies scrambling for scarce supplies when prices were rising, and perhaps in the future among OPEC governments for customers at times of stagnating or falling prices. And for the companies, intensified competition over the long run was likely to mean a decline in profit margins.

Specifically, in the temporary downturn that the world oil market took in 1981, the large inventories accumulated in 1979 and 1980 turned into a mixed blessing. By 1981 as prices first stagnated and then sagged slightly, the companies faced a difficult choice: mounting storage and capital charges if they continued to hold on to their excess inventories or direct losses and further downward price pressure if they sold them off.

The domestic scene, which in the 1980s was bound to become crucial for the oil companies, also held contradictory elements. The phasing out of price controls, decided upon toward the end of the Carter administration and accelerated after Reagan's advent, promised a powerful boost to the oil industry's domestic earnings just when changing relations with OPEC governments put their foreign prospects under a cloud. The Windfall Profits Tax—another part of Carter's second energy program —diverted a sizable portion of those added earnings to the federal treasury. But under the ambitious synthetic fuels program of federal subsidies for the production of oil from shale rock, and of oil or gas from coal, those tax receipts were to be returned in part to one segment of the industry. Carter administration experts estimated that receipts from the windfall tax by 1990 might amount to anywhere from $146 billion to $270 billion, and that $88 billion of that latter amount would be spent on synthetic fuels. Under Reagan's first budget, adopted in the summer of 1981, the Windfall Profits Tax was cut in half, and the synthetic fuels program substantially reduced.

PREACHING, PRICING, AND THE LITTLE ENGINE THAT
COULD

The lifting of price controls had been recommended by Jimmy
Carter almost as a counsel of despair. The energy program he had
proposed at the time of his Moral Equivalent of War in the spring of 1977
had been completely emasculated by Congress in the following year. The
"gas guzzler tax," which would have created a powerful disincentive
against the purchase—and hence the manufacture—of cars with poor
fuel economy, was rejected outright. Also rejected was a standby tax
on gasoline that Carter had hoped to apply so as to discourage petroleum imports as they came to exceed certain maximum limits in the
future.

Among the measures that survived the congressional ordeal were a set
of automobile efficiency standards that mandated an improved performance for new cars up to a level of 27.5 miles per gallon by 1985; the
removal of price controls on certain categories of natural gas; a program
for converting some power stations from petroleum to coal; and a variety
of tax credits for home insulation and solar heating. After eighteen
months in Congress, the "moral equivalent of war" had turned into the
immoral equivalent of a multiple skirmish.

Meanwhile as our oil consumption set new records and our imports
declined only slightly below the all-time high of 1977, the Carter administration came under severe criticism from our allies: for example, at
the Economic Summit meeting in Venice in June 1980. The leaders of
Western European nations and of Japan were keenly aware of some of
the global oil realities that Americans had so long chosen to ignore.
American per-capita consumption of energy was more than twice as high
as in other leading industrial countries. Some of this, of course, was due
to our higher standard of living; but even for each unit of gross national
product, our energy consumption was 44 percent higher than that of
West Germany, 74 percent higher than that of Japan, and as much as
86 percent higher than that of France. The most glaring contrast was in
transportation. In 1979 European gasoline prices were two to three times
as high as in the United States—ranging from $1.39 per gallon in Britain
to $1.87 in West Germany and $2.25 a gallon in Italy and France. Not
surprisingly, Europeans were driving fuel-efficient cars that were averag-
ing over 20 miles to the gallon compared to our sorry record of fuel
economy dropping from 14.4 miles to the gallon in 1962 to a unprece-

dented low of 13.1 miles to the gallon in 1973 and inching back up to 14.1 miles to the gallon by 1978.

It was clear to Japanese and European leaders that our price controls and other patchwork energy policies were boosting our own oil imports at a time when they were strenuously limiting theirs. Thus between 1974 and 1979, West European imports declined by 2.5 percent; and ours rose by 5.9 percent per year. In relative terms, oil imports constituted only one-fifth of total energy consumption in the United States, as against one-half in the European Economic Community, and over two-thirds in Japan. This meant that whatever impact a given OPEC price increase might have on the production costs of American industry and on our balance of payments, the strain on Europe would be twice—and that on Japan three and one half times—as great. But in absolute terms, our oil imports were as large as Europe's and far larger than Japan's. Hence our oil purchases were a major factor in putting upward pressure on world prices. OPEC's impact on America was only slight; but America was OPEC's best customer so that our consumption patterns were a major factor in handing OPEC its recurrent opportunity to escalate world prices.

We are a country richly endowed in domestic energy, yet we insisted on living high on the OPEC oil barrel as well. Four-fifths of American energy consumption, as of the late 1970s, continued to be supplied by our domestic resources of petroleum, natural gas, and coal—as well as minor amounts of nuclear energy and hydroelectric power. And those American domestic energy resources were larger than the total energy consumption, domestic and imported, used by the average European or Japanese. Yet we insisted on supplementing our ample domestic supplies with a flow of imports that might seem like a mere trickle to us but was bound to seem to anyone looking from abroad like a major stream. The American's after-dinner snack turned out to be as large as his friend's supply of daily bread. And our oil imports for frills were raising the energy costs for Europe's and Japan's bare essentials.

Minor irritations added to such interallied friction. Following the opening of the Transalaska pipeline, production from the North Slope reached 1.1 million barrels daily in 1978 and 1.5 million in 1979—an amount equivalent to the production of the United Arab Emirates or of Mexico, or to half the oil consumption of France or of West Germany. Valdez, the southern terminal of the pipeline, was 1200 miles by sea from Seattle, but West Coast refineries were unable to handle the full amount of additional supplies from Alaska. Valdez was also 3300 miles from Yokohama, and economic logic would have required the excess of Alaskan oil to be exported to Japan—with the foreign-exchange earnings helping to cover the cost of our imports to the East Coast. But Congress, in the midst of taking President Carter's 1977 energy program to pieces, was in no mood to listen to such economic reason: No exports from Alaska were allowed; instead, much of the oil had to be laboriously trans-shipped from ocean-going tankers via smaller vessels through the Panama Canal to make the six- or seven-thousand-mile journey to U. S. Atlantic ports. In 1974 Henry Kissinger had eloquently explained to West Europeans and Japanese the urgent need for a common energy policy among the major industrial nations—lest they be caught in "a vicious cycle of competition, autarchy, rivalry, and depression, such as led to the collapse of the world order in the thirties." The International Energy Agency had been set up in Paris in response to those urgings in order to plan such a coordinated energy approach. But now, with its newly found Alaskan oil, the United States itself was setting a prime example of shortsighted protectionism. Naturally, such contradictory behavior left our allies with little respect for either our energy policy or our economic leadership.

Just how far apart the industrial nations were in coordinating their energy policies became apparent in 1979 and 1980. As the shutdown of Iran's wells early in 1979 sent prices soaring, Europeans, Japanese, and Americans alike scrambled for the spot market, where prices rose from $13 in 1978 to over $40 late in 1979 and again late in 1980. The second OPEC oil price shock crucially depended on this competitive bidding-up of the price, which empirically demonstrated the new prices that a jittery traffic would bear.

No wonder that President Carter at Venice in June 1980 was being put on the defensive by his colleagues such as Chancellor Helmut Schmidt of West Germany, President Valéry Giscard d'Estaing of France, and Prime Minister Masayoshi Ohira of Japan. The year before, Carter had offered his second major energy program, vowing to "limit" our oil imports to 8.2 million barrels daily for 1979, and "not one drop more than" 8.6 mb/d, in 1980 or later years. By 1990 he hoped that the portion of the Windfall Profits Tax spent on encouraging synthetic fuels would have added 2.5 mb/d derived from coal or shale. In view of the failure of his 1977 Moral Equivalent of War program, Carter's main device for restraining consumption now was the phasing out of price controls, which would let the consumer bear the full brunt of the oil price rise, combined with a windfall profits tax, which would limit the extra earnings of the oil industry.

Price decontrol had been adopted almost as a last resort—but, lo and behold, it worked. In 1979 our oil imports—at 7.9 million barrels daily —stayed a bit below Carter's immediate target; in 1980, instead of rising slightly as he had foreseen, they dropped by as much as 20 percent. The phasing out of price controls happened to coincide with the second oil price shock on the world market, and the combined effect on American consumption was dramatic. The decline in oil use in 1979/80 was twice as large as at the time of price controls in 1973/74. By mid-1981, our oil imports and our oil consumption were, for the first time, both back below their 1973, pre-embargo levels. The American consumer, it turned out, was prepared to respond instantly and intelligently to such price signals as the doubling of gasoline prices from $0.70 to $1.40 per gallon. Not only did drivers become more careful of their mileage, but car buyers made a headlong rush from the fuel-inefficient products of Detroit to the economical Toyotas and Volkswagens.

In the automobile industry, the result was a clamor for subsidies to the bankrupt Chrysler Corporation, and pressure for "voluntary" restraints on Japanese car exports. But the effect on gasoline consumption and oil imports would be felt for years to come, as the proportion of twenty-five- or thirty-mile-per-gallon compacts to the ten- or fifteen-mile gas guzzlers steadily increased over the years. Ever since the crisis of 1973, Americans had been exhorted to mend their wasteful ways and wearned that we might all freeze in the dark some day soon—but gasoline prices had not risen much beyond the cost of living, and everyone had driven much as before. Now it turned out that Americans were not addicts to their wasteful ways. A little pricing will save a lot of preaching.

When my children were small, one of their favorite stories that I would read to them at bedtime was about the Little Engine That Could.

Once upon a time there was a railroad train all filled with circus animals and toys and candy for the children. But it got stranded at the bottom of a hill. Its engine "simply could not go another inch." Three other engines that happened to pass by all haughtily refused to help. One said it was a Passenger Engine that would not move freight. One was a freight engine that would not move animals or clowns. The third was a Rusty Old Engine that said "I must rest my weary wheels." But then "The very little engine came chug, chug, chugging along." Right away it offered to help. And "she said 'I think I can. I think I can. I think I can.' And she hitched herself to the little train." And at the top of the hill she puffed proudly: " 'I thought I could. I thought I could. I thought I could. . . .' "

The story, suitably translated from the railway to the automobile age, symbolizes the solution to America's energy problem in the late twentieth century. The "big engines that couldn't" (or "wouldn't") were the Buicks and Dodges, the Mercurys and Pontiacs of the 1960s and 1970s. They encased their hapless inmates in several tons of solid armor plate, but they were so mean and clumsy that they delivered no more than eight or ten miles to the gallon. And then came the "little engines that could" —the Toyotas and Volkswagens and Hondas, which Americans insisted on importing from Japan or Germany in growing numbers in the 1970s; and the Chevrolet Chevettes, Plymouth Horizons, and Ford Mustangs that Detroit—two energy crises and one near-bankruptcy later—learned to build right here at home and delivered 25 or 30 or even 40 miles to the gallon.

Of course, there will be other ingredients in the great American energy solution of the 1980s and 1990s. More off-shore drilling will add to conventional petroleum supplies, and price deregulation may make available more natural gas. Perhaps coal gasification and liquefaction (that is, synthetic gas and oil from coal) can at last stand on their own feet without the invariably corrupting effect of government subsidies on sound business management. Power stations can shift back from oil to coal, perhaps with "cogeneration" of steam for district heat to pay for the added cost of proper antipollution safeguards. More efficient technologies can reduce the "transmission losses" (the energy used up in heating high voltage wires and inducing static in radios miles away, which now wastes a sizable proportion of all electric power), and thus give us more flexibility in locating power stations near coal mines. Some sectors of the chemical industry may be able to shift back from oil to coal as well. Slurry pipelines may prove to be an efficient way of transporting coal—perhaps to cities such as Los Angeles that have to supply their water at great distance in any case. Home owners can install better insulation and get used to more economic thermostat settings for heating and air conditioning, thus saving on their own fuel bills and the nation's bill for oil imports. There is a wide-open fronteir for ingenuity, and every little bit helps.

There even is a place in such a comprehensive energy solution for the big or medium-sized engines of the railroad age. A revitalized rail system will be able to haul coal from mines in the Midwest and the Rocky Mountains to markets and export harbors on the East and West coasts —and compete with the airlines for intercity traffic and with the private automobiles for metropolitan commuting. It is, above all, an efficient, high-speed rail system that keeps down the energy consumption for transport in such countries as France and Japan.

Still and all, efficient automobiles remain the single most important ingredient in the over-all energy solution, and this for several concurrent reasons.

• A larger proportion of oil consumption is burned up in automobile engines in America than in any other major industrial country.

• Technologies now in the experimental stage (such as oil and gas from shale or coal) will take a decade or more to develop for a mass market. Other technologies (for example, solar or fusion energy) are unlikely to find mass application before the twenty-first century. But the technology for producing 35- or even 50-mile-per-gallon cars already is well known and could be fully applied in a few years.

• Of all energy-using equipment—such as power stations, furnaces for heating, or industrial equipment or residential buildings—automobiles (along with household utensils) have the shortest natural lifespan. The average age of cars on the roads is only six years. Hence any improvement in automobile efficiency will make itself felt sooner than other changes in energy-use patterns.

• A massive shift to other forms of transportation—subways, urban and intercity buses, railroads—involve large capital expenditures or considerable readaptation of life styles, or both. By contrast, 40-mile-per-gallon cars would require no such expenses or readaptation and they would allow us to commute to work or drive to the supermarket as freely as before but using one-third the energy getting there.

• A detailed comparision of energy-use patterns in all major industrial countries shows that American industry is by and large more energy efficient than its European and Japanese competition. In residential and commercial heating and cooling, the differences are largely accounted for by climate. The most glaring contrast is in transportation. The U.S. is a more sparsely populated country, and Americans travel more and farther than do Europeans and Japanese—but they also burn up one and a half times as much fuel doing it.

No *DEUS EX MEXICO*

The fuel-efficient cars that Detroit was at last beginning to produce represented a sober, pragmatic approach to the energy problem, equally far from the moralizing of the cosmic pessimists—who insist that we are being punished for our wasteful ways of the past and that doomsday is near—and the wishful thinking of the blithe optimists—who assure us that there is plenty more oil and that it is OPEC whose collapse is imminent. The answer to the pessimists is that despondency and self-flagellation have never solved any problem yet. And one important reminder to the wishful thinkers is that the real problem is not the supply of oil but its price.

Oil finds in the late 1960s and 1970s in the North Sea, Alaska, and Mexico have been impressive. Singly they have each added as much as a new Kuwait, or Venezuela, or Iraq. Taken together, they have helped reduce OPEC's share of world oil from 53 percent in 1973 to 38 percent in 1981. But OPEC's influence has long extended far beyond the thirteen members of the organization. The threats of shutdown in Libya in 1970 and the abrupt production cutbacks in Saudi Arabia and other countries in 1973 made OPEC into the marginal producer, and, as any student of Economics 101 will tell you, market prices are set at the margin. The new oil finds, therefore, have added to supplies but not changed the price.

Occasionally, a newly exporting country, such as Nigeria in the late 1960s or Mexico in the mid-1970s, may give a slight discount until its market share is established. If the transportation route is significantly shorter between a given exporter and importer—as between the United States and Mexico—there is a small transport premium to be divided between them. Otherwise, all exports follow the prevailing—that is, the OPEC—price. North Sea oil from the United Kingdom and from Norway is usually exported at prices comparable to Libyan and Algerian oil of equally high quality. Non-OPEC producers such as Malaysia, Trinidad, and Oman have quietly followed OPEC's lead. Soviet oil is exported to Western countries, and even to Eastern European communist states, at prices comparable to Persian Gulf oil. And of course even American domestic producers have followed the OPEC lead as soon as price controls have been lifted.

In the late 1970s there were widespread press reports freely suggesting that Mexico's new oil finds would make it into another Saudi Arabia. And soon there was speculation that perhaps our American import needs could be fully supplied from Western hemisphere sources, if only the United States could persuade Mexico and Canada to form a common energy market. There are two reflections that will quickly dispel this pleasant fantasy. First, some of the estimates of Mexican reserves encouraged by the government vastly overstated the actual amounts of oil discovered—usually by lumping together "proven" and "probable" reserves, and reserves of oil and of natural gas (under the conveniently fuzzy label of "hydrocarbon reserves"). In fact, Mexico's proven reserves are only one-fourth as large as those of Saudi Arabia. Second, there are no blandishments that will induce our southern or northern neighbors to sell their oil to us below world prices, and at those prices it makes little difference where the oil comes from. There is, for our energy problems of the late twentieth century, no *deus ex Mexico*.

By contrast, the pragmatic, little-engine-that-could approach has important indirect benefits. In the late 1970s, almost half of our oil came from imports; hence as soon as the total amount of oil used began to decline, the saving in imports was more than twice as great. For example, in 1980 American oil consumption was down 9 percent from 1979, but imports were down as much as 30 percent; in the first half of 1981, imports declined by another 13 percent. Indeed, 1980 imports were barely four-fifths of the target President Carter had set in his second energy program of 1979, and by mid-1981 the United States, thanks to decontrol and rising world prices, had reduced imports by as much as President Carter had hoped to obtain by 1990 from his costly and ambitious synfuels program.

This better American performance had as much to do as did high Saudi production with creating the miniglut of 1981. Together, Americans and Saudis were hastening the day when economic forces might bring OPEC back to a unified price structure, with small and predictable increases, as long advocated by the Saudis. The improved American record was also bound to brighten the prospects for future energy cooperation with Europeans and Japanese, such as the standby emergency oil-sharing program developed by the International Energy Agency.

Indeed, there were numerous ways in which lower oil consumption improved our prospects for weathering any future political interruptions of supply. We noted in the last chapter that declining rates of normal OPEC production have automatically enhanced the relative size of Saudi Arabia's spare capacity. The same is true for the Strategic Petroleum Reserve in the United States.

The SPR was one of the more purposeful aspects of President Carter's original energy program of 1977. It got off to a slow start—only 67 million barrels, or about a week's worth of imports, by the end of 1978, and 91 million barrels the next year. But in 1981 the Reagan administration took advantage of softening oil prices to resume the buildup of the Strategic Reserve. Once the SPR reaches its preliminary target of 500 million barrels, it might be drawn down in an emergency at a rate of 1.5 million barrels daily, thus compensating for an entire year for the loss of 17 percent of our imports at the record 1977 rate, or as much as 27 percent at the more modest mid-1981 rate. And for about three months, such storage could compensate even for a cutoff of anywhere from two-thirds to all of our imports—an extremely unlikely contingency. It will be recalled that the production cuts accompanying the Arab embargo reduced the over-all level of world oil imports by up to 7 percent for a period of about three months, and those to the United States somewhat less. Indeed by 1982 or 1983, it will not be impossible to imagine a situation where Saudi reserve production capacity and U.S. reserve storage might compensate for several months for the loss of production from any two OPEC countries.

Perhaps the time might come soon when our Strategic Petroleum Reserve and similar stocks might be thought of as antidotes not just against physical interruptions in supply but also against sharp increases in price. In short, stored oil such as the SPR might in future serve as a buffer stock to prevent the sort of panic buying and price driving that proved so disastrous in 1979 and 1980.

On the world petroleum scene, the price jump of 1979/80 had reduced consumption and imports and thus belatedly encouraged the forces of price moderation. On the political scene, the trends were far more contradictory. Yet even in a region as turbulent as the Middle East was bound to be in the 1980s, it was true that every move toward peace, as between Egypt and Israel at Camp David, and every explosion prevented, as in the Iraq-Iran war or in the Lebanese crisis of the spring of 1981, was likely to encourage the forces of moderation and enhance the prospects for peace and security. Just as the United States, as the leading petroleum consumer and importer, played the crucial role in tempering the petroleum scene, so the United States, as the leading superpower intimately involved in the Middle East, would have to take the lead in numerous ways in calming the forces of political conflict.

8

LEADING FROM STRENGTH:
AMERICA AND THE MIDDLE EAST

PEACE AT CAMP DAVID

On March 26, 1979, three weary but elated men assembled in front of television cameras on the White House lawn to sign the Egyptian-Israeli peace treaty. It was a moment of signal triumph for Anwar el-Sadat, Menachem Begin, and Jimmy Carter.

For President Sadat, the signing was the culmination of the political strategy he had pursued, off and on, since his accession in 1970: an honorable peace with Israel that would regain Egypt's territories and put an end to three decades of futile belligerence; an about-face in international alignment from Moscow to Washington; and a chance to tackle Egypt's pressing economic problems with a liberal economic policy and American aid.

For Prime Minister Menachem Begin, it was a moment of political vindication. As leader of the Jewish terrorist underground in the mid-1940s he had done his part to bring about the departure of the British from Palestine. But when Israel became independent in 1948, it had been his bitter antagonists, such as Chaim Weizmann and David Ben Gurion, with their moderate rhetoric and their compromises, who had become the founders of the new state; whereas Begin was relegated to leadership of a small and extreme party in perpetual opposition. Then, in 1977, a change of electoral fortunes had finally brought him to power. He had outlived Weizmann and Ben Gurion. Let history acknowledge them as the founders of the state; it would be he, Menachem Begin, whom future generations would remember as the peacemaker.

Jimmy Carter signed as a witness only, yet it was fitting that he should play the host. At Camp David the previous September, he had labored long and hard to snatch agreement from the jaws of failure. In the checkered record of Carter's presidency, the Mideast peace treaty of 1979 stands out as the greatest achievement. Without active American participation, without promises of massive military and economic assistance to both sides, and without Jimmy Carter's singleminded, almost desperate, dedication, Egyptians and Israelis might never have overcome the legacy of a generation of hostility and suspicion.

The signing of the treaty marked a mid-point in a five-year process of recurrent, intensive negotiations. The exploratory moves had been made after Carter's accession in January 1977 and Begin's election victory of March; they culminated in Sadat's dramatic visit to Jerusalem in November 1977, when he assured his listeners in the Knesset that "we welcome you among us with full security and safety." The basic principles of the peace treaty had been hammered out in a thirteen-day marathon session at Camp David, Maryland, on September 5–17, 1978—and it was only natural that the treaty and the process of diplomacy that produced it should be remembered as the Camp David accords. Its most tangible provision, the evacuation of Israeli forces from the Sinai peninsula, was not scheduled to be completed until April 1982. On the much thornier question of peace between Israel and the Arab Palestinians—and of the future of the West Bank, the Gaza Strip, and East Jerusalem —the Washington treaty created no more than a framework for negotiations for political autonomy as a possible preliminary to ultimate settlement. Only developments over the next several years would show whether the Camp David accords would be a first step toward such an over-all settlement or a decisive step away from it.

Simple logic had long required that Arabs and Israelis should make peace. Nasser's threat to drive Israel into the sea and the Palestine Liberation Organization's vow "to liquidate the Zionist presence in Palestine" had remained empty boasts; the PLO, indeed, had come closer to destroying the governments of Jordan and Lebanon than of Israel. Hostility toward Israel had poisoned the politics of an entire Arab generation, made the more radical governments and organizations heavily dependent on the Soviet Union, and exposed Arab discord and weakness for all to see. Israel had fought four wars in twenty-five years—three of them ending in victory and the fourth in a standoff. Yet in view of the ratio of populations and territories, no victory by Israelis over Arabs could ever be final. Ultimately, Israel's security could be guaranteed not by further victories but only by peace agreements with its neighbors.

For successive administrations in Washington, there was much urgency behind such arguments. The Arab-Israeli conflict had opened the doors wide to Soviet influence in the Middle East at a time when Soviet power had been contained in Europe and, thanks to the Sino-Soviet conflict, was receding in the Far East. The 1973 war had propelled Washington and Moscow into their most serious confrontation since the Cuban missile crisis of 1962; and by interrupting major oil supplies it had threatened the Western powers and Japan with economic disaster.

The events of 1973, nonetheless, constituted not only a danger but also an opportunity. The military standoff, to which Washington's actions had notably contributed, had restored Arab pride and given Israelis a new sense of vulnerability; in sum it had made both sides receptive to the logic of peace. For two decades the Soviet Union had exploited Arab-Israeli enmity; now it was up to the United States to take advantage of the possibilities of reconciliation.

But here the argument, by its simple logic, ran into a dilemma: should the many obstacles to a lasting peace be removed by a piecemeal or a comprehensive approach?

Israel in 1967 or 1973 had been at war with Egypt, Syria, and Jordan; and since 1975 the Israeli-Lebanese frontier had posed the gravest threats to peace. Issues that must be resolved in making peace included the future of territories occupied by Israel in 1967 (the West Bank, Gaza, the Sinai peninsula, and the Golan heights); the definition of Israel's future boundaries; the Palestinians' demand for a state of their own and for a right to return; the future both of the wells on the Gulf of Suez that were supplying much of Israel's oil and of the settlements that successive Israeli governments had allowed—or encouraged—to be established in parts of the Sinai and the West Bank; and, thorniest of all, the question of Jerusalem. A comprehensive approach would bring together all the parties at once, say at a conference in Geneva, as well as Americans and Russians as facilitators and guarantors of such a settlement. A piecemeal approach, on the contrary, would bring together only two of the principal parties at any one time—say, Israelis and Egyptians or Israelis and Syrians—perhaps with active American mediation; and it would take up the issues one by one.

A comprehensive approach was implicit in the resolutions (numbers 242 and 338) adopted in the United Nations Security Council after the wars of 1967 and 1973, which blandly juxtaposed opposing demands, such as Israel's for "secure and recognized boundaries" and the Arabs' for evacuation of occupied territories. A comprehensive approach also had long been championed by the United States Department of State. More recently it had been embodied in a detailed blueprint drawn up by a study group at the prestigious Brookings Institution, of which Carter's national security adviser Zbigniew Brzezinski had been a prominent member. A truly comprehensive solution, so its advocates hoped, would commit all parties to peace; it would leave no Arab country with the stigma of having broken ranks by making a separate agreement; it would offer to Israel a full peace rather than a partial truce. Comprehensive talks would provide a chance for mutual accommodation over a wide range of issues; and the result would prove durable because it would remove all likely areas of friction in advance.

The critics remained unconvinced by such reasoning. By trying to address all issues at once, you would risk maximizing the disagreements, and delay on the thornier issues would impede all progress on the easier ones. By assembling all parties at one single conference, you would strengthen the hand of those—Syrians, PLO, Soviets—least interested in peace; or as Kissinger put it, "A comprehensive approach . . . would inherently favor the radicals by giving the most intransigent governments a veto over the entire process." Granted that the Russians might try to sabotage any peace settlement after its conclusion, it did not follow that they must be given a decisive say in its very formulation. The pragmatic course—so the champions of the piecemeal approach insisted —was to take up the easiest issues first and work gradually up to the harder parts of the agenda. And by concentrating first on the more moderate Arabs and on the less contentious issues, you would establish a precedent of accommodation and compromise and build up a momentum that eventually would allow you to solve the remaining issues.

In the aftermath of the October War, Henry Kissinger had followed the piecemeal approach. He had adjourned the Geneva conference after only a single perfunctory session in December 1973. Then, in successive exercises of his celebrated "shuttle diplomacy," he had negotiated three disengagement agreements. The first, on January 18, 1974, had taken Israeli troops back to the western shore of the Suez Canal. The last, also between Israel and Egypt, had secured a further Israeli withdrawal behind the strategic Mitla and Gidi mountain passes and from the Abu Rudeis oil field. This agreement, on September 4, 1975, had allowed Sadat to reopen the canal and to rebuild the devastated cities along its route; and Israel had been reassured by undertakings of large amounts of American military and economic aid and of American reconnaissance, which would substitute for the intelligence that Israel had been able to gather from the now evacuated mountain positions. An agreement of June 25, 1974, between Israel and Syria had created a small demilitarized zone along the Golan Heights, and thus reduced the danger of a renewed outbreak on that front.

Kissinger's piecemeal approach had succeeded brilliantly where earlier comprehensive attempts, such as the United Nations resolutions, the Jarring mission, and the Rogers Plan, had failed. The September 1975 agreement had resulted in the first major Israeli withdrawal from the 1967 lines and allowed Egypt to restore control over all populated parts of its territory. The Golan agreement had brought into the disengagement process even the truculent Syrian dictator Hafez el-Assad. But Kissinger's success had had its heavy price. First there had been a severe strain in American-Israeli relations—indeed, President Ford in March 1975 had ordered an over-all "reassessment." And eventually there had been American commitments to Israel of unprecedented magnitude: not only arms and economic aid far beyond earlier levels, but also a commitment that Washington would not deal with the PLO until it recognized Israel. Above all, it soon became clear that the agreements of 1974 and 1975 would not be the prelude to further agreements or even negotiations. America had expended its full leverage on no more than a partial agreement. Sadat indeed had regained his canal and his cities, but most of the Sinai remained occupied. Israel was no nearer to being recognized by her neighbors, let alone to peaceful relations with them. There had not even been an attempt to deal with the Palestinian issues. And since the momentum had run out, a totally new effort would be required to breathe new life into the peace process.

It was widely taken for granted that such a new approach would have to await the voters' verdict on President Ford in November 1976 and on Prime Minister Yitzhak Rabin in March 1977—the diplomacy of democracies often limps along from election date to election date—and that, this time, it must be a comprehensive approach. Indeed, the Carter administration made much progress during the spring and summer of 1977 in removing, one by one, the obstacles to a second Geneva conference. Carter emphasized that the Palestinians should have their own "homeland" and must "participate in the determination of their own future." Since a separate PLO delegation would have been unacceptable to Israel, Sadat proposed a careful scheme whereby a Palestinian professor teaching at a university in the United States would join a single, composite Arab delegation. A joint U.S.–Soviet communiqué on October 1, 1977, defined the terms on which Washington and Moscow would act as co-chairmen at Geneva.

But then it turned out that Sadat and Begin had taken things into their own hands. After months of preliminary secret contacts in Morocco and Romania, Sadat announced dramatically: "There is no time to lose. I am ready to go the ends of the earth. . . . I am ready to go . . . to the Knesset, to discuss peace with the Israeli leaders." Begin promptly extended the invitation. The main purpose of Sadat's visit to Jerusalem, on November 20, 1977, was to remove the "psychological barrier" that in his estimate constituted "70 percent of the whole problem."

It would seem that the prospect of having to deal, however indirectly, with Palestinian representatives had alarmed Begin, and that the American-Soviet communiqué had alarmed Sadat as well. Israel had reason to consider the Soviet Union its most implacable enemy, and Sadat, who had dramatically broken with the Soviets in 1972, had no desire to see them reappear as peacemakers and peacekeepers in the Middle East. Both men may have been wary of the complications that the presence of other Arabs would bring to Geneva. Sadat was eager for direct negotiations that would create an irresistible momentum for a general peace. Perhaps Begin was eager to make an agreement with Sadat now so as to avoid having to make agreements with other Arabs later; if so, the seeds of many future difficulties were sown at the start.

In any case, the comprehensive approach was now out, and the piecemeal approach in. Even Jimmy Carter, his Geneva hopes shattered, conceded, on second thought, that "it's much more important to have direct negotiations between Egypt and Israel than to have us acting as a constant dominant intermediary." Nonetheless, it became amply apparent during the following months and years that Egyptians and Israelis would have a hard time talking to each other at length or fruitfully without a continual American presence: hence the session at Camp David in September 1978, and hence the signing ceremony at the White House the following March.

There was some hope, certainly among the Egyptian and American participants, that Camp David at last would combine the best of the piecemeal and comprehensive approaches. It set up a strict timetable for full Israeli evacuation of the occupied Egyptian territories and for establishment of full diplomatic relations between the two countries. It offered a second timetable for talks on the West Bank, Gaza, and East Jerusalem. Sadat was clear that he saw in Camp David a first step toward a comprhensive peace: his bold initiative had overcome the "wall . . . of suspicion" and shown other Arabs the way to peace and recovery of territories. And Carter was full of hope that moderate Arab governments —Saudi Arabia and perhaps Jordan—would almost at once join in the peace process.

But Begin had flatly refused to allow any formal linkage between the Sinai and the Palestinian parts of the agreement, and the negotiations had almost fallen apart over this. The explanations offered by the American negotiators in a number of "side letters" inevitably sounded somewhat lame. Any strict reading of the treaty's text tended to support the critics' contention that Sadat had indeed been lured into signing a separate peace. The Saudis, far from joining, were firm and vocal in their condemnation of the Camp David approach. The PLO chimed in with dark warnings that the United States would be punished for its betrayal, and that all tangible American interests throughout the Middle East would be held to ransom. Many Israelis were fearful that a change in government in Cairo—indeed a single assassin's bullet—might shatter their hopes for peace.

Nonetheless, the agreement between Egypt and Israel proved viable, and the evacuation of Sinai and the normalization of relations went through several successive stages according to the original schedule. The Saudis, far from imposing any new embargoes, kept their oil production at record levels for most of the three years after Camp David. Their diplomatic break with Egypt expressed their disapproval of Sadat's unilateral move; yet it was not accompanied by ejection of the hundreds of thousands of Egyptian workers from Saudi Arabia, which economically would have hurt both sides. The PLO seemed to be at a low ebb and for some years brought off no terrorist spectaculars. By mid-1981 there were even distinct signs that both Saudi Arabia and some of the PLO leaders, notably chairman Yassir Arafat, were prepared to enter some process of peace negotiation. Above all, there was no change in Egyptian policy even when the assassin's bullet did strike in Cairo and Sadat was replaced with his chosen successor, Hosni Mubarak.

Supporters of the Camp David process could claim that it was the crucial move toward peace. Without Egypt, no other state could risk war against Israel. Thus the protracted Arab-Israeli conflict had been reduced from its earlier cataclysmic proportions to those of an ordinary conflict—of the sort with which the Middle East is replete. True, the Washington treaty did not bring peace to the region: no one treaty and no number of signatories could do that; but it removed the most prominent and recurrent threat of war. Whereas Arab and Israeli eyes used to be fixed on the wrongs of the past, the treaty helped many of them refocus their attention on the dangers of the present and the future. When Russia moved into Afghanistan at the end of 1979, it was Iraq— long a Soviet client—and Saudi Arabia that led other Islamic states in denouncing the invasion. When Iraq's power-hungry leader, Saddam Hussein, launched his attack on Iran, the neighboring Saudis turned to the United States for the latest in defense equipment.

Critics could object that Camp David not only had failed to settle the Palestine question but, by freeing Israel's southwestern flank, had seriously impaired any prospects for later settlement. The growing normalization of Egyptian-Israeli relations had left the Begin government free, in mid-1981, to bomb Iraq's nuclear reactor and to sharpen its confrontation with Syria in Lebanon. The talks on Palestinian autonomy envisaged by the Washington treaty, spluttered along inconclusively through much of 1979 and 1980, and after a prolonged lapse were resumed—with no better prospect—late in 1981.

One major difficulty was that Egypt was not an authorized spokesman for the Palestinians under Israeli occupation, let alone for those in exile; and an assassination campaign by the PLO was directed against all those in Gaza or on the West Bank who showed any inclination to cooperate with Sadat or to endorse the Camp David process. Even an Israeli government wholly dedicated to peace with Arab Palestinians would have found it difficult to make meaningful concessions in the preliminary negotiations—since Sadat could make no reciprocal concessions, and since further points would have to be conceded to resident Palestinians, Jordanians, PLO, or whomever, once the negotiations began in earnest.

The second difficulty was that Israeli authorities in a dozen years of occupation had not encouraged any political leadership to form among West Bank or Gaza residents with whom Israel could have constructively negotiated. The Jordanian political machine on the West Bank had long since decayed; and although Israel's opposition Labor party from time to time talked about preferring a "Jordanian option" in future negotiations, the fact was that the Arab League in 1974 had unanimously recognized the PLO as the sole authorized spokesman for the Palestinian people. The PLO's victory in most of the mayoral and town council elections on the West Bank in April 1976 and growing diplomatic recognition in the world at large further enhanced its apparent legitimacy. Yet the PLO's solemnly stated fundamental aim of a secular Palestinian state implied the destruction of Israel, and the PLO's condemnation of the Camp David peace was quick and categoric.

The most serious obstacle to progress on the Palestinian question was Begin's growing intransigence. His May 1979 Palestine autonomy plan envisaged for West Bank and Gaza residents "personal," not territorial autonomy; reserved crucial issues such as land and water to the Israeli occupation authorities; and generally seemed designed as a vehicle for perpetuating rather than for phasing out the military occupation. Before 1977 Israeli governments had allowed new Jewish settlements on the West Bank only in thinly populated areas nearest the pre-1967 border. Begin, far from suspending such activity for the duration of the negotiations with Egypt, authorized or condoned a growing stream of settlements throughout the entire West Bank. The Israeli election of 1981, in which Begin's Likud bloc gained 48 out of 120 seats (as against only 43 in 1977) showed that his truculence enhanced rather than diminished his popularity with the voters. Begin's coalition of August 1981 did not include Moshe Dayan or Ezer Weizman, who had played crucial roles in the negotiations with Egypt, and generally was far more homogeneous and extremist than that of 1977, which had carried him through Camp David.

CRISIS IN IRAN AND AFGHANISTAN

While Egypt and Israel were proceeding on their tortuous road toward peace, the rush of other events demonstrated that there were many tensions and dangers in the Middle East quite unrelated to the Arab-Israeli conflict. On January 16, 1979—four months after Camp David and two months before the Washington treaty—the shah fled from Iran; on February 1, the Ayatollah Ruhollah Khomeini made his triumphal return from exile, hailed by the masses as the rightly guided Imam, who would bring Shiite Iran back from a thousand years of the kingdom of darkness to God's own kingdom of light. On May 20, the government of Israel announced its plan for Palestinian autonomy, and on May 25 Israeli forces evacuated el-Arish, the largest town on the Sinai peninsula. On November 4, left-wing militants occupied the American embassy in Tehran, seizing some fifty hostages. On November 20, five hundred men variously described as zealots or trained guerrillas, occupied the holy mosque in Mecca, to be ejected only twenty-six days later by Saudi units with the help of French special forces. On December 26, the Soviets invaded Afghanistan, and on January 23, 1980, President Carter declared the Persian Gulf a region of American "vital interest." Three days later Israel completed evacuating the Western two-thirds of Sinai, and on February 26, Egypt and Israel, after more than three decades, exchanged ambassadors for the first time. On April 24, an attempt to rescue the Tehran hostages by American military force ended in utter fiasco in a remote Iranian desert. On September 4, 1980, Iraq launched its invasion of Iran's oil-rich Khuzistan province. On January 20, 1981, the Tehran hostages were at last released, after more than fourteen months of captivity.

The Iranian revolution caught Washington totally unprepared. In the quarter century since the CIA had helped restore the shah to his throne, the Iranian monarchy had become ever more central to Washington's strategic thinking—and ever more remote from its own population. In the mid-1950s, Iran was the centerpiece of Dulles's "Northern Tier" conception of Middle East defense against threats from the Soviet Union. In the following decades, although the shah was a driving force in the OPEC revolution of 1971–73 and was not above occasional flirtations with Moscow, Washington supplied Iran with a growing stream of weapons. Both Kissinger and Brzezinski considered the shah's Iran a major asset for regional stability. No one in Washington seems to have reflected how crucially such calculations depended on the regime's domestic support, or how rapidly this support was eroding under the combined impact of the influx of oil money and American weapons and of the regime's growing reliance on its odious secret police. Perhaps the single-minded concentration of Carter's Middle Eastern experts on the problems of Arab-Israeli peace made them the less prepared for the upheaval in Iran.

When the shah's difficulties became obvious in the fall of 1978, some of those experts saw the shah's salvation in timely concessions and liberalization; others saw it in resolute repression; and each side, with a growing sense of urgency, took its case to the media. If only the shah would commit himself to sincere enough reforms he might lead the country toward constitutional monarchy. If only the U.S. Navy could bring an aircraft carrier (two weeks' journey away in the Philippines) to warn off the Soviets, then the Iranians could be left to settle their differences and Washington would try to live with whatever the result. If only the shah would leave the country briefly, perhaps the monarchy could be saved for his son. If only a coalition could be patched together between the shah and the National Front, or Khomeini and the army. If only the CIA, instead of suspending all intelligence gathering in a friendly country, had forecast the impending storm. If only the National Security Council had ordered a timely study of the resurgence of Islam.

None of this was of any help to the shah. His own vacillation and Washington's public musings only embittered and emboldened the opposition, which had long denounced the shah as America's puppet. And in the eyes of the rest of the world, America's prestige came to be the more inexorably involved in his downfall.

The Iranian revolution created a power vacuum. In Tehran there were successive bloody purges, continuing factional struggles, and armed gangs sporadically taking the law into their own hands. As usual on such occasions in Iranian history, the outlying provinces took advantage of this confusion by defying the authority of the center. The danger of the situation seemed to be emphasized by the Soviet invasion of neighboring Afghanistan—which brought Russian forces within less than 400 miles by air of the Strait of Hormuz, through which more than half of the world's oil imports was passing. In contrast to the previous year's irresolution, Carter now decided to take a strong, immediate stand: "Any attempt by any outside force to gain control of the Persian Gulf region will be regarded as an assault on the vital interests of the United States of America, and such an assault will be repelled by any means necessary, including military force." To lend emphasis to American disapproval of the action in Afghanistan, he ordered grain shipments to the Soviet Union suspended and American participation in the 1980 Moscow Olympics cancelled. And with evident White House encouragement, the statement about America's vital interests in the Gulf came to be referred to as the "Carter Doctrine."

Meanwhile, the handling of the hostage crisis undercut such assertions of strength. For well over a year, day in day out, Americans in impotent anger watched on their television screens the misfortunes and outrages inflicted on fifty-two fellow citizens. Such publicity in itself was a major victory for the Iranian fanatics—for it was bound to feed their macabre fantasies of their own global power and of the cosmic evil embodied in Carter and the United States. Economic sanctions were proclaimed against Iran as early as December 1979, but diplomatic relations were not broken until April 7, 1980. For months Carter used the hostage crisis as an excuse to avoid meeting Senator Edward Kennedy, his rival for the Democratic presidential nomination, in direct debate. Repeatedly he emphasized that the survival of the hostages was his paramount consideration. Yet when the military rescue attempt was launched in April 1980, even its advocates admitted that the operation if "successful" might save the lives of no more than half the captives. When the mission ran into trouble because a helicopter crashed into a cargo plane in a supposedly well-rehearsed refueling maneuver, Carter called off the operation and dramatically proclaimed the failure to the world at large. Even the so-called government in Tehran did not learn of the rescue mission until this announcement. In sum, Carter's handling of the protracted crisis is best described as erratic.

Some critics of the Carter Doctrine have held that the president overreacted. The Soviets had moved not into the Persian Gulf, where Carter promised to defend "vital interests" with "military force"; rather they had moved into Afghanistan to shore up a shaky pro-Soviet government in Kabul that was slipping from Moscow's grip. Their move was essentially defensive, and there was no evidence that it was part of any longer-range plan of regional expansion. Indeed, some of the more hopeful critics concluded, widespread anti-Soviet guerrilla activity might yet turn Afghanistan into Moscow's "Vietnam."

Such criticisms were ill founded. The invasion of Afghanistan was indeed an ominous development. Moscow had established its influence or control over a number of countries in the region—first Egypt and Iraq in the fifties and sixties; then smaller countries at the periphery such as South Yemen, Somalia, or Ethiopia in the 1970s; then once again more central countries such as Libya and Syria in the late 1970s. But events in Egypt, Iraq, and Somalia showed that any country at some physical distance retained the possibility of reversing this drift into the Soviet camp. In Eastern Europe, the Soviets had invaded Hungary in 1956 and Czechoslovakia in 1968 to force faltering satellite regimes back into line. In Afghanistan they used the same technique for the first time to expand their sphere of control beyond the 1945 lines. If the Russians managed to consolidate their position in Afghanistan, the takeover was likely to become irreversible, and put them in an even stronger position to put political and military pressure on neighboring Iran.

Carter's strategic perception of the Afghanistan crisis and the long-term dangers it posed to the Gulf can thus hardly be faulted. What may rightly be questioned is the tactics and timing of a pronouncement such as the "Carter Doctrine." For it soon became embarrassingly clear that there had been no advance coordination with actual or potential allies, or even among White House, State Department, and Pentagon. The Russian threat to the Gulf was as yet hypothetical and remote in time. If it materialized, the paramount question might indeed become where America and its allies would draw the line. In the meantime, however, many prior questions arose.

Who would be our allies in the region? Saudi Arabia's role would obviously be crucial, because of its vast territory and vaster oil resources. Yet the Saudis remained unwilling to enter openly into any defense arrangement with Washington or to make available any bases. As long as the Palestinian question remained unsettled, their fear was that any such overt alignment would jeopardize their relations with most other Arab countries. Perhaps they also remembered Kissinger's vague threat of December 1974 of using force against unspecified oil fields. And in any case, it was not their habit to rush into any major new policy without careful study—or obvious need. Later in 1980, when Iraq's attack on Iran suggested a more immediate military danger to themselves, they did not hesitate to ask for immediate help from Washington—in the form of advanced reconnaissance planes known as AWACS (airborne warning and control systems).

What would be the attitude of our major allies outside the region? If the Persian Gulf was "vital" to the United States, surely it was five or six times as vital to those allies. The Gulf in 1979 supplied 77 percent of Japan's oil needs, 59 percent of Western Europe's, and 12 percent of America's. Yet Chancellor Helmut Schmidt ruled out West German participation in any military action to protect the Gulf oil fields or shipping lanes, and the Japanese referred to the antiwar clause of their constitution. Perhaps those allies had lived too long under the American protective umbrella to develop a more activist attitude overnight. Perhaps they were uneasy over America's impulsiveness—and aware that even the most successful military action was likely to interrupt the flow of oil first and restore it only much later.

Among the allies, the French were most accustomed to diplomatic-military initiatives in Africa or the Middle East, and their naval forces in the Indian Ocean were third in size after America's and Russia's. For all those reasons they would be the most valuable partners in any military action that might be required. Yet the French were jealous of their independence, and from time to time insisted on cultivating close relations with nations with whom the United States was at odds, such as Qaddafi's Libya, Khomeini's Iran, or Saddam Hussein's Iraq. Above all, since their withdrawal from NATO's military command structure, they were willing to cooperate only quietly and behind the scenes rather than overtly in response to solemn "doctrines."

And finally, *what forces would the United States put behind any line drawn around the Persian Gulf if and when the time came?* When Carter made his pronouncement in January 1980, our nearest naval base was the Indian Ocean island of Diego Garcia, 3000 miles from the Gulf's oil fields. The British had a long-standing arrangement for use of military facilities in Oman, located at the vital Strait of Hormuz; and the French had a naval base at Djibouti nearly 2000 miles away. Arrangements for American use of Egyptian airfields and negotiations for use of naval facilities in Oman, Somalia, and Kenya were completed only later in 1980 and 1981. Above all, American military planners were only beginning to develop their strategy for the Persian Gulf region and to coordinate the roles that the navy, air force, or seaborne and airborne troops might play. Although the creation of a "Rapid Deployment Force" was announced in March 1980, it remained painfully obvious for some time that it was not much of a force, and that its deployment would be far from rapid. The aborted hostage rescue attempt of April 1980 only emphasized Washington's lack of preparation—or military judgment. Only in June 1981 did Reagan's Defense Secretary Caspar Weinberger settle a prolonged interservice feud between the army and the marine corps and order that the forces assigned to the Persian Gulf region be transformed into a separate regional command—by the end of 1982.

Fortunately, the Soviet threat proved less acute than Carter had feared. Tenacious resistance throughout the rural areas of Afghanistan committed Soviet forces to a protracted struggle. The attack from Iraq strengthened Iranian cohesion, at least for the moment. The crisis in Poland provided a major distraction for Kremlin policy makers from whatever might have been their Middle Eastern plans beyond the occupation of Afghanistan. Although Begin's growing militancy for the moment frustrated all hopes for a wider Arab-Israeli settlement, the Camp

David agreement held as between Egypt and Israel, and evacuation of the remainder of Sinai was expected by April 1982. Even the hostages were released on the very day Jimmy Carter turned over his office to Ronald Reagan.

Reagan's tough statements, during the campaign and after his election, characterizing the Iranian captors as "criminals," "kidnappers," and "barbarians" may have served to speed the release of the hostages; and Carter's stand on "vital interests" in the Persian Gulf a year earlier accorded broadly with Reagan's inclination to subordinate most foreign-policy questions to the global Soviet threat. In applying this paramount concern to the Middle East, Secretary of State Alexander Haig spoke of the need "to develop a consensus of strategic concerns throughout the region."

Such a plea for consensus was a vast improvement on John Foster Dulles's rigid notion three decades earlier of a formal, regionwide defense pact. Yet Reagan's and Haig's early approach to the Middle East also posed many dangers of oversimplification. There were many Middle Eastern problems of concern to the United States that could be neither wished away nor readily subsumed under the rubric of East-West confrontation—foremost among such problems being the Palestine question and the continuing risk that local conflicts posed to the flow of oil from the Middle East. And there was the danger—under Reagan as under Carter—that an impulsive, piecemeal approach, far from allowing any latent consensus to come to the fore, would aggravate the existing dissensions.

The Reagan administration's early relations with Israel and Saudi Arabia provided a good illustration. The Carter administration had been emphatic that Begin's settlement policy on the West Bank was a flagrant violation of international law; and it had regularly condemned Israel's frequent military incursions into southern Lebanon. By contrast, Ronald Reagan, in his pre-election television debate with Jimmy Carter, suggested that those settlements were politically unwise rather than illegal. And Secretary of State Haig, on his visit to Israel in April 1981, reassured Israeli leaders that such actions to protect Israel from guerrilla incursions were entirely appropriate. A country as dependent on the United States as Israel is tends to be acutely sensitive to such nuances of attitude and expression, and it is not too much to suggest that such Washington pronouncements encouraged Begin's subsequent militancy, including the confrontation with Syria in May 1981 and the large-scale air raid on Beirut in July. When Washington responded by suspending the previously scheduled delivery of advanced American warplanes to Israel, Begin's reaction in turn was one of surprise and disappointment. The mission to the region on which President Reagan dispatched American ambassador Philip C. Habib prevented an immediate Syrian-Israeli confrontation in Lebanon in the spring and summer of 1981 and even succeeded in drawing the Saudis closer into the process of multilateral diplomacy. Yet when the Reagan administration went forward with earlier plans to sell five advanced reconnaissance planes (AWACS) to Saudi Arabia for delivery later in the decade, the reaction was one of acute alarm in Israel and among its friends in the United States.

By October 1981, Reagan obtained approval for the AWACS deal, but not without expending considerable political capital on the effort: the House of Representative overwhelmingly passed a resolution of disapproval—which failed by a single vote in the Senate. A "Memorandum of Understanding" on "strategic cooperation," signed by the Reagan and Begin governments on November 30 needed no congressional approval. Yet it contained few specifics, and in its generalities perpetuated the previous fallacy that the Soviet threat alone would be enough to create a strategic consensus between the United States and various Middle Eastern countries.

It was high time for Washington to try to pull together these and other potentially conflicting strands in our Middle Eastern policy. Such a reassessment would do well to combine an analysis of the situation as it emerged from the Camp David peace process with a broader consideration of the successes and reversals of our Middle Eastern policy in the decades since the Truman Doctrine of 1947.

MIDDLE EAST ALIGNMENTS AND REALIGNMENTS

Ever since 1947 the United States had sought to secure the political independence of the Middle East from the European colonialism of the past and from any Soviet colonialism of the future. Our eagerness to see an end to European domination of the region first expressed itself in encouraging the termination of the British mandate over Palestine. The line against Soviet expansion was drawn first in the Truman Doctrine, by providing military assistance to Greece and Turkey and by insisting on Soviet evacuation from the northern regions of Iran.

Those policies were a striking success. The British began their imperial withdrawal with Palestine in 1948 and concluded it in the Gulf emirates in 1971; and Eisenhower's strong stand in 1956 made it clear that the United States would not allow that process of decolonization to be reversed. In defining the relations of its own oil companies with Middle Eastern countries in this postcolonial era, the United States went to some trouble—and expense in the form of tax revenues foregone—to avoid the sort of confrontation that embittered British-Iranian relations at the time of Mossadegh's nationalization attempt. The Soviets, in response to Truman's firm stand, relinquished their pressure on Turkey and completed their evacuation of Iran. Since the 1950s, to be sure, they have established close relations first with Nasser's Egypt and Kassem's Iraq, then with South Yemen and Ethiopia, and then with Qaddafi's Libya and Assad's Syria. But since their withdrawal from Iran's Azarbaijan province in 1947, they did not again cross their immediate Middle Eastern frontier until their invasion of Afghanistan in December 1979.

Nonetheless, the very successes of America's Middle Eastern policy conjured up new and unexpected problems. The states of the region, having escaped with American help from European and Soviet domination, soon filled the resulting power vacuum with the din of their quarrels. The recurrent Arab-Israeli wars poisoned relationships between the United States and many of the Arab countries. The smoldering feud between Greece and Turkey since the late 1950s embroiled America's two allies on NATO's southern flank. The massive inflow of arms into the region from the Soviet Union, the United States, and Western Europe exacerbated those intraregional quarrels, aggravated the pattern of domestic repression, and made of military officers the most effective contenders for political power. The Truman Doctrine stopped the Soviets' frontal pressure, but it did not prevent political leaders in Cairo, Baghdad, or Damascus from opening the back door to Soviet influence. The generous "fifty-fifty" agreements between American oil companies and Middle Eastern governments in the 1950s made it easier for those governments to escalate the price of oil in the 1970s. The inflow of oil money accelerated the arms race and heightened the regional and domestic tensions. And those tensions—notably during the war of 1973 and the Iranian revolution of 1979—served to endanger the supply of oil and to drive the price further up. Since the 1970s, the American-Soviet confrontation has also come to focus once again on the Middle East. In sum, the Middle East in the last decade has become the world's center of oil and of turmoil.

The United States, in the decades since the Second World War, has clearly been the outside power with the most decisive influence in the Middle East—a circumstance that has been demonstrated again and again from the time of the Truman Doctrine, the Azarbaijan crisis, and Israel's independence in 1947/48 to the time of the disengagement agreements of 1974/75 and the Camp David peace of 1978/79. This fundamental fact of American preponderance in the Middle East has probably been far more obvious to seasoned imperialists in London, Paris, or Moscow—or indeed to long-time victims of imperialism in Cairo, Damascus, or Tehran—than to common American citizens or even to the policy makers in Washington. American power in the Middle East grew as a result of many separate decisions, in response to numerous seemingly unrelated crises. There never was any intention to transform the region into an American empire. Nor even was there any occasion for formulating a long-range over-all design—any Middle Eastern equivalent, say, of the Marshall Plan for European reconstruction and unification. Surely whatever American empire may have evolved in the Middle East over the years has been acquired in that proverbial fit of absent-mindedness. And when policy makers in Washington did put their minds to the region, they tended to see it in distinct segments, such as Turkey, Iran, the Arab Countries, and Israel.

Close relations developed with Turkey as a result of the Truman Doctrine, a generous American program of economic aid, and Turkish efforts to make the transition from a one-party system to a full-fledged democracy. But attempts to form a Middle Eastern alliance centered on Turkey and Egypt did not succeed. Turkish governments in the 1950s and 1960s were eager to strengthen their relations with Western Europe: in 1952 Turkey joined the North Atlantic Treaty Organization, and in 1963 it became an associate member of the European Economic Community. By contrast, Ankara governments remained reluctant to become involved in Middle Eastern affairs—except at Washington's specific request, as in the formation of the abortive Baghdad Pact in 1955. Even the Department of State in Washington assigned Turkey to its European, rather than its Middle Eastern, bureau.

American relations were even closer with Israel, widely admired by Americans as a pioneering democracy not unlike their own, and the only Middle Eastern country with a large, autonomous constituency among American voters and political leaders. There have been recurrent moments of strain, or even crisis, in governmental relations between Washington and Jerusalem—most recently during the 1973 war, at the time immediately prior to the disengagement agreement of 1975, and in the wake of Israeli bombings in Iraq and Lebanon in 1981. Nonetheless, America's commitment to Israel's survival as an independent state has remained an unquestioned axiom of United States policy toward the Middle East.

This intimate relationship between Israel and America was bound to create recurrent difficulties in our relations with the Arab countries. And there was a tendency, partly as a result, to conceive of our interests in the Arab world narrowly as centering only around petroleum. Americans would have been content to keep their interests in Israel and in oil quite separate—except that Arab governments, on occasions such as the 1973 embargo, emphatically connected them.

The need to formulate a more integrated policy for the Middle East was perceived in Washington chiefly in response to the Soviet threat, which was, after all, regionwide; hence, the efforts in the early 1950s to establish a Middle East Command or a Middle East Defense Organization centered on Egypt and perhaps Turkey. Yet even here a more segmented view soon prevailed. When John Foster Dulles traveled to the region in the spring of 1953 to assess the prospects of a regional defense pact, he had concluded that the countries at the core of the region, such as Egypt, were too preoccupied with their conflict with Israel or their colonial memories to fit into any such scheme. Instead, the best plan would be to rally the "northern tier" of nations, such as Turkey, Iran, and Pakistan, which showed more "awareness of the danger." The geographic distinctions thus established were maintained throughout the 1950s and 1960s. American relations with Nasser's Egypt remained highly antagonistic, and those with other Arab countries mostly strained or aloof. And Washington felt little need to reassess relations with Iran as they developed since the CIA's plot to restore the shah and since Dulles's own ill-fated Baghdad Pact project of northern tier defense.

By the 1970s Dulles's northern tier conception had long since disintegrated. American-Iranian relations, linked ever more closely to the shah's personal fortunes, had come to rest on a number of convenient fallacies: that the task of "policing" such a region as the Gulf after the British departure could be delegated to some other government; that a regime as repressive and unpopular as the shah's would make a suitable candidate for "regional policeman"; that such a regime would be strengthened rather than weakened by massive arms supplies; that, in a showdown, such a regime could be saved, by American advice or active help, from the wrath of its own people—or that a regime thus saved would be worth saving. As a final irony, the Pentagon began to worry that, in the confusion of the Iranian revolution, some of the advanced weapons earlier lavished on the shah might now fall into Soviet hands.

Thus our Middle Eastern policies evolved and rigidified in bits and pieces over a quarter-century. Then came the high political drama of the 1970s: the Yom Kippur-War, Sadat's Jerusalem visit, the peace at Camp David, the revolution in Iran, and the occupation of Afghanistan. Each event had the effect of putting into question one or more of the policy assumptions inherited from the 1950s. Taken together, they amounted to a realignment of strategic dimensions:

- Egypt, which had been Moscow's best friend in the region in Nasser's day, was eager under Sadat to join an anti-Soviet coalition;
- Iran, far from serving as anyone's "policeman," was convulsed by revolution and xenophobia;
- the occupation of Afghanistan brought the Soviets closer to the center of the region than they had been in thirty years;
- the Iranian upheaval emphasized the continuing importance of Turkey as a geographic barrier between the Soviet Union and the Arab countries;
- oil, once a source only of multinational company profits, was now a burden of American and global economic dependence;
- Saudi Arabia, no longer a remote desert kingdom, had become a global financial power with aspirations to regional political leadership; and
- Camp David, by making peace on the major front, showed the Arab-Israeli gap to be no longer unbridgeable and, by implication, held out new hope for Arab-American relations.

From a purely strategic point of view, America's loss in Iran and gain in Egypt compensated for each other. Imagine for a moment that the shah's regime had fallen in the days of Nasser's alliance with Moscow: the result would have been to make any future Soviet bid for Middle East dominion quite irresistible. Or imagine, on the contrary, that the shah's domestic position had been secure: Sadat's Egypt and Iran then might have formed the nucleus of a regionwide defense pact that would have surpassed John Foster Dulles's fondest dreams.

As things stand—with Iran out and Egypt in—one might think of a scheme of anti-Soviet defense of the Middle East that included Turkey and the Arab countries in the West's sphere, left Afghanistan in Soviet hands, and kept the status of Iran and the Persian Gulf undefined. At best, in the event of a Soviet occupation of Iran, such a defense line might be moved forward to the Zagros mountains, including on the Western side the Iranian oil fields in Khuzistan and the northern shore of the Strait of Hormuz. This presumably would have been the military strategy implicit in Carter's proclamation of the Gulf as an area of America's vital interest. But such a line drawn across the map could not begin to encompass the true strategic problem: for it overlooks the realities of oil, of warfare in a nuclear age, and of the inhabitants of the Middle East —whose defense presumably is in question.

Such a line, drawn across, or north of, the Persian Gulf could serve our strategic interests best if it did *not* become the baseline for any military operations. The Gulf is only some 600 miles by air from the Soviet Union—and 9,000 miles from the United States. Oil fields, pipelines, and tanker ports are highly vulnerable to attack by air, from the sea, or on the ground. The Iraq-Iran war quickly knocked out most Iranian oil exports for three months, and Iraq's for about a year. In the future, the Saudi and Iraqi pipelines to Yanbu will provide a limited alternative to the Hormuz route. Yet if the entire Gulf became a theater of operations, the industrial world would most likely be deprived of as much as half its normal oil imports for the duration of the fighting and perhaps for months beyond. The loss of oil supplies would be three or four times as large as during the 1973 embargo or the Iranian revolution —a scenario close to the "actual strangulation" that Kissinger feared. Such a "defense" would be madness; it would, at least for a time, destroy the vital interests it was intended to protect. Nor would such a "defense" elicit much sympathy from our allies in Europe of Japan, for whom oil from the Gulf is many times more vital.

Because of those risks to the oil, it is hard to see the United States limiting any confrontation with the Soviets to such a Gulf war: almost inevitably, the conflict would quickly escalate to a global and nuclear level. Nor is it easy to conceive of the Soviet Union provoking such a regional war—partly because of this risk of nuclear escalation, but, above all, because so many less risky options are available.

In 1980 Soviet tanks enabled Libya's Qaddafi to conquer the state of Chad, temporarily extending his control southward across the entire Sahara. South Yemen and Ethiopia are now firmly under Soviet control, and there have been intermittent efforts to expand that control into neighboring Somalia or North Yemen. In Iran, President Abolhassan Bani-Sadr was deposed early in 1981; and what little cohesion remained in the Iranian revolutionary regime seemed to depend on the revered figure of the octogenarian ayatollah. Upon his death, if not before, the power struggle in Tehran and the provinces was sure to intensify, and factions trained or supported by Moscow were almost certain to play a prominent part. This conjured up the prospect of a communist takeover either ministry by ministry, as in Czechoslovakia in 1945–48, or province by province, as in China in 1934–49. And a Soviet dominated Iran would not only be in direct control of a major source of oil in Khuzistan, it would also be in artillery, torpedo, and fighter plane range of the Middle East's remaining flow of oil. Whether the United States would have a chance to limit the damage of such a Soviet takeover—for example, by pushing to the Zagros mountain line—would depend not only on our military preparedness but also on such fortuitous factors as an Iranian —or other neighboring—government asking for timely help.

In Europe and the Far East, Soviet and Western strategic interests were carefully delimited by the armistice lines drawn at the end of the Second World War, and the absence of such lines clearly has contributed to making the Middle East a recurrent arena of American-Soviet confrontation. Considering the remarkable stability over the decades of the line first drawn across Europe in the Yalta agreement of 1945, it might be thought that Washington and Moscow could avoid such future confrontations by drawing a Yalta line across the Middle East.

Such a conclusion would be both fallacious and dangerous, for at least four reasons:

• In 1945 millions of Allied troops were poised to invade Germany— Russians from the East, Americans and other allies from the West. The movement of such massive armed forces created an urgent need for clearly defined lines, lest American and Soviet troops inadvertently become involved in a further war against each other. In the Middle East today, there is no such obvious urgency for drawing a line.

• Those same troops in 1945 provided a massive and automatic enforcement machinery for the lines drawn. In the Middle East today there is no comparable machinery.

• As Western Europe recovered from the Second World War, the instinct of self-preservation of its people, expressed in plans such as the European Defense Community and the North Atlantic Pact, helped perpetuate the original Yalta line. The experience in Korea and Vietnam shows that, in the absence of such a spirit of collective self-defense, even the most clearly drawn lines will not prevent war.

- In 1945, Soviet and American armed forces in Europe were of comparable strength, with the likely balance in favor of the U.S. Today in the Middle East, the U.S. would be negotiating from a position of far greater weakness. There is little incentive, therefore, for the Soviets either to sign an agreement that would be fair to Western interests, or to observe such an agreement after it were signed. Seven years before Yalta, in 1938, another group of allied leaders met at Munich with Hitler himself to confirm the line by which he proposed to annex the German-speaking Sudeten region of Czechoslovakia and to accept his verbal guarantees of peace in their lifetime; six months later, Hitler's forces occupied the remainder of Czechoslovakia. A Middle Eastern Yalta in the 1980s could all too easily turn into a Middle Eastern Munich instead.

REFOCUSING OUR POLICY

It would be equally foolish to ignore the Soviet threat to the Middle East; to assume that it can be removed by the bold proclamation of a doctrine or contained at the stroke of a pen; or to think of it as leading to a military confrontation to be fought with the weapons of the Second World War—a confrontation in which our own distance from the theater of war and the vulnerability of the West's oil supplies would prove to be decisive handicaps. Just as we need to reexamine the geographic pieces of the Middle East kaleidoscope after the shifts and reversals of the 1970s, so we have to find a broader perspective to integrate the military, diplomatic, economic, and cultural dimensions of our relations with the peoples of the Middle East. A purely defensive stance would in fact make a poor defense—because an exclusively military approach risks giving away the game to the Soviets.

Whether we like it or not, indeed whether we know it or not, we have been in competition with the Soviets in the Middle East since the days not just of Stalin and Truman but of Lenin and Wilson. As the Bolshevik revolution in the 1920s and 1930s lost its universalist fervor, the Soviets in that competition have increasingly relied on the naked elements of power—on the political intrigue of secret communist parties, on military occupation in Azerbaijan or Afghanistan, on the export of MIGs and Kalashnikovs, on Cuban military instructors and East German police officers. On our side, CIA plots, helicopters and transport planes, F-15s and AWACS, battleships and aircraft carriers have been recurrent and often indispensable parts—but on balance minor parts—of our total inventory. More important have been the colleges founded by American missionaries and the technical education that generations of Middle Easterners have received in the United States, the American expertise that has opened the underground riches of Middle East petroleum to human exploitation, the commercial enterprise of American banks and consulting firms, the diversity of ideas and the confidence in technical progress embodied in the contemporary American ethos. Logically enough, in the intense political maneuvering that has dominated the Middle East in recent decades, the Arabs have relied on Moscow for weapons of war and on Washington for mediation for peace.

Sixty years ago, when America's competition with Bolshevism in the Middle East first took shape, President Wilson's emissaries were naïve indeed—and more than a little condescending—to think that the United States, in its "self-sacrificing spirit," could readily bring "a democratic state," "complete religious liberty," and "economic development" to the peoples of the Middle East. Yet the intellectual devotion of college teaching and the pragmatic ingenuity of manufacturing that Dr. King and Mr. Crane represented have remained America's most pervasive influence on the modern Middle Eastern scene.

The breadth and yet the indivisibility of this American impact has probably been more apparent to Middle Easterners than to ourselves. When Turkey felt threatened by the Soviet Union in the 1940s, it appealed for American military and diplomatic support but also undertook an ambitious transformation of its political system from a party dictatorship into a democratic multiparty system; and although Turkey has experienced several reversals in that movement, notably in 1960 and 1980, the broad process of democratization is strongly entrenched and supported by the vast majority of the population. Similarly, when Sadat broke with the Soviet Union, made peace with Israel, and offered a *de facto* alliance to the United States, he also embarked on a program of liberalization of the economy and of the political processes that have generated their own momentum and won broad popular support. In Saudi Arabia, the first petroleum minister, Abdullah Tariki, studied at the University of Texas, and his successor, Ahmad Zaki Yamani, at the Harvard Business School. And today the Saudi elite take it for granted that their fortunes are tied to the economic future of the capitalist West and of the United States in particular. When the Palestinian movement was on the point of entering the peace negotiations in 1977, a Palestinian-

American professor was to have been its representative at Geneva. The cultural links are closest of all between the United States and Israel. More than twice as many Jews live in the United States as do in Israel, and the United States is the most frequent destination for the sizable number of Israelis who leave their country. The political program that led to the creation of the state of Israel was adopted in 1942 at the Biltmore Hotel in New York. And over the years, the annual fund drive of the United Jewish Appeal and, more recently, United States government aid have been the principal sources of Israel's external capital.

Egypt, Turkey, Saudi Arabia, Israel—these are the countries in the Middle East with which we have had the most varied historic ties. Today, they are important in the region because of the size of their territory, population, military power, oil production, or some combination of those factors. They are also likely to be the countries that will weigh most heavily in the formulation of specific details of our Middle Eastern policy for the remainder of this century. (Whether Iran, which ranks after Saudi Arabia in area and after Turkey and Egypt in population, can be added to this list in the future as a fifth country will depend on circumstances very largely beyond American control.)

There were no serious problems between the United States and Egypt during the final years of Sadat's reign. He had boldly made peace with Israel, and thus decisively contributed to the political stability of the region. He shared the Carter and Reagan administrations' apprehensions about Soviet penetration in the Middle East and Africa—indeed he tended to see Soviet control of South Yemen, Soviet and Cuban military assistance to Ethiopia, Libya's massive purchase of Soviet arms, and Libya's presence in Chad as parts of a coordinated Soviet strategy of encircling Egypt; and his response was to make available Egyptian military facilities for strategic use by American forces.

Sadat's peace policy, nonetheless, was both a strength and, in the short run, a weakness. It allowed Egypt to turn away from futile wars with Israel and from Nasser's grandiose ambitions for regional dominance and global stature; and it promised to regain for Egypt all of the territories occupied by Israel in 1967. But the Camp David peace also laid Sadat open to the charge of having deserted the common Arab cause—a criticism widely voiced by a broad range of domestic opposition, and, in varying degrees of shrillness, by other Arab governments from Saudi Arabia to Libya. The major problem of Egypt remains the massive pressure of overpopulation which threatens to cancel out any gains of economic development. Even here, Sadat's liberalization of the economy offered a more hopeful approach than had Nasser's socialist austerity; and American foreign aid and private investment contributed to the gradual improvement.

Sadat's assassination brought about no fundamental change in Egypt's domestic or foreign policy. The assassination was carried out by a small group of Muslim fundamentalists during a military parade celebrating the eighth anniversary of the October 1973 war. The government of Hosni Mubarak quickly managed to quell the scattered riots that followed. And while decisively moving against the fundamentalist radicals, Mubarak managed to effect an early reconciliation with prominent secularist opponents of Sadat, such as Mohammed Hassanein Heikal who had been Egypt's leading journalist in Nasser's day. In his foreign policy, Mubarak confirmed Egypt's commitment to the Camp David accords and to military cooperation with the United States. Once the Sinai evacuation phase of the Washington treaty was fully implemented, it was possible that Mubarak's modest and systematic leadership might mend Egypt's relations with Saudi Arabia and other moderate Arab countries—where Sadat's flamboyance and brusqueness had needlessly widened the rift. And any improvement in Egyptian-Arab relations was likely to strengthen the Mubarak regime's domestic stability as well.

Turkish-American relations came under a cloud in 1974, when Turkish forces intervened on Cyprus under a disputed provision of the 1960 treaty that guaranteed the island's binational constitution. In response, the United States Congress suspended military aid; Turkey closed its American bases, except those under NATO; Greece left the NATO military structure; and a dispute over territorial rights in the Aegean Sea further embittered Greek-Turkish relations. When American military aid to Turkey was resumed, Ankara and Washington negotiated a new agreement on military bases. By 1980 Greece returned to full NATO membership, and there were active efforts, with U.N. and U.S. participation, to settle the Cyprus dispute.

In Turkey itself, Atatürk's cultural revolution, which transformed a traditional Islamic society into a modern nation-state in the 1920s, has been a full success. But the introduction of democracy since the 1940s and rapid economic development since the 1950s have suffered temporary setbacks. In the late 1970s, for example, weak coalition governments failed to control reckless foreign-exchange spending, mounting unemployment, and endemic terrorism from right and left that claimed over two hundred lives each month—thus provoking the peaceful military coup of September 12, 1980. Turkey's ruling generals are committed to a return to democracy; and they are even more determined than were the major civilian parties to cooperating with the United States, within NATO and bilaterally, against any Soviet attack. There has been some reluctance to extend that cooperation to possible American military action in the Middle East—both because of Turkey's strong economic ties with Arab countries and because of legitimate doubts as to what form such American action might take. Yet the government of General Kenan Evren tried to overcome such difficulties by pursuing what it called a "multidimensional" foreign policy.

There has been much talk about the "special relationship" between the United States and Saudi Arabia, which includes many facets. The sheer extent of the kingdom's area, and its location on both the Persian Gulf and the Red Sea, make it of supreme importance in any American strategic calculations for the Middle East as a whole. The United States is Saudi Arabia's major trade partner, and a large portion of the huge Saudi financial surplus is invested in the United States, notably in government obligations. And Saudi Arabia is a conservative regime that feels strongly committed to the capitalist global order in which the United States plays the central role.

The most critical link is the obvious one between the leading exporter and importer of oil; of necessity it is a close but tense relationship—both sides want a sale, the seller at a higher and the buyer at a lower price. Luckily for the Saudis, American companies, in their search for profits, opened the kingdom's vast oil reservoirs as they converted the world's economy from coal to oil. Luckily for us, the Saudis in recent years, for good reasons of their own, have preferred to see the price of oil rise slowly and steadily rather than steeply and suddenly. But let us not forget that it was the Saudis who contrived the 1973 price revolution and accompanied it with a bold attempt to coerce our foreign policy. The Saudis themselves are sure to remember our own inconsistencies. In 1974 Kissinger hinted at invading their oil fields, but since 1978 the Carter and Reagan administrations have offered them some of our most advanced weapons and badgered them to enter into a formal defense agreement. When the Saudis increased their oil production in mid-1979, Carter expressed his gratitude for this "Fourth of July present"; but his energy secretary had the bad judgment of asking for Saudi approval of a buildup of our Strategic Petroleum Reserve—intended, presumably, to make us immune to any future oil embargoes. And time and again members of the Washington inner circle have expressed their misconception that a solution to the Palestine problem is a necessary inducement for a moderate Saudi oil policy. In sum, what is needed in American-Saudi relations is a more consistent American policy, based on a clearer recognition of where our interests diverge and where they overlap.

The half-finished agenda of Camp David remains the fundamental fact in Israel's relations with its Middle Eastern neighbors and with the United States. Perhaps Prime Minister Begin has received too little of the credit for the half that was accomplished and too much of the blame for the half that was not. He showed courage in agreeing to surrender all of Sinai, and perhaps no leader with less impeccably nationalist credentials could have made his fellow Israelis accept that part of the deal. For abandoning the Sinai peninsula meant returning oil fields that had made Israel largely self-sufficient; losing precious minutes of warning time in case of future aerial attack; and evacuating a number of Israeli settlements—all in return for the promise of peace with their most powerful Arab neighbor and the hope that the peace would hold. Begin shows no such courage or generosity with regard to the Palestinian issues. On the West Bank his stand comes close to the most intransigent Israeli position: that Judea and Samaria (as he insists on calling the region) are lands of Biblical promise where Jews may settle as of right, and that there will never be a separate Palestinian state—although he fails to spell out the implication of permanent annexation.

The June 1981 Israeli elections may have brought about a further hardening of positions, due in part to the growing assertiveness of the second generation of Israeli immigrants from Morocco, Yemen, Iraq, and other Middle Eastern countries. In their former home countries, their parents were discriminated against by Arabs; on arrival they faced the condescension of the old Zionist establishment—mostly of European Jews strongly identified with Labor—to whom this influx of "Oriental Jews," or Sephardim, represented Israel's prime social problem. To the second generation Sephardim, Begin's policies provide a perfect expression of their resentment both of Arabs and of the old Labor establishment. Politics to them also is intensely personal, and the election rallies of the spring of 1981 resounded to their chants of "Begin King of Israel."

Camp David has secured for Israel peace on the southern, Sinai front —but it has led to more intense military clashes on the northern, Lebanese front. Only a peace on all fronts would allow Israel to reduce its overgrown military establishment with its heavy burden on the economy and its galloping rate of inflation. (Israel today maintains under arms a larger proportion of its population and devotes to defense a larger proportion of its national product than almost any other country in the world.) Nor has the withdrawal from Sinai altered the basic demographic facts: Arabs now constitute about one-third of the residents of Israel and the occupied Palestinian territories (West Bank, Gaza, East Jerusalem), and given their higher birth rates might outnumber Jews by the end of the century. Hence, moderate Israelis recognize that a solution to the Palestine problem is necessary to safeguard the Jewish and democratic character of their society and the health of their economy. But between such an abstract recognition and an actual peace agreement there remains a wide, and perhaps unbridgeable gap.

An alternative Israeli government, led by the Labor (Alignment) party, would most likely be more conciliatory with regard to the West Bank and Gaza. Still, it remains an open question whether the concessions that *any* Israeli government would make would be sufficient to resolve the Palestinian issues. The pre-1977 Labor-led coalitions also encouraged Israeli settlements on the West Bank, although in a more limited and clearly defined area; and in the 1981 campaign Labor did not dare attack Begin's settlement policy outright. Neither Labor nor any other responsible group would consider redividing Jerusalem; and no major group so far has expressed any willingness to accept a separate Palestinian state on the West Bank and in Gaza, or even to negotiate with the PLO.

The obstacles to peace are at least as formidable on the other side. In 1974 Arab governments recognized the PLO as the "sole legitimate representative of the Palestinian people"—thus barring any "Jordanian option," or Palestinian peace settlement negotiated between Israel and King Hussein. And one can hardly blame Israelis for refusing to deal with the PLO as long as it officially proclaims that its aim is "armed struggle" in order "to liquidate the Zionist presence in Palestine," and as long as it rejects as "fundamentally invalid" (or "null and void") the establishment of Israel, the Balfour Declaration of 1917, and even the 1947 partition plan for Palestine. In the wake of Camp David, there were some signs of a possible rapprochement between Jordan, Syria, and the PLO that might have led to a joint negotiating position—but soon there was renewed sharp friction between Jordan and Syria. On his visit to the United States in August 1981, President Sadat proposed mutual and simultaneous recognition of Israel and the PLO as the logical next step; and that same month, Foreign Minister Prince Fahd of Saudi Arabia called for renewed negotiations on the principle that "all states of the region should be able to live in peace." Yet once again, between such sentiments and principles and actual—let alone successful—negotiations there remained a wide gap.

LIVE AND LET LIVE

The United States should remain alert to any opportunities for bridging, or at least narrowing, that gap. Perhaps growing criticism of Begin's intransigence among Israel's supporters in the United States will have a moderating effect. Perhaps progress in the autonomy talks mandated by Camp David and toward actual autonomy for the West Bank and Gaza can create a new political structure among resident Palestinians with whom further negotiations can proceed. Perhaps there must be a new start so as to bring King Hussein, or even the PLO—or both— into the negotiating process. Perhaps Saudi Arabia, with its immense financial resources can try again to follow up on Prince Fahd's suggestion and help crystallize a new joint approach on the Arab side—despite the initial failure of such an effort in December 1981. Perhaps both Arabs and Israelis, instead of invoking the other side's intransigence as their alibi, will start testing each other's willingness for negotiation and accommodation. Perhaps Mayor Teddy Kollek's plans for decentralized neighborhood government in Jerusalem will serve as a concrete example of how Jews and Palestinian Arabs can live in peace. Perhaps moderate Israelis and Palestinians will both come to recognize that a small and landlocked sovereign Palestinian state need not pose a military threat to Israel. The opportunities for accommodation are, after all, as numerous as the arenas of conflict. It took a decade from Sadat's break with Moscow in 1972 to the scheduled final evacuation of Sinai in 1982; if a serious start is made soon, perhaps peace between Israelis and Palestinians will break out in the 1990s.

In seeking to facilitate and hasten this potential peace process, the United States must clearly bear in mind what a Palestinian peace can and what it cannot accomplish. It would not bring peace to the region as a whole; it would only remove the single most persistent cause of war. It would not remove the danger of Soviet penetration of the region, but it would close the door on Moscow's prime opportunity of the past. It would not ensure peace on all of Israel's frontiers forever, but it would allow Israelis to devote more of their energies to the tasks of peaceful development. It would not convert all Arabs into friends and allies of the United States or even establish brotherhood and unity among Arabs themselves; yet it would remove the single most stubborn obstacle to Arab-American cooperation. It would not roll back, or even stabilize, the price of oil, but it would defuse some of the regional turmoil that tends to escalate that price.

When and how the peace process will start will depend largely on the parties themselves. We can facilitate peace but we cannot impose it. If Sadat and Begin had not begun to talk in Jerusalem and Cairo, none of Jimmy Carter's efforts at Camp David would have been to any avail. Our intensive preparations for a Geneva conference in 1977 helped to keep up the momentum, and may even have precipitated Sadat's Jerusalem visit. But earlier on, we did not even anticipate such crucial develop-ments as Sadat's break with Moscow or Begin's willingness to trade the Sinai for peace with Egypt; and any direct pressure from Washington to bring about either of those developments would clearly have been coun-terproductive.

Ultimately, the success of Camp David depended on a fortunate com-bination of long-range planning and improvisation in responding to short-term developments. In developing his peace plan in the spring and summer of 1977, President Carter could rely on a long set of precedents and nearly a decade of detailed and varied preparations: William Scran-ton's proposal of "even-handedness," the Jarring Mission and the Rogers plan of 1970/71, Kissinger's shuttle diplomacy, the Brookings study, and the combined expertise of the State Department and the National Secu-rity Council. Nonetheless, it is to the lasting credit of Carter's team, including Secretary of State Cyrus Vance and Security Adviser Zbigniew Brzezinski, that at the crucial moment they were able to shift from the comprehensive Geneva approach on which they had labored so hard to the piecemeal approach dictated by Sadat's Jerusalem trip. Without detailed exploration, and without a clear notion of America's ultimate aims, no successful diplomatic effort could ever have been launched. Without tactical flexibility in responding to the desires of others and to unforeseen events, no such effort could have been completed. Steadiness in the pursuit of long-term aims and adaptability in the choice of short-term means is one of the secrets of success in a region with as many intersecting interests as the Middle East.

By contrast, the risks of planning without flexibility are suggested by the near collapse of Carter's peace effort when Sadat and Begin took things into their own hands. The danger of impulsively responding to events without long-term planning are illustrated by the Iranian hostage crisis and our handling of the Afghanistan invasion. And Washington's discomfiture during the Iranian revolution shows what can happen when long-range planning and short-term responsiveness both are lacking.

Camp David combined not only planning and flexibility, but also elements of the seemingly opposite comprehensive and piecemeal approaches. Carter's preparations for a Geneva conference had explored the positions of all concerned—including Israelis, Egyptians, Palestinians, Saudis, Syrians, Jordanians, and even Russians. Sadat's and Begin's bold initiatives thereupon bypassed the "veto" which, in Kissinger's view, any comprehensive approach risks giving to "the most intransigent governments." In the future, comprehensive explorations toward peace should at a minimum include Israel and her Eastern neighbors: Palestinians, Syrians, Jordanians, and Saudis. Perhaps the Soviets also should be included in the exploratory process; and perhaps the agenda should be broadened to include Lebanon, and thereby insure some meaningful participation by Syria. But if one or another of those parties should prove unwilling to contribute to a genuine settlement, the others should be prepared to go ahead anyhow. Just as the Brookings Institution's report *Toward Peace in the Middle East* of 1975 provided a reasoned basis for Carter's Middle East peace efforts in 1977, so perhaps a recent thoughtful report by the Seven Springs Center entitled *The Path to Peace* of 1981 can help set the agenda for American peace efforts in the early 1980s. Among the virtues of that report is that it seeks to define possible approaches and necessary procedures, but leaves the formulation of concrete solutions to the actual process of negotiation.

What we must guard against most, in our Middle East diplomacy as in our energy policy, are lingering delusions of omnipotent grandeur and sudden fits of dejection and despair. There is no quick, magic solution to the world's oil problems; yet OPEC does not have us over a barrel, nor need we freeze in the dark. Instead, we can price our energy consumption at replacement cost, reduce our imports, and build up a buffer stock against sudden rises in price or drops in supply. There is no master plan that will bring permanent peace to the Middle East—nor need we see conflict get out of hand or escalate into a Third World War. Instead, we can help defend our friends against external aggression when they ask for such help; and we can mediate conflicts as we did in the lengthy and tortuous Camp David process. By discouraging the forces of aggression and encouraging the forces of peaceful change within the region, we can reduce the likelihood of regional wars and revolutions with their risks to the supply of oil.

Happily, each of our efforts will support and reinforce the others. Reduced dependence on oil imports and a larger Strategic Petroleum Reserve will dispel any notions of an "oil weapon" to be used against us and will allow us to face with greater equanimity the political risks of the Middle Eastern scene. Progress toward Palestinian settlement will improve our relations with Saudi Arabia. A modest level of readily deployable United States forces in the region will help discourage possible acts of aggression—for example, against the Sudan by Libya, against North Yemen by South Yemen, or against Kuwait by Iraq. Better American relations with a stabler Middle East will make more credible any "nuclear umbrella" that we may wish to hold over parts of the area so as to discourage Soviet adventurism. In such an environment, Turkey will be less reluctant to extend its defense commitments southward. Perhaps even the Iranian revolution, in a later, more moderate phase, will begin to reestablish tolerable relations with the United States.

In sum, in a more peaceful Middle East of the future, there should be room for Arabs, Israelis, Turks, and Iranians; for traditional monarchies, fundamentalist Muslim regimes, and "people's democracies"; for genuine democracies and for military regimes; for allies of either the United States or the Soviet Union and for neutrals; and for oil-producing countries and for importers of oil. Our aim for the Middle East should not be uniformity or American domination, but a pattern of peaceful pluralism—of live and let live.

Appendix

STATISTICAL TABLES

Table 1: Oil in the United States

	1960	1973	1974	1979	1980	1981*
Proved Reserves, January 1 (in billion barrels)	31.7	36.3	35.3	27.8	26.5	26.4
Proved Reserves/Current Production Ratio (in years)	12.5	10.5	10.7	8.3	8.4	8.4
Oil Use (in million barrels daily—mb/d)						
Domestic oil produced	8.0	11.0	10.5	10.1	10.2	10.2
+ Foreign oil imported	1.6	6.0	5.9	7.9	6.2	5.3
Total oil consumed**	9.7	16.9	16.2	17.9	16.4	15.5
Strategic Petroleum Reserve						
In million barrels	—	—	—	91.2	107.8	173.0
In days of imports	—	—	—	12	17	32
Oil Prices (in dollars per barrel—$/bbl)						
Domestic crude oil	2.88	3.89	6.87	12.64	21.59	32.71
Imported crude oil	—	—	—	23.45	36.06	35.87
Refiner acquisition cost	—	—	9.07	17.72	28.07	36.13
Cost of Oil Imports (in $billion)	1.2	7.1	25.4	55.2	78.5	82.6
U.S.Oil Companies (net revenue in $ billion)						
Domestic	1.9	4.1	6.4	12.8	15.6	—
+ Foreign	1.0	7.5	10.0	18.7	19.6	—
Total net revenue	2.9	11.7	16.4	31.5	35.2	

Sources: US Dept. of Energy, Energy Information Administration. *Annual Report to Congress 1980* 3 vols. (Washington D.C., 1981), vol. 2 [reserves, SPR, prices]; *BP Statistical Review of the World Oil Industry 1980* (London: British Petroleum Co., 1981) [oil use]; Chase Manhattan Bank, *Statistical Analysis of a Group of Oil Companies* (annual) and *The Petroleum Situation*, (quarterly) [oil companies]; *Petroleum Intelligence Weekly; Oil and Gas Journal* [1981 data]
*Latest data available
**Totals may not add because of rounding and stock changes.

TABLE 1 AND FIGURE 1: OIL IN THE UNITED STATES

In the decades before the oil shock of 1973, consumption increased "as if there were no tomorrow." In 1968 Americans used twice as much oil as they had in 1950 and in 1978, three times as much (18.2 million barrels daily being the all-time maximum reached that year). Foreign oil imports in the 1960s were limited by the import quota, or "drain America first," program. But proven reserves failed to keep pace with demand, and the declining reserves : production ratio (the oil industry's "ready-shelf inventory") indicated the growing strain on resources (see Chapter 4).

Discovery of the giant field in northern Alaska in 1969 made a one-time addition of about 9 billion barrels to reserves, and the opening of the Transalaska pipeline in 1977 similarly boosted production for the next few years. (Production figures in table 1 include, and reserve figures exclude, oil obtained as a by-product of natural gas; hence line 2 is larger than line 1 divided by line 3.) Although drilling increased sharply in the 1970s, the trend of discovery and production was downward. Growing demand was met from imports, which doubled between 1960 and 1970 and quadrupled by 1973. (Note that figures are for *net* imports, excluding minor amounts reexported, mostly from Puerto Rico and the Virgin Islands.) The dip in consumption and, consequently, imports in 1974/75 was due as much to recession as to the OPEC price explosion—since price controls on domestic crude oil and gasoline kept the consumer in a "fool's paradise of cheap energy" (see Chapter 7).

Consumption and imports set new records in 1976–78, until the phasing out of controls and OPEC's second price explosion caused a sharp drop: "a little pricing will save a lot of preaching" (Chapter 7). The Strategic Petroleum Reserve was being built up steadily. By mid-1981 it was adequate to compensate for a 13 percent drop in oil on the world market, such as occurred during the embargo of 1973/74, for more than eight months; and as imports continued to decline the reserve grew proportionately larger.

The crude oil prices paid by refineries, or "refiner acquisition cost," is a composite, or weighted average, of the crude oil price at the wellhead (including, in the mid 1970s, "old oil," "new oil," etc.), and the landed cost of imports plus transportation from the domestic oil field or landing port to the refinery. The gap between the domestic and foreign price gradually narrowed in 1979–81 as price controls were being phased out. The landed cost of imported oil in turn represents a weighted average of OPEC and other foreign crude oil prices (see table 3) plus transportation.

The growing profits of the U.S. oil industry resulted in part from the steady rise in domestic prices—the industry's "current slice of the two-trillion-dollar pie" of vastly appreciated underground reserves—and in part from inventory profits at times of sharp OPEC price rises.

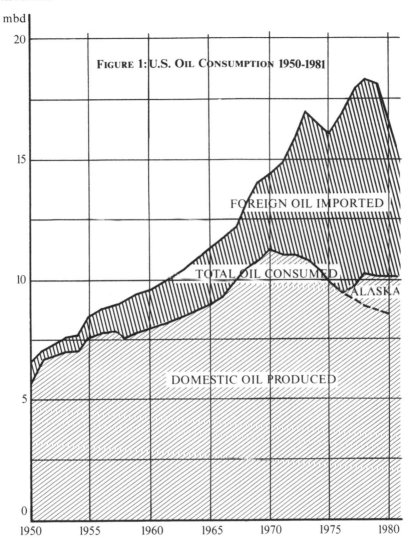

FIGURE 1: U.S. OIL CONSUMPTION 1950-1981

FOREIGN OIL IMPORTED

TOTAL OIL CONSUMED

ALASKA

DOMESTIC OIL PRODUCED

Table 2:

	United States		
	1960	1973	1979
Total Energy Consumed			
In millions of tons oil-equivalent (toe)	1035	1793	1877
In toe per capita	5.7	8.5	8.5
In toe per $ of GDP	1.11	1.15	1.04
Total Oil Consumed, in millions of tons (mt)	457	813	868
% of total energy consumed	44	45	46
Oil Imported (mt)*	83	305	415
% of total energy consumed*	8	17	22
Energy Used for Transportation (mt)	232	409	435
% of total energy consumed	23	23	23
Passenger Car Efficiency (mpg)	14.3	13.1	14.3

Sources: International Energy Agency, *Energy Policies and Programs of IEA Countries* (Paris, IEA. 1981), pp. 309f, 145f., 190f, 20, 26. Last line: EIA, *Annual Report to Congress 1980*, p. 195.

TABLE 2: ENERGY IN INDUSTRIAL COUNTRIES

Table 2 compares the United States with the two other leading industrial countries. Energy use in West Germany is fairly typical of Western Europe —higher than in France and Italy, lower than in the Netherlands and Sweden. Japan's energy use is the lowest per capita among major industrial countries but well within the European range when compared to gross domestic product. After completing their switch from coal in the 1960s, Europe and Japan became, in the 1970s, more heavily dependent on oil than was the United States.

Throughout the period, Americans were using twice as much energy per capita as Europeans and nearly three times as much as the Japanese. Even per unit of national income, Germans and Japanese in 1979 used, respectively, 43 percent and 44 percent less energy than we did. Since only 22 percent of our total energy came from foreign oil in 1980 (or 15 percent in 1981), it follows that with more careful use of energy we could phase out all oil imports, become totally self-sufficient in energy—and still maintain the highest living standard in the industrial world. Yet in absolute terms our oil imports in 1979 were as large as the total oil consumption of West Germany and Japan combined: "our imports for frills raise their prices for essentials" (see Chapter 7).

The major contrast was in transportation, which uses up twice as large a share of total energy in the United States as in the other countries. Americans inhabit

Energy in Industrial Countries

| | West Germany | | | Japan | |
1960	1973	1979	1960	1972	1979
146	266	288	94	342	370
2.6	4.3	4.7	1.0	3.1	3.2
0.61	0.62	0.58	0.69	0.69	0.59
31	148	145	29	260	263
22	56	51	31	76	71
29	147	146	31	280	277
20	55	51	33	82	75
16	32	39	12	44	51
11	11	13	12	13	14
–	–	–	–	–	–

*These figures reflect not only consumption but also additions to stocks and petroleum used by refineries and, hence, some of them exceed the immediately preceding lines.

a larger country, are more mobile, and have developed a more dispersed, suburban style of living; but they also have been using far less efficient means of transportation, notably low-mileage, gas-guzzling passenger cars. This makes "the little engine that could" (chapter 7) such an essential ingredient in solving our energy problem and reducing OPEC's price-gouging opportunities: our addiction to high-priced oil is OPEC's only oil weapon. The 1978/79 increase in gasoline prices prompted the most dramatic improvement in average gasoline mileage for our passenger car fleet—from 14.3 miles per gallon in 1979 to 15.2 in 1980—a larger increase in one year than in the previous five years. At first, the "little engines that could" were imported from Japan and Germany, but now they are made in Detroit as well. As they continue to rejuvenate our automobile fleet, they may be expected to reduce our total oil consumption and imports even more dramatically throughout the 1980s.

Unfortunately, tables 1 and 2 reflect the continuing confusion in energy measurement. Table 2 is based on metric tons, a unit of weight conforming to the international system. Table 1 is based on barrels of 42 gallons, the traditional measure of volume used by the American oil industry. For crude oils of average specific gravity, 1 ton equals 7.33 barrels; hence 1 barrel per day is equivalent to 49.8 tons per year.

Table 3:

| | Production (million barrels daily) | | | | | Production Capacity |
	1960	1973	1974	1979	1980	1981	1981
Iran	1.06	5.90	6.06	3.18	1.48	1.32	3.0**
Iraq	1.00	2.02	1.97	3.48	2.65	0.90	4.0**
Kuwait	1.69	3.08	2.60	2.56	1.69	1.12	2.8
Libya	–	2.18	1.52	2.09	1.79	1.12	2.1
Saudi Arabia	1.31	7.71	8.62	9.84	10.26	9.81	11.3
United Arab Emirates	–	1.53	1.67	1.83	1.71	1.50	2.5
Subtotal	5.1	22.4	22.5	23.0	19.6	15.8	25.7
Other OPEC	2.8	8.9	8.6	8.5	7.6	6.7	8.8
Total OPEC	**7.9**	**31.3**	**31.1**	**31.4**	**27.3**	**22.5**	**34.4**
World	**22.0**	**58.5**	**58.6**	**65.8**	**62.6**	**58.9**	
OPEC as % of World	36	53	53	48	44	38	

Sources: *BP Statistical Review of the World Oil Industry,* annual [production]; *Petroleum Intelligence Weekly,* Feb. 22, 1982 [1981 production and capacity]; *Petroleum Economist,* June 1981 [Revenue]; International Monetary Fund, *International Financial Statistics,* annual and monthly [Financial Reserves]; D.A. Rustow and John F. Mugno, *OPEC Success and Prospects* (New York: 1976), p. 131 [1960 revenue]; 1981 revenue figures estimated.

TABLE 3: MIDDLE EAST OIL

In 1950, the United States produced half the world's oil, in 1980 less than one-sixth. Conversely, the Middle East's share in world production rose from one-sixth in 1960 to over one-third in 1973, declining slightly since then. In 1960, Venezuela joined with Iran, Iraq, Kuwait, and Saudi Arabia to found OPEC, with other Third World members joining as their oil exports increased: Qatar 1961, Indonesia and Libya 1962, United Arab Emirates 1967/74, Algeria 1969, Nigeria 1971, Ecuador and Gabon 1973. The organization's combined production rose from 36 percent of the world total in 1980 to over half in the early 1970s, and declined again to 40 percent in 1980. Similarly, its share of world exports reached a high of 87 percent in 1973–74, and by 1980 declined to 63 percent.

The increase in oil income of OPEC countries has been phenomenal. For the six leading Middle Eastern countries shown on table 3 that income increased

Middle East Oil

Government Oil Revenue ($billion)						Financial Reserves ($billion, Dec. 31)					
1960	1973	1974	1979	1980	1981	1960	1973	1974	1979	1980	1981
0.29	4.1	17.5	20.8	11.6	11.1	0.18	1.2	8.4	15.4	15.5*	–
0.27	1.8	5.7	20.3	26.5	9.8	0.26	1.5	3.3	–	–	–
0.47	1.9	7.0	16.0	18.3	15.7	0.07	0.5	1.4	3.0	3.9	4.1
–	2.3	6.0	14.8	23.2	16.0	0.08	2.1	3.6	6.5	13.1	9.0
0.36	4.3	22.6	55.5	104.2	113.5	0.19	3.9	14.3	19.5	23.4	32.2
–	0.9	5.5	12.4	19.2	19.5	–	0.1	0.5	1.5	2.0	3.2
1.37	15.4	64.3	139.8	203.0	185.6	0.70	9.4	31.4	53.0	65.7	–
0.93	7.1	26.2	48.2	69.1	79.3	0.61	5.2	15.8	21.5	28.4	–
2.30	**22.5**	**90.5**	**188.0**	**272.1**	**264.9**	**1.3**	**14.6**	**47.2**	**74.4**	**94.1**	**87.1**
						60.0	183.6	220.3	398.0	455.0	–
						2.2	7.9	21	19	21	–

* Latest figure available ** Before Iraq-Iran War of October 1980
Totals may not add because of rounding. Saudi Arabia and Kuwait include one-half each of Neutral Zone.

elevenfold between 1960 and 1973 and one-hundredfold by 1979. From 1979 to 1981, their production fell by 36% but their revenues increased by 35%. OPEC's accumulated financial reserves also increased spectacularly, tripling between 1960 and 1973, quadrupling by 1974, and doubling once again between 1974 and 1980. Yet financial reserves, which were as high as 7 months' income in 1960 and 1973, by 1980 were down to 4 months' income—a clear indication that OPEC countries have little difficulty adjusting their expenditure to their rising incomes. (Note, however, that the IMF figures for "international reserves" here given have in recent years excluded gold, and thus are somewhat understated.)

OPEC's share in world financial reserves rose from 2 percent in 1960 to 21 percent in 1974 but has remained at that level quite steadily, which indicates that the rest of the world has largely adjusted to OPEC's rising prices by inflating its currencies.

	Population (million) mid 1980	Oil Reserves billion barrels Jan. 1, 1981	years production
Table 4:			
Iran	37.5	57.5	106
Iraq	13.1	30.0	85
Kuwait	1.4	67.9	110
Libya	3.0	23.0	35
Saudi Arabia	8.4	168.0	45
United Arab Emirates	0.8	30.4	46
6 Middle Eastern Countries	**64.0**	**376.8**	**53**
Other OPEC	271.1	57.5	21
OPEC	**335.2**	**434.4**	**43**

Sources: *UN Monthly Statistical Bulletin* [population]; *Oil and Gas Journal,* Dec. 29, 1980 [oil reserves]; US Department of Energy, *1980 International Energy Annual* and *Petroleum Intelligence Weekly* [prices]. For oil production, revenues and financial reserves, see table 3.

TABLE 4: OPEC: HAWKS VERSUS DOVES

OPEC's largest oil reserves are found, by and large, in the least populated countries. Thus the six major Middle Eastern producers listed here (and on table 3) have a combined population less than Nigeria's (77 million) and less than half of Indonesia's (152 million), yet their oil reserves are more than six times as large as those of the seven OPEC members not listed. The contrast is even sharper in per-capita incomes from oil, which range from $24,000 in the United Arab Emirates to $12,000 or $13,000 for Kuwait and Saudi Arabia to

OPEC: Hawks versus Doves

Per Capita Gov't Oil Revenues $ 1980	Financial Reserves	Oil Price		$/bbl Jan. 1 1980	1981	1982
		1973	1974			
300	400	2.40	11.04	30.37	37.00	34.20
2,000	–	2.38	10.85	27.96	35.96	33.46
13,500	2,900	2.31	10.74	27.50	35.50	32.30
7,800	4,400	2.87	11.98	34.50	40.78	36.50
12,400	2,800	2.41	10.84	26.00	32.00	34.00
24,000	2,500	2.47	11.75	29.56	36.56	35.50
3,200	**1,026**					
255	105	–	–	25.20 to 29.99	32.88 to 40.02	32.88 to 36.52
811	**281**					

only about $250 for the non-Middle Eastern producers. The result is that the oil-rich underpopulated countries have favored slow and predictable price rises, and the populous countries with more modest oil resources have tried to charge what the traffic will bear—with Libya siding with the hawks more for political than economic reasons (see Chapter 6). The gap in the doves' and hawks' prices was widest in 1980/81.

Table 5:

Military Expenditure
(million constant dollars)

Country	1950	1960	1970	1975	1979
Afghanistan	–	–	43	47	59*
Egypt	206	513	2,271	5,756	2,840
Iran	212	577	1,906	10,168	4,943
Iraq	58	313	841	2,049	1,988
Israel	57	189	2,016	3,160	3,068
Jordan	56	181	279	246	387
Libya	–	13	331	1,048	1,579*
Saudi Arabia	–	–	2,094	9,430	14,640
Sudan	27	67	255	152	290
Syria	58	170	429	1,088	1,937
Turkey	609	892	1,448	2,351	1,968
MIDDLE EAST	1,436	3,372	12,583	36,537	36,999

Sources: Stockholm International Peace Research Institute, *World Armament and Disarmament: SIPRI Yearbook 1980* (London, 1981), pp. 20ff. [military expenditure 1950–1979 in constant 1978 dollars] and pp. 96f. [arms imports in constant 1975 dollars]. International

The Middle East Arms Race

Military Expenditure 1980				Personnel in Armed Forces 1979		Arms Imports millions of constant dollars		
dollar million	*dollar per head*	*as % of gov't spending*	*as % of GNP*	*-000s*	*as % of men 18 to 45*	*1970–75*	*1975–79*	*major supplier*
–	–	–	–	–	–	60	253	USSR
2,168*	54*	42.0*	13.2*	395	5.6	2,181	–	USSR
4,200	110	12.3	23.8*	415	5.9	2,053	6,229	USA
2,700	202	24.0	10.9*	212	10.1	336	2,418	USSR
5,200	1,333	32.0	23.2	166	22.8	1,688	2,008	USA
420	127	22.3	10.9*	6/	12.0	–	2,615	USA
448*	162*	19.5*	2.4*	42	8.5	656	3,151	France 1970–74 USSR 1975–79
20,704	2,518	28.1	15.0*	45	2.6	324	2,806	USA
245	13	12.7	3.9*	68*	–	96	232	USSR 1970–74 France 1975–79
4,040	459	30.5	13.1	228	15.5	2,320	1,170	USSR
2,921	54	22.0	4.2	566	6.7	–	–	USA
						10,156	23,777	

Institute of Strategic Studies, *The Military Balance,* annual [expenditure 1980, personnel].
* Latest figure available

TABLE 5: THE MIDDLE EAST ARMS RACE

One way that Middle Eastern countries have managed to spend much of their rapidly mounting oil income is by taking off into a headlong arms race. The increases in military spending by Iran, until the fall of the shah, by Libya under Qaddafi, and by Saudi Arabia are particularly striking. Other countries have received financial aid for arms purchases from friendly oil-producing countries or from the superpowers.

The over-all military burden is heaviest, in terms of military spending as a share of national income and of personnel in the armed forces, for Israel and her Arab neighbors—Jordan, Syria, and Egypt. As Middle Easterners play the game "clubs are trumps" (see Chapter 1).

Military secrecy, the vagaries of Third World government statistics, and the difficulties of currency comparisons over time make all figures in table 5 approximate at best. Thus for Libya in 1977 SIPRI gives a military spending figure of $1,579 million in 1978 dollars, and IISS a figure of $338 million in current dollars.

I have employed a more comprehensive definition of the Middle East than either of my sources. Thus I have added Afghanistan, Libya, and Sudan (and in the first block of columns, Turkey) to SIPRI's Middle East totals, which also include smaller countries not here listed, such as Lebanon, Kuwait, and the two Yemens. The last three columns are based on data for the six leading arms importers in each Third World region—Middle East, South Asia, and North Africa—as defined by SIPRI. This accounts for the omission of Jordan in 1970/74 and Egypt in 1975/79, which temporarily took seventh place in SIPRI's Middle East, and of Turkey, which SIPRI defines as outside the Third World.

Notes

Prologue

Page 1: "The occasion was notable . . ." Henry A. Kissinger, *The White House Years* (Boston: Little Brown, 1979), p. 51.

Page 17: "Reduction of inflation" and following. "Declaration of the Venice Economic Summit," June 23, 1980, points 4, 7, 30, 27, 19, and 34; the "tolerable" goals for 1990 are detailed in point 17. See *New York Times,* June 24, 1980.

Page 20: If somehow Americans could wean themselves. Or, as one might put it in doggerel:
"The whole might of OPEC/Would be worth not one kopeck/If only we could toil/Without imported oil."
Dankwart A. Rustow, "Oil in the 1980's: A Question of Supply," *New York Times* January 6, 1980, p. III–14.

Chapter 1

Page 25: Did not have to be "opened up." Dankwart A. Rustow, "The Political Impact of the West," *Cambridge History of Islam,* 2 vols. (London: Cambridge University Press, 1970), 1:674.

Page 27: "Widening control over nature . . ." Dankwart A. Rustow, *A World of Nations: Modernization and Political Leadership* (Washington, D.C.: Brookings, 1967), p. 3; see also Cyril E. Black, *The Dynamics of Modernization* (New York: Harper, 1966).

Page 27:   Napoleon's appeal. Referring to the Mamluks, Egypt's ruling
            class during the Ottoman period, he went so far as to assert:
            ". . . more than the Mamluks I respect God, his Prophet, and
            the Quran" (J. C. Hurewitz, *The Middle East and North Africa
            in World Politics,* 3 vols. [New Haven: Yale University Press,
            vol. 1, 1975; vol. 2, 1979], 1:116f). Only the first two volumes of
            this invaluable collection of documents have been published to
            date, covering the period until 1945 and cited hereafter as
            "Hurewitz, *Middle East.*" For the more recent period, see the
            same author's earlier work, *Diplomacy in the Near and Middle
            East,* 2 vols. (Princeton: Van Nostrand, 1956), cited hereafter as
            "Hurewitz, *Diplomacy.*"

Page 29:   "Power belongs to God . . ." Koran, Surah 63:8. Cf. Wilfred
            Cantwell Smith, *Islam in Modern History* (Princeton: Princeton
            University Press, 1957), p. 41: "The fundamental spiritual crisis
            of Islam . . . stems from an awareness that something is awry
            between the religion which God has appointed and the historical
            development of the world which he controls."

Page 29:   "Cutting edge . . ." Lewis V. Thomas in L. V. Thomas and R.
            N. Frye, *The United States and Turkey and Iran* (Cambridge,
            Mass.: Harvard University Press, 1957), p. 136.

Page 30:   Şinasi. Cf. Bernard Lewis, *The Emergence of Modern Turkey,* 2d
            ed. (London: Oxford University Press, 1968), pp. 136f.

Page 30:   "Temporary" occupation hard to terminate. John Marlowe, *An-
            glo-Egyptian Relations 1800–1953* (London: Cresset Press,
            1954), p. 253.

Page 32:   Britain's declaration of Egypt's "independence." Hurewitz, *Mid-
            dle East,* 2:298–301.

Page 32:   T. E. Lawrence, *Revolt in the Desert* (London: J. Cape, 1927) and
            Seven Pillars of Wisdom (Garden City: Doubleday, 1935).

Page 33:   The Balfour Declaration and the relevant passage from the
            League of Nations Covenant will be found in Hurewitz, *Middle
            East,* 2:106, 179f.

Page 34:   "Politics running on . . ." Gertrude Bell, *The Letters of Gertrude
            Bell,* 2 vols., ed. Lady Florence Bell (London: Benn, 1927),
            2:533.

Page 36:   "Pussy-footing imperialism . . ." Bernard Lewis, "Democracy in
            the Middle East: Its State and Prospects," *Middle Eastern
            Affairs* 6, no. 4 (April 1955): 105. The same thought, in slightly
            different wording, is expressed in Bernard Lewis, *The Middle
            East and the West* (Bloomington: Indiana University Press,
            1964), p. 59.

Page 37:   "Independence is never given ..." Ja'far al-Askari in George E. Kirk, *A Short History of the Middle East* (New York: Praeger, 1949), p. 137.

Page 40:   British leaders impressed with Zionists. See the biographical sketch of Sir Mark Sykes by his son Christopher Sykes, *Two Studies in Virtue* (New York: Knopf 1953), pp. 107–235. The elder Sykes was the British government's top expert on the Middle East; he is best known for the Sykes-Picot agreement of 1916, which defined British and French territorial interests in the Middle East and became the basis for the postwar partition into mandates.

Page 40:   "Full support" for Arab unity. Foreign Secretary Anthony Eden's speech at Mansion House, May 29, 1941, in Hurewitz, *Middle East,* 2:628. The response was Nuri Said's "Fertile Crescent Scheme." See p. 44 below and Hurewitz, ibid., pp. 628–30.

Page 41:   Nations . . . historical process. I have elaborated these historical comparisons in my article "Nation," *International Encyclopedia of the Social Sciences,* 17 vols. (New York: Macmillan, 1968), 11:7–14. and my book *A World of Nations,* ch. 2.

Page 42:   For estimates of the linguistic and religious composition of the population of Middle Eastern countries, see Dankwart A. Rustow, *Middle Eastern Political Systems* (Englewood-Cliffs, N.J.: Prentice-Hall, 1971), p. 22.

Page 44:   Arab League whose membership grew . . . The seven founding members were Egypt, Iraq, Lebanon, Syria, Transjordan (later called Jordan), Saudi Arabia, and Yemen. The governments of other Arab-speaking countries joined as they attained independence: Libya 1953; the Sudan 1956; Tunisia and Morocco 1958; Somalia 1960; Kuwait and Mauritania 1961; Algeria 1962; Southern Yemen 1967; Bahrain, Oman, Qatar, and United Arab Emirates 1971; Djibouti 1977. The Palestine Liberation Organization was admitted as an observer in 1967 and a member in 1976. Egypt's membership was suspended in 1979, following its signature of the Washington peace treaty with Israel.

Page 49:   "Our problem is an Egyptian problem." Saad Zaghlul, leader of the Egyptian nationalist delegation at the Paris peace conference and later prime minister, in Anwar G. Chejne, "Egyptian Attitudes Toward Pan-Arabism," *Middle East Journal* 11, no. 3 (1957): 253.

Page 50:   "Ottoman" or "Turkish" nation. Dankwart A. Rustow, "The Modernization of Turkey in Historical and Comparative Perspective," in Kemal H. Karpat, ed., *Social Change and Politics in Turkey* (Leiden: Brill, 1973), pp. 93–120, esp. p. 106.

Page 51: "Concentric circles." Gamal Abdul Nasser, *Egypt's Liberation: Philosophy of the Revolution* (Washington, D.C.: Public Affairs Press, 1955), pp. 109–14.

Page 51: "Render Unto Caesar . . ." Matthew 22:21.

Page 51: Muslim leaders and brotherhoods. Lewis, *Middle East and the West,* p. 100.

Page 52: Afghani. See Nikki R. Keddie, *Sayyid Jamāl al-Dīn "al-Afghā-nī": A Political Biography* (Berkeley: University of California Press, 1972).

Page 53: Limiting conscription. See Lewis, *Emergence of Modern Turkey,* pp. 116, 218, 337f.

Page 53: ". . . but one tooth left in its jaw." The poem was composed by Mehmed Âkif. Its first two stanzas, not including the line quoted, are known as the "Independence March" and are the official anthem of the Republic of Turkey. Âkif himself, however, whose religious-fundamentalist opinions were at odds with Atatürk's policy of secularization, chose voluntary exile in Egypt. See my article, "Mehmed Âkif's 'Independence March'," *Journal of the American Institute for the Study of Middle Eastern Civilization,* 1, no. 3/4 (autumn-winter 1980/81): 112–17.

Page 54: Clubs are trump. Thomas Hobbes, *English Works,* ed. Sir William Molesworth (London: J. Bohn, 1839–45), 6:122.

Page 55: "If the Army does not do this job . . ." Nasser, *Egypt's Liberation,* p. 31. On the role of the soldiers in Middle Eastern politics, see J. C. Hurewitz, *Middle East Politics: The Military Dimension* (New York: Praeger, 1969).

Page 59: The Middle East, one of the most highly armed regions. For details, see table 5 in the Appendix.

CHAPTER 2

Page 62: American University of Beirut. See George Antonius, *The Arab Awakening* (New York: H. Hamilton, 1938), pp. 41ff. "When account is taken of its contribution to the diffusion of knowledge, of the impetus it gave to literature and science, and of the achievement of its graduates, it may justly be said that its influence on the Arab revival, at any rate in its earlier stage, was greater than that of any other institution" (p. 43). A Jesuit institution established the first Arab printing press in Beirut in 1847 (p. 44). In Egypt there were similar British institutions of higher education, for example Victoria College in Alexandria. One of its graduates recalls a football match that made the spectators feel not as Greek, British, Arab, Muslim, Copt, Catholic, but as plain "Victorians." Edward Atiyah, *An Arab Tells His Story* (London: J. Murray, 1946), pp. 55ff.

Page 63:   First woman graduate. See Halide Edib [Adivar], *The Turkish Ordeal* (New York: Century, 1928).

Page 64:   Atatürk and an American mandate. For Turkish sources see Dankwart A. Rustow, "The Political Impact of the West," *Cambridge History of Islam,* 1:693.

Page 64:   Wilson's recommendation to the peace conference. Hurewitz, *Middle East,* 2:66.

Page 64:   ". . . qualified to go to Syria . . ." In Harry N. Howard, *The King-Crane Commission* (Beirut: Khayat, 1963), p. 37.

Page 65:   General Syrian Congress. The resolution is in Hurewitz, *Middle East,* 2:180–82.

Page 65:   The King-Crane report. Ibid., 2:191–99; the passages quoted are from articles 1, 5, and 6.

Page 67:   "Poor Wilson." In D. A. Rustow, "The Army and the Founding of the Turkish Republic," *World Politics* 11, no. 4 (July 1959): 636.

Page 67:   ". . . placing American citizens . . . at a disadvantage." See the statement of the U.S. Ambassador to the British Foreign Office, May 12, 1920, in Hurewitz, *Middle East,* 2:216.

Page 68:   Biltmore program. Ibid., 2:595–97.

Page 70:   ". . . collapse of world order." Kissinger's opening address at the Washington Energy Conference, February 11, 1974. Cf. D. A. Rustow and John F. Mugno, *OPEC: Success and Prospects* (New York: New York University Press for Council on Foreign Relations, 1976), p. 51.

Pages 72–73:   A single linguistic majority. See the statistical table in D. A. Rustow, *World of Nations,* appendix 1.

Page 73:   Ninety-five percent of exports go to or from industrial countries. My calculation is from 1973 trade figures in *United Nations Statistical Yearbook 1974,* pp. 56f., where the noncommunist industrial and nonindustrial countries are labeled "developed" and "developing market economies."

Page 75:   Support for Israel . . . a humanitarian anxiety. See Hurewitz, *Middle East,* 2:811–19. A report by Earl G. Harrison, American member of the Intergovernmental Committee on Refugees (August 1945), warned that "To anyone who has visited the concentration camps and who has talked with the despairing survivors, it is nothing short of calamitous to contemplate that the gates of

Palestine should be soon closed. . . . No other single matter is, therefore, so important from the viewpoint of Jews . . . who have known the horrors of the concentration camps as is the disposition of the Palestine question" (ibid., p. 815). Hurewitz notes that the report, "which received President Truman's prompt endorsement, contributed substantially to molding early postwar American public opinion in favor of Zionism" (ibid., p. 811).

Page 77:   "The area south of Batum and Baku . . ." The document became known with the American capture of German foreign office archives in 1945 (ibid., p. 561).

Page 77:   "If I do not give help . . ." Fuat Köprülü, in Dankwart A. Rustow, "Foreign Policy of the Turkish Republic," in R. C. Macridis, ed., *Foreign Policy in World Politics* (Englewood-Cliffs, N.J.: Prentice Hall, 1958), p. 308.

Page 79:   Colonial powers withdrawing. France had withdrawn from Syria and Lebanon under duress in 1946. The British timetable of evacuation turned out to be: Palestine 1948, Egypt 1949 (except Suez 1956), Iraq 1955, Sudan 1956, Jordan 1956, Somalia 1960, Cyprus 1960, Kuwait 1961, Aden (South Yemen) 1967, Libya 1969, Trucial Sheikhdoms (United Arab/Emirates) 1971.

Page 79:   The right to station forces in Egypt. Both the Anglo-Egyptian Treaty of 1936 and the 1951 proposal for a Middle East Command obliged Egypt "in the event of war, imminent danger of war [,] or apprehended international emergency" to allow "the use" of its "ports, aerodromes [airfields] and means of communication." Only the addition of a comma and the substitution of "airfields" for "aerodromes" betrayed that this time the document had received its final editing in Washington, not London. See Hurewitz, *Diplomacy,* 2:204, 330.

Page 95:   For the text of the Baghdad Pact, see Hurewitz, ibid., p. 390. The quote is from art. 1. I have listed the members in order of their accession. The United States, without ever formally joining the pact, became a member of its military committee in 1957 and joined its planning staff in 1958.

Page 80:   Nuri Said had been the author of the Fertile Crescent unity scheme of 1942 (see chapter 1), which was soon overtaken by Egypt's rival Arab League proposal.

Page 80:   "Corrupt clique installed by imperialism." In George Lenczowski, *The Middle East in World Affairs,* 4th ed. (Ithaca, N.Y.: Cornell University Press, 1980), p. 289.

Page 80:   John Foster Dulles's speech on the Near and Middle East of June 1, 1953, is reprinted in Hurewitz, *Diplomacy,* 2:342.

Page 82:   "... Arabs will naturally turn toward the West ..." Nasser's statement of September 3, 1954, is quoted by Lenczowski, *The Middle East in World Affairs,* p. 527.

Page 83:   Washington's warning to Britain and France. Oil shipments via Suez were interrupted because Egypt blocked the canal at the time of the Anglo-French landing; also Saudi Arabia and Iraq declared an embargo on shipments to Britain and France. The canal was reopened, and the embargo lifted, in March 1957. In November 1956, the U.S. Office of Defense Mobilization had prepared a plan for emergency oil shipments to be put into effect "as soon as Hammarskjöld made a statement indicating Anglo-French compliance." This led Europeans "to believe that we were forcing Britain and France to withdraw from Suez by withholding oil from them" (Sherman Adams, *Firsthand Report* [New York: Harper, 1961], pp. 266f.). Cf. Harold Lubell, *Middle East Oil Crises and Western Europe's Energy Supplies* (Baltimore: Johns Hopkins, 1963).

Page 87:   "Arab cold war." Malcolm H. Kerr, *The Arab Cold War: Gamal 'Abd al-Nasir and His Rivals* (London: Oxford University Press, 1970).

CHAPTER 3

Page 93:   Iraq petroleum concession. In fact, the holdings were just under one-quarter; 23.75 percent of the Iraq Petroleum Company was owned each by Shell, Anglo-Iranian (later known as British Petroleum), and Compagnie Française des Pétroles; and 11.875 percent each by Exxon and Mobil. The remaining 5 percent of the shares were held by Calouste Sarkis Gulbenkian, an enterprising Armenian who had arranged for the original petroleum concession from the Ottoman sultan. (See Ralph Hewins, *Mr. Five Per Cent* [London: Hutchison, 1957].) The same IPC shareholding formula was applied to concessions in other former Ottoman territories, such as Qatar and the United Arab Emirates—as well as Palestine, Transjordan, Syria, Lebanon, and Cyprus, where little or no oil was ever found.

Page 93:   Middle Eastern petroleum reserves. For two competent analyses of Middle Eastern oil in the immediate postwar period, see Raymond F. Mikesell and Hollis B. Chenery, *Arabian Oil* (Chapel Hill: University of North Carolina Press, 1949) and Charles Issawi and Mohammed Yeganeh, *The Economics of Middle Eastern Oil* (New York: Praeger, 1962).

Page 94:   "Bookkeeping notations . . . to minimize its tax bill." M. A.

Adelman, *The World Petroleum Market* (Baltimore: Johns Hopkins, 1972), p. 161.

Page 94:   A single network of oil companies. In the crucial years from 1947 to 1954, major company participation was distributed as follows:

	Iran*	Iraq	Kuwait	Saudi Arabia
Exxon		x		x
BP	x	x	x	
Shell		x		
Gulf			x	
Texaco				x
Socal				x
Mobil		x		x

*After 1954, all 7 companies held shares in Iran.

Page 95:   "The conversation ends in conspiracy . . ." Adam Smith, *The Wealth of Nations,* 1776, Bk I, ch. 10 (New York: Penguin [Pelican Classics], 1970), p. 232.

Page 95:   "As if it had originated in Texas." John M. Blair, *The Control of Oil* (New York: Pantheon, 1976), p. 113. The system was technically known as the "Galveston basing point." For example, the price of Middle Eastern oil sold in Naples would be calculated on the basis of prices prevailing at the Texas port of Galveston, plus freight charges for the trip to Naples from Galveston (5,600 miles) rather than from the Persian Gulf (4,000 miles). The effect, of course, was that low-cost Middle East oil at no destination would underbid the higher-cost American oil.

Page 95:   Seven companies control 65 percent of petroleum reserves. Issawi and Yeganeh, *The Economics of Middle Eastern Oil,* p. 61.

Page 96:   Conflict coming to a head in Iran. Outside the Middle East, Mexico had nationalized the holdings of foreign oil companies as early as 1938. That time the companies had won even more decisively: their operations in Mexico were shut down, and development of Mexico's oil reserves on a large scale postponed, in effect, for over thirty years.

Page 97:   Long ton versus short ton. See Rustow and Mugno, *OPEC,* p. 5.

Page 97:   Ghavam's intricate legal argument. He reasoned that Mossadegh's law made it illegal to negotiate without parliamentary approval, that parliament's term had expired, and that new elections could not be held while foreign troops remained on Iranian soil. (This indeed was a surprisingly prescient provision of the 1906 constitution.) When the Russians had completed their withdrawal, in part under strong American diplomatic pressure, Ghavam claimed "changed circumstances" and a rebellion in the ranks of his own party: "We cannot impose our will . . . on representatives elected by universal suffrage." Quoted in George E. Kirk, *The Middle East 1945–1950* "Survey of International Affairs" (London: Oxford University Press, 1954), p. 86.

Page 99:   Did Mossadegh succeed or fail? Stanley Hoffmann has succinctly illustrated the problem of time perspective: "Metternich had succeeded by 1825 and failed by 1848, and writers disagree whether he had succeeded or failed by 1914" (*Contemporary Theory in International Relations* [Englewood-Cliffs, N.J.: Prentice-Hall, 1960], p. 36).

Page 100:   Iranian consortium of 1954. The agreement will be found in Hurewitz, *Diplomacy,* 2:348–83. As revised in 1955, the allocation of shares was as follows: BP 40 percent, Shell 14 percent; Exxon, Gulf, Mobil, Socal, and Texaco 7 percent each; CFP (the French partner in the Iraq concession) 6 percent; a group of "independent" U.S. companies 5 percent.

Page 100:   To drop a major antitrust suit. President Truman, just before leaving office in January 1953, instructed the Justice department to convert the criminal antitrust case against the "International Oil Cartel" into a civil suit. In August, just two weeks before the restoration of the shah with help from the CIA, President Eisenhower's National Security Council transferred responsibility for this civil suit from the antitrust division of the Justice department to the State Department—surely an arrangement unprecedented in legal history. See Blair, *The Control of Oil,* p. 73. (The author had been in charge of preparing the antitrust prosecution that thus came to naught; he speaks with knowledge—and barely audible frustration.) While the suit was still pending, the oil companies were represented by the firm of Sullivan and Cromwell—from which Eisenhower's secretary of state, John Foster Dulles, was on leave.

Page 100:   "Accumulating financial reserves . . ." See Appendix, table 3. For the ratio of those reserves to expenditures on annual imports, see Rustow and Mugno, *OPEC,* p. 138.

Page 101:   "Transfer of tax revenue . . . to the Middle East." J. E. Hartshorn describes the details of the system in *Politics and World Oil Economics* (New York: Praeger, 1962), p. 199.

Page 101:   "Alternative for . . . controversial foreign aid . . ." Robert B.
                Krueger, *The United States and International Oil* (New York:
                Praeger, 1975), p. 71.

Pages 101–2:   Route by which Gulf oil reached its markets. About one-third
                of the oil from the Gulf states went via the Indian Ocean to Japan
                and other Asian destinations. Most Iraqi and Saudi production
                (23 percent of the regional total) went by two different pipelines
                to the Mediterranean and thence by tanker to Europe. The re-
                mainder (43 percent)—mostly from Kuwait and Iran—went to
                Europe via Suez.

Page 102:   "Growing Middle Eastern expertise . . ." Dankwart A. Rustow,
                "Dependability and Dependence: Political Prospects for Middle
                East Oil," in *Oil Imports and the National Interest* (New York:
                Petroleum Industry Research Foundation, 1971), p. 39. When I
                wrote the article, late in 1970, some industry experts vigorously
                objected to my conclusion that "nationally controlled [oil] oper-
                ations would prove technically feasible in [most] countries
                . . . in the 1970s and in . . . the Gulf sheikhdoms somewhat later."
                But Algeria nationalized while my essay was in page proof in
                February 1971; the Arab Gulf states, led by the Saudis, reached
                an agreement on gradual nationalization in 1972, and Libya and
                Iraq nationalized unilaterally in 1973. For the detailed chronol-
                ogy, see Rustow and Mugno, *OPEC,* pp. 156ff.

Page 104:   On Mattei see Paul Frankel, *Mattei: Oil and Power Politics* (New
                York: Praeger, 1966). The label for the companies was popula-
                rized by Anthony Sampson's book *The Seven Sisters: The Great
                Oil Companies and the World They Made* (New York: Viking,
                1975). In astronomical legend since the days of classical antiq-
                uity, "seven sisters" was a name for the Pleiades.

Page 105:   Successful bids by "independents." A veteran IPC official com-
                plains of the "severity . . . beyond compare" of the terms ob-
                tained by the governments. See Stephen Helmsley Longrigg, *Oil
                in the Middle East* (London: Oxford University Press, 1954), p.
                215; cf. p. 209n.

Page 107:   Prices cut by as much as one-half. In 1958, the posted price for
                Saudi Arabian Light had been $2.08 per barrel. By the end of the
                1960s, the actual price had dropped to $1.30. By the spring of
                1970 it was between $1 and $1.10. See Adelman, *World Petro-
                leum Market,* p. 191.

Page 107:   Per capita energy as an indicator of development: See e.g. Black,
                Dynamics of Modernization.

Page 110:   Nigeria in 1971. Qatar (1961), Ecuador, and Gabon (both 1973) brought the total membership to thirteen, their exports have remained insignificant. In 1974 Abu Dhabi's membership was extended to the United Arab Emirates as a whole, Dubai and Sharjah being the other oil producing emirates.

Page 110:   The "Declaratory Statement." Reprinted in Rustow and Mugno, *OPEC,* pp. 166–72, and analyzed ibid., pp. 7–9.

Page 112:   "After cash must come control." Peregrine Fellowes, "Living Dangerously—Can Europe Really Afford to Rely on Middle East Oil?" *The New Middle East* (October 1971), p. 26.

Page 112:   "The actual tactics . . ." The sentence is from Rustow and Mugno, *OPEC,* p. 21.

Page 113:   Aramco's 1950 tax bill. Cf. Krueger, *U.S. and International Oil,* p. 52. Total taxes in 1950/51 increased by only 9.4 percent on production that had increased as much as 40 percent.

CHAPTER 4

Page 118:   "Ready-shelf inventory." Reserves are "proven" by a costly process of drilling holes in close enough proximity to establish the precise width and depth of oil-bearing strata and thus the volume of oil in the given field. If previously known reserves are drawn down, it is time to stake out the dimensions of other known fields —hence Adelman's grocery-store metaphor. See M. A. Adelman, "The World Oil Cartel: Scarcity, Economics, and Politics," *Economics and Business* 16, no. 2 (summer 1976): 10. If the fields being newly "proven" turn out much smaller than expected, it is time to begin a process of exploration in other promising areas, thus starting a process followed by discovery, "proving," and installation of producing equipment that may take a decade or more. A twelve-year reserves/production ratio thus gives adequate warning when this process of exploration must be started.

Page 118:   Proven reserves. The "proving" of the major oil field on the North Slope of Alaska in 1970 increased the reserves/production ratio temporarily. After the opening of the Transalaska pipeline in 1977, the North Slope also raised the production figures temporarily; yet the 1970 peak of U.S. domestic production has never again been reached.

Page 121:   "Supply . . . for more than a thousand years." The remark was made in April 1944 by Eugene Holman, vice-president of Standard Oil of New Jersey (now Exxon), quoted in Benjamin Shwadran, *The Middle East, Oil, and the Great Powers,* 3d ed.

(New York: Wiley, 1973), p. 333. In 1947 Jersey Standard—apparently not fully convinced of its own argument about a millennium of domestic supplies—joined the Aramco consortium.

Page 122: "Largest subsidy . . . in U.S. history." Blair, *The Control of Oil,* p. 182. He calculates its value at "slightly" over $50 billion for the first decade of its operation, but the program lasted fourteen years.

Page 122: "Drain America First." S. David Freeman, *Energy: The New Era* (New York: Walker, 1974), p. 117. The author was head of the president's energy policy planning staff in 1967–71 and later of the Ford Foundation's Energy Policy Project.

Page 123: More oil off the American market. It is impossible to calculate exactly what the quantity of oil imports would have been in the absence of the quota program—since lower prices would have increased over-all consumption. Arab production cuts during the embargo averaged 2.77 million barrels a day (calculated from Rustow and Mugno, *OPEC,* p. 137, line 2). American oil imports, in the years that the quota program was being phased out, increased by almost exactly that amount—from 3.42 mb/d in 1970 to 6.26 mb/d in 1973, or by 2.84 mb/d. Note, however, that the embargo lasted only five months and the quota program as long as fourteen years.

Page 123: Cost of an adequate storage program. On storage costs in this period, cf. Adelman, *World Petroleum Market,* p. 269; and Sam Schurr and Paul Homan, *Middle Eastern Oil and the Western World* (New York: Elsevier, 1971), p. 81.

Page 126: Palestinian refugees. For Palestinian Arab population figures before and after 1967, see Fred J. Khouri, *The Arab-Israeli Dilemma* (Syracuse: Syracuse University Press, 1968), pp. 377–79.

Page 128: "Liquidate the Zionist presence . . ." Art. 15 of the "Palestine National Covenant" of June 1968 (available from office of the PLO's Permanent Observer to the United Nations).

Page 132: See William B. Quandt, *Decade of Decisions* (Berkeley, Calif.: University of California Press, 1977), p. 123. The author served as Middle East specialist on the staff of the National Security Council first under Kissinger and then again under Brzezinski.

Pages 132–33: "Who asked them to leave?" In T. B. Millar, "Soviet Policy East and West of Suez," *Foreign Affairs* 49, no. 1 (October 1970): 19.

Page 136: Akins's Algiers speech. Cf. Adelman, "Is the Oil Shortage Real?" pp. 80f. For Akins's rebuttal, see his article "The Oil

Crisis: This Time the Wolf Is Here," *Foreign Affairs* 51, no. 3 (April 1973): 462–90 at 473.

Page 136:   The other OPEC members scented their opportunity. The discussion of Qaddafi's financial negotiations is adapted from Rustow and Mugno, *OPEC,* pp. 20–22.

Page 138:   Meanwhile, Qaddafi had nationalized. For the chronology of nationalizations, see ibid., pp. 156–59.

Page 140:   "Raising the price of crude oil." Louis Kraar, "OPEC Is Starting to Feel the Pressure," *Fortune,* May 1975, p. 186.

Page 141:   The price at the Persian Gulf. Adelman, *World Petroleum Market,* p. 190.

CHAPTER 5

Page 145:   Climax of the high drama. See D. A. Rustow, "Petroleum Politics 1951–1974: A Five-Act Drama Reconstructed," *Dissent* 21, no. 2 (spring 1974): 144–53.

Page 146:   Dayan on the cease-fire. *New York Times,* October 31, 1973, p. 16.

Page 147:   OPEC's aggregate oil revenues, see the appendix.

Page 148:   Sadat's earlier political career: See his memoirs *Revolt on the Nile* (New York: John Day, 1957), pp. 57, 139.

Page 149:   Sadat interview. Arnaud de Borchgrave, "Battle is Now Inevitable," *Newsweek,* April 9, 1973, pp. 44ff.

Page 150:   ". . . the Arabs may well come to us." Kissinger, *White House Years,* p. 559.

Page 150:   Enver Pasha. See D. A. Rustow, "Enwer Pasha," *Encyclopaedia of Islam,* new edn. (Leiden: E. J. Brill, 1959–), 2:698–702.

Page 151:   "Vintage Sadat." Kissinger, *White House Years,* p. 1299.

Page 153:   Yamani's visit to the United States. His lecture was given to the Middle East Institute. He had been making the same proposals to the relevant government officials. On Saudi Arabia's tactics toward the United States see D. A. Rustow, "U.S.–Saudi Relations and the Oil Crises of the 1980s," *Foreign Affairs,* 55, no.3 (April 1977): 494–516.

Page 154:   Akins, "The Oil Crisis," p. 468.

Page 154:   "Time is running out . . ." Internal Aramco memoranda reprinted in the Hearings of Senator Church's Subcommittee on Multinational Corporations, *Multinational Petroleum Companies and Foreign Policy* (Washington, D.C., G.P.O. 1974), pt. 7, pp. 504, 506. (Cited hereafter as *Church Committee Hearings.*)

Page 155:   "Can the Arabs Really Blackmail Us?" by Robert E. Hunter,

New York Times Magazine, September 23, 1973, pp. 25, 98–108; the quotation is from p. 25. In Hunter's own estimate, the Arab notion that the United States could "deliver" Israel was an "illusion"; at most Washington could help bring Arabs and Israelis together to work things out on their own. Hunter subsequently served on the staff of National Security Adviser Zbigniew Brzezinski.

Page 155:   "The Arab Oil Squeeze." *Newsweek,* September 17, 1973. The young man turned out to be an American Jew from Brooklyn who had bought a bedouin costume on a recent trip to Israel.

Page 155:   ". . . whether markets will find oil." Ian Seymour (editor of *Middle East Economic Survey), New York Times,* October 7, 1973, p. III–1. For Nixon's press conference on September 5, 1973, see ibid., September 6, 1973.

Page 156:   Specifics of the embargo. See *U.S. Oil Companies and the Arab Oil Embargo,* a report by the Federal Energy Administration to Senator Church's subcommittee, January 27, 1975; for its effects, see the careful estimates by Robert B. Stobaugh, "The Oil Companies in the Crisis," in Raymond Vernon, ed, *The Oil Crisis: In Perspective* (New York: Norton 1976), pp. 179–202.

Page 156:   ". . . draw attention of the world to the Arab cause . . .". Statement of the Organization of Arab Petroleum Exporting Countries, March 18, 1974; the document bears the earmarks of Saudi draftsmanship; Syria and Libya dissented.

Page 157:   Saudi Arabia . . . international reserves. See the monthly publication of the International Monetary Fund, *International Financial Statistics,* various issues, line 1-d of the respective country tables. For Saudi Arabia, lines 1-d and 3-d should be added to compute the total of reserves; the latter, since mid-1975, represents "other assets" of the Saudi Arabian Monetary Agency— which, in practice, are a different form of holding international reserves.

Page 158:   ". . . not to ship the oil at all . . ." George Keller of Aramco, *Church Committee Hearings,* part 7, p. 418.

Page 159:   Yamani interview. Oriana Fallaci, "A Sheik Who Hates to Gamble," *New York Times Magazine* September 14, 1975, p. 19.

Page 159:   The U.S. . . . to show its "appreciation": Yamani's remarks at a press conference at the December 1976 OPEC meeting. See *Keesing's Contemporary Archives,* 1977, p. 28320.

Page 160:   "Provoked . . . the embargo." "Choose between . . . oil and . . . Israel." In, respectively, *U.S. Oil Companies,* the Federal Energy Administration; and R. E. Hunter, "Can the Arabs."

Page 161:   "In a stalemate . . ." Kissinger, *The White House Years,* p. 360, paraphrasing Egyptian Foreign minister Mahmoud Fawzi. He comments that "Fawzi's last point was, of course, precisely the strategic opportunity I perceived for the United States" (p. 360f.). Thus there seems to have been a convergence of American and Egyptian thinking at the highest levels.

Page 162:   Kissinger as "even-handed." Note that in his memoirs (ibid., p. 50f.) he implies that Scranton's remark was ill-advisedly candid, rather than inaccurate in reflecting Kissinger's and Nixon's embryonic Middle Eastern policy.

Page 162:   "Logistical headache." The authors of the FEA report felt the hangover of those headaches keenly enough to use the entire quoted phrase twice within three pages (pp. 2, 5).

Page 163:   Shortfalls in the U.S., Western Europe, and Japan. See the import figures in U.S. Bureau of Mines, *Petroleum Statement Monthly;* cf. Stobaugh, "The Oil Companies."

Page 163:   Comparative oil import dependence. Cf. Rustow and Mugno, *OPEC,* pp. 42f. and table 2 in the appendix.

Page 163:   "Who Won the Yom Kippur and Oil Wars?" My article appeared in *Foreign Policy,* no. 10 (Winter 1974/75), pp. 166–75. The editor, who received the manuscript shortly after President Ford's "doomsday speech" (see chapter 5), at first gasped audibly on the telephone and complained that my anaysis was wildly out of line with prevailing Washington views of the moment. It was.

Page 165:   Mobil ads. In *New York Times,* op-ed. page, May 11, September 21, October 5, and November 30, 1972; and on January 18 and April 12, 1973. (Additional ads, not here quoted, appeared on March 1 and April 19, 1973.) The whole series was reprinted on pp. 20f. of *New York Times,* January 2, 1974.

Page 167:   U.S. energy prices and energy-consuming devices between 1950 and 1970. See U.S. Department of Energy, Energy Information Administration, *Annual Report to Congress 1980,* 3 vols., (Washington, D.C., 1981), 2:21, 195ff. This is an invaluable compendium of data on petroleum and other forms of energy; cited hereafter as EIA, *Report 1980.* For earlier data, see Sam Schurr et al., *Energy in the American Economy, 1850–1975* (Baltimore: Johns Hopkins, 1960).

Page 170:   "Mass merchandising" of gasoline. Blair, *The Control of Oil,* p. 238.

Page 171:   Lichtblau's talk was delivered to a seminar at Johns Hopkins University. See "Arab Role Denied in Oil Shortage," *New York Times,* September 20, 1973.

Page 171:   FEO tended to credit early estimates of U.S. shortage. Richard

B. Mancke, *Squeaking By: U.S. Energy Policy Since the Embargo* (New York: Columbia University Press, 1976), pp. 20, 161.

Page 171:   FEO policies aggravated shortages. Ibid., p. 25. State-by-state percentages, ibid. pp. 30ff.

Page 174:   Kissinger's "vicious cycle" and Ford's "doomsday" statements. In Rustow and Mugno, *OPEC*, pp. 49ff., on which some of the above summary is based. Levy's article appeared in *Foreign Affairs*, vol. 59, no. 1 (summer 1980). Bergsten's articles have been reprinted in C. Fred Bergsten, *Toward a New International Economic Order: Selected Papers, 1972–1974* (Lexington, Mass: Lexington Books, 1975), pp. 381–421.

Page 174:   "Is the Oil Shortage Real?" by M. A. Adelman,

Page 246:   Jackson thundered. In Sampson, *Seven Sisters*, p. 270.

Page 175:   Bizarre theory: Akins stated his views on CBS-TV's "Sixty Minutes" program on May 4, 1980. Kissinger earlier had refused to be interviewed for the program because he believed CBS was about to do a "hatchet job." (*New York Times*, April 29, 1980, p. B14). Akins had been abruptly dismissed as ambassador to Riyadh in 1975 when, in a Saudi television appearance, he had tried to explain away Kissinger's implied invasion threat of December 1974. Akins himself had been the target for similar finger-pointing by Professor Adelman; see chapter 4. In sober fact, neither the shah nor any other OPEC governments needed much prompting, from Kissinger, Akins, or anyone, to raise the price of oil as the opportunity offered itself.

Page 175:   "Actual strangulation." Kissinger's interview was published in *Business Week* on January 13, 1975, but widely reported in the press by late December 1974.

Page 175:   Øystein Noreng, *Oil Politics in the 1980s: Patterns of International Cooperation* (New York: McGraw Hill, 1978).

Page 176:   "Chiselling and cheating." Adelman, "Is the Oil Shortage Real?" p. 87.

Page 176:   Estimates of needed investments in energy alternatives. Caroll L. Wilson, "A Plan for Energy Independence," *Foreign Affairs*, 51, no. 4 (July 1973): 657–75, and Thomas O. Enders, "OPEC and the Industrial Countries," ibid., 53, no. 4 (July 1975): 632.

Page 178:   The Ford Foundation study. Summarized in *A Time to Choose: America's Energy Future* (Cambridge, Mass, Ballinger 1974). See also "Resources for the Future," Joel Darmstadter et al., *How Industrial Societies Use Their Energy* (Baltimore, Md.: Johns Hopkins 1977).

Page 178:   "Farewell to Oil" and the following. The articles appeared respectively in *Commentary*, May 1974; *U.S. News and World Report*, December 3, 1973, and November 26, 1973; *Newsweek*, November 19, and November 12, 1973; *Time*, September 17, 1973; *U.S. News*, May 12, 1975; *Newsweek*, September 29, 1975; *Foreign Affairs*, April 1973 and summer 1980.

Page 178:   "Is the World Oil Scarcity Now Becoming a Surplus?" and the following. *U.S. News*, June 17, 1974; *Time*, October 29, 1974; *Newsweek*, March 3, 1975; *Environment*, September 1974; *Fortune*, April 7, 1974 and May 1975.

Pages 178–79:   "Oil: America's Huge Stake . . ." and the following. *U.S. News*, October 22, 1973; *New Republic*, October 20, 1973; *Newsweek*, July 23, 1973; *New York Times Magazine*, September 23, 1973; *Forbes*, September 15, 1975; *New Republic*, March 30, 1974.

Page 179:   "Arabian Fantasy" and the following. *Harper's*, January 1974; *Foreign Policy*, winter 1972–73; *U.S. News*, January 14, 1974; *Vital Speeches*, April 1974; *Newsweek*, July 2, 1973.

Page 179:   "Who's to Blame . . . ?" and following. *Newsweek*, December 3, 1973; *Progressive*, February 1974; *Nation*, June 18, 1973; *Motor Trend*, April 1974; *Nation*, February 15, 1975; *Newsweek*, January 14, 1975.

Page 179:   "Calling OPEC's Bluff . . ." and following. *New Republic*, July 5, 1975; *Harper's*, March 1975; *Dun's Review*, February 1975; *U.S. News*, February 18, 1974; *Time*, January 19, 1976.

CHAPTER 6

Page 181:   Joseph Kraft, "Letter from Iran," *The New Yorker*, December 18, 1978, p. 134.

Page 184:   Above-normal oil stocks in mid-1980. Comparing world-wide inventory levels for 1978 and 1980, the excess in the first three quarters of 1980 was 800 million, 700 million, and 530 million barrels. In the fourth quarter, as a result of the Iraq-Iran war, excess inventories declined to 140 million barrels. (For detailed figures, see U.S. Department of Energy, *International Energy Indicators*, May 1981, pp. 8f. A somewhat different set of figures is reflected on the graph of Exxon Corporation, *World Oil Inventories* [New York: Exxon 1981], p. 8.) By comparison the shortfall in Iran at the time of the strike (December 1979 to March 1980) totaled only 249 million barrels compared to immediate prestrike levels. (My calculations from *Petroleum Intelligence Weekly*, January 29, 1979, p. 9, and February 24, 1980, p. 9; hereafter cited as *PIW*.)

Page 187:   Yamani's truculent announcement. He told NBC's "Meet the
             Press" on April 29, 1981, that "this glut was anticipated by Saudi
             Arabia. . . . We engineered the glut . . . in order to stabilize the
             price of oil." Saudi production would not be cut "until we unify
             the price of oil."

Page 187:   "Cash and control." See above, p. 112.

Page 187:   "Best-of-practices doctrine." See above, pp. 111 and 140.

Page 188:   Seeing their production decline to one-half or less. By August
             1981 Libya's production had dropped to 39 percent and Nig-
             eria's to 35 percent of its 1980 levels.

Page 189:   "OPEC is not to blame." At the height of the 1980 price rise,
             the monthly *OPEC Bulletin* featured two such apologetic arti-
             cles by OPEC officials: "Why OPEC Is Not to Blame," by
             Adnan al-Janabi, May 1980, pp. 15–19; and "OPEC Is a Scape-
             goat," by Hamid Zaheri, June 1980. pp. 44–46.

Page 190:   Beyond "national requirements." The phrase is from the "Long-
             Term Strategy" report discussed below, p. 20.

Page 190:   "King Midas' dilemma." Rustow, "U.S.–Saudi Relations," p.
             511.

Page 190:   The "backward-bending supply curve," of course, is a prime
             indication of a monopolistic rather than competitive market.

Page 191:   Oil incomes of the 1970s and the Iranian revolution. See Walter
             J. Levy, "The Years That the Locust Hath Eaten: Oil Policy and
             OPEC Development Prospects," *Foreign Affairs* 57, no. 2 (win-
             ter, 1978/79): 286–305.

Page 192:   "Persian Gulf production . . . to zero." S. Fred Singer, "A Crisis
             —For OPEC," *New York Times,* March 31, 1981; see also his
             articles "The Coming Revolution in World Oil Markets" and
             "The World's Falling Need for Oil," *Wall Street Journal* Febru-
             ary 4 and April 21, 1981.

Page 193:   "They can't blacklist us all." *New York Times,* July 13, 1981, p.
             D4:4.

Page 195:   A country's oil reserves . . . its population. For details see table
             4 (OPEC: Hawks *vs.* Doves) in the Appendix.

Page 200 A: Saudis cut production "perhaps to show their displeasure . . ."
             William B. Quandt, *Saudi Arabia in the 1980s: Foreign Policy,
             Security, and Oil* (Washington, D.C.: Brookings, 1981), p. 116.

Page 200:   OPEC's mini price war of 1977. See D. A. Rustow, "Middle East
             Oil: International and Regional Developments," *Middle East
             Contemporary Survey,* ed. Colin Legum, vol. 2 (New York and
             London: Holmes & Meier, 1979), p. 218f.

Page 201:   "Long-Term Strategy." The report was approved by the Ministerial Committee in London on February 22, 1980, Although it was not officially released, "confidential" xerox copies soon became widely available; my account is based on one in my possession. Summaries of the report have appeared in the trade press: for example, *PIW,* May 12, 1980 (see ibid., April 20, 1981, for proposed revisions), and *Platt's Oilgram,* May 6, 1980.

Page 202:   Formula in the "deep freeze." Yamani's remarks at a conference in London, September 28, 1981 in (*PIW,* October 5, 1981, supplement, p. 1).

Page 204:   "Chiselling and Cheating," see above, p. 176.

Page 205:   Intra-OPEC price war. For a detailed scenario for such a price war in the mid-1970s, see Rustow and Mugno, *OPEC,* pp. 100–102. In 1976 the Saudis could still have made money by producing at maximum if the price had dropped by as much as 40 percent. In the mid-1980's scenario outlined earlier in Chapter 6, they could hold out even longer.

Page 207:   Oil export routes . . . vulnerable. Cf. Dankwart A. Rustow, "OPEC and the Political Future of the World Oil Market," *Selected Studies on Energy—Background Papers for Energy: The Next Twenty Years,* ed. Hans H. Landsberg (Cambridge, Mass.: Ballinger, 1980), pp. 393–419, esp. 404ff.

Page 212:   Loosening of the international monetary system. For an excellent analysis of OPEC's impact in speeding up that process, see Adam Smith, *Paper Money* (New York: Summit Books, 1981), chapters 7–10.

CHAPTER 7

Page 216:   Oil consumption grew faster in the 1960s. See D. A. Rustow, "Europe in the Age of Petroleum," *The Euro-American System,* ed. E. O. Czempiel and D. A. Rustow (Boulder, Col.: Westview, 1976), pp. 93–108.

Page 216:   "Ready-shelf inventory." See above, p. 118.

Page 216:   "Drain America." See p. 122.

Page 220:   Refiner acquisition cost: EIA, *Report 1980,* II, 91. Note that the "refiner acquisition cost" is slightly above the "wellhead price" of domestic and the "landed cost" of imported oil. The difference is accounted for by transportation and storage costs and profit by the producer or importer; it ranged from $0.14 for imports in 1976 to $2.64 for domestic oil in 1980. See also table 1 in appendix.

Page 221:   The nation's thirst for oil imports. The figures given in the text refer to gross imports, which then dominated the public discussion. For net import figures see table 1 in the appendix. The difference is accounted for mostly by a small amount of oil reexported from tanker ports or refineries in Puerto Rico or the Virgin Islands to nearby Caribbean destinations.

Page 221:   "Another Alaska:" Rustow, "U.S.–Saudi Relations . . . ," p. 498.

Page 221:   Russell Baker, "A Meow in Search of an Enemy," *New York Times,* April 27, 1977.

Page 222:   "Two trillion dollars." Robert Stobaugh and Daniel Yergin, "Energy: An Emergency Telescoped," *Foreign Affairs* 58, no. 3 (spring 1980): 87.

Page 223:   Chase Bank. See below, p. 226 and table 1 in appendix.

Page 224:   *Fortune's* "500" list is published every May for the previous year. Exxon stayed at the top of the list in 1975 and 1976, dropped back to second place in 1977 and 1978, and once again rose to the top in 1979. The effect of OPEC's two major price increases on this ranking is unmistakable.

Pages 225:   Companies had long since recouped their investments. For detailed calculations, see Issawi and Yeganeh, *Economics of Middle Eastern Oil,* pp. 42, 121; they estimate that total investments by major Western oil companies in the Middle East from 1926 to 1960 amounted to $2.4 billion at historic cost, and that net income from Middle Eastern operations from 1948 to 1960 averaged $1.4 billion annually.

Page 226:   Domestic production and wellhead prices (1975–1980). See EIA, *Annual Report 1980,* 2:49, 87.

Page 226:   "Chase Group." Chase Manhattan Bank, *The Petroleum Situation* 6, no. 1 (January 1982).

Page 228:   U.S. energy consumption figures per capita and per unit of gross domestic product. See the careful calculations in Joel Darmstadter et al., *How Industrial Societies Use Their Energy,* pp. 223f., and the follow-up study by Joy Dunkerley, *International Comparisons of Energy Consumption* (Washington, D.C., 1978).

Page 229:   Oil imports as percentage of total energy consumption. My calculations from *BP Statistical Review of the World Oil Industry 1980* (London, British Petroleum Co. 1981), pp. 26, 32. This is the most useful and up-to-date single source of information on world oil.

Pages 231–32: *The Little Engine That Could,* by Watty Piper (New York: Platt & Munck, 1961), passim.

Page 233:   Energy used in the transportation sector in the United States and other industrial countries. Darmstadter et al., *How Industrial Societies,* pp. 70ff., 223.

Page 235:   Mexican reserves. *Oil and Gas Journal,* estimates for January 1, 1981, are 44 billion barrels for Mexico—as against 165 bn for Saudi Arabia, 64.9 bn for Kuwait, 63 bn for the USSR, 57.5 bn for Iraq, and 26.4 bn for the United States. Thus Mexico ranked fifth and the United States sixth.

CHAPTER 8

Page 238:   Sadat's Knesset speech. Reprinted in his book *In Search of Identity* (New York, Harper 1978), pp. 330–43; the quote is from p. 335.

Page 238:   "Liquidate the Zionist presence." See the Palestinian National Charter, adopted at the national congress of the PLO in Cairo, July 1–17, 1968, Art. 15.

Page 240:   Brookings Report, *Toward Peace in the Middle East,* Report of a Study Group (Washington, D.C., 1975).

Page 240:   "A comprehensive approach . . ." Kissinger, *White House Years,* p. 559.

Page 242:   "Determination of their own future." Carter at Aswan, Egypt, May 1, 1977.

Page 242:   Palestinian professor. The leading candidate was Edward Said, professor of English at Columbia. He is the author of *The Question of Palestine* (New York, Random House, 1980).

Page 242:   "Go . . . to the Knesset." Sadat in the People's Assembly, Cairo, November 9, 1977.

Pages 242–43: "Psychological barrier"; "wall of suspicion." Sadat, *In Search,* p. 336.

Page 242:   "Important to have direct negotiations." Carter at his news conference, November 30, 1977 (*New York Times,* December 1).

Page 245:   The PLO and the West Bank. See Menahem Milson, "Making Peace with the Palestinians," *Commentary* 71 (May 1981): 25–35.

Page 246:   Persian Gulf . . . "vital interest." Carter's declaration of January 23, 1980, in *New York Times,* January 24, p. 12

Page 248:   Critics of the Carter Doctrine: See for example George F. Kennan, "The Renaissance of American Foreign Policy," *New York Times,* February 1, 1980 (op-ed page).

Page 249:   No advance coordination for the Carter doctrine. "As far as is known, neither the current [Reagan] administration nor the previous [Carter] one has ever conducted a detailed study of the implications of the policy or its alternatives." David D. Newsom, "America EnGulfed," *Foreign Policy,* no. 43 (summer 1981), p. 17. The author, a State Department career official and Middle

East specialist, and under-secretary of state for Political Affairs from 1978 to 1981, was in a position to know.

Page 250: Not much of a force. The point is driven home by James R. Schlesinger, who served as secretary of defense under Nixon and Ford and of energy under Carter, in an article entitled "Rapid(?) Deployment(?) Force(?)" *Washington Post,* September 24, 1980.

Page 251: Reagan's tough statements on hostages. He called the crisis a "humiliation and a disgrace," referred to the Iranian captors as "nothing better than criminals and kidnappers," and insisted that the United States must not "pay ransom for people that have been kidnapped by barbarians." (*New York Times,* October 22, p. 1:6, December 25, p. 4:5, and December 2, p. 1:5)

Page 251: "Consensus of strategic concerns": Secretary of State Haig, testifying before the House Foreign Affairs Committee on March 18, 1980, stated that it was "fundamentally important to begin to develop a consensus of strategic concerns throughout the region among Arab and Jew, and to be sure that the overriding danger of Soviet inroads is not overlooked."

Page 254: "Absent-mindedness." Great Britain, according to a common saying, had acquired her empire in a "fit of absent-mindedness."

Page 254: Turkey and the EEC. See Dankwart A. Rustow and Trevor Penrose, *Turkey and the Community* (Brighton: Sussex European Research Centre, 1981).

Page 255: Plans for a Middle East Defense Organization and Dulles's "Northern tier." See above chapter 2.

Page 259: Soviet-American competition in the Middle East since 1917. Cf. D.A. Rustow, "The Appeal of Communism to Islamic Peoples," in J. Harris Proctor, ed., *Islam and International Relations* (Durham, N.C.: University of North Carolina Press, 1963), pp. 40–60

Page 260: Dr. King and Mr. Crane. See above, chapter 2.

Page 261: More than twice as many Jews in the United States. In 1967, it was estimated that out of total of 1.8 million Jews throughout the world, 5.9 million (42 percent) lived in the United States, 2.7 million (19 percent) in the Soviet Union, and 2.4 million (18 percent) in Israel. *Encyclopedia Judaica* 16 vols. (Jerusalem: Encyclopedia Judaica, 1971–72), 13:894f.

Page 262: Turkish-American relations. Turkey in the late 1970s. See my article "Turkey's Travails," *Foreign Affairs* 58, no. 1 (fall 1979): 82–102.

Page 263: The "special relationship" between the U.S. and Saudi Arabia. See the well-informed and balanced account by William B.

Quandt, *Saudi Arabia in the 1980s,* especially chapters 8 and 9.

Page 264: Begin showed courage. Begin's view of life and of courage is summed up in a statement from his memoirs that "Life is one long chain of revolts and surrenders, which are sometimes so intertwined that one cannot distinguish between them." Menachem Begin, *The Revolt,* rev. ed. (New York: 1977), p. 149. Perhaps it is fair to say that at Camp David he surrendered on the Sinai question,—in one single intertwined act—revolted against a settlement on the issue of Palestine.

Page 265: Israel under arms. Ratios of military personnel to population. See Appendix Table 5

Page 265: Israel's Jewish and Arab populations before and after 1967. See chapter 4.

Page 265: PLO the "sole legitimate representative." Unanimous resolution of the Arab League's summit meeting at Rabat, October 1974; even King Hussein, rather than let himself be outvoted, supported the resolution.

Page 265: "Liquidate the Zionist presence." The passages are quoted from the Palestine National Charter, Arts. 9, 15, 19, and 20.

Page 266: Prince Fahd's statement on Palestine peace. *New York Times,* August 9, 1981, p. 6.

Page 266: Neighborhood government. See Teddy Kollek, "Jerusalem Present and Future," *Foreign Affairs* 59, no. 5 (summer 1981): 1041–49.

Page 266: Small sovereign state. A persuasive argument was made by a leading Palestinian intellectual teaching at the American University of Beirut. See Walid Khalidi, "Thinking the Unthinkable: A Sovereign Palestinian State." Ibid. 56, no. 4 (July 1978): 695–713.

Page 350 A: "The Path to Peace." Joseph N. Greene, Jr., Philip M. Klutznick, Harold H. Saunders, and Merle Thorpe, Jr., *The Path to Peace: Arab-Israeli Peace and the United States* (Mount Kisco, N.Y.: Seven Springs Center, October 1981) Of the coauthors, Klutznick was former president of the World Jewish Congress; and Saunders, as a high State Department official, was crucially involved in the Middle East peace negotiations throughout the 1970s.

Index

Abd al-Qadir, 52
Abdullah al-Salim al-Sabah, emir of Kuwait, 15, 24, 161, 185
Abdullah, emir of Transjordan, 34, 44
Abu Dhabi, 45, 109
Adelman, M. A., 94, 118, 141–42, 174, 176, 204, 216
Aden, 16, 25
Afghanistan, 25, 38, 84
  linguistic patterns in, 42
  Soviet occupation of, 18, 88, 206, 209, 244, 246, 247, 248–50, 253, 256
Airborne Warning and Control System, *see* AWACS
Akins, James E., 136, 154, 155, 164, 175
Alawis, 34, 38
Algeria, 38, 48, 52, 69, 72, 85, 128
  oil industry of, 103, 110, 135, 136, 154, 195
  population of, 195–96
American University of Beirut (AUB), 62
Amin, Idi, 197
Anglo-American Committee of Inquiry (1946), 68, 79
Anglo-Egyptian Treaty (1936), 79
Anglo-Iranian Oil Company, 78, 96, 181
  see also British Petroleum Company
anti-Semitism, 40, 41, 67
antitrust suits, 94, 105, 121

Arab Caliphate of Islam, 32, 33
Arab Federation, 44
Arabian-American Oil Company (Aramco), 77, 95, 96, 98, 105, 158, 200, 225
  fifty-fifty agreement of, 101
  Saudi rate of participation in, 146–47, 153
  Saudi warnings to, 154, 155
  tax bills of, 113–14
Arab-Israeli conflict, 16, 49, 55, 79, 124–31
  Arab advantage in, 126–27, 239
  cold war vs., 80–81, 161
  gap of perception and, 126
  Gaza Strip and, 50, 125, 126, 238, 239, 244, 245, 265, 266
  Kissinger's disengagement agreements and, 240–41
  Kissinger's view of importance of, 15, 17, 161
  1979 treaty in, 151, 199, 200, 206, 238, 242–45
  oil prices and, 18, 146, 156, 199, 224
  origins of, 38–41
  peace negotiations and, 18, 19, 58–59, 127, 129, 130, 146, 147–52, 153, 159, 162, 199–200, 206, 237–45, 250–51, 256, 261, 264–69

Levy, Walter J., 174, 175
Lewis, Bernard, 36
Libya, 38, 45, 48, 84, 133–40
  British relations with, 16, 138
  military coups in, 57, 133
  oil industry of, 92, 103, 105–7, 109, 110,
    116, 134–40, 141, 146, 154, 188, 195,
    197, 224, 225, 227
  Soviet relations with, 76, 85, 197,
    257
  U.S. base in, 131, 132, 134
Lichtblau, John H., 171
Limits to Growth (Meadows *et al.*), 168
London *Times*, 132–33
Lybyer, Albert Howe, 64–66

McCarthy, Eugene, 16
Mahdi, the ("Redeemer"), 52
Malaysia, oil industry of, 140–41, 234
mandate system, 33–35, 36, 38, 63–67
Marathon, 104, 106
Marshall Plan, 70–71, 72, 75, 122, 174
Mattei, Enrico, 104, 106
Meadows, Dennis, 168
Meir, Golda, 129, 148
Mexico, oil industry of, 140–41, 152,
  234–35
Middle East Command, proposal for
  (1951), 79, 85, 123, 255
military politics, 54–59, 73, 124, 197
Miller, Otto N., 154–55, 165
missionaries, 62, 63, 260
Mobil, 94, 96, 154, 175, 193
  energy crisis advertised by, 165, 224
Mohammed, 25, 26, 51
Mohammed Riza Pahlevi, shah of Iran, 99,
  131, 132, 146, 175, 176, 185
  fall of (1979), 43, 159, 181, 184, 246–
    47
  restoration of (1953), 16, 78, 181–82,
    246, 255
Monroe Doctrine, 61
Montgomery, George R., 64–66
Morocco, 38, 44, 48
Mossadegh, Mohammed, 16, 78, 97–100,
  108, 110, 112, 115–16, 181–82
Mubarak, Hosni, 59, 243, 262
Mubarak, Sheikh, emir of Kuwait, 24
mullahs, 182
Muslim Brotherhood, 52
Mussolini, Benito, 150
Mustafa Kemal, *see* Atatürk

Nader, Ralph, 168
Nagib, Mohammed, 58, 79
Napoleon I, emperor of France, 27–28, 29,
  35, 62, 126
Nasser, Gamal Abdul, 36, 51, 52, 78, 80,
  81–85, 87, 123, 238
  compensatory fantasy of, 150–51
  death of, 127, 134, 148
  military coup of (1952), 55, 58, 79, 81,
    101, 133
  pan-Arabism of, 44–45, 48, 49, 58, 85,
    127, 133, 134, 149, 157
  Sadat compared to, 148–49, 151, 261–62
  Six-Day War and, 125, 126, 127
National Front (Iranian), 78, 97, 99, 182
National Iranian Oil Company, 98, 99
nationalism:
  European, 28, 41–42, 48, 50, 62–63
  self-determination and, 28, 33, 63, 67
  see also Arab nationalism; *specific coun-
    tries*
nationalization:
  failure of, 78, 98–100
  legality of, 98
  of oil, 137, 138, 141, 164, 166, 224, 225;
    see also Iranian crisis
  of Suez Canal, *see* Suez crisis
national security, oil and, 120–21, 122, 170,
  197, 205–13, 249–50
National Security Council, U.S., 121, 267
national unity, requirements of, 41–42
Naval Petroleum Reserve, 121, 122
Neutral Zone, oil concession in, 105
Newsweek, 149–50, 154, 155
New York Times, 154, 155, 165, 191–92
New York Times Magazine, 155
New Zealand, 71
Nigeria:
  oil industry of, 103, 110, 136–37, 140,
    143, 162, 188, 195, 227, 234
  population of, 195–96
Nixon, Richard, 15, 16, 24, 129, 147, 155,
  158, 160, 161, 166, 182, 185
  energy policy of, 117, 218, 222
Noreng, Øystein, 175
North Atlantic Treaty Organization
  (NATO), 69, 77, 80, 81, 131, 132, 254,
  262, 263
northern tier defense, 16, 80, 81, 83, 84,
  246, 255
North-South dialogue, 175
Norway, oil industry of, 140–41, 234